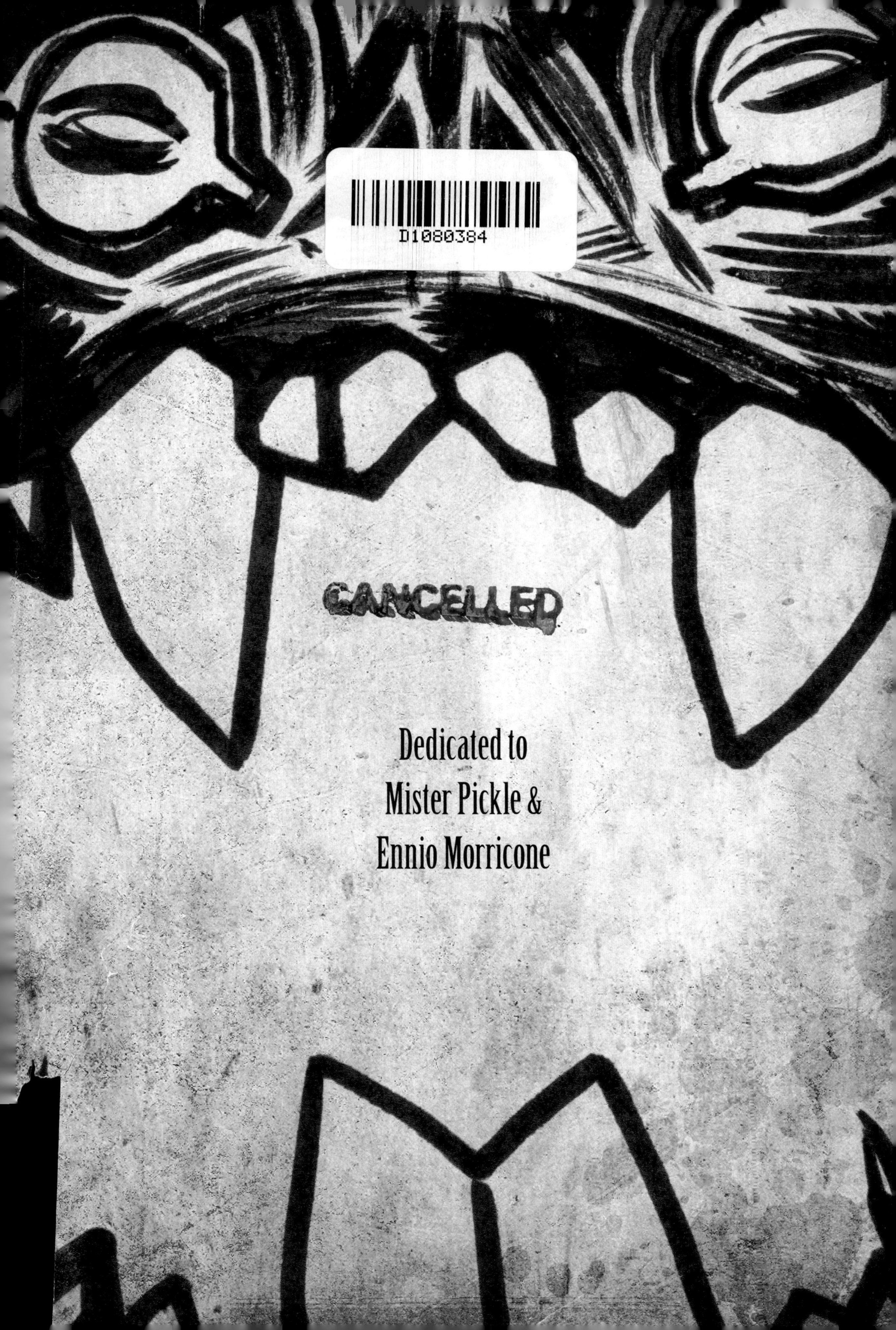

Dedicated to
Mister Pickle &
Ennio Morricone

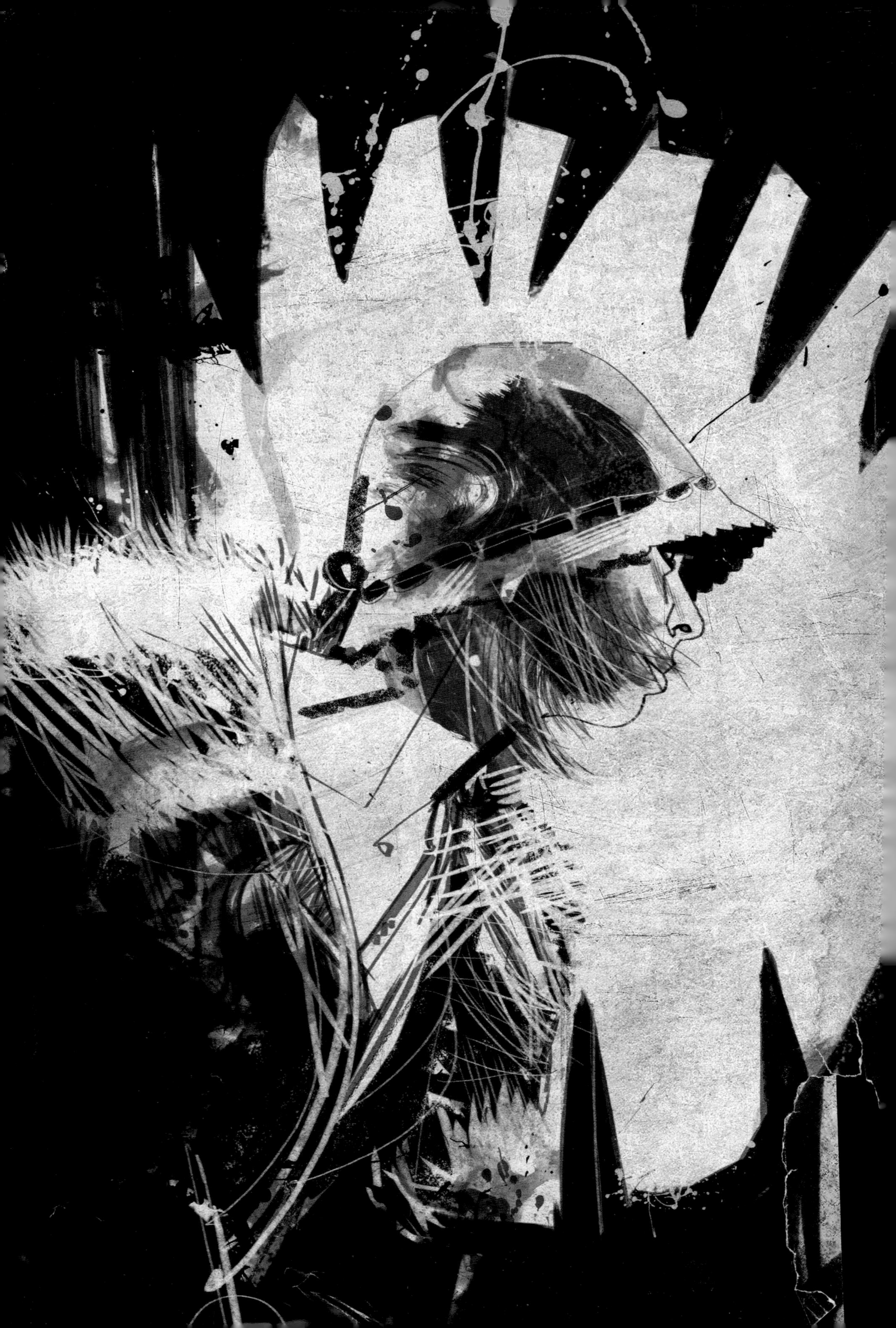

INTRODUCTION

The word is "Ferd" — as in "Fake Nerd" — and it was coined by Mister Damon Lindelof.

Damon is a pal of mine, the producer on the recent *Star Trek* movie, sometime Marvel Comics writer and co-creator of *Lost*. As you can imagine, The Force is strong in this one and his nerd credentials are impeccable. People talk of high-powered meetings where Damon kicks back in his vintage *Star Wars* t-shirts and you only have to check out one nano-second of his smash-hit TV show to spot the million comic-book and geek-culture references he and his writers have peppered through every episode. He's the real deal and we love him for it, but since *Iron Man* made half a billion, Raimi's *Spider-Man* averaged eight hundred million, and *The Dark Knight* shattered the big ten figures, the sharks have come circling. Because comics is where the money is, my friends, and the suits are faking nerd.

Even my agent, God bless him, is trying to get in on the act, and just getting it ever-so-slightly wrong when we have lunch together. He waxes nostalgic about "Kirby's Spider-Man" and "The Green Lanterns" title he enjoyed so much as a kid. But I know he's faking, and in his heart of hearts, he knows I bloody know. Why does it bug me so much? I'll tell you why, True Believer: Because we've been training for this moment since we opened our first comic. While friends were hitting home runs down the park, we were cataloguing our *Micronauts* collection. While others were getting hands in bras, we were impressed by just how smooth John Romita Sr.'s inks made Gil Kane's pencils look and thought he rivalled Ditko himself in terms of Spider-Man's action poses. It only takes four years to be a lawyer and four or five years to qualify as a doctor, but it's taken our entire lives to collect all this shit in our heads. This is our vocation, and with the exception of a lucky few, most of us don't even get a DIME for our expertise. Thus, you can imagine my frustration when I meet a Ferd through work. My spider-sense just TINGLES.

So what's this got to do with *Turf* writer Jonathan Ross?

Well, Jonathan's the real deal too. Yes, he's a TV big-shot, best described to an American as Letterman, Stern, Siskel and Ebert all rolled up in a Saville Row suit. But you know deep down that he'd rather be writing *Spider-Man* than interviewing Madonna or Tarantino or Tom Cruise or any of those people he talks to every week. He might have the biggest chat show in the country, host the most respected movie review program and radio show, but nothing seemed to bring him more pleasure than the Steve Ditko documentary he wrote for the BBC arts channel with a reverence and consideration normally only reserved for a Heller or a Wolfe. I've liked him since his first TV appearance in 1987 where he outed himself as one of us at a time when being a nerd had as much social status as an IRA terrorist or a local pedophile. We're talking about a man who doesn't just have one copy of *Amazing Fantasy* #15: He has his bagged copy, his wall-displayed copy and a "reading" copy for his desk.

He's got *Detective Comics* #27, *Action Comics* #1 and complete runs of pretty much anything you can think of. He's got the best collection of original comic book art in the country and possibly even the world. But this doesn't make him a comic book professional. A great reader doesn't always make a great writer. I'm just trying to hammer home that he's not some smarmy media player hoping to cash in on a passing fad. He's wanted this for as long as he can remember and it brought me great pleasure to hook him up with artist Tommy Lee Edwards.

Tommy, as discerning readers know, was my collaborator on *Marvel 1985* a couple of years back, and I was feeding Jonathan the pages as they were coming in as I knew he'd dig them. I'm an art snob. No, seriously, I'm a snooty bitch when it comes to something I love, and believe me when I say there's really less than ten guys in the entire industry right now that I truly rate. Tommy Lee makes my top five and has a unique style that I fell in love with the moment I saw it. There's a quiet naturalism here, a classic approach to layout and inks that evokes a little Alex Toth, a little Gene Colan, a touch of Dan Spiegel and all the other greats who make it look so effortless. When I talked Jonathan into actually writing down all these ideas he's had over the years and finally doing his dream job, I could think of no-one I'd rather pair him with than Tommy. It was like when Brad met Angelina on *Mr. and Mrs. Smith*: These guys just wanted to fuck and create little comic books as soon as possible.

Their first result is the book you're reading now. Welcome to *Turf* and a very conscious break from the action-driven, decompressed storytelling that's been oh-so-fashionable in comics since the turn of the decade. Yes, I hang my head in shame with the rest when I say it takes longer to have a pee than read the dialogue in one of my books. But Jonathan grew up loving Don McGregor and Alan Moore and all those guys who used to give you value for money and bang with your buck. This is a reaction to all these books you can read standing in the store. Something you can really get your teeth into, if you'll pardon the expression.

Mark Millar
Glasgow, Scotland
9 March 2011

Chapter One

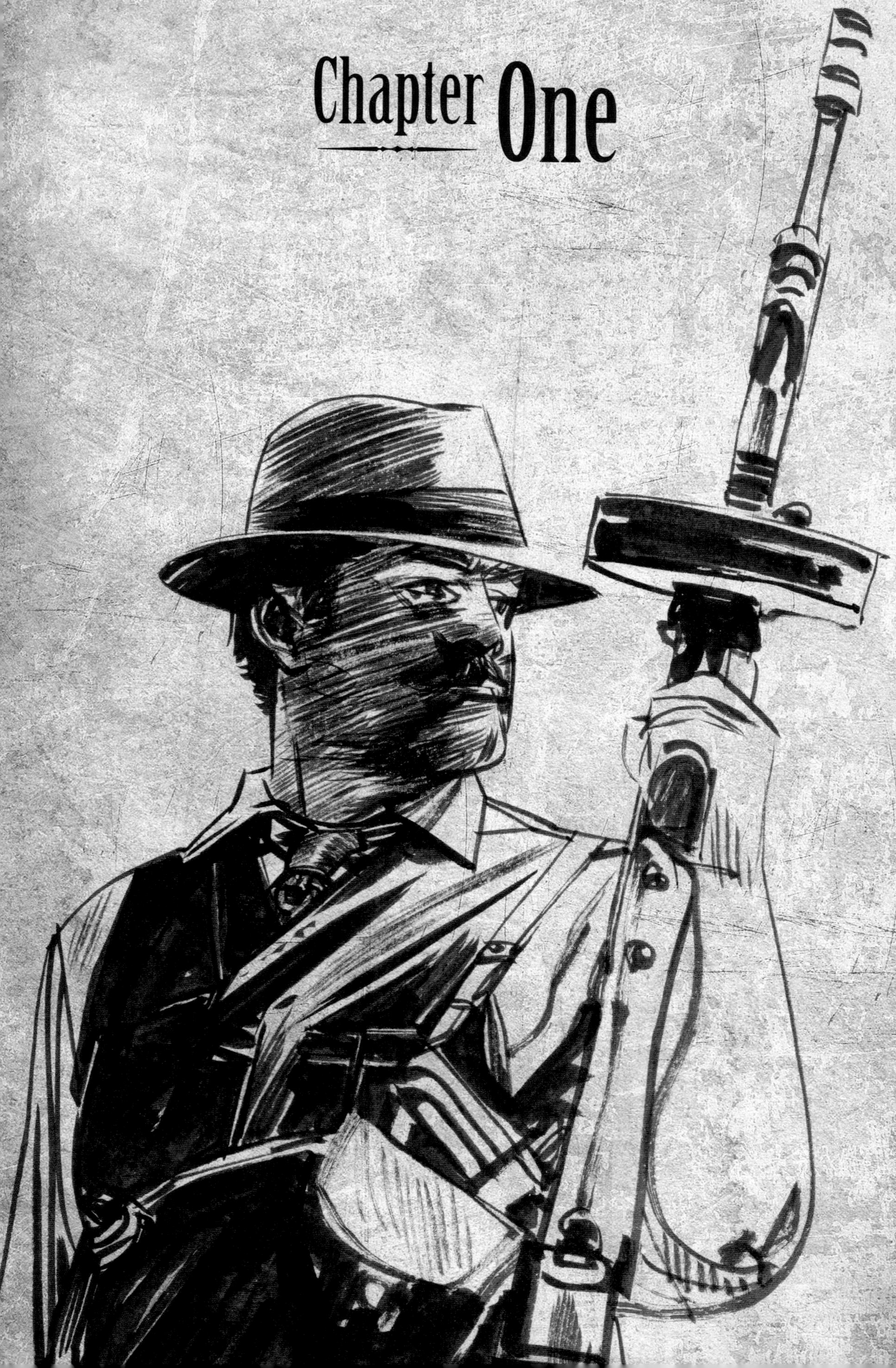

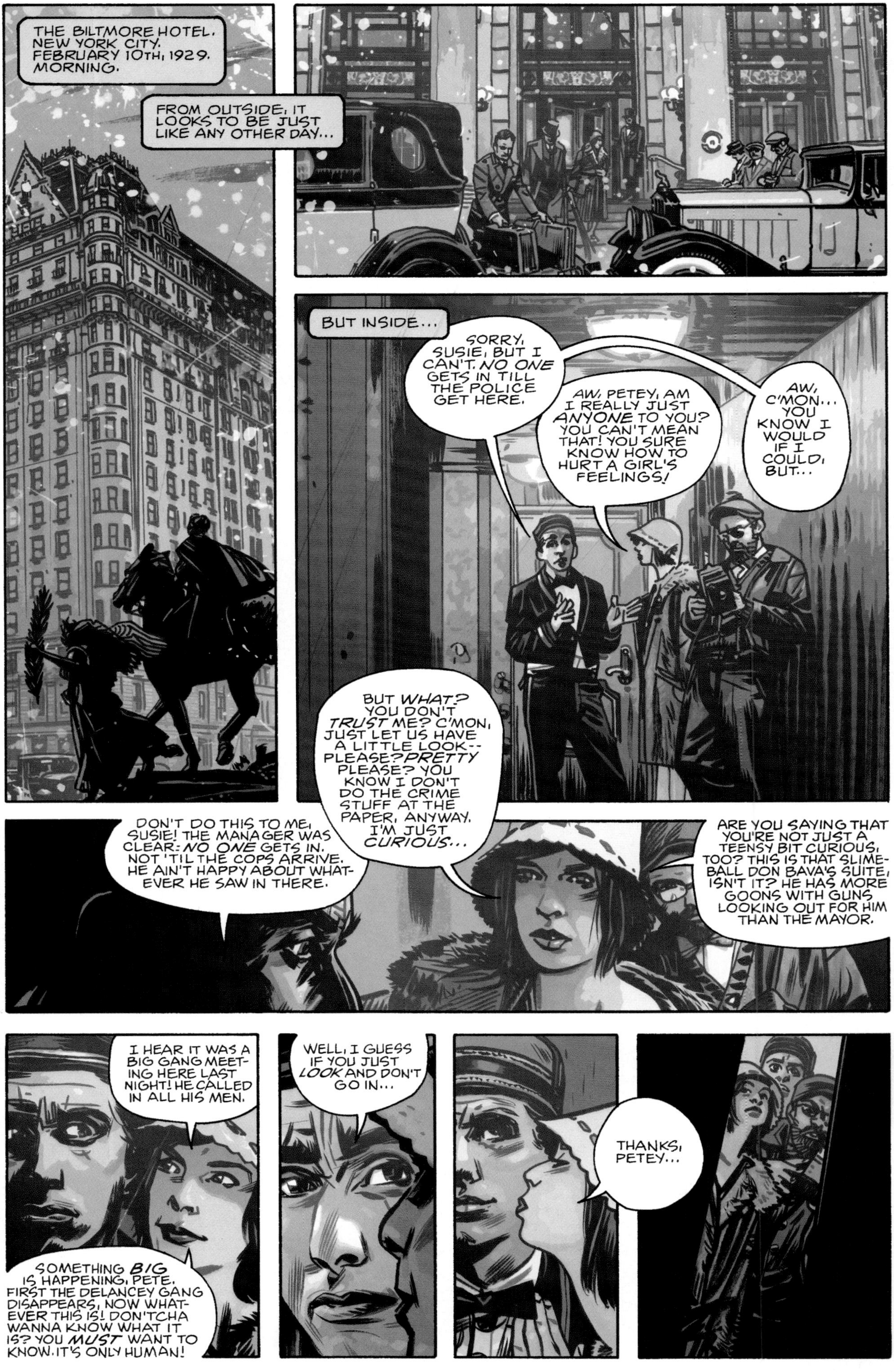
THE BILTMORE HOTEL, NEW YORK CITY. FEBRUARY 10TH, 1929. MORNING.
FROM OUTSIDE, IT LOOKS TO BE JUST LIKE ANY OTHER DAY...
BUT INSIDE...
SORRY, SUSIE, BUT I CAN'T. NO ONE GETS IN TILL THE POLICE GET HERE.
AW, PETEY, AM I REALLY JUST ANYONE TO YOU? YOU CAN'T MEAN THAT! YOU SURE KNOW HOW TO HURT A GIRL'S FEELINGS!
AW, C'MON... YOU KNOW I WOULD IF I COULD, BUT...
BUT WHAT? YOU DON'T TRUST ME? C'MON, JUST LET US HAVE A LITTLE LOOK-- PLEASE? PRETTY PLEASE? YOU KNOW I DON'T DO THE CRIME STUFF AT THE PAPER, ANYWAY. I'M JUST CURIOUS...
DON'T DO THIS TO ME, SUSIE! THE MANAGER WAS CLEAR: NO ONE GETS IN. NOT 'TIL THE COPS ARRIVE. HE AIN'T HAPPY ABOUT WHATEVER HE SAW IN THERE.
ARE YOU SAYING THAT YOU'RE NOT JUST A TEENSY BIT CURIOUS, TOO? THIS IS THAT SLIMEBALL DON BAVA'S SUITE, ISN'T IT? HE HAS MORE GOONS WITH GUNS LOOKING OUT FOR HIM THAN THE MAYOR.
I HEAR IT WAS A BIG GANG MEETING HERE LAST NIGHT! HE CALLED IN ALL HIS MEN.
SOMETHING BIG IS HAPPENING, PETE. FIRST THE DELANCEY GANG DISAPPEARS, NOW WHATEVER THIS IS! DON'TCHA WANNA KNOW WHAT IT IS? YOU MUST WANT TO KNOW. IT'S ONLY HUMAN!
WELL, I GUESS IF YOU JUST LOOK AND DON'T GO IN...
THANKS, PETEY...

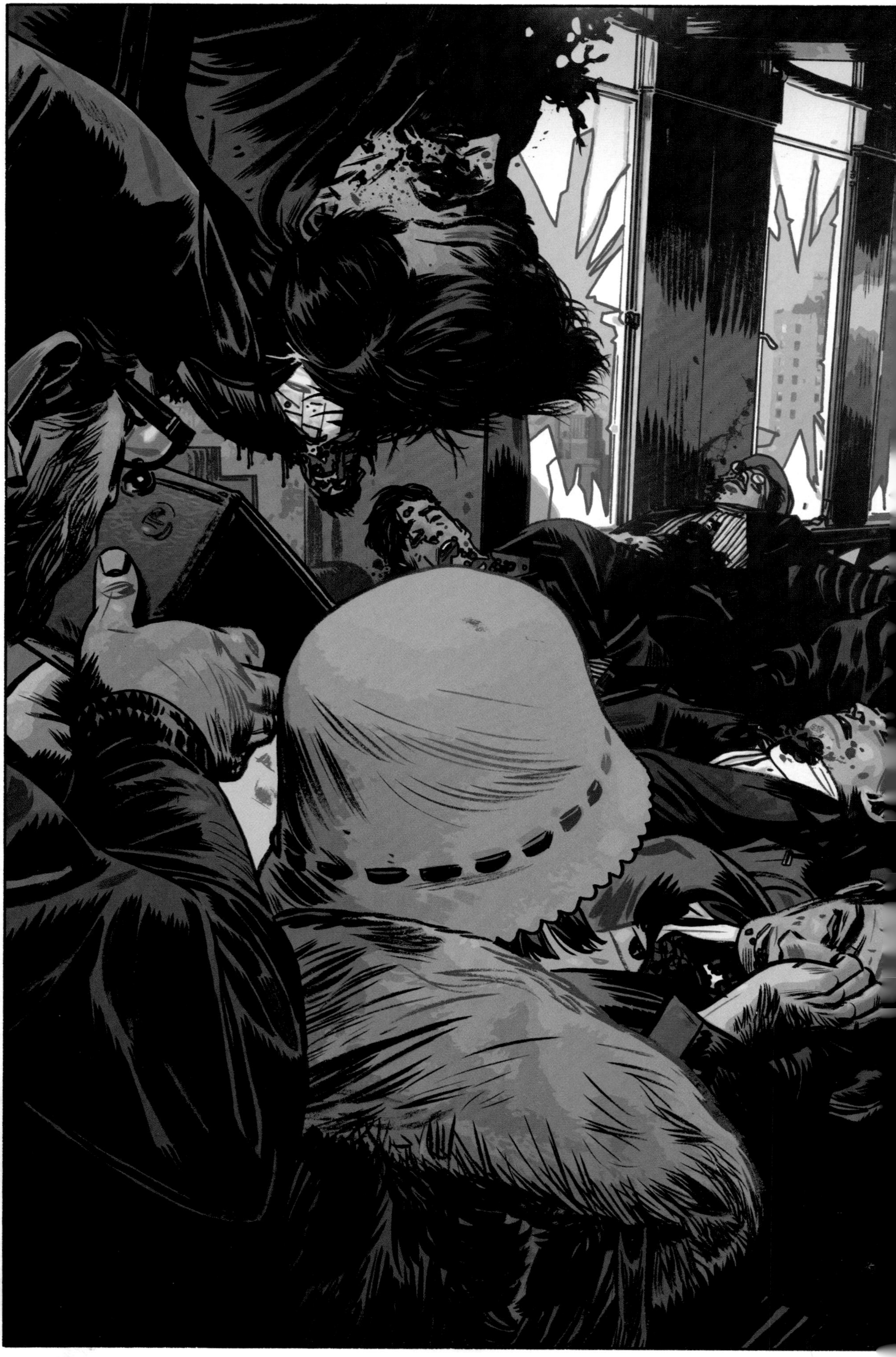

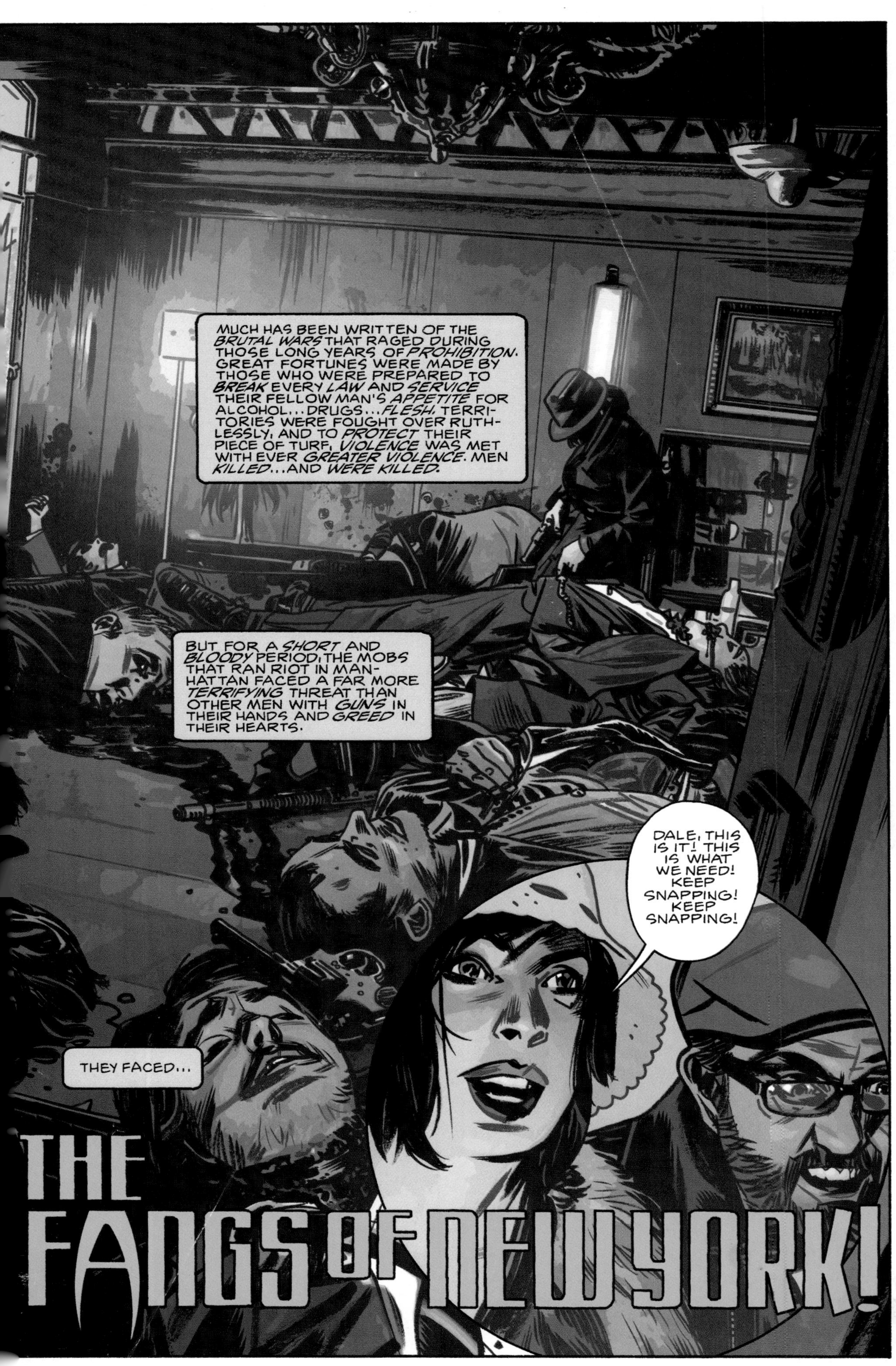
MUCH HAS BEEN WRITTEN OF THE BRUTAL WARS THAT RAGED DURING THOSE LONG YEARS OF PROHIBITION. GREAT FORTUNES WERE MADE BY THOSE WHO WERE PREPARED TO BREAK EVERY LAW AND SERVICE THEIR FELLOW MAN'S APPETITE FOR ALCOHOL... DRUGS... FLESH. TERRITORIES WERE FOUGHT OVER RUTHLESSLY, AND TO PROTECT THEIR PIECE OF TURF, VIOLENCE WAS MET WITH EVER GREATER VIOLENCE. MEN KILLED... AND WERE KILLED.
BUT FOR A SHORT AND BLOODY PERIOD, THE MOBS THAT RAN RIOT IN MANHATTAN FACED A FAR MORE TERRIFYING THREAT THAN OTHER MEN WITH GUNS IN THEIR HANDS AND GREED IN THEIR HEARTS.
DALE, THIS IS IT! THIS IS WHAT WE NEED! KEEP SNAPPING! KEEP SNAPPING!
THEY FACED...
THE FANGS OF NEW YORK!

ONE DAY EARLIER...NEW YORK CITY, FEBRUARY 9TH, 1929. EARLY EVENING.

MANY WOULD SAY IT'S THE *GREATEST CITY* ON THE FACE OF THE EARTH. THE HIGHEST BUILDINGS. THE FASTEST CARS.

THE MOST GLAMOROUS PEOPLE ALL GETTING TO KNOW EACH OTHER AT THE WILDEST PARTIES.

AND DESPITE THE FACT IT'S *ILLEGAL*, THE GREATEST NUMBER OF UNDERGROUND DIVES AND BARS AND JAZZ CLUBS SELLING *BOOZE* IN THE WHOLE OF THE UNITED STATES OF AMERICA.

PLACES WHERE A THIRSTY MANHATTANITE CAN GRAB A LITTLE *REFRESHMENT* TO HELP KEEP THAT PARTY *SWINGING*.

AND *BOY*, DOES IT SWING. *HARDER* AND *FASTER* THAN EVER BEFORE...

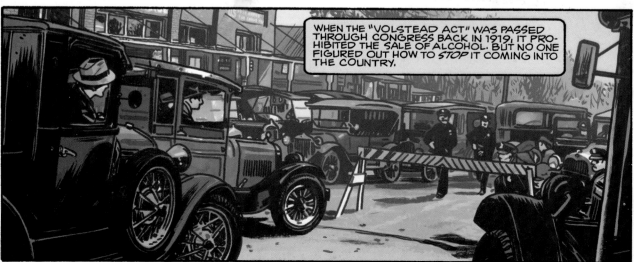

WHEN THE "VOLSTEAD ACT" WAS PASSED THROUGH CONGRESS BACK IN 1919, IT PRO-HIBITED THE SALE OF ALCOHOL. BUT NO ONE FIGURED OUT HOW TO *STOP* IT COMING INTO THE COUNTRY.

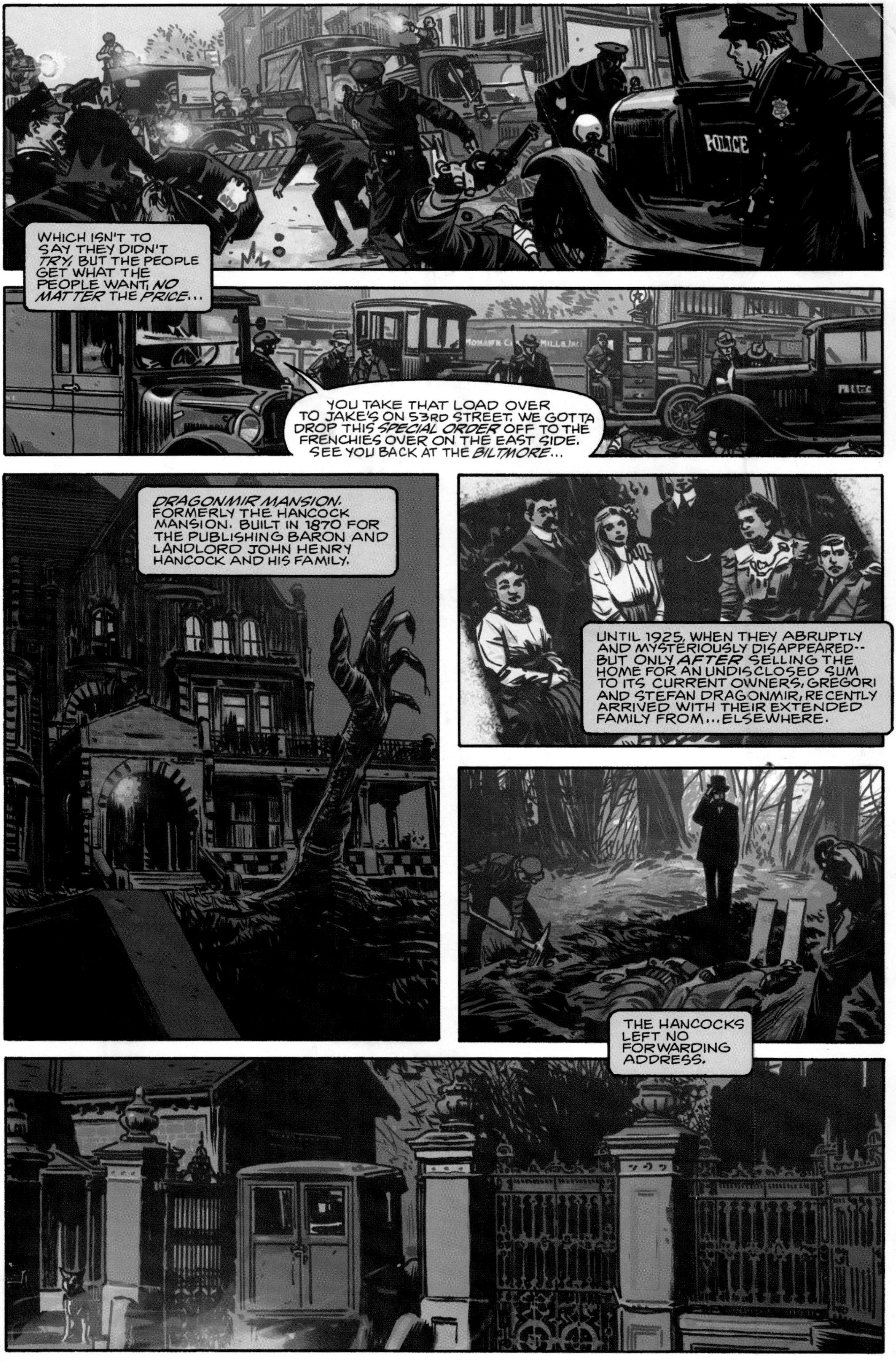
WHICH ISN'T TO SAY THEY DIDN'T *TRY*, BUT THE PEOPLE GET WHAT THE PEOPLE WANT, *NO MATTER* THE *PRICE*...
POLICE
YOU TAKE THAT LOAD OVER TO JAKE'S ON 53RD STREET. WE GOTTA DROP THIS *SPECIAL ORDER* OFF TO THE FRENCHIES OVER ON THE EAST SIDE. SEE YOU BACK AT THE *BILTMORE*...
DRAGONMIR MANSION. FORMERLY THE HANCOCK MANSION. BUILT IN 1870 FOR THE PUBLISHING BARON AND LANDLORD JOHN HENRY HANCOCK AND HIS FAMILY.
UNTIL 1925, WHEN THEY ABRUPTLY AND MYSTERIOUSLY DISAPPEARED-- BUT ONLY *AFTER* SELLING THE HOME FOR AN UNDISCLOSED SUM TO ITS CURRENT OWNERS, GREGORI AND STEFAN DRAGONMIR, RECENTLY ARRIVED WITH THEIR EXTENDED FAMILY FROM... ELSEWHERE.
THE HANCOCKS LEFT NO FORWARDING ADDRESS.

HOOCH, I UNNER-STAN. GUNS AND DOPE I UNNERSTAN, RIGHT. GIRLS, I *REALLY* UNNERSTAN. BUT STEALIN' *BLOOD* FROM HOSPITALS AND BRINGIN' IT TO THIS PLACE DON'T MAKE NO SENSE AT ALL.

THE BOSS SAYS WE DO IT, WE DO IT, AN' WE BETTER DO IT *QUICK*. THE DON CALLED A MEET TONIGHT. MOST OF THE FAMILY GONNA BE THERE.

DON'T FEEL RIGHT, THAT'S ALL. JUST DON'T FEEL RIGHT. WE SHOULDN'T BE DEALING WITH THESE PEOPLE.

AW, TELL IT TO THE BOSS. THEIR MONEY'S SAME COLOR AS EVERBUDDY ELSE'S, THEY WANNA BUY BLOOD INSTEAD O' BOOZE, WHO CARES? LEAST IT AIN'T YERS.

YOU ARE SURE, STEFAN? TO ACT ALONE LIKE THIS VILL GIVE YOUR BROTHER NO CHOICE. HE HASS YET TO DISCOVER THE TRUTH ABOUT YOUR ACTIONS WITH THE DELANCEY FAMILY.

IF YOU CONTINUE ON THIS PATH, THEN HE VILL ASSUME YOU MEAN TO TAKE CHARGE OF THE CLAN.

IS THAT WHAT YOU MEAN TO DO, STEFAN?

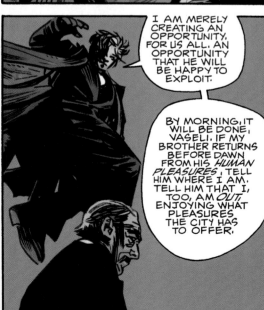

I AM MERELY CREATING AN OPPORTUNITY, FOR US ALL. AN OPPORTUNITY THAT HE WILL BE HAPPY TO EXPLOIT.

BY MORNING, IT WILL BE DONE, VASELI. IF MY BROTHER RETURNS BEFORE DAWN FROM HIS *HUMAN PLEASURES*, TELL HIM WHERE I AM. TELL HIM THAT I, TOO, AM *OUT*, ENJOYING WHAT PLEASURES THE CITY HAS TO OFFER.

IT VILL BE AS YOU VISH, STEFAN. ENJOY YOUR LITTLE... PARTY.

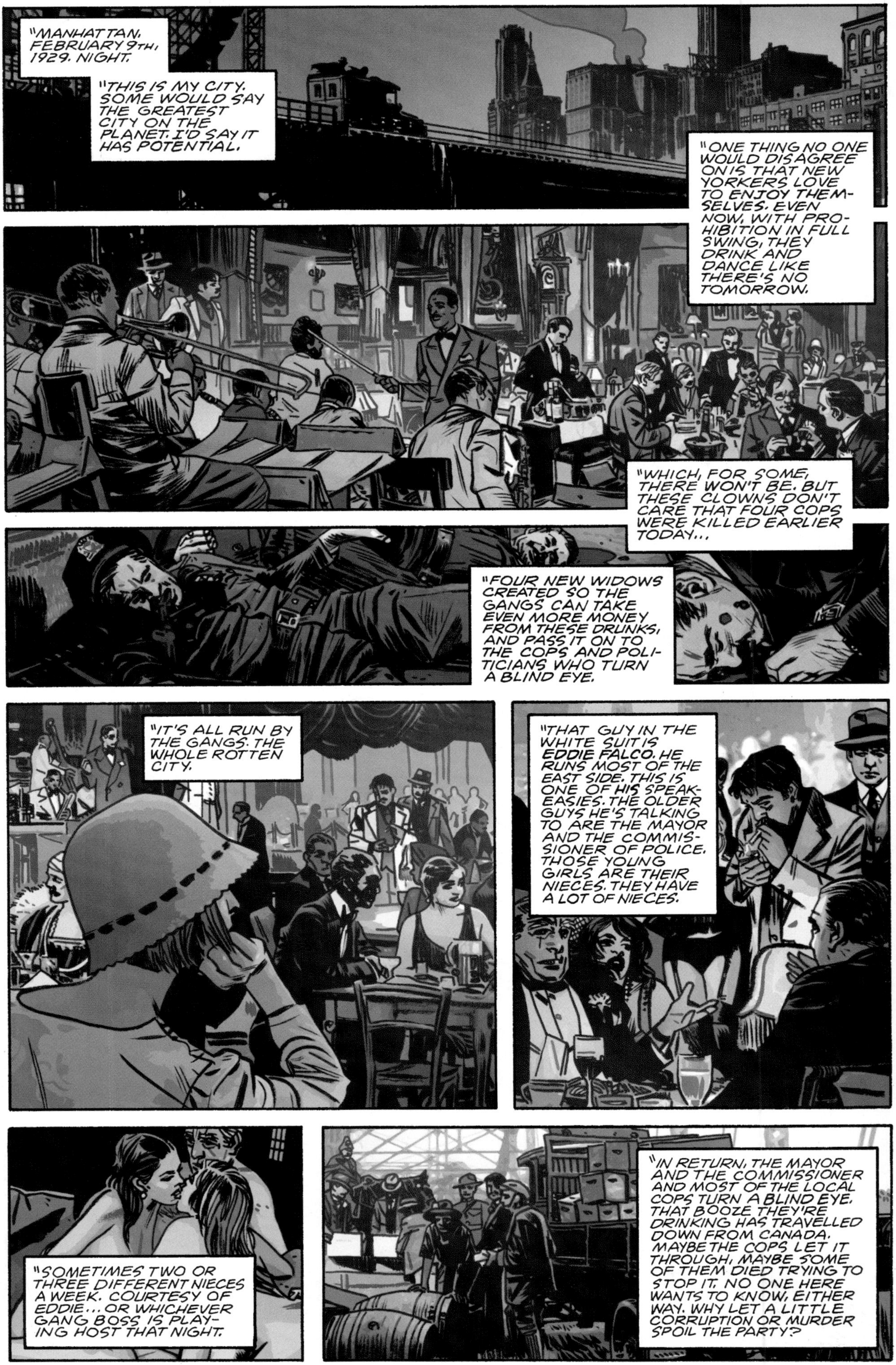
"MANHATTAN. FEBRUARY 9TH, 1929. NIGHT.
"THIS IS MY CITY. SOME WOULD SAY THE GREATEST CITY ON THE PLANET. I'D SAY IT HAS POTENTIAL.
"ONE THING NO ONE WOULD DISAGREE ON IS THAT NEW YORKERS LOVE TO ENJOY THEMSELVES. EVEN NOW, WITH PROHIBITION IN FULL SWING, THEY DRINK AND DANCE LIKE THERE'S NO TOMORROW.
"WHICH, FOR SOME, THERE WON'T BE. BUT THESE CLOWNS DON'T CARE THAT FOUR COPS WERE KILLED EARLIER TODAY...
"FOUR NEW WIDOWS CREATED SO THE GANGS CAN TAKE EVEN MORE MONEY FROM THESE DRUNKS, AND PASS IT ON TO THE COPS AND POLITICIANS WHO TURN A BLIND EYE.
"IT'S ALL RUN BY THE GANGS. THE WHOLE ROTTEN CITY.
"THAT GUY IN THE WHITE SUIT IS EDDIE FALCO. HE RUNS MOST OF THE EAST SIDE. THIS IS ONE OF HIS SPEAKEASIES. THE OLDER GUYS HE'S TALKING TO ARE THE MAYOR AND THE COMMISSIONER OF POLICE. THOSE YOUNG GIRLS ARE THEIR NIECES. THEY HAVE A LOT OF NIECES.
"SOMETIMES TWO OR THREE DIFFERENT NIECES A WEEK. COURTESY OF EDDIE... OR WHICHEVER GANG BOSS IS PLAYING HOST THAT NIGHT.
"IN RETURN, THE MAYOR AND THE COMMISSIONER AND MOST OF THE LOCAL COPS TURN A BLIND EYE. THAT BOOZE THEY'RE DRINKING HAS TRAVELLED DOWN FROM CANADA. MAYBE THE COPS LET IT THROUGH, MAYBE SOME OF THEM DIED TRYING TO STOP IT. NO ONE HERE WANTS TO KNOW, EITHER WAY. WHY LET A LITTLE CORRUPTION OR MURDER SPOIL THE PARTY?

"WELL, *I'D* LIKE TO SPOIL THE PARTY. AND ONE DAY I WILL. I'LL WRITE THE STORY OF THIS LOUSY, STINKING PLACE, AND THE CROOKED COPS AND CORRUPT POLITICIANS AND, ADMITTEDLY, HANDSOME GANGSTERS THAT WILL BLOW IT ALL APART."

BUT FOR NOW, I'M JUST THE SOCIETY REPORTER FOR THE GOTHAM HERALD. I COVER WEDDINGS, CHARITY GALAS, DEBUTANTE BALLS, THE STUFF NO ONE WANTS TO READ ABOUT ...UNLESS THEY WERE THERE. WHICH REMINDS ME...

COME ON, DALE, LET'S GO. WE NEED TO BE ACROSS TOWN AT THE BILTMORE. THE *LADIES FOR CHRISTIAN COOKING* FUNDRAISER SHOULD BE POSITIVELY *JUMPING* BY NOW. AND I NEED TO ASK MRS. VAN DYKE HOW SHE MANAGES TO DO SO MUCH FOR HER MANY CHARITIES AND STILL FINDS TIME TO EAT THREE LUNCHES A DAY.

CAN'T I FINISH MY LEMONADE FIRST? IT'S GOT A REAL KICK. *YOU* SHOULD TRY IT!

NO, THANKS. YOU SHOULDN'T BE DRINKING, EITHER. I BROUGHT YOU HERE FOR RESEARCH. YOU KNOW AS WELL AS I DO THAT INNOCENT MEN MIGHT HAVE BEEN MURDERED TO BRING THAT BOOZE HERE.

IT'S NO WONDER YOU DON'T DATE MUCH, KILLJOY. SO I LIKE TO DRINK--WHO DOESN'T?

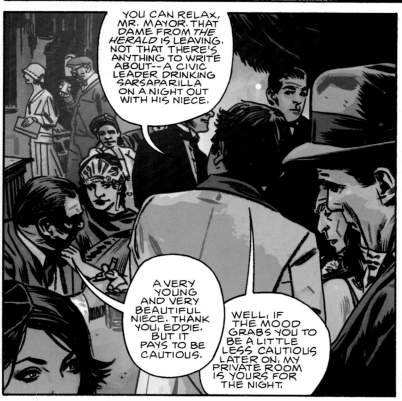

YOU CAN RELAX, MR. MAYOR. THAT DAME FROM *THE HERALD* IS LEAVING. NOT THAT THERE'S ANYTHING TO WRITE ABOUT-- A CIVIC LEADER DRINKING SARSAPARILLA ON A NIGHT OUT WITH HIS NIECE.

A VERY YOUNG AND VERY BEAUTIFUL NIECE. THANK YOU, EDDIE. BUT IT PAYS TO BE CAUTIOUS.

WELL, IF THE MOOD GRABS YOU TO BE A LITTLE LESS CAUTIOUS LATER ON, MY PRIVATE ROOM IS YOURS FOR THE NIGHT.

AND ALTHOUGH I *HATE* TO TALK BUSINESS IN FRONT OF HIS HONOR HERE, HAVE YOUR MEN TURNED UP ANYTHING ON DELANCEY AND HIS BOYS? NO ONE'S SEEN OR HEARD FROM ANY OF THEM FOR DAYS NOW. ANYTHING WE SHOULD KNOW? ANY CHANGES IN OUR SPECIAL RELATIONSHIP?

DON'T BE PARANOID, EDDIE. IF THE DELANCEY GANG HAS GONE, THEN IT MUST HAVE BEEN ONE OF THE OTHER OUTFITS. IT'S NOT US. WE DON'T KNOW ANYTHING YET. I HAVE MY MEN LOOKING INTO IT. O'LEARY IS IN CHARGE. YOU KNOW O'LEARY, RIGHT, EDDIE?

OH, WE KNOW O'LEARY, DON'T WE, TONY? AND WE KNOW JUST WHERE TO FIND HIM.

O'LEARY KNOWS TO OFFER YOU HIS FULL CO-OPERATION. HE'S AN AMBITIOUS COP. HE'LL GO FAR.

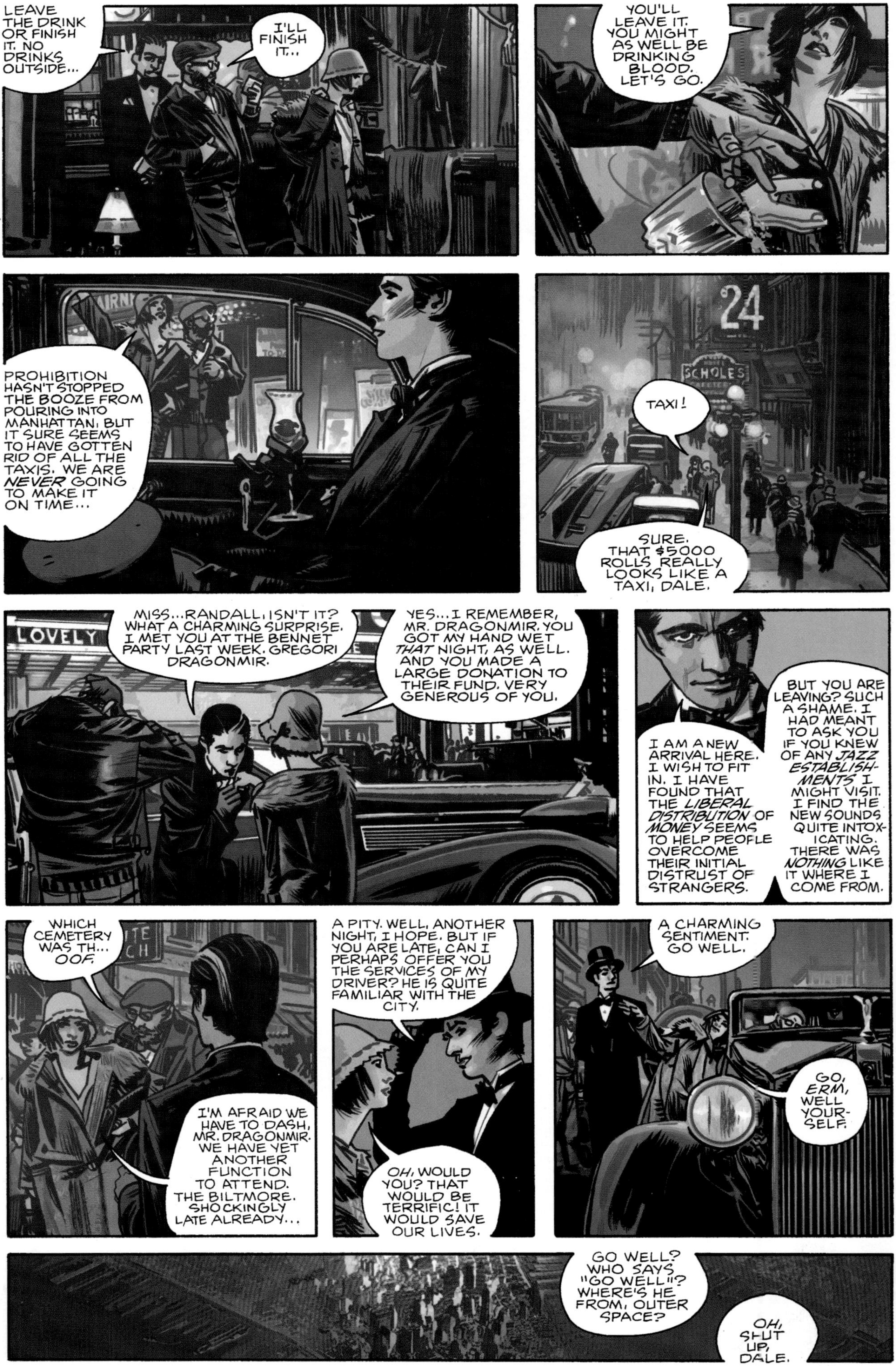
LEAVE THE DRINK OR FINISH IT. NO DRINKS OUTSIDE...
I'LL FINISH IT...
YOU'LL LEAVE IT. YOU MIGHT AS WELL BE DRINKING BLOOD. LET'S GO.
PROHIBITION HASN'T STOPPED THE BOOZE FROM POURING INTO MANHATTAN, BUT IT SURE SEEMS TO HAVE GOTTEN RID OF ALL THE TAXIS. WE ARE *NEVER* GOING TO MAKE IT ON TIME...
24
SCHOLE'S
TAXI!
SURE. THAT $5000 ROLLS REALLY LOOKS LIKE A TAXI, DALE.
LOVELY
MISS...RANDALL, ISN'T IT? WHAT A CHARMING SURPRISE. I MET YOU AT THE BENNET PARTY LAST WEEK. GREGORI DRAGONMIR.
YES...I REMEMBER, MR. DRAGONMIR. YOU GOT MY HAND WET *THAT* NIGHT, AS WELL. AND YOU MADE A LARGE DONATION TO THEIR FUND. VERY GENEROUS OF YOU.
I AM A NEW ARRIVAL HERE. I WISH TO FIT IN. I HAVE FOUND THAT THE *LIBERAL DISTRIBUTION* OF *MONEY* SEEMS TO HELP PEOPLE OVERCOME THEIR INITIAL DISTRUST OF STRANGERS.
BUT YOU ARE LEAVING? SUCH A SHAME. I HAD MEANT TO ASK YOU IF YOU KNEW OF ANY *JAZZ ESTABLISHMENTS* I MIGHT VISIT. I FIND THE NEW SOUNDS QUITE INTOXICATING. THERE WAS *NOTHING* LIKE IT WHERE I COME FROM.
WHICH CEMETERY WAS TH... *OOF.*
I'M AFRAID WE HAVE TO DASH, MR. DRAGONMIR. WE HAVE YET ANOTHER FUNCTION TO ATTEND. THE BILTMORE. SHOCKINGLY LATE ALREADY...
A PITY. WELL, ANOTHER NIGHT, I HOPE. BUT IF YOU ARE LATE, CAN I PERHAPS OFFER YOU THE SERVICES OF MY DRIVER? HE IS QUITE FAMILIAR WITH THE CITY.
OH, WOULD YOU? THAT WOULD BE TERRIFIC! IT WOULD SAVE OUR LIVES.
A CHARMING SENTIMENT. GO WELL.
GO, *ERM,* WELL YOURSELF.
GO WELL? WHO SAYS "GO WELL"? WHERE'S HE FROM, OUTER SPACE?
OH, SHUT UP, DALE.

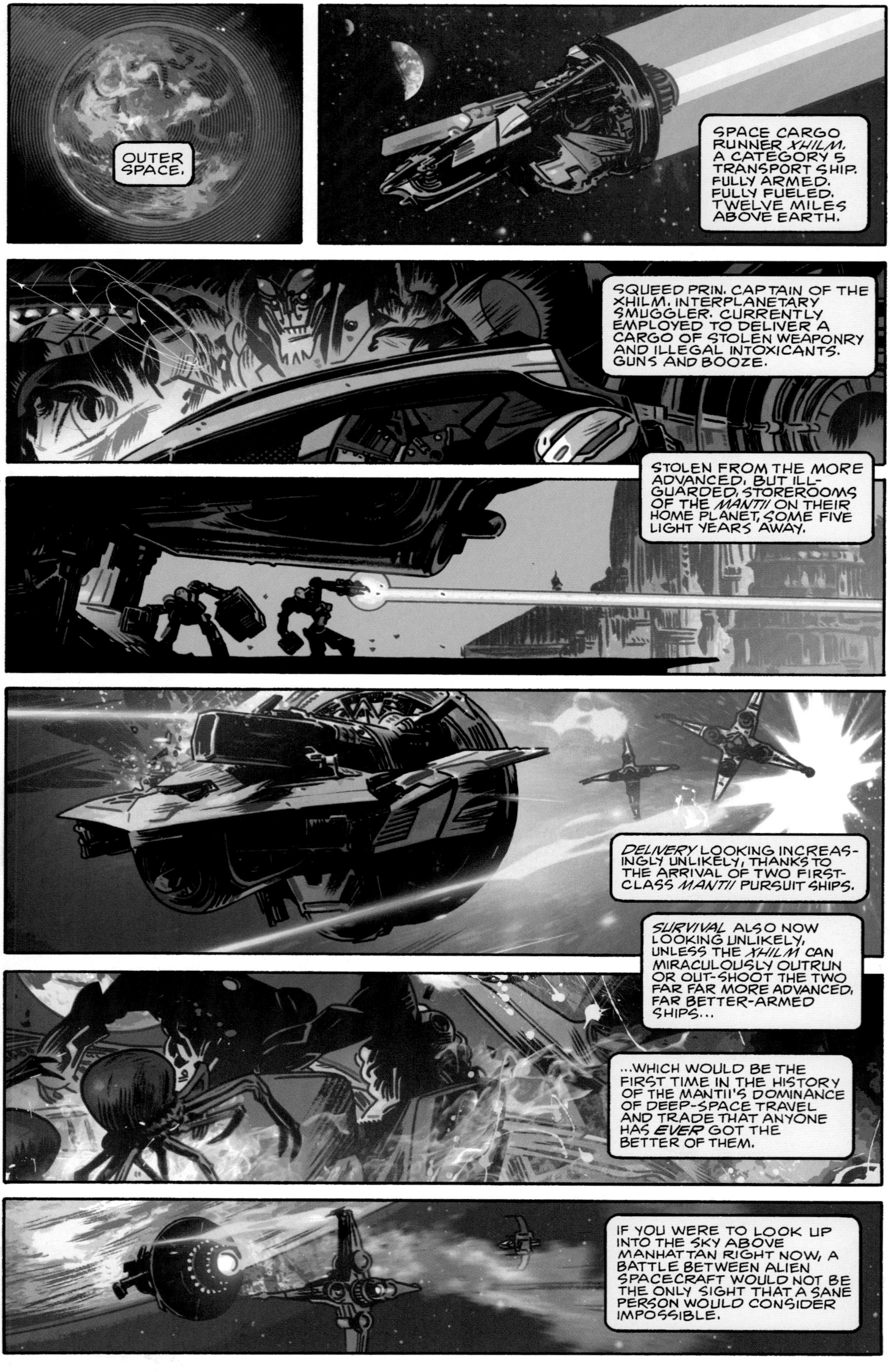
OUTER SPACE.
SPACE CARGO RUNNER XHILM. A CATEGORY 5 TRANSPORT SHIP. FULLY ARMED. FULLY FUELED. TWELVE MILES ABOVE EARTH.
SQUEED PRIN. CAPTAIN OF THE XHILM. INTERPLANETARY SMUGGLER. CURRENTLY EMPLOYED TO DELIVER A CARGO OF STOLEN WEAPONRY AND ILLEGAL INTOXICANTS. GUNS AND BOOZE.
STOLEN FROM THE MORE ADVANCED, BUT ILL-GUARDED, STOREROOMS OF THE MANTII ON THEIR HOME PLANET, SOME FIVE LIGHT YEARS AWAY.
DELIVERY LOOKING INCREASINGLY UNLIKELY, THANKS TO THE ARRIVAL OF TWO FIRST-CLASS MANTII PURSUIT SHIPS.
SURVIVAL ALSO NOW LOOKING UNLIKELY, UNLESS THE XHILM CAN MIRACULOUSLY OUTRUN OR OUT-SHOOT THE TWO FAR FAR MORE ADVANCED, FAR BETTER-ARMED SHIPS...
...WHICH WOULD BE THE FIRST TIME IN THE HISTORY OF THE MANTII'S DOMINANCE OF DEEP-SPACE TRAVEL AND TRADE THAT ANYONE HAS EVER GOT THE BETTER OF THEM.
IF YOU WERE TO LOOK UP INTO THE SKY ABOVE MANHATTAN RIGHT NOW, A BATTLE BETWEEN ALIEN SPACECRAFT WOULD NOT BE THE ONLY SIGHT THAT A SANE PERSON WOULD CONSIDER IMPOSSIBLE.

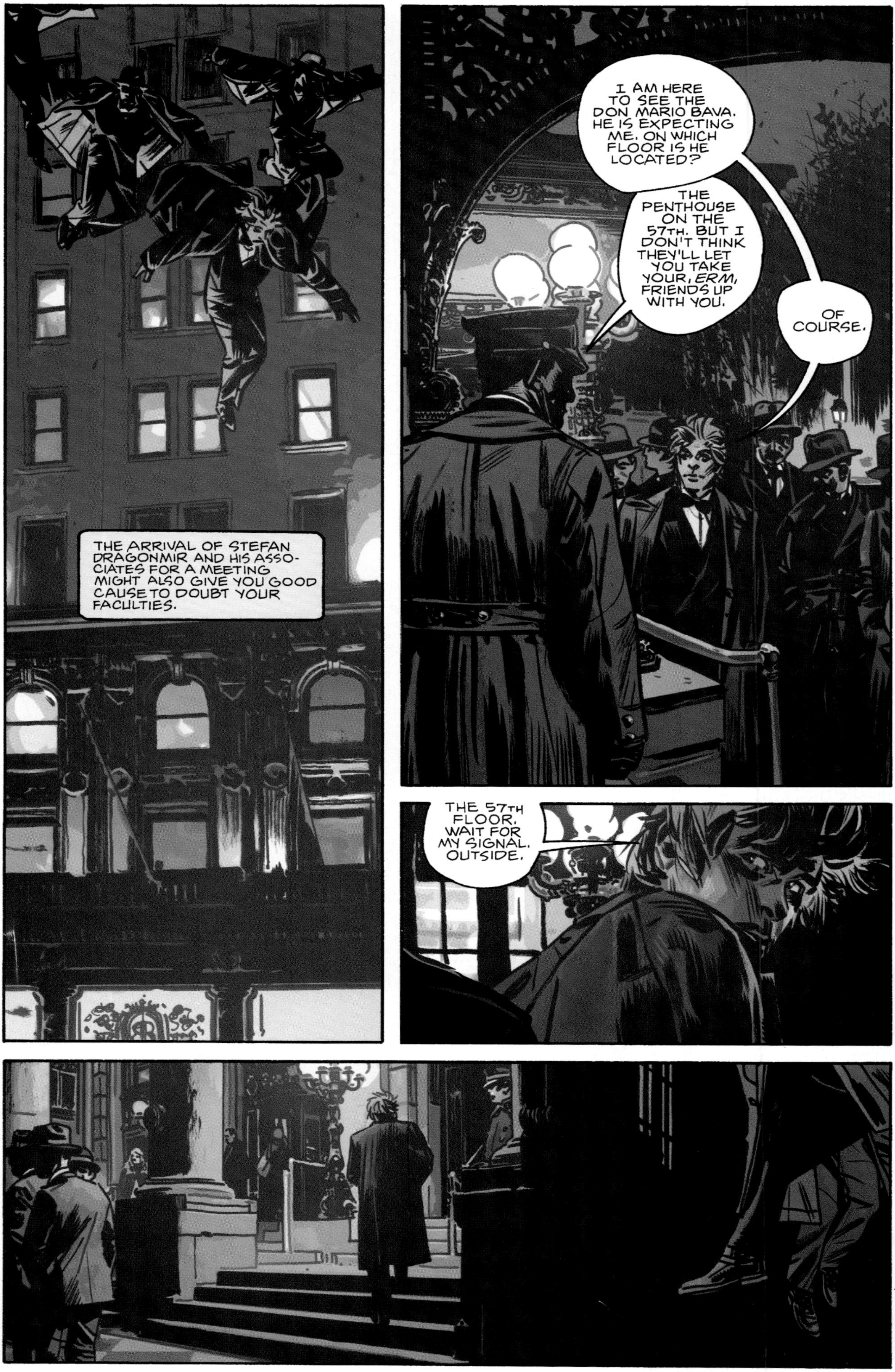
THE ARRIVAL OF STEFAN DRAGONMIR AND HIS ASSOCIATES FOR A MEETING MIGHT ALSO GIVE YOU GOOD CAUSE TO DOUBT YOUR FACULTIES.
I AM HERE TO SEE THE DON MARIO BAVA. HE IS EXPECTING ME. ON WHICH FLOOR IS HE LOCATED?
THE PENTHOUSE ON THE 57TH. BUT I DON'T THINK THEY'LL LET YOU TAKE YOUR, *ERM*, FRIENDS UP WITH YOU.
OF COURSE.
THE 57TH FLOOR. WAIT FOR MY SIGNAL. OUTSIDE.

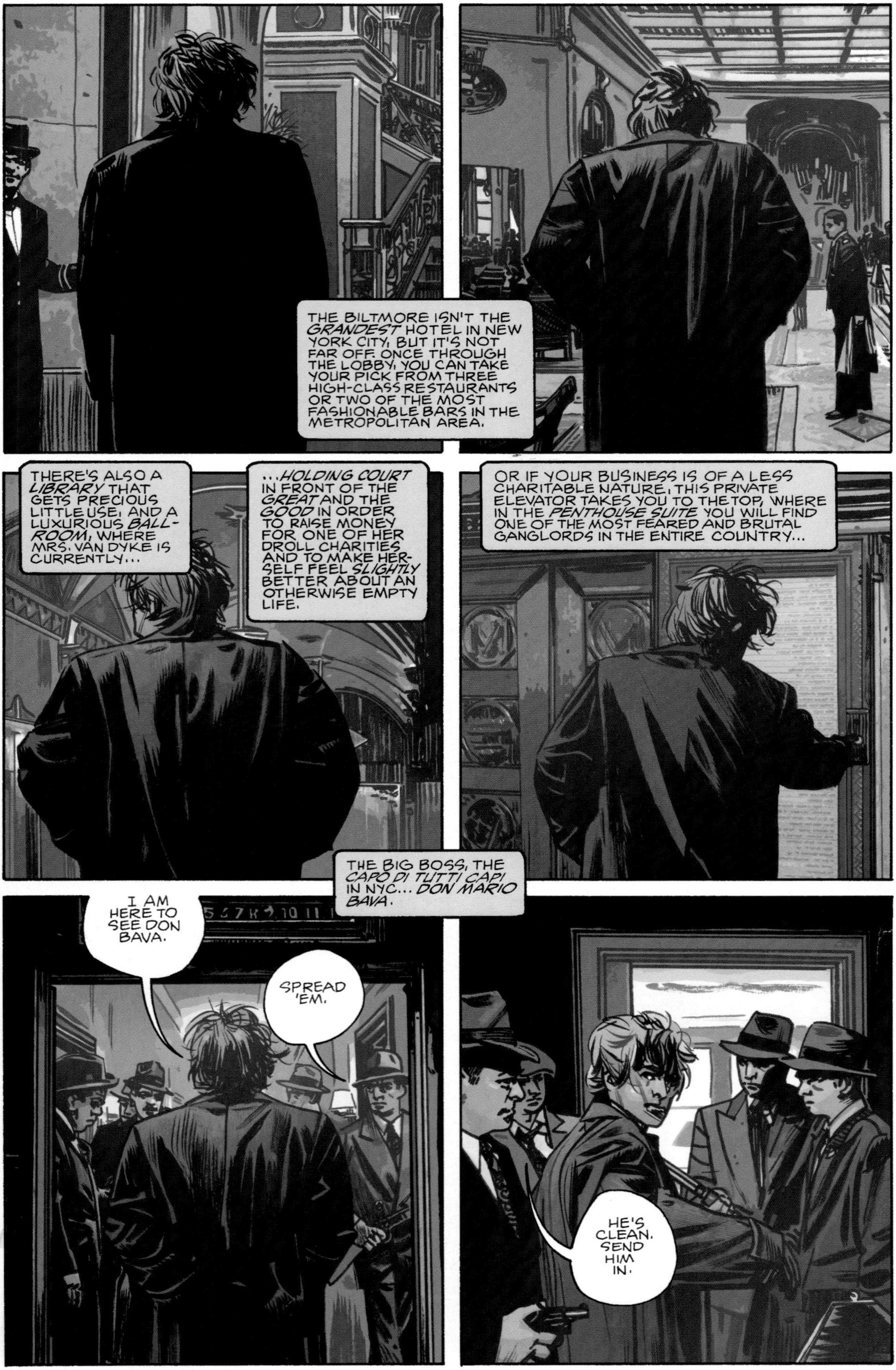
THE BILTMORE ISN'T THE *GRANDEST* HOTEL IN NEW YORK CITY, BUT IT'S NOT FAR OFF. ONCE THROUGH THE LOBBY, YOU CAN TAKE YOUR PICK FROM THREE HIGH-CLASS RESTAURANTS OR TWO OF THE MOST FASHIONABLE BARS IN THE METROPOLITAN AREA.
THERE'S ALSO A *LIBRARY* THAT GETS PRECIOUS LITTLE USE, AND A LUXURIOUS *BALL-ROOM*, WHERE MRS. VAN DYKE IS CURRENTLY...
...*HOLDING COURT* IN FRONT OF THE *GREAT* AND THE *GOOD* IN ORDER TO RAISE MONEY FOR ONE OF HER DROLL CHARITIES AND TO MAKE HER-SELF FEEL *SLIGHTLY* BETTER ABOUT AN OTHERWISE EMPTY LIFE.
OR IF YOUR BUSINESS IS OF A LESS CHARITABLE NATURE, THIS PRIVATE ELEVATOR TAKES YOU TO THE TOP, WHERE IN THE *PENTHOUSE SUITE* YOU WILL FIND ONE OF THE MOST FEARED AND BRUTAL GANGLORDS IN THE ENTIRE COUNTRY...
THE BIG BOSS, THE *CAPO DI TUTTI CAPI* IN NYC... *DON MARIO BAVA*.
I AM HERE TO SEE DON BAVA.
SPREAD 'EM.
HE'S CLEAN. SEND HIM IN.

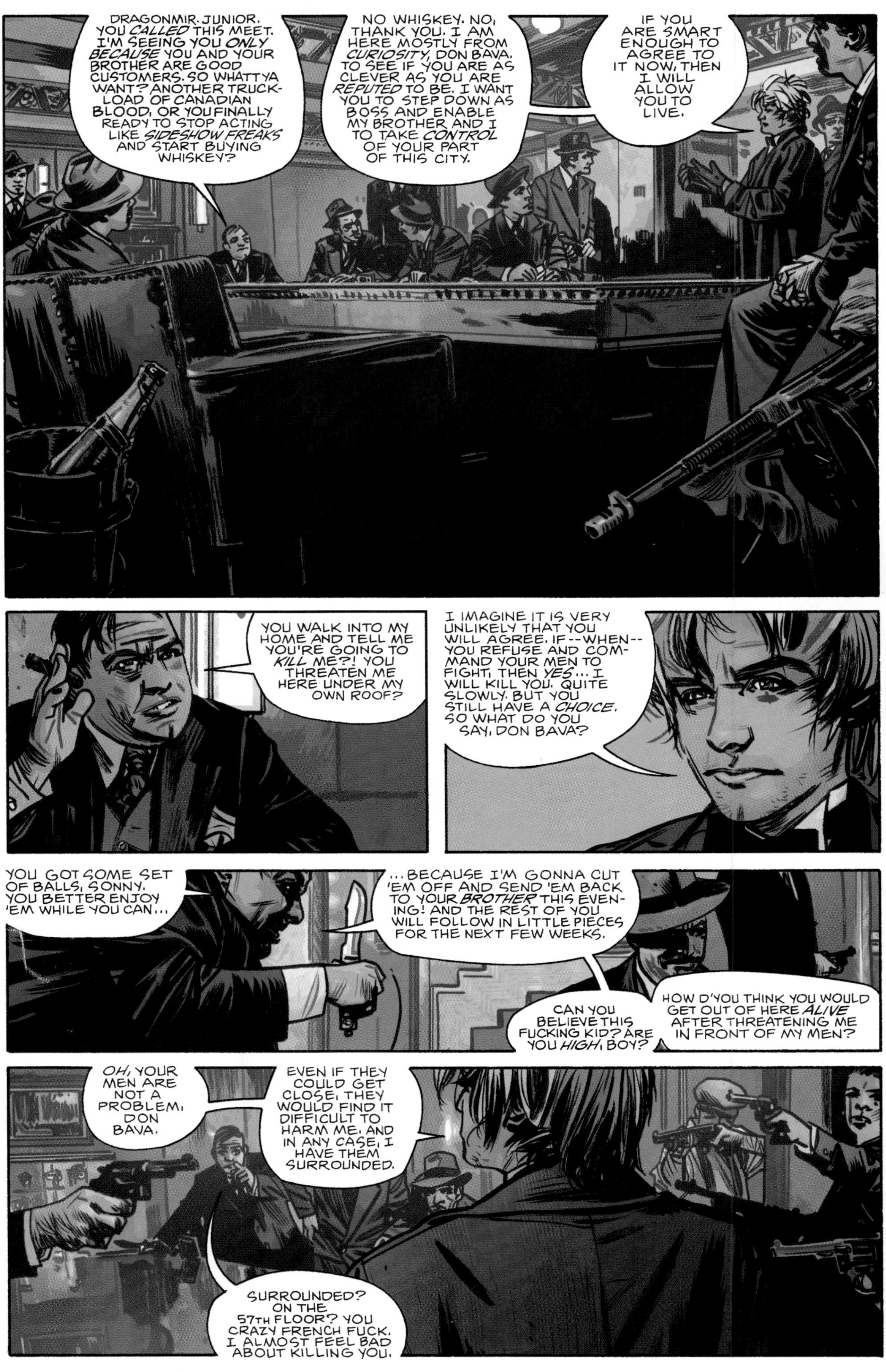
DRAGONMIR. JUNIOR. YOU CALLED THIS MEET. I'M SEEING YOU ONLY BECAUSE YOU AND YOUR BROTHER ARE GOOD CUSTOMERS. SO WHATTYA WANT? ANOTHER TRUCK-LOAD OF CANADIAN BLOOD, OR YOU FINALLY READY TO STOP ACTING LIKE SIDESHOW FREAKS AND START BUYING WHISKEY?
NO WHISKEY. NO, THANK YOU. I AM HERE MOSTLY FROM CURIOSITY, DON BAVA. TO SEE IF YOU ARE AS CLEVER AS YOU ARE REPUTED TO BE. I WANT YOU TO STEP DOWN AS BOSS AND ENABLE MY BROTHER AND I TO TAKE CONTROL OF YOUR PART OF THIS CITY.
IF YOU ARE SMART ENOUGH TO AGREE TO IT NOW, THEN I WILL ALLOW YOU TO LIVE.
YOU WALK INTO MY HOME AND TELL ME YOU'RE GOING TO KILL ME?! YOU THREATEN ME HERE UNDER MY OWN ROOF?
I IMAGINE IT IS VERY UNLIKELY THAT YOU WILL AGREE. IF--WHEN--YOU REFUSE AND COMMAND YOUR MEN TO FIGHT, THEN YES... I WILL KILL YOU. QUITE SLOWLY. BUT YOU STILL HAVE A CHOICE. SO WHAT DO YOU SAY, DON BAVA?
YOU GOT SOME SET OF BALLS, SONNY. YOU BETTER ENJOY 'EM WHILE YOU CAN...
...BECAUSE I'M GONNA CUT 'EM OFF AND SEND 'EM BACK TO YOUR BROTHER THIS EVENING! AND THE REST OF YOU WILL FOLLOW IN LITTLE PIECES FOR THE NEXT FEW WEEKS.
CAN YOU BELIEVE THIS FUCKING KID? ARE YOU HIGH, BOY?
HOW D'YOU THINK YOU WOULD GET OUT OF HERE ALIVE AFTER THREATENING ME IN FRONT OF MY MEN?
OH, YOUR MEN ARE NOT A PROBLEM, DON BAVA.
EVEN IF THEY COULD GET CLOSE, THEY WOULD FIND IT DIFFICULT TO HARM ME. AND IN ANY CASE, I HAVE THEM SURROUNDED.
SURROUNDED? ON THE 57TH FLOOR? YOU CRAZY FRENCH FUCK. I ALMOST FEEL BAD ABOUT KILLING YOU.

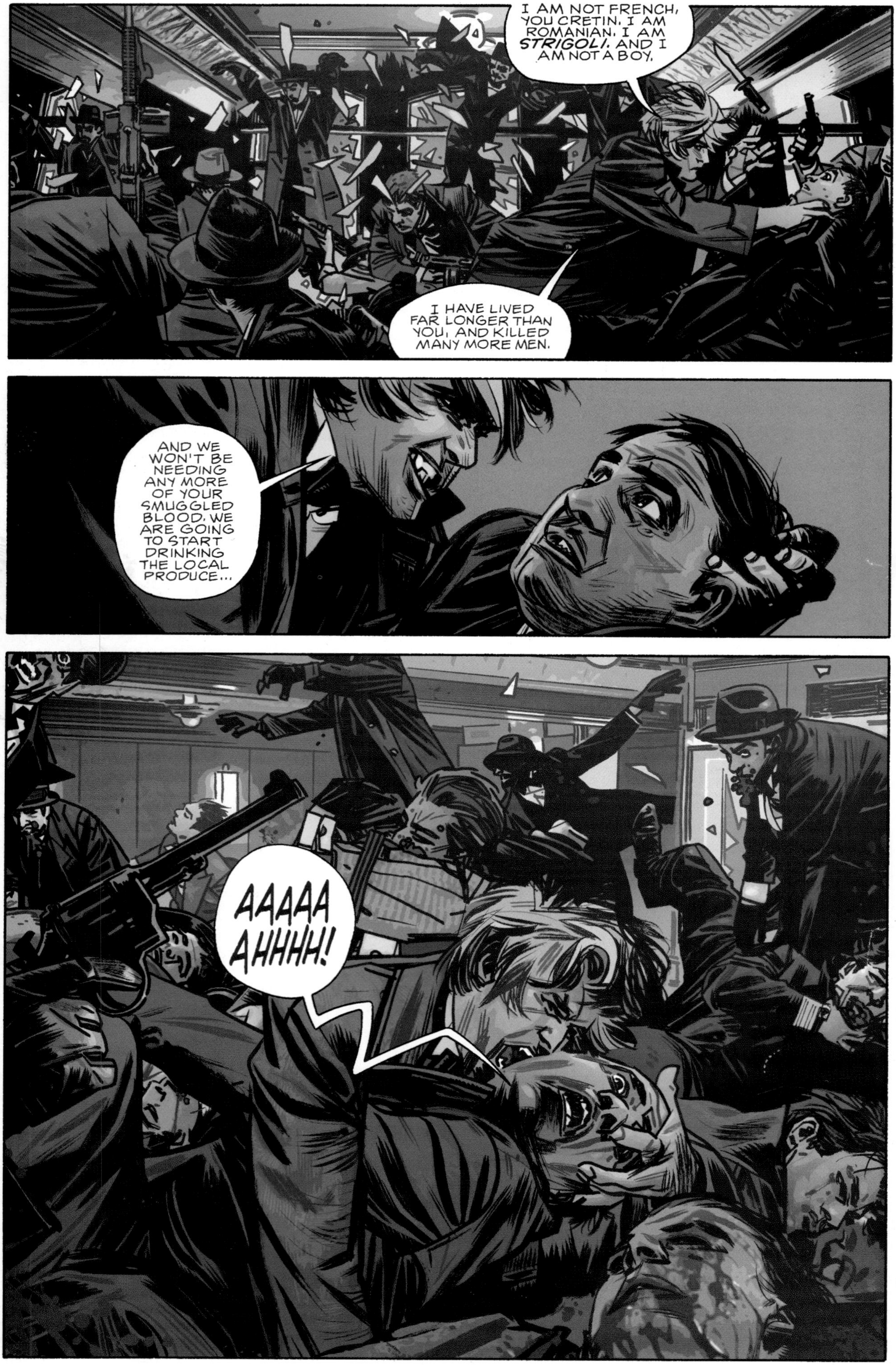
I AM NOT FRENCH, YOU CRETIN. I AM ROMANIAN. I AM *STRIGOLI*. AND I AM NOT A BOY.
I HAVE LIVED FAR LONGER THAN YOU, AND KILLED MANY MORE MEN.
AND WE WON'T BE NEEDING ANY MORE OF YOUR SMUGGLED BLOOD. WE ARE GOING TO START DRINKING THE LOCAL PRODUCE...
AAAAA AHHHH!

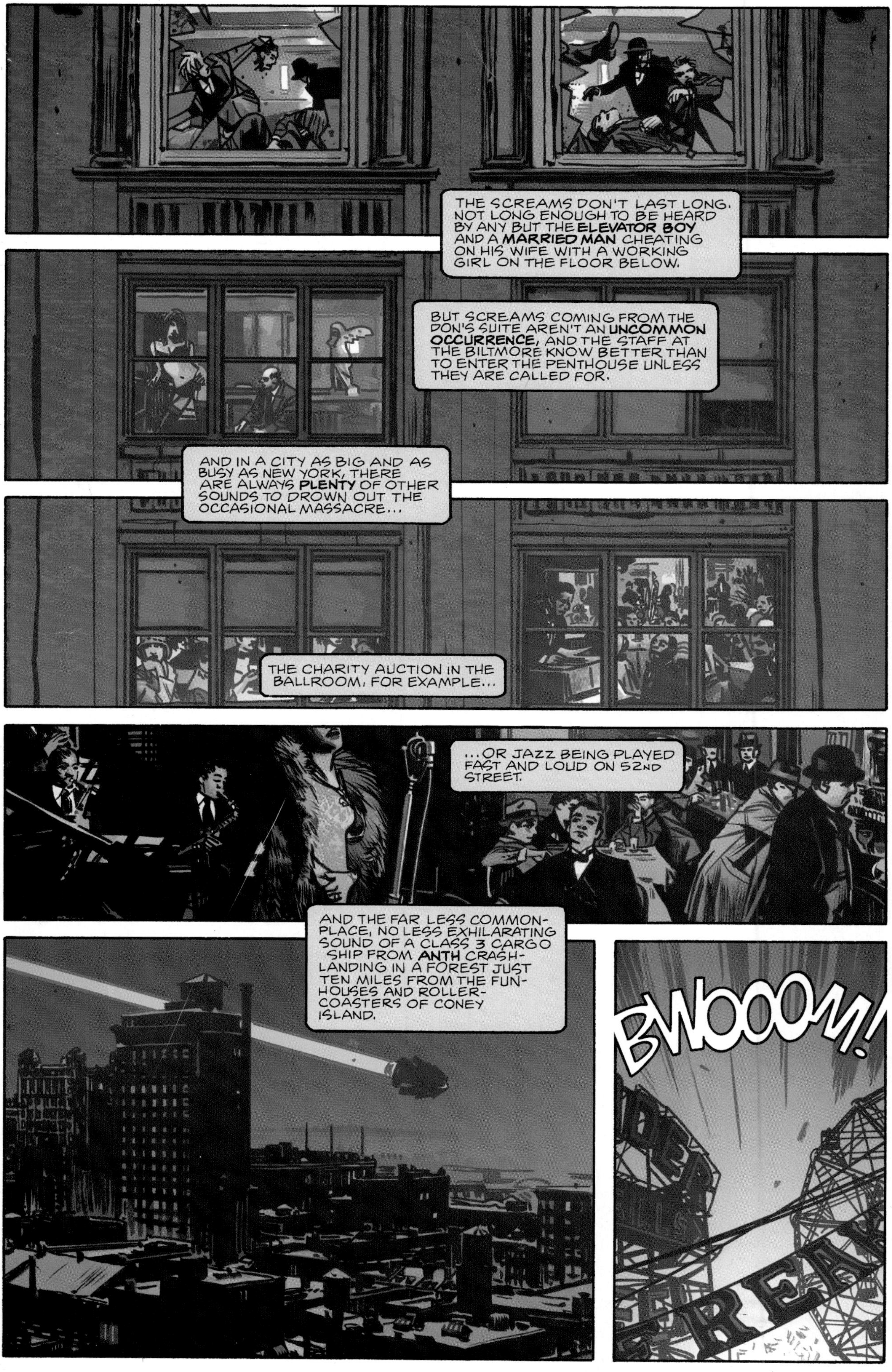
THE SCREAMS DON'T LAST LONG. NOT LONG ENOUGH TO BE HEARD BY ANY BUT THE ELEVATOR BOY AND A MARRIED MAN CHEATING ON HIS WIFE WITH A WORKING GIRL ON THE FLOOR BELOW.
BUT SCREAMS COMING FROM THE DON'S SUITE AREN'T AN UNCOMMON OCCURRENCE, AND THE STAFF AT THE BILTMORE KNOW BETTER THAN TO ENTER THE PENTHOUSE UNLESS THEY ARE CALLED FOR.
AND IN A CITY AS BIG AND AS BUSY AS NEW YORK, THERE ARE ALWAYS PLENTY OF OTHER SOUNDS TO DROWN OUT THE OCCASIONAL MASSACRE...
THE CHARITY AUCTION IN THE BALLROOM, FOR EXAMPLE...
...OR JAZZ BEING PLAYED FAST AND LOUD ON 52ND STREET.
AND THE FAR LESS COMMONPLACE, NO LESS EXHILARATING SOUND OF A CLASS 3 CARGO SHIP FROM ANTH CRASH-LANDING IN A FOREST JUST TEN MILES FROM THE FUNHOUSES AND ROLLERCOASTERS OF CONEY ISLAND.
BWOOOM!

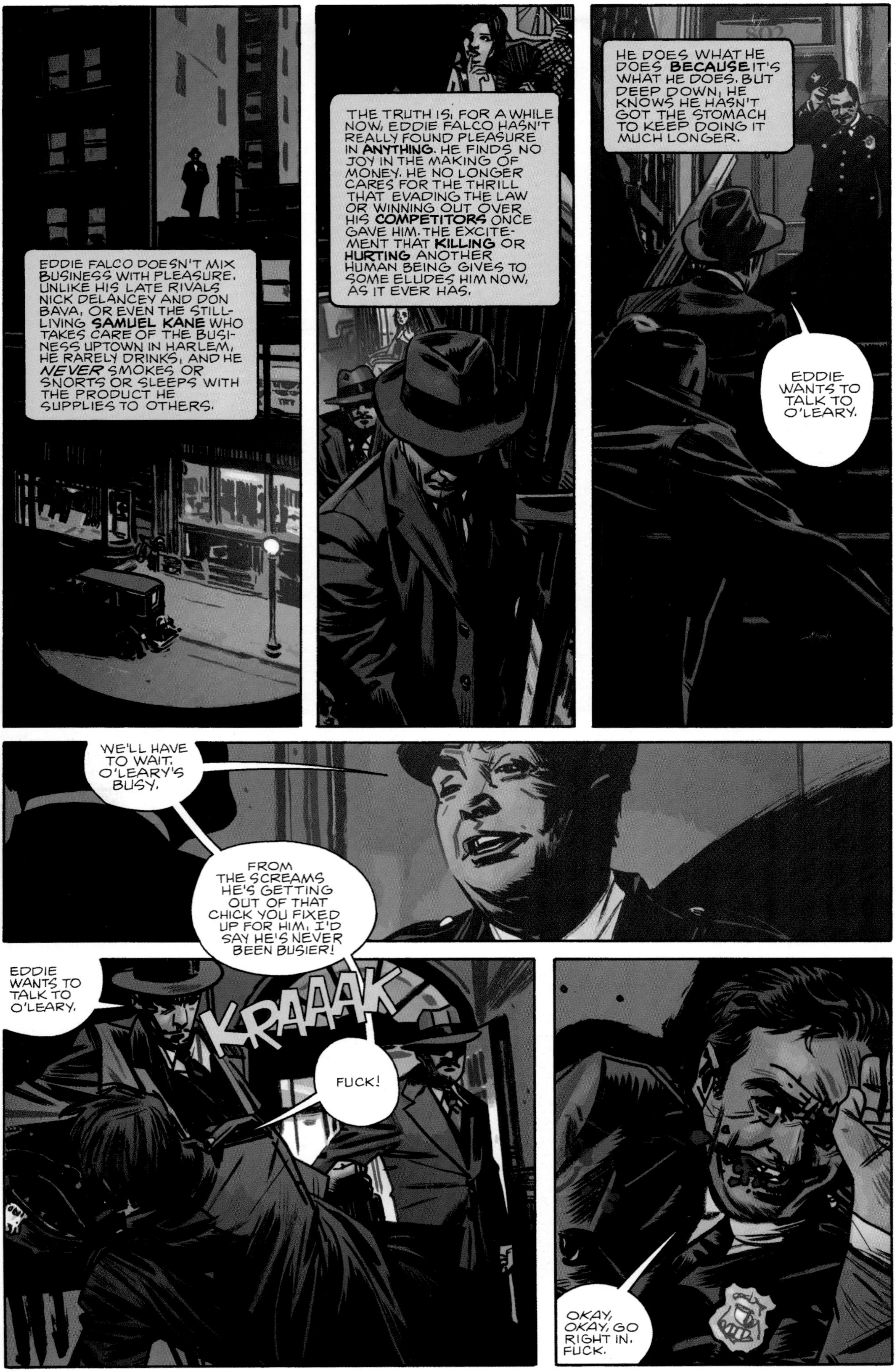

EDDIE FALCO DOESN'T MIX BUSINESS WITH PLEASURE. UNLIKE HIS LATE RIVALS NICK DELANCEY AND DON BAVA, OR EVEN THE STILL-LIVING **SAMUEL KANE** WHO TAKES CARE OF THE BUSINESS UPTOWN IN HARLEM, HE RARELY DRINKS, AND HE ***NEVER*** SMOKES OR SNORTS OR SLEEPS WITH THE PRODUCT HE SUPPLIES TO OTHERS.
THE TRUTH IS, FOR A WHILE NOW, EDDIE FALCO HASN'T REALLY FOUND PLEASURE IN **ANYTHING**. HE FINDS NO JOY IN THE MAKING OF MONEY. HE NO LONGER CARES FOR THE THRILL THAT EVADING THE LAW OR WINNING OUT OVER HIS **COMPETITORS** ONCE GAVE HIM. THE EXCITEMENT THAT **KILLING** OR **HURTING** ANOTHER HUMAN BEING GIVES TO SOME ELUDES HIM NOW, AS IT EVER HAS.
HE DOES WHAT HE DOES **BECAUSE** IT'S WHAT HE DOES. BUT DEEP DOWN, HE KNOWS HE HASN'T GOT THE STOMACH TO KEEP DOING IT MUCH LONGER.
EDDIE WANTS TO TALK TO O'LEARY.
WE'LL HAVE TO WAIT. O'LEARY'S BUSY.
FROM THE SCREAMS HE'S GETTING OUT OF THAT CHICK YOU FIXED UP FOR HIM, I'D SAY HE'S NEVER BEEN BUSIER!
EDDIE WANTS TO TALK TO O'LEARY.
KRAAAK
FUCK!
OKAY, OKAY, GO RIGHT IN. FUCK.

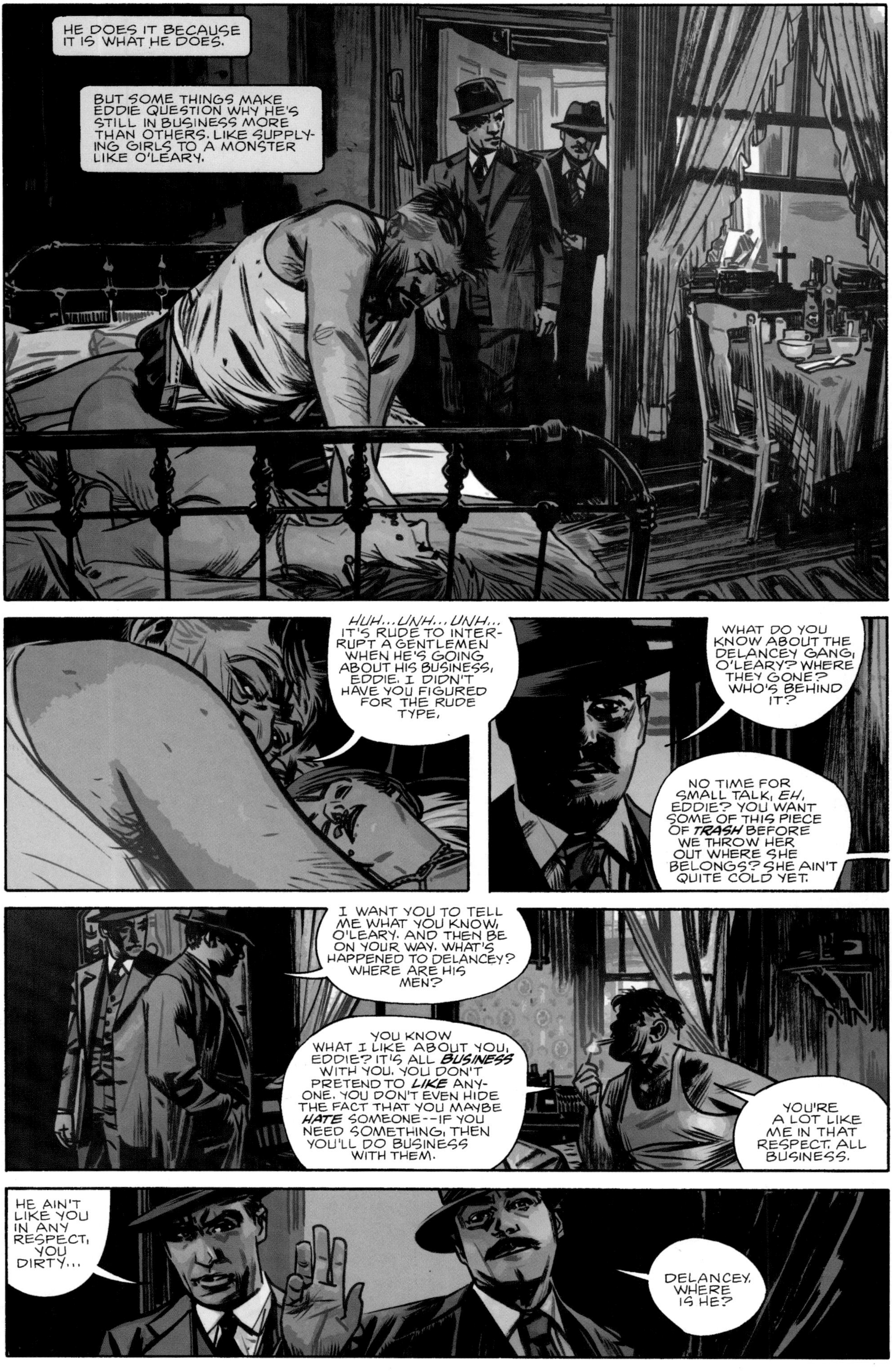
HE DOES IT BECAUSE IT IS WHAT HE DOES.
BUT SOME THINGS MAKE EDDIE QUESTION WHY HE'S STILL IN BUSINESS MORE THAN OTHERS. LIKE SUPPLYING GIRLS TO A MONSTER LIKE O'LEARY.
HUH... UNH... UNH... IT'S RUDE TO INTERRUPT A GENTLEMEN WHEN HE'S GOING ABOUT HIS BUSINESS, EDDIE. I DIDN'T HAVE YOU FIGURED FOR THE RUDE TYPE.
WHAT DO YOU KNOW ABOUT THE DELANCEY GANG, O'LEARY? WHERE THEY GONE? WHO'S BEHIND IT?
NO TIME FOR SMALL TALK, EH, EDDIE? YOU WANT SOME OF THIS PIECE OF TRASH BEFORE WE THROW HER OUT WHERE SHE BELONGS? SHE AIN'T QUITE COLD YET.
I WANT YOU TO TELL ME WHAT YOU KNOW, O'LEARY. AND THEN BE ON YOUR WAY. WHAT'S HAPPENED TO DELANCEY? WHERE ARE HIS MEN?
YOU KNOW WHAT I LIKE ABOUT YOU, EDDIE? IT'S ALL BUSINESS WITH YOU. YOU DON'T PRETEND TO LIKE ANYONE. YOU DON'T EVEN HIDE THE FACT THAT YOU MAYBE HATE SOMEONE--IF YOU NEED SOMETHING, THEN YOU'LL DO BUSINESS WITH THEM.
YOU'RE A LOT LIKE ME IN THAT RESPECT. ALL BUSINESS.
HE AIN'T LIKE YOU IN ANY RESPECT, YOU DIRTY...
DELANCEY. WHERE IS HE?

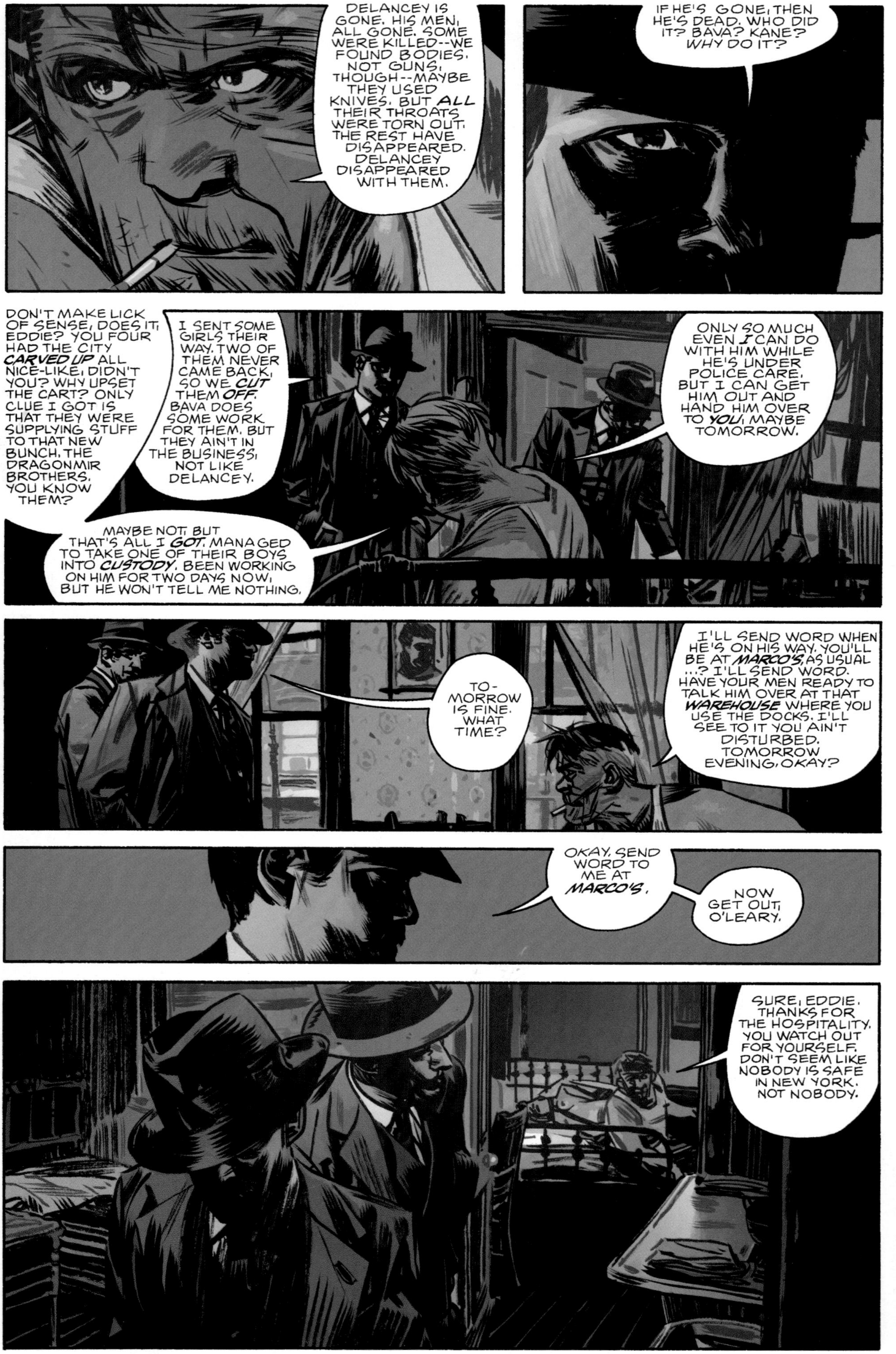
DELANCEY IS GONE. HIS MEN, ALL GONE. SOME WERE KILLED--WE FOUND BODIES. NOT GUNS, THOUGH--MAYBE THEY USED KNIVES. BUT ALL THEIR THROATS WERE TORN OUT. THE REST HAVE DISAPPEARED. DELANCEY DISAPPEARED WITH THEM.
IF HE'S GONE, THEN HE'S DEAD. WHO DID IT? BAVA? KANE? WHY DO IT?
DON'T MAKE LICK OF SENSE, DOES IT, EDDIE? YOU FOUR HAD THE CITY CARVED UP ALL NICE-LIKE, DIDN'T YOU? WHY UPSET THE CART? ONLY CLUE I GOT IS THAT THEY WERE SUPPLYING STUFF TO THAT NEW BUNCH, THE DRAGONMIR BROTHERS. YOU KNOW THEM?
I SENT SOME GIRLS THEIR WAY. TWO OF THEM NEVER CAME BACK, SO WE CUT THEM OFF. BAVA DOES SOME WORK FOR THEM, BUT THEY AIN'T IN THE BUSINESS, NOT LIKE DELANCEY.
MAYBE NOT, BUT THAT'S ALL I GOT. MANAGED TO TAKE ONE OF THEIR BOYS INTO CUSTODY. BEEN WORKING ON HIM FOR TWO DAYS NOW, BUT HE WON'T TELL ME NOTHING.
ONLY SO MUCH EVEN I CAN DO WITH HIM WHILE HE'S UNDER POLICE CARE. BUT I CAN GET HIM OUT AND HAND HIM OVER TO YOU, MAYBE TOMORROW.
TO-MORROW IS FINE. WHAT TIME?
I'LL SEND WORD WHEN HE'S ON HIS WAY. YOU'LL BE AT MARCO'S, AS USUAL ...? I'LL SEND WORD. HAVE YOUR MEN READY TO TALK HIM OVER AT THAT WAREHOUSE WHERE YOU USE THE DOCKS. I'LL SEE TO IT YOU AIN'T DISTURBED. TOMORROW EVENING, OKAY?
OKAY. SEND WORD TO ME AT MARCO'S.
NOW GET OUT, O'LEARY.
SURE, EDDIE. THANKS FOR THE HOSPITALITY. YOU WATCH OUT FOR YOURSELF. DON'T SEEM LIKE NOBODY IS SAFE IN NEW YORK. NOT NOBODY.

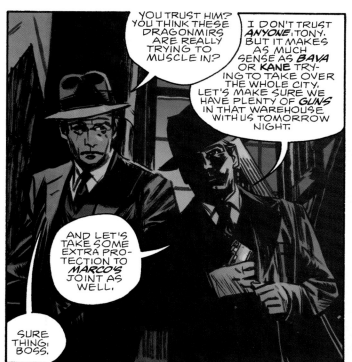

YOU TRUST HIM? YOU THINK THESE DRAGONMIRS ARE REALLY TRYING TO MUSCLE IN?

I DON'T TRUST *ANYONE*, TONY. BUT IT MAKES AS MUCH SENSE AS *BAVA* OR *KANE* TRYING TO TAKE OVER THE WHOLE CITY. LET'S MAKE SURE WE HAVE PLENTY OF *GUNS* IN THAT WAREHOUSE WITH US TOMORROW NIGHT.

AND LET'S TAKE SOME EXTRA PROTECTION TO *MARCO'S* JOINT AS WELL.

SURE THING, BOSS.

AND ONCE O'LEARY'S GONE, HAVE SOMEONE TAKE CARE OF THAT GIRL'S *BODY.* WE AIN'T SUPPLYING HIM WITH GIRLS ANYMORE, YOU GOT THAT? WHEN THIS OVER, I WANT YOU TO TAKE CARE OF THAT *PIG.*

IT'LL BE A PLEASURE, BOSS. A PLEASURE.

I THINK YOU HAVE DONE IT *WELL,* O'LEARY. MY MASTER WILL BE PLEASED. HE WILL TAKE CARE OF YOU.

HAPPY TO BE OF SERVICE. WHEN HE KILLS THAT EDDIE PRICK, ASK HIM TO MAKE IT SLOW, WILL YOU?

HE WILL DO WHAT-EVER HE WISHES TO DO.

"HOPE HE MAKES IT SLOW."

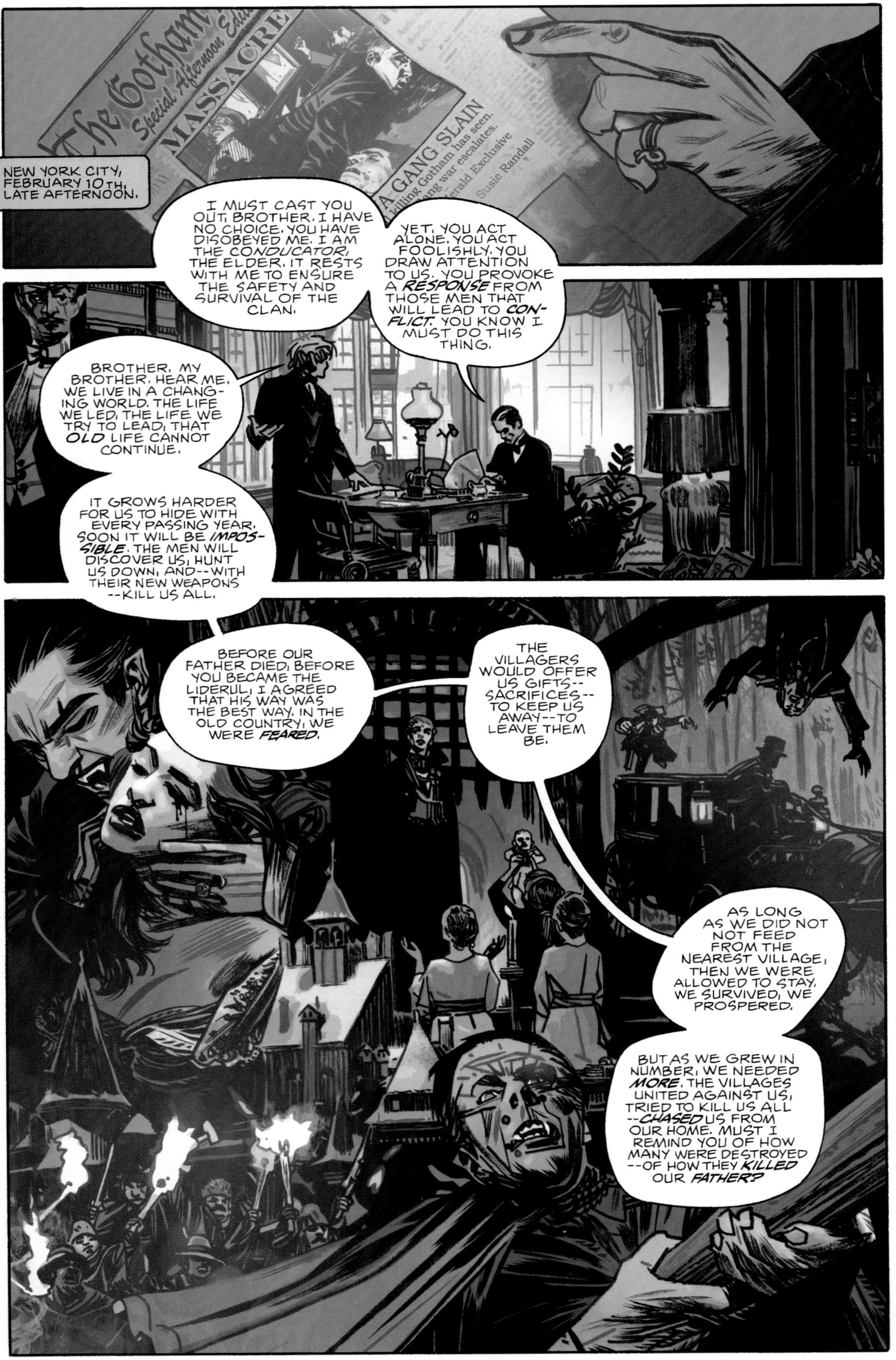
MASSACRE
A GANG SLAIN
Susie Randall
NEW YORK CITY, FEBRUARY 10TH, LATE AFTERNOON.
I MUST CAST YOU OUT, BROTHER. I HAVE NO CHOICE. YOU HAVE DISOBEYED ME. I AM THE *CONDUCATOR*, THE ELDER. IT RESTS WITH ME TO ENSURE THE SAFETY AND SURVIVAL OF THE CLAN.
YET, YOU ACT ALONE. YOU ACT FOOLISHLY. YOU DRAW ATTENTION TO US. YOU PROVOKE A ***RESPONSE*** FROM THOSE MEN THAT WILL LEAD TO ***CONFLICT.*** YOU KNOW I MUST DO THIS THING.
BROTHER. MY BROTHER. HEAR ME. WE LIVE IN A CHANGING WORLD. THE LIFE WE LED, THE LIFE WE TRY TO LEAD, THAT ***OLD*** LIFE CANNOT CONTINUE.
IT GROWS HARDER FOR US TO HIDE WITH EVERY PASSING YEAR. SOON IT WILL BE ***IMPOSSIBLE***. THE MEN WILL DISCOVER US, HUNT US DOWN, AND--WITH THEIR NEW WEAPONS --KILL US ALL.
BEFORE OUR FATHER DIED, BEFORE YOU BECAME THE LIDERUL, I AGREED THAT HIS WAY WAS THE BEST WAY. IN THE OLD COUNTRY, WE WERE ***FEARED***.
THE VILLAGERS WOULD OFFER US GIFTS-- SACRIFICES-- TO KEEP US AWAY--TO LEAVE THEM BE.
AS LONG AS WE DID NOT NOT FEED FROM THE NEAREST VILLAGE, THEN WE WERE ALLOWED TO STAY. WE SURVIVED, WE PROSPERED.
BUT AS WE GREW IN NUMBER, WE NEEDED ***MORE***. THE VILLAGES UNITED AGAINST US, TRIED TO KILL US ALL --***CHASED*** US FROM OUR HOME. MUST I REMIND YOU OF HOW MANY WERE DESTROYED --OF HOW THEY ***KILLED*** OUR ***FATHER?***

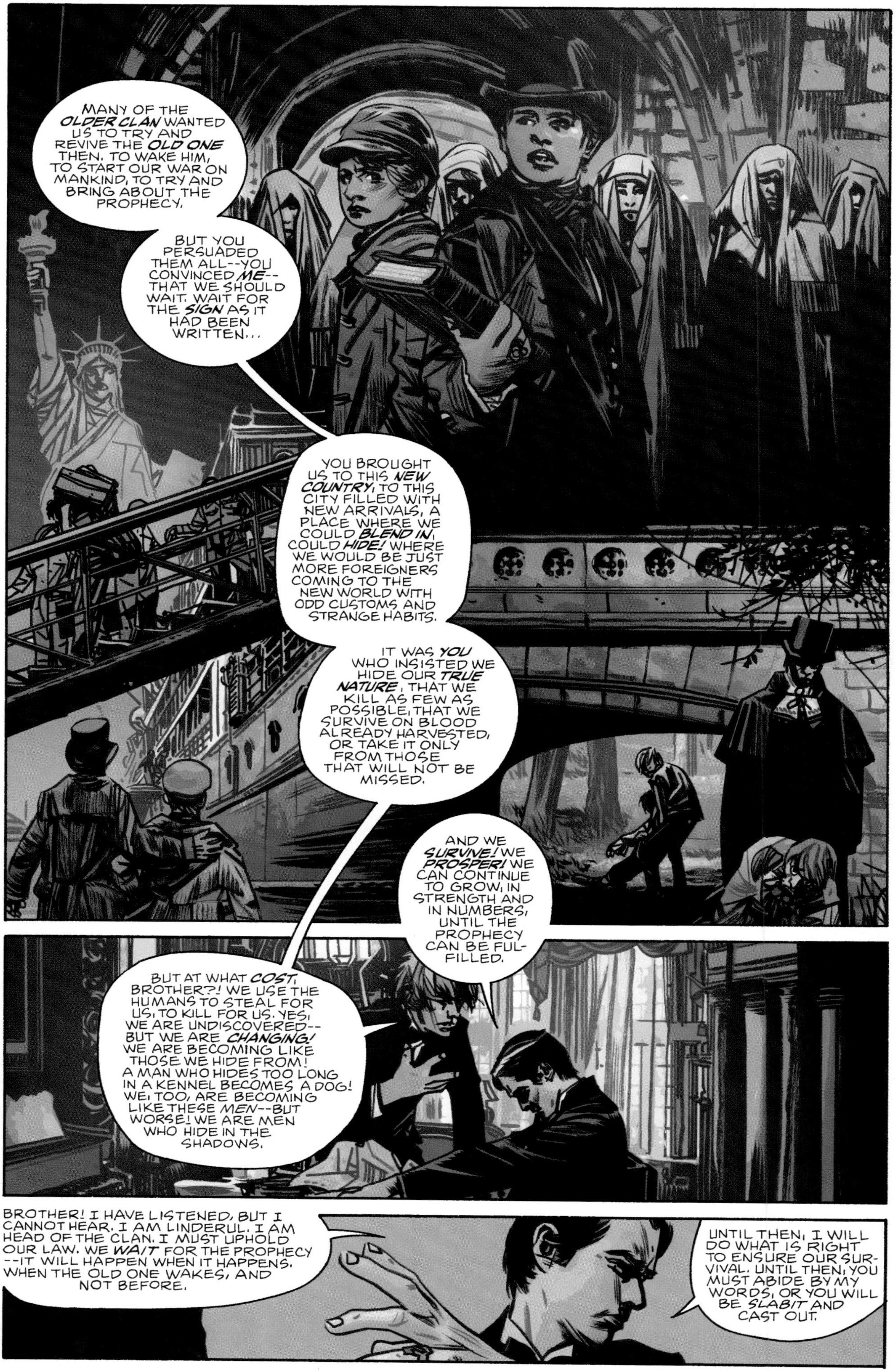
MANY OF THE OLDER CLAN WANTED US TO TRY AND REVIVE THE OLD ONE THEN. TO WAKE HIM, TO START OUR WAR ON MANKIND, TO TRY AND BRING ABOUT THE PROPHECY.
BUT YOU PERSUADED THEM ALL--YOU CONVINCED ME--THAT WE SHOULD WAIT. WAIT FOR THE SIGN AS IT HAD BEEN WRITTEN...
YOU BROUGHT US TO THIS NEW COUNTRY, TO THIS CITY FILLED WITH NEW ARRIVALS, A PLACE WHERE WE COULD BLEND IN, COULD HIDE! WHERE WE WOULD BE JUST MORE FOREIGNERS COMING TO THE NEW WORLD WITH ODD CUSTOMS AND STRANGE HABITS.
IT WAS YOU WHO INSISTED WE HIDE OUR TRUE NATURE, THAT WE KILL AS FEW AS POSSIBLE, THAT WE SURVIVE ON BLOOD ALREADY HARVESTED, OR TAKE IT ONLY FROM THOSE THAT WILL NOT BE MISSED.
AND WE SURVIVE! WE PROSPER! WE CAN CONTINUE TO GROW, IN STRENGTH AND IN NUMBERS, UNTIL THE PROPHECY CAN BE FUL-FILLED.
BUT AT WHAT COST, BROTHER?! WE USE THE HUMANS TO STEAL FOR US, TO KILL FOR US. YES, WE ARE UNDISCOVERED--BUT WE ARE CHANGING! WE ARE BECOMING LIKE THOSE WE HIDE FROM! A MAN WHO HIDES TOO LONG IN A KENNEL BECOMES A DOG! WE, TOO, ARE BECOMING LIKE THESE MEN--BUT WORSE! WE ARE MEN WHO HIDE IN THE SHADOWS.
BROTHER! I HAVE LISTENED, BUT I CANNOT HEAR. I AM LINDERUL. I AM HEAD OF THE CLAN. I MUST UPHOLD OUR LAW. WE WAIT FOR THE PROPHECY --IT WILL HAPPEN WHEN IT HAPPENS. WHEN THE OLD ONE WAKES, AND NOT BEFORE.
UNTIL THEN, I WILL DO WHAT IS RIGHT TO ENSURE OUR SUR-VIVAL. UNTIL THEN, YOU MUST ABIDE BY MY WORDS, OR YOU WILL BE SLABIT AND CAST OUT.

YOU ARE WRONG, GREGORI. YOUR WEAKNESS *SICKENS* ME! TO SEE YOU BARGAIN WITH THESE FOOLS *DISGUSTS* ME! THEIR GRASP ON THE CITY IS WEAK, AND WE ARE *STRONG*, WE HAVE ALWAYS BEEN STRONG. YOU WOULD WAIT AND WAIT LIKE OUR FATHER UNTIL THESE NEW YORK MEN *ALSO* RISE UP AND CHASE US OUT. WE SHOULD RULE THIS CITY OF FOOLS! WE CAN RULE THIS COUNTRY! WE *WILL* RULE THE PLANET, AND THEY WILL BE OUR SERVANTS AND OUR FOOD, AS IT HAS BEEN FORETOLD IN THE PROPHECY. WE MUST *WAKE* THE OLD ONE *NOW*! SO WAS IT WRITTEN, SO SHALL IT BE!

YOU MUST FIND THE COURAGE, BROTHER, TO... *UNHHHH!*

I AM NOT WEAK. NOR DO I LACK COURAGE. I FOLLOW THE OLD WAYS BECAUSE THAT IS WHAT SEPARATES US FROM *THEM*. THE OLD ONE WILL WAKE WHEN HE IS READY, NOT BEFORE. THE PROPHECY WILL BE FULFILLED WHEN IT IS TIME, NOT WHEN YOU CHOOSE. ALL YOU WILL ACHIEVE WITH THIS MADNESS IS TO SEE OUR KIND DESTROYED, OR FORCED TO LIVE LIKE RATS AGAIN, FORAGING AND HIDING IN THE SHADOWS.

FOREVER.

YOU WILL *STOP* THESE ATTACKS ON THE GANG LEADERS. YOU WILL REMAIN IN THE HOUSE, YOU WILL *OBEY* MY *WILL* AS LIDERUL OF THE CLAN, OR YOU WILL BE CAST OUT. YOU WILL BE WEAKENED, AND CAST OUT. THAT IS MY WILL.

VASELI, ASSIST MY BROTHER.

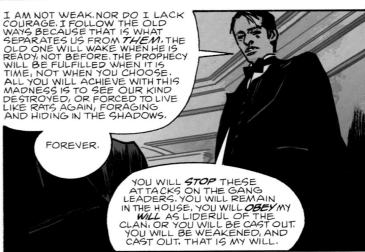

YOU ARE RRIGHT, STEFAN. HE HASH BECOME VEAK. FOR QUESHTIONING HIS RULE, YOU SHOULD BE DEAD. BUT HE LETSH YOU LIVE. HE CANNOT KILL HIS BROTHER.

ACHH, HE IS VEAK, LIKE HUMAN. YOU MUSSSHT KILL HIM, THEN, AND BECOME LINDERUL. I VVILL GATHER THE COUNSEL. WE VILL MEET SOON...

WHAT MUST BE, MUST BE. SEND WORD IF HE LEAVES. FALCO'S MEN SHOULD BE GATHERED AT THE WAREHOUSE. I DO NOT WISH TO HAVE THEM WAIT TOO LONG. THE AGE OF MEN IS ENDING. THE AGE OF THE VAMPIR BEGINS.

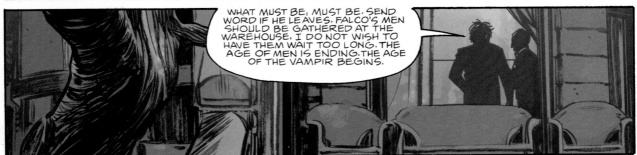

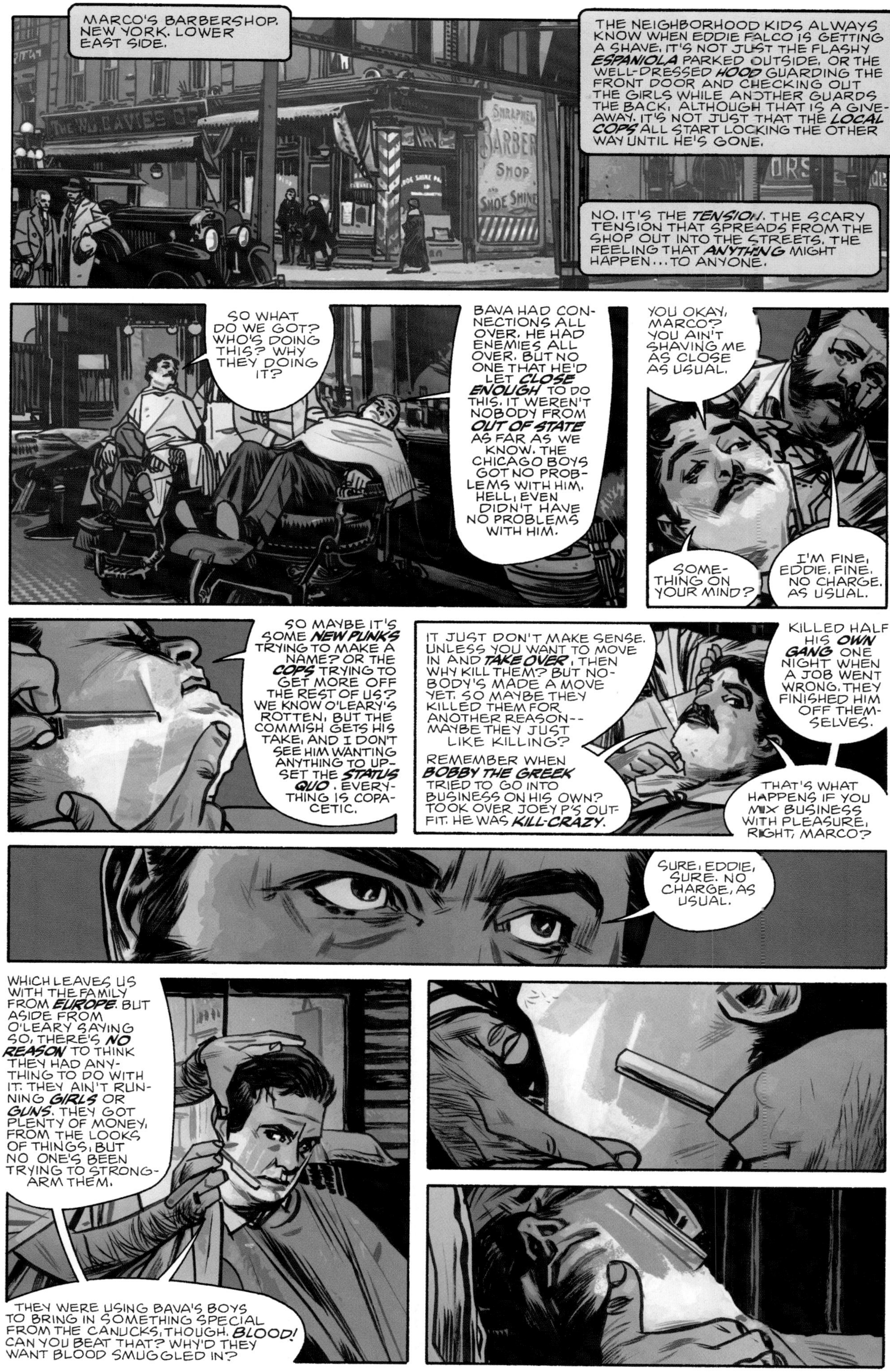
MARCO'S BARBERSHOP. NEW YORK. LOWER EAST SIDE.
THE NEIGHBORHOOD KIDS ALWAYS KNOW WHEN EDDIE FALCO IS GETTING A SHAVE. IT'S NOT JUST THE FLASHY ESPANIOLA PARKED OUTSIDE, OR THE WELL-DRESSED HOOD GUARDING THE FRONT DOOR AND CHECKING OUT THE GIRLS WHILE ANOTHER GUARDS THE BACK, ALTHOUGH THAT IS A GIVE-AWAY. IT'S NOT JUST THAT THE LOCAL COPS ALL START LOCKING THE OTHER WAY UNTIL HE'S GONE.
BARBER SHOP AND SHOE SHINE
NO. IT'S THE TENSION. THE SCARY TENSION THAT SPREADS FROM THE SHOP OUT INTO THE STREETS. THE FEELING THAT ANYTHING MIGHT HAPPEN... TO ANYONE.
SO WHAT DO WE GOT? WHO'S DOING THIS? WHY THEY DOING IT?
BAVA HAD CONNECTIONS ALL OVER. HE HAD ENEMIES ALL OVER. BUT NO ONE THAT HE'D LET CLOSE ENOUGH TO DO THIS. IT WEREN'T NOBODY FROM OUT OF STATE AS FAR AS WE KNOW. THE CHICAGO BOYS GOT NO PROBLEMS WITH HIM. HELL, EVEN DIDN'T HAVE NO PROBLEMS WITH HIM.
YOU OKAY, MARCO? YOU AIN'T SHAVING ME AS CLOSE AS USUAL.
SOMETHING ON YOUR MIND?
I'M FINE, EDDIE. FINE. NO CHARGE. AS USUAL.
SO MAYBE IT'S SOME NEW PUNKS TRYING TO MAKE A NAME? OR THE COPS TRYING TO GET MORE OFF THE REST OF US? WE KNOW O'LEARY'S ROTTEN, BUT THE COMMISH GETS HIS TAKE, AND I DON'T SEE HIM WANTING ANYTHING TO UPSET THE STATUS QUO. EVERYTHING IS COPACETIC.
IT JUST DON'T MAKE SENSE. UNLESS YOU WANT TO MOVE IN AND TAKE OVER, THEN WHY KILL THEM? BUT NOBODY'S MADE A MOVE YET. SO MAYBE THEY KILLED THEM FOR ANOTHER REASON-- MAYBE THEY JUST LIKE KILLING?
REMEMBER WHEN BOBBY THE GREEK TRIED TO GO INTO BUSINESS ON HIS OWN? TOOK OVER JOEY P'S OUTFIT. HE WAS KILL-CRAZY.
KILLED HALF HIS OWN GANG ONE NIGHT WHEN A JOB WENT WRONG. THEY FINISHED HIM OFF THEMSELVES.
THAT'S WHAT HAPPENS IF YOU MIX BUSINESS WITH PLEASURE, RIGHT, MARCO?
SURE, EDDIE, SURE. NO CHARGE, AS USUAL.
WHICH LEAVES US WITH THE FAMILY FROM EUROPE. BUT ASIDE FROM O'LEARY SAYING SO, THERE'S NO REASON TO THINK THEY HAD ANYTHING TO DO WITH IT. THEY AIN'T RUNNING GIRLS OR GUNS. THEY GOT PLENTY OF MONEY, FROM THE LOOKS OF THINGS, BUT NO ONE'S BEEN TRYING TO STRONG-ARM THEM.
THEY WERE USING BAVA'S BOYS TO BRING IN SOMETHING SPECIAL FROM THE CANUCKS, THOUGH. BLOOD! CAN YOU BEAT THAT? WHY'D THEY WANT BLOOD SMUGGLED IN?

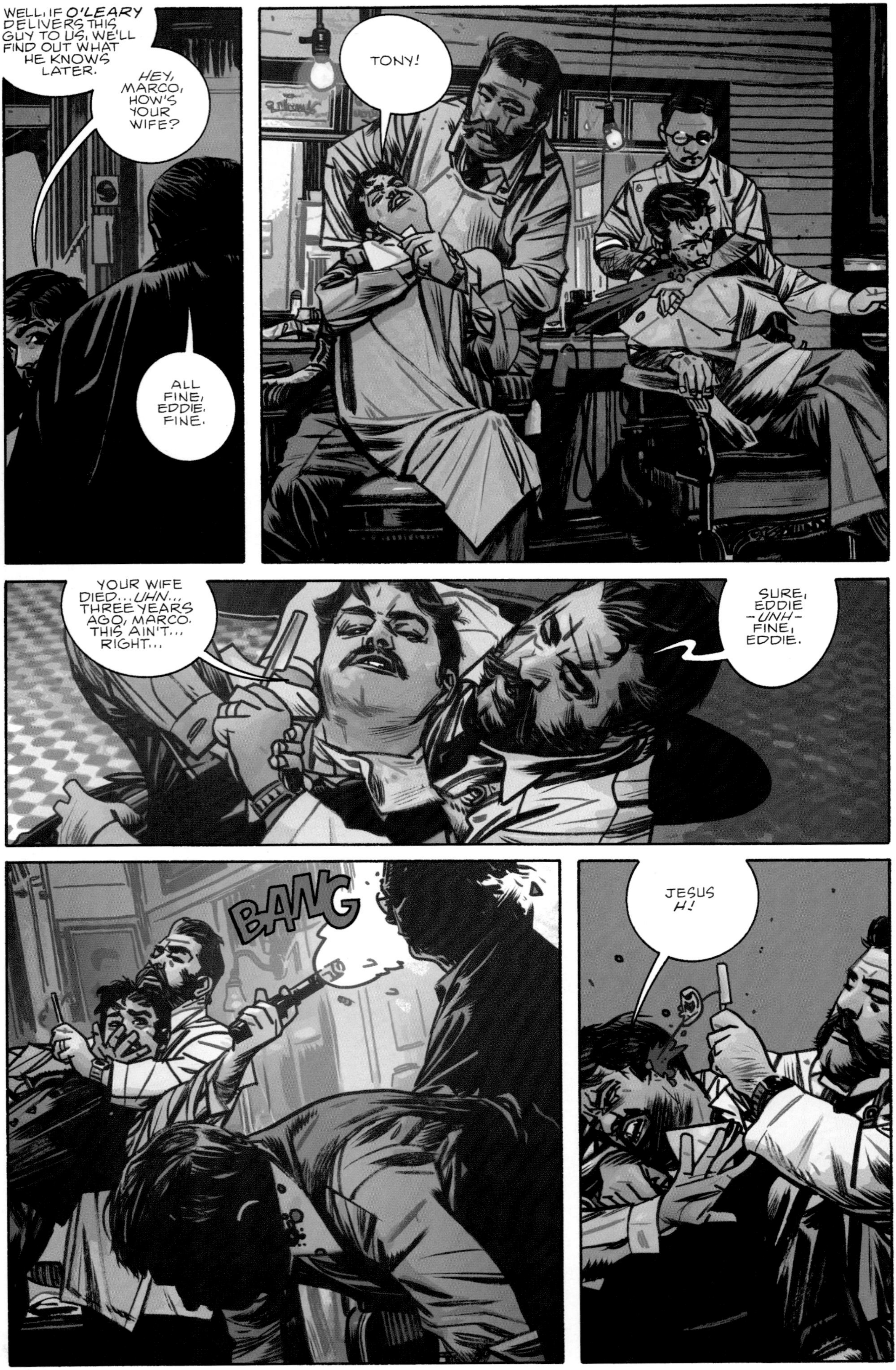
WELL, IF O'LEARY DELIVERS THIS GUY TO US, WE'LL FIND OUT WHAT HE KNOWS LATER.
HEY, MARCO, HOW'S YOUR WIFE?
ALL FINE, EDDIE. FINE.
TONY!
YOUR WIFE DIED... UHN... THREE YEARS AGO, MARCO. THIS AIN'T... RIGHT...
SURE, EDDIE -UNH- FINE, EDDIE.
BANG
JESUS H!

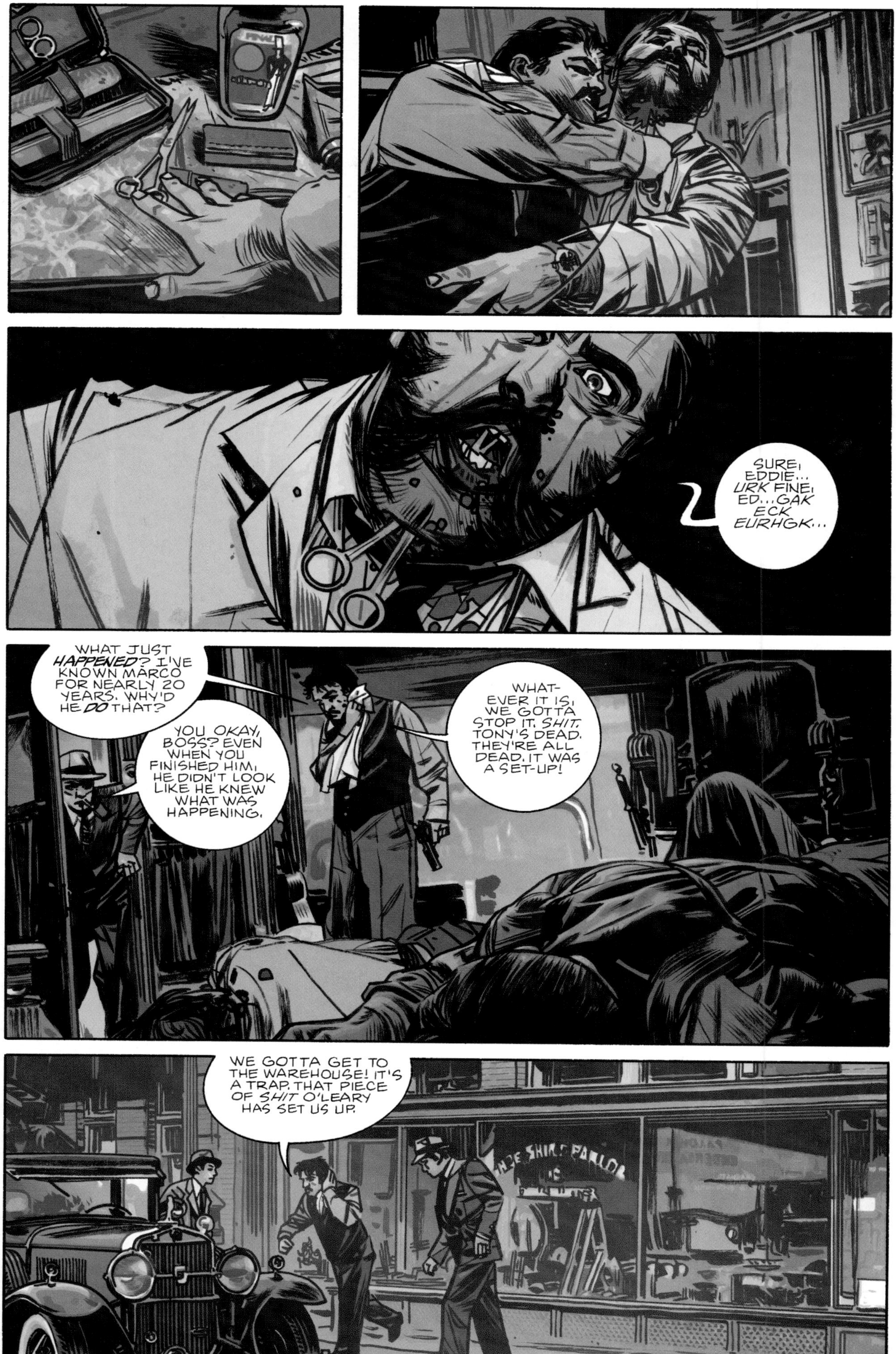
SURE, EDDIE... URK FINE, ED...GAK ECK EURHGK...
WHAT JUST HAPPENED? I'VE KNOWN MARCO FOR NEARLY 20 YEARS. WHY'D HE DO THAT?
YOU OKAY, BOSS? EVEN WHEN YOU FINISHED HIM, HE DIDN'T LOOK LIKE HE KNEW WHAT WAS HAPPENING.
WHAT-EVER IT IS, WE GOTTA STOP IT. SHIT. TONY'S DEAD. THEY'RE ALL DEAD. IT WAS A SET-UP!
WE GOTTA GET TO THE WAREHOUSE! IT'S A TRAP. THAT PIECE OF SHIT O'LEARY HAS SET US UP.

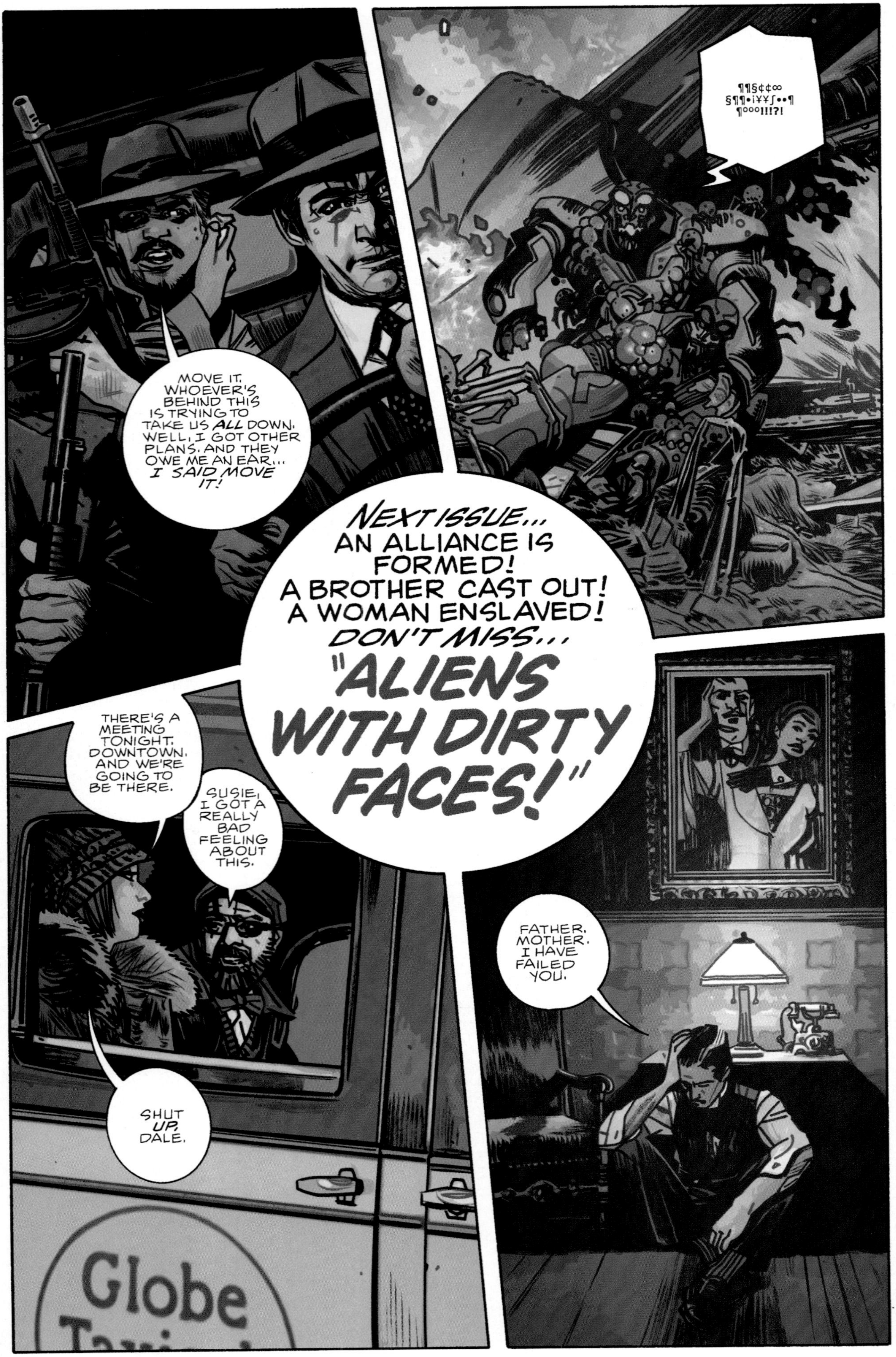
MOVE IT. WHOEVER'S BEHIND THIS IS TRYING TO TAKE US ALL DOWN. WELL, I GOT OTHER PLANS. AND THEY OWE ME AN EAR... I SAID MOVE IT!
NEXT ISSUE... AN ALLIANCE IS FORMED! A BROTHER CAST OUT! A WOMAN ENSLAVED! DON'T MISS... "ALIENS WITH DIRTY FACES!"
THERE'S A MEETING TONIGHT, DOWNTOWN. AND WE'RE GOING TO BE THERE.
SUSIE, I GOT A REALLY BAD FEELING ABOUT THIS.
SHUT UP, DALE.
Globe
FATHER. MOTHER. I HAVE FAILED YOU.

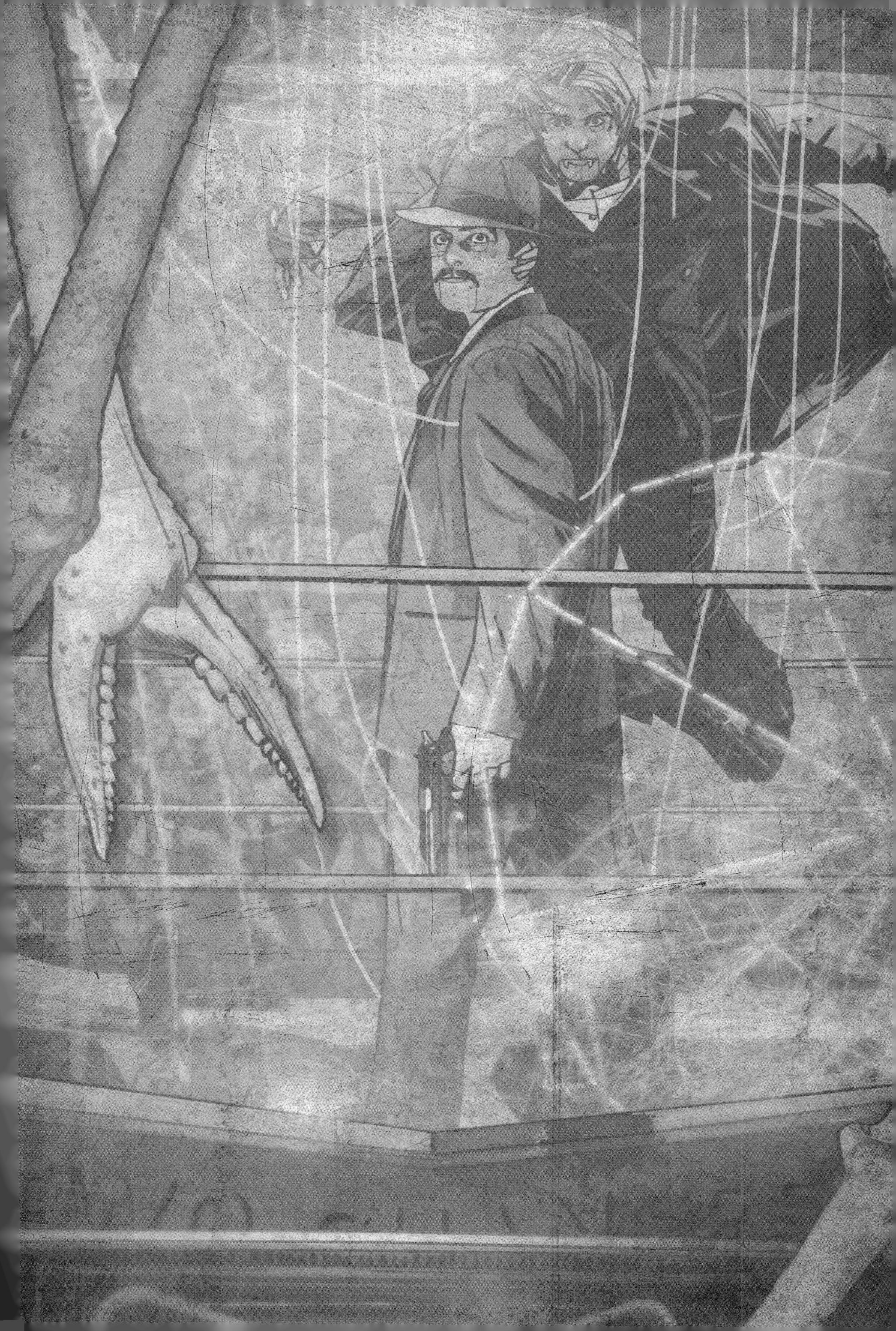

Chapter Two

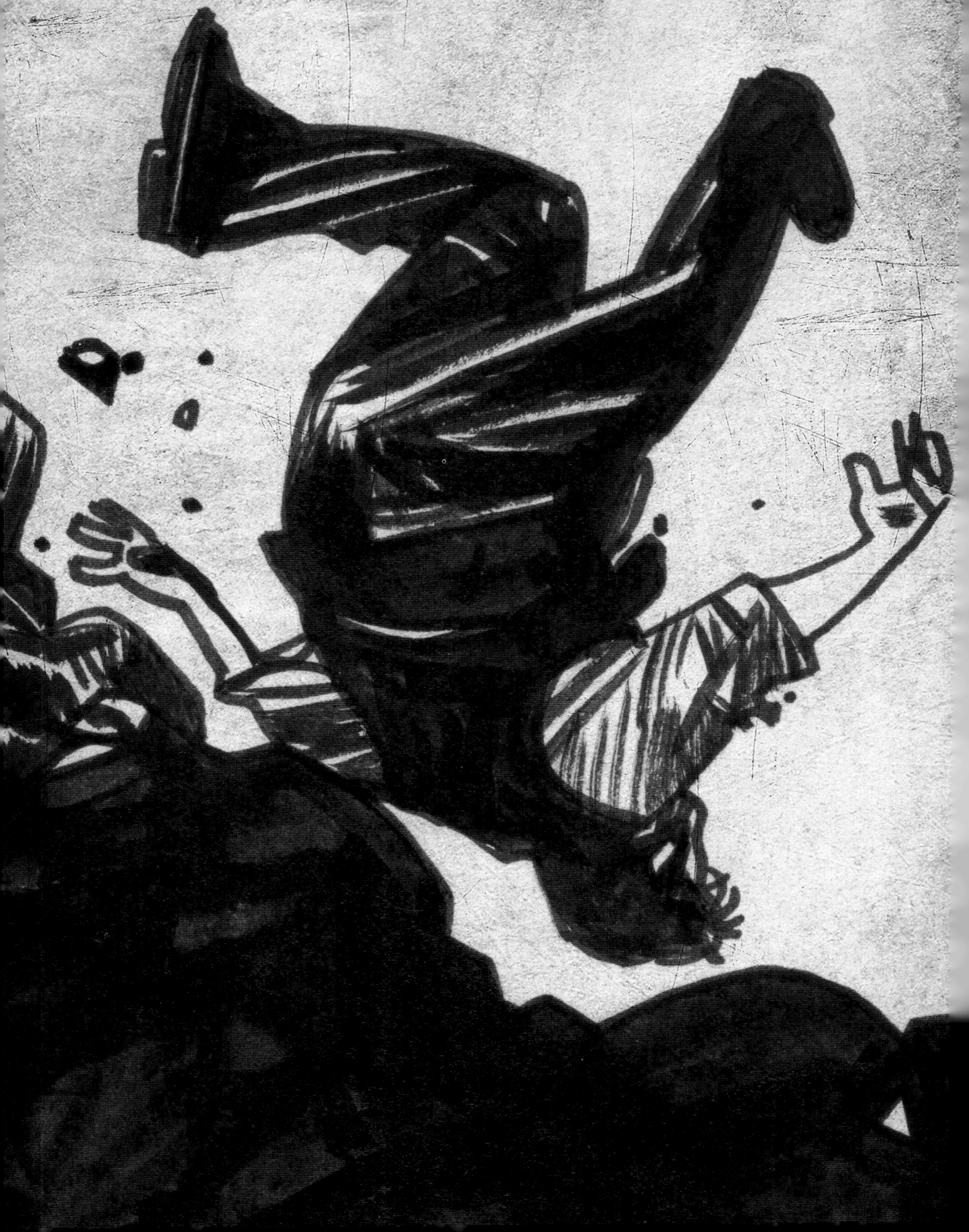

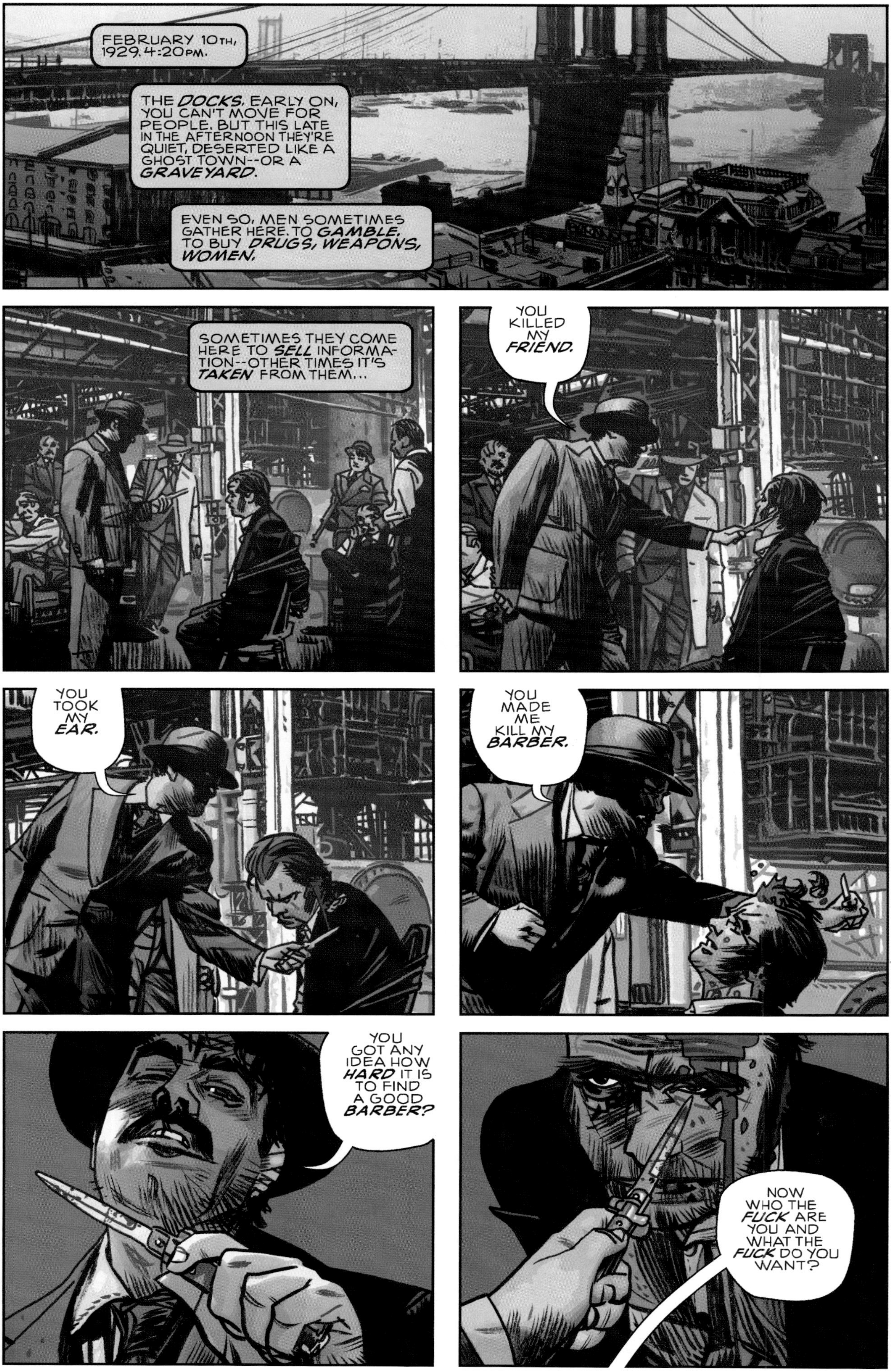
FEBRUARY 10TH, 1929. 4:20PM.
THE DOCKS. EARLY ON, YOU CAN'T MOVE FOR PEOPLE. BUT THIS LATE IN THE AFTERNOON THEY'RE QUIET, DESERTED LIKE A GHOST TOWN--OR A GRAVEYARD.
EVEN SO, MEN SOMETIMES GATHER HERE. TO GAMBLE. TO BUY DRUGS, WEAPONS, WOMEN.
SOMETIMES THEY COME HERE TO SELL INFORMATION--OTHER TIMES IT'S TAKEN FROM THEM...
YOU KILLED MY FRIEND.
YOU TOOK MY EAR.
YOU MADE ME KILL MY BARBER.
YOU GOT ANY IDEA HOW HARD IT IS TO FIND A GOOD BARBER?
NOW WHO THE FUCK ARE YOU AND WHAT THE FUCK DO YOU WANT?

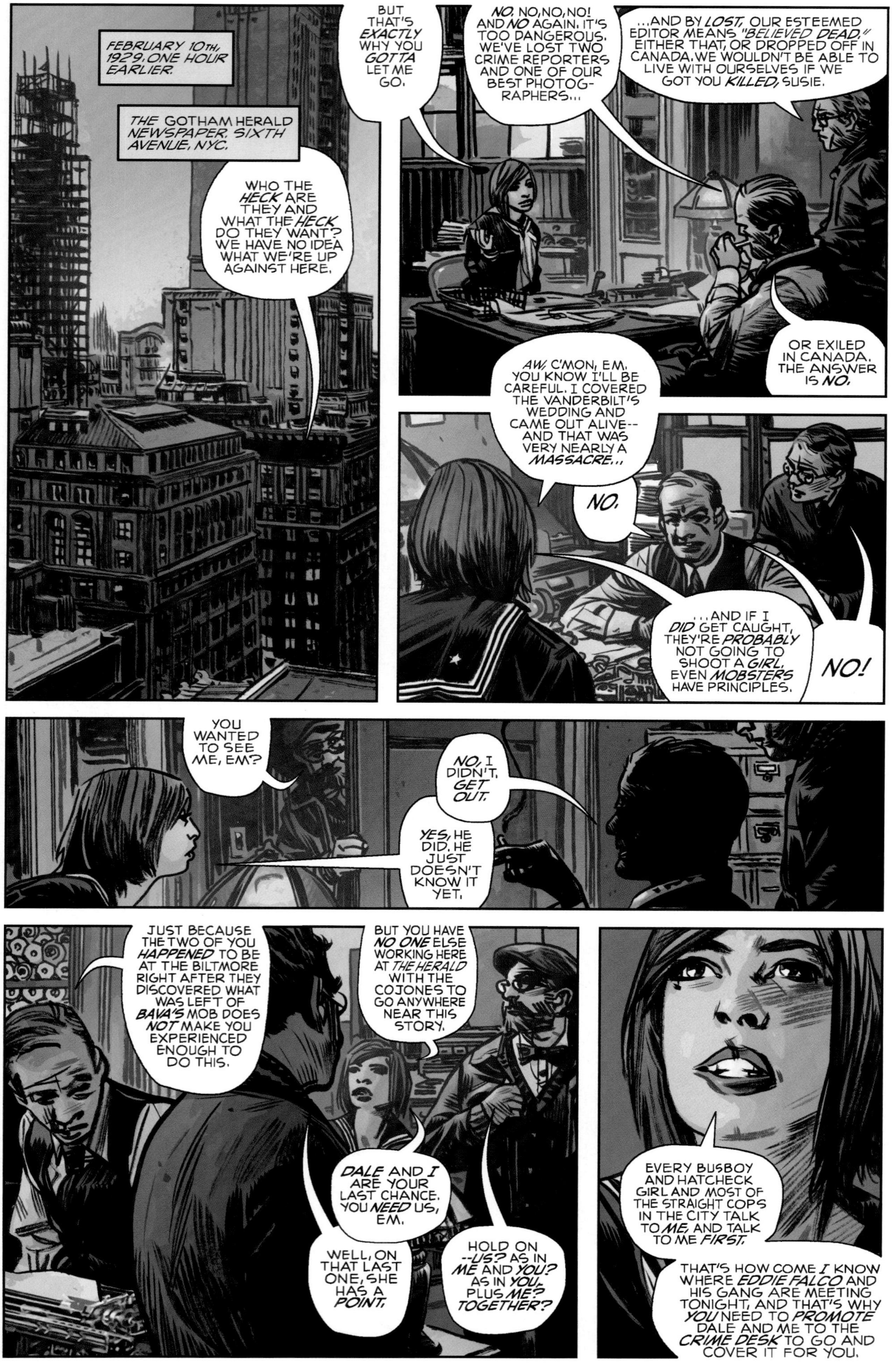
FEBRUARY 10TH, 1929, ONE HOUR EARLIER.
THE GOTHAM HERALD NEWSPAPER, SIXTH AVENUE, NYC.
WHO THE HECK ARE THEY AND WHAT THE HECK DO THEY WANT? WE HAVE NO IDEA WHAT WE'RE UP AGAINST HERE.
BUT THAT'S EXACTLY WHY YOU GOTTA LET ME GO.
NO, NO, NO, NO! AND NO AGAIN. IT'S TOO DANGEROUS. WE'VE LOST TWO CRIME REPORTERS AND ONE OF OUR BEST PHOTOG-RAPHERS...
...AND BY LOST, OUR ESTEEMED EDITOR MEANS "BELIEVED DEAD." EITHER THAT, OR DROPPED OFF IN CANADA. WE WOULDN'T BE ABLE TO LIVE WITH OURSELVES IF WE GOT YOU KILLED, SUSIE.
OR EXILED IN CANADA. THE ANSWER IS NO.
AW, C'MON, EM. YOU KNOW I'LL BE CAREFUL. I COVERED THE VANDERBILT'S WEDDING AND CAME OUT ALIVE-- AND THAT WAS VERY NEARLY A MASSACRE...
NO.
...AND IF I DID GET CAUGHT, THEY'RE PROBABLY NOT GOING TO SHOOT A GIRL. EVEN MOBSTERS HAVE PRINCIPLES.
NO!
YOU WANTED TO SEE ME, EM?
NO, I DIDN'T. GET OUT.
YES, HE DID. HE JUST DOESN'T KNOW IT YET.
JUST BECAUSE THE TWO OF YOU HAPPENED TO BE AT THE BILTMORE RIGHT AFTER THEY DISCOVERED WHAT WAS LEFT OF BAVA'S MOB DOES NOT MAKE YOU EXPERIENCED ENOUGH TO DO THIS.
BUT YOU HAVE NO ONE ELSE WORKING HERE AT THE HERALD WITH THE COJONES TO GO ANYWHERE NEAR THIS STORY.
DALE AND I ARE YOUR LAST CHANCE. YOU NEED US, EM.
WELL, ON THAT LAST ONE, SHE HAS A POINT.
HOLD ON --US? AS IN ME AND YOU? AS IN YOU, PLUS ME? TOGETHER?
EVERY BUSBOY AND HATCHECK GIRL AND MOST OF THE STRAIGHT COPS IN THE CITY TALK TO ME, AND TALK TO ME FIRST.
THAT'S HOW COME I KNOW WHERE EDDIE FALCO AND HIS GANG ARE MEETING TONIGHT, AND THAT'S WHY YOU NEED TO PROMOTE DALE AND ME TO THE CRIME DESK TO GO AND COVER IT FOR YOU.

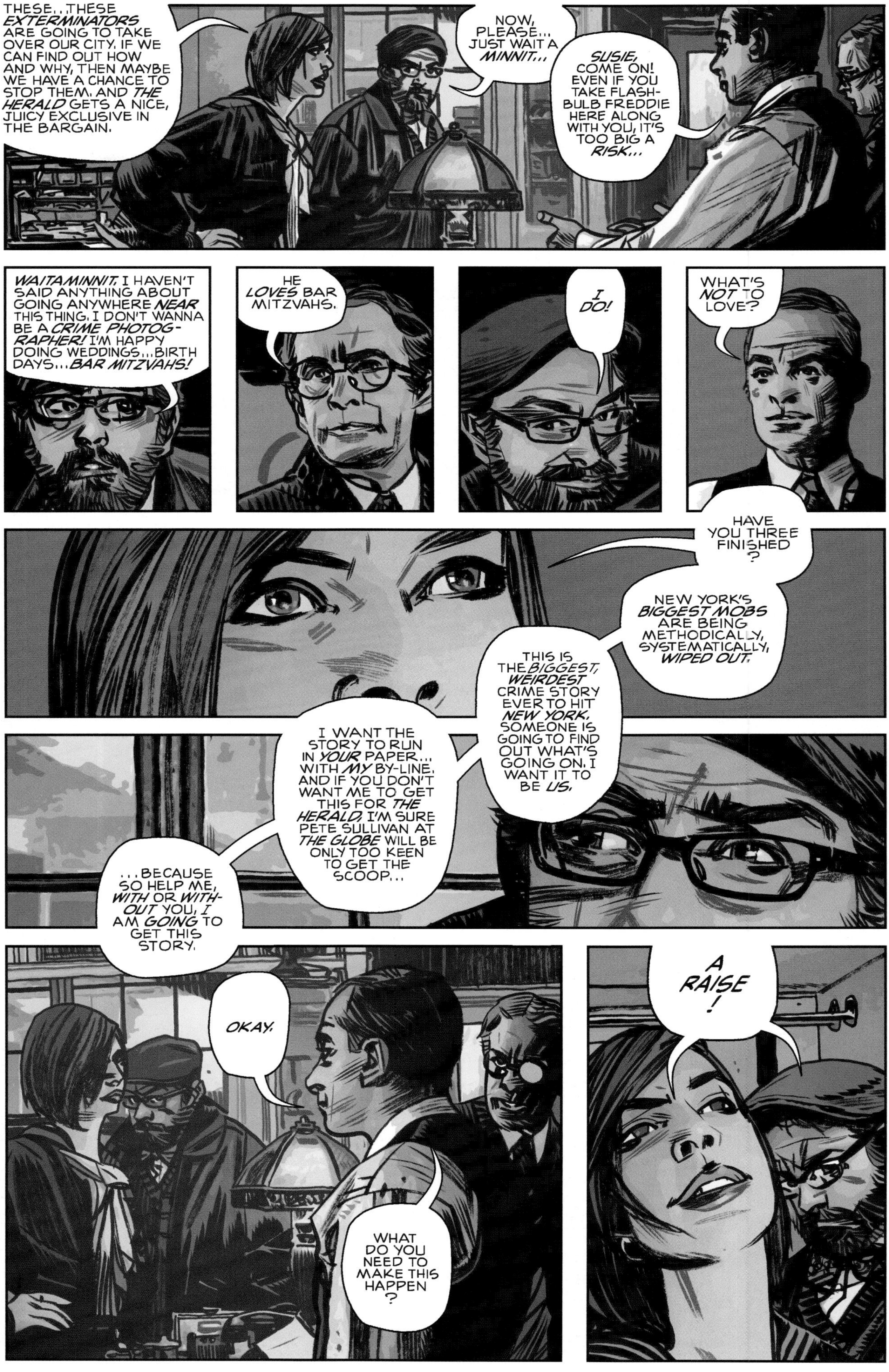
THESE...THESE *EXTERMINATORS* ARE GOING TO TAKE OVER OUR CITY. IF WE CAN FIND OUT HOW AND WHY, THEN MAYBE WE HAVE A CHANCE TO STOP THEM. AND *THE HERALD* GETS A NICE, JUICY EXCLUSIVE IN THE BARGAIN.
NOW, PLEASE... JUST WAIT A *MINNIT*...
SUSIE, COME ON! EVEN IF YOU TAKE FLASH-BULB FREDDIE HERE ALONG WITH YOU, IT'S TOO BIG A *RISK*...
WAITAMINNIT, I HAVEN'T SAID ANYTHING ABOUT GOING ANYWHERE *NEAR* THIS THING. I DON'T WANNA BE A *CRIME PHOTOGRAPHER!* I'M HAPPY DOING WEDDINGS...BIRTH DAYS...*BAR MITZVAHS!*
HE *LOVES* BAR MITZVAHS.
I DO!
WHAT'S *NOT* TO LOVE?
HAVE YOU THREE FINISHED ?
NEW YORK'S *BIGGEST MOBS* ARE BEING METHODICALLY, SYSTEMATICALLY, *WIPED OUT.*
THIS IS THE *BIGGEST, WEIRDEST* CRIME STORY EVER TO HIT *NEW YORK.* SOMEONE IS GOING TO FIND OUT WHAT'S GOING ON. I WANT IT TO BE *US.*
I WANT THE STORY TO RUN IN *YOUR* PAPER... WITH *MY* BY-LINE. AND IF YOU DON'T WANT ME TO GET THIS FOR *THE HERALD,* I'M SURE PETE SULLIVAN AT *THE GLOBE* WILL BE ONLY TOO KEEN TO GET THE SCOOP...
...BECAUSE SO HELP ME, *WITH* OR *WITHOUT* YOU, *I* AM *GOING* TO GET THIS STORY.
OKAY.
WHAT DO YOU NEED TO MAKE THIS HAPPEN ?
A RAISE !

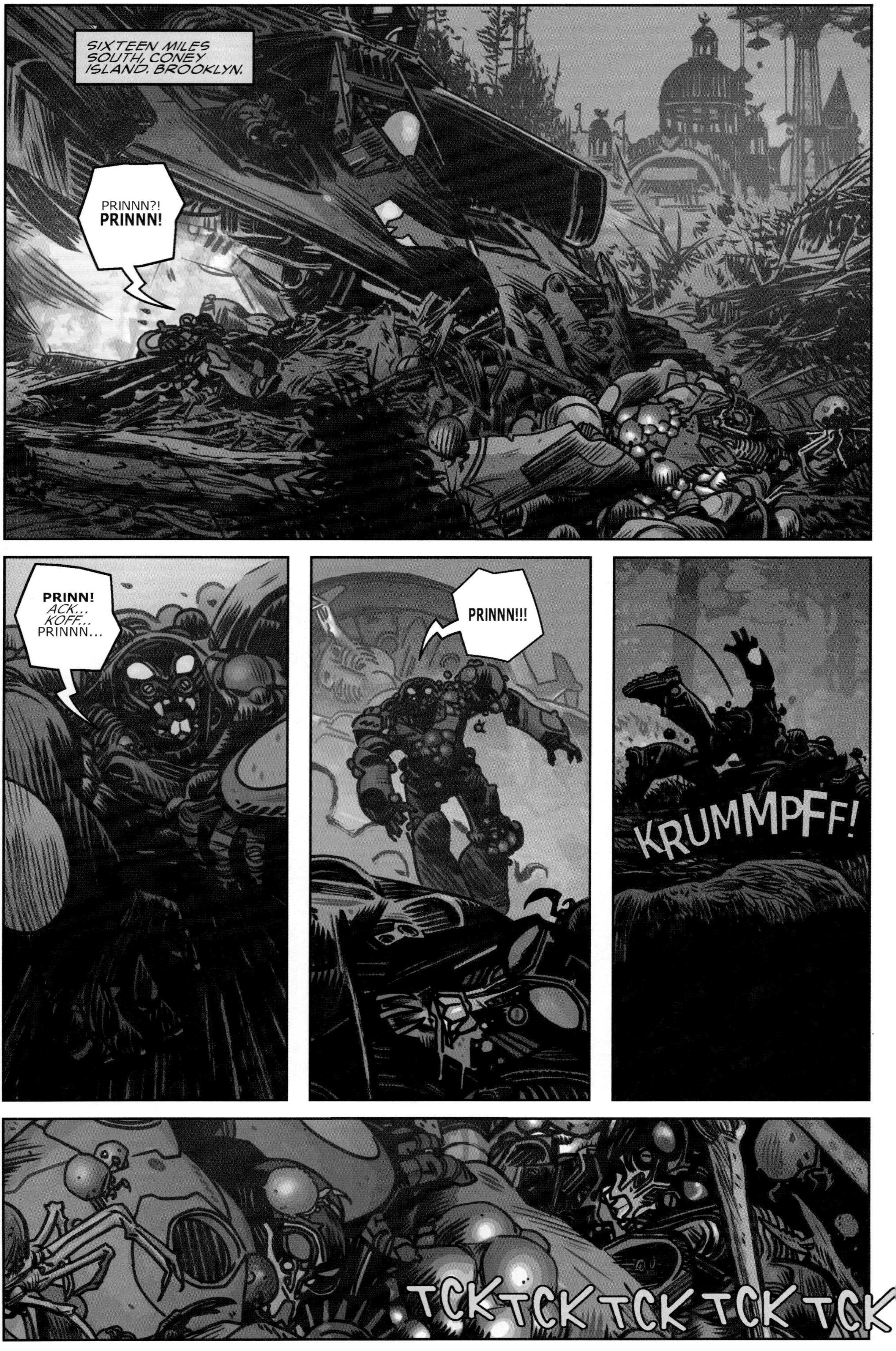
SIXTEEN MILES SOUTH, CONEY ISLAND, BROOKLYN.
PRINNN?! **PRINNN!**
PRINN! *ACK... KOFF...* PRINNN...
PRINNN!!!
KRUMMPFF!
TCK TCK TCK TCK TCK

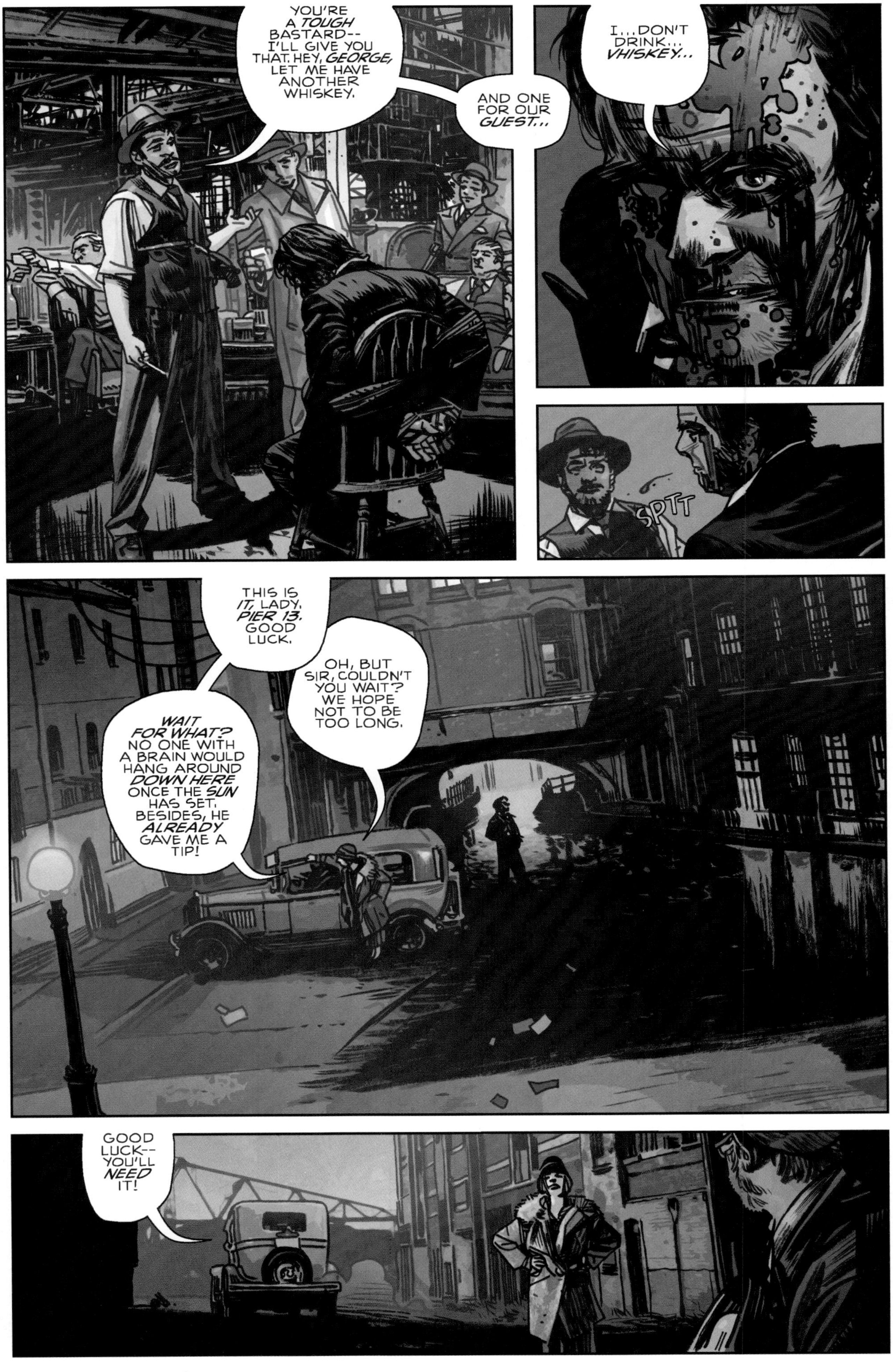
YOU'RE A TOUGH BASTARD-- I'LL GIVE YOU THAT. HEY, GEORGE, LET ME HAVE ANOTHER WHISKEY.
AND ONE FOR OUR GUEST...
I...DON'T DRINK... WHISKEY...
SPTT
THIS IS IT, LADY. PIER 13. GOOD LUCK.
OH, BUT SIR, COULDN'T YOU WAIT? WE HOPE NOT TO BE TOO LONG.
WAIT FOR WHAT? NO ONE WITH A BRAIN WOULD HANG AROUND DOWN HERE ONCE THE SUN HAS SET. BESIDES, HE ALREADY GAVE ME A TIP!
GOOD LUCK-- YOU'LL NEED IT!

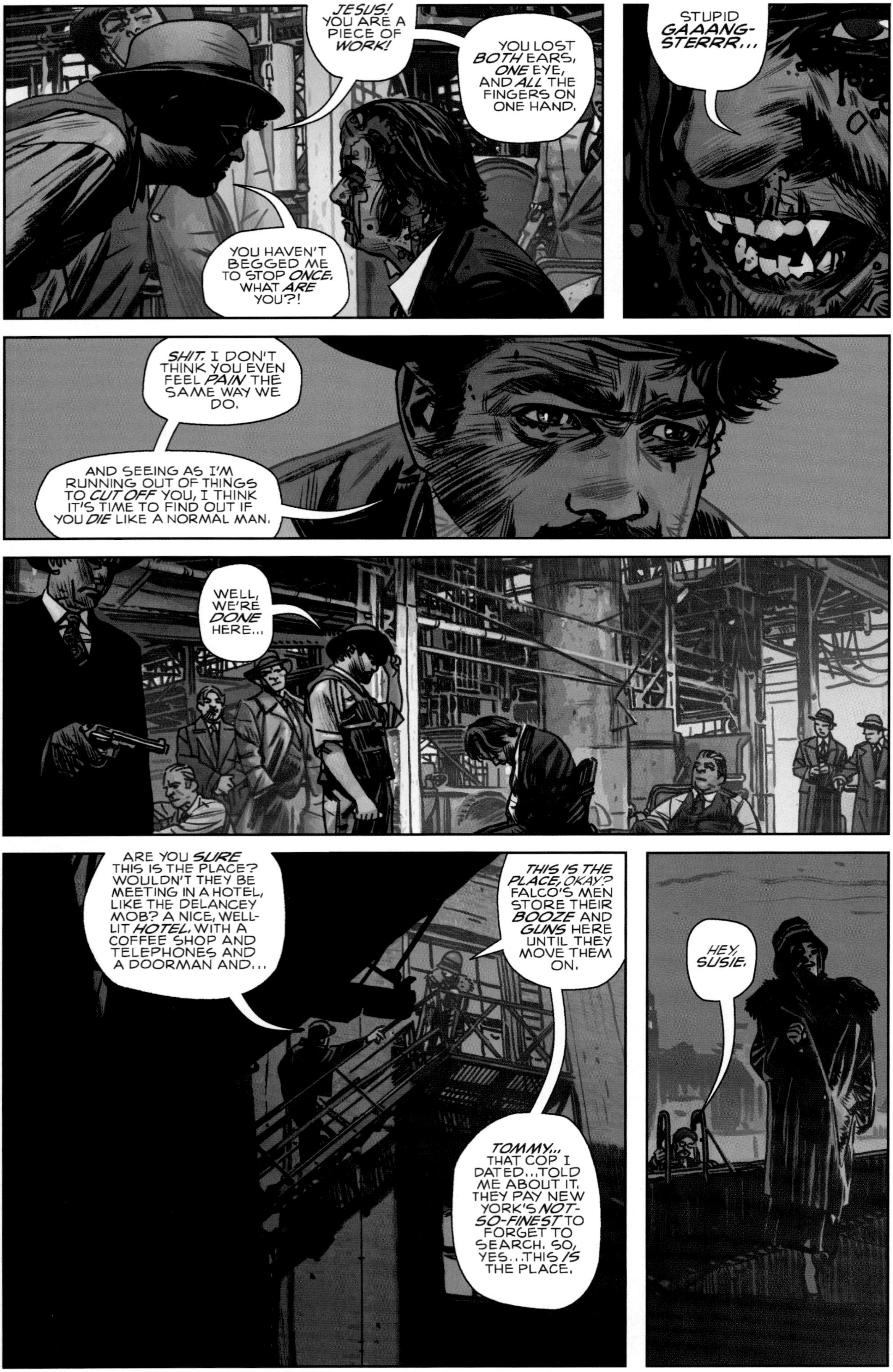
JESUS! YOU ARE A PIECE OF WORK!
YOU LOST BOTH EARS, ONE EYE, AND ALL THE FINGERS ON ONE HAND.
YOU HAVEN'T BEGGED ME TO STOP ONCE. WHAT ARE YOU?!
STUPID GAAANG-STERRR...
SHIT. I DON'T THINK YOU EVEN FEEL PAIN THE SAME WAY WE DO.
AND SEEING AS I'M RUNNING OUT OF THINGS TO CUT OFF YOU, I THINK IT'S TIME TO FIND OUT IF YOU DIE LIKE A NORMAL MAN.
WELL, WE'RE DONE HERE...
ARE YOU SURE THIS IS THE PLACE? WOULDN'T THEY BE MEETING IN A HOTEL, LIKE THE DELANCEY MOB? A NICE, WELL-LIT HOTEL, WITH A COFFEE SHOP AND TELEPHONES AND A DOORMAN AND...
THIS IS THE PLACE, OKAY? FALCO'S MEN STORE THEIR BOOZE AND GUNS HERE UNTIL THEY MOVE THEM ON.
TOMMY... THAT COP I DATED... TOLD ME ABOUT IT. THEY PAY NEW YORK'S NOT-SO-FINEST TO FORGET TO SEARCH. SO, YES... THIS IS THE PLACE.
HEY, SUSIE.

I'M SORRY, BUT AFTER TONIGHT, I'M *THROUGH.* I'M NOT CUT OUT FOR ALL THIS EXCITEMENT. I JUST WANT TO TAKE *PICTURES* OF PEOPLE.

GANG-STERS ARE PEOPLE.

NICE PEOPLE. NICE, *NORMAL* PEOPLE. PEOPLE WHO SMILE WHEN THEY SEE A CAMERA. I AIN'T CUT OUT FOR THIS, SUSIE. I HAVEN'T GOT YOUR *GUTS.* I HAVEN'T GOT YOUR... *AMBITION.*

I'LL STAY WITH YOU *TONIGHT,* BUT THIS IS *IT.*

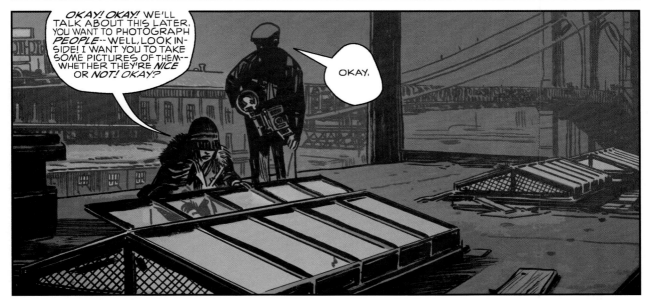

OKAY! OKAY! WE'LL TALK ABOUT THIS LATER. YOU WANT TO PHOTOGRAPH *PEOPLE*-- WELL, LOOK INSIDE! I WANT YOU TO TAKE SOME PICTURES OF THEM-- WHETHER THEY'RE *NICE* OR *NOT!* OKAY?

OKAY.

THIS IS FOR TONY, AND FOR MARCO.

AND TO RID THE WORLD OF WHATEVER THE HELL *YOU* ARE...

KLICK

LAST CHANCE...

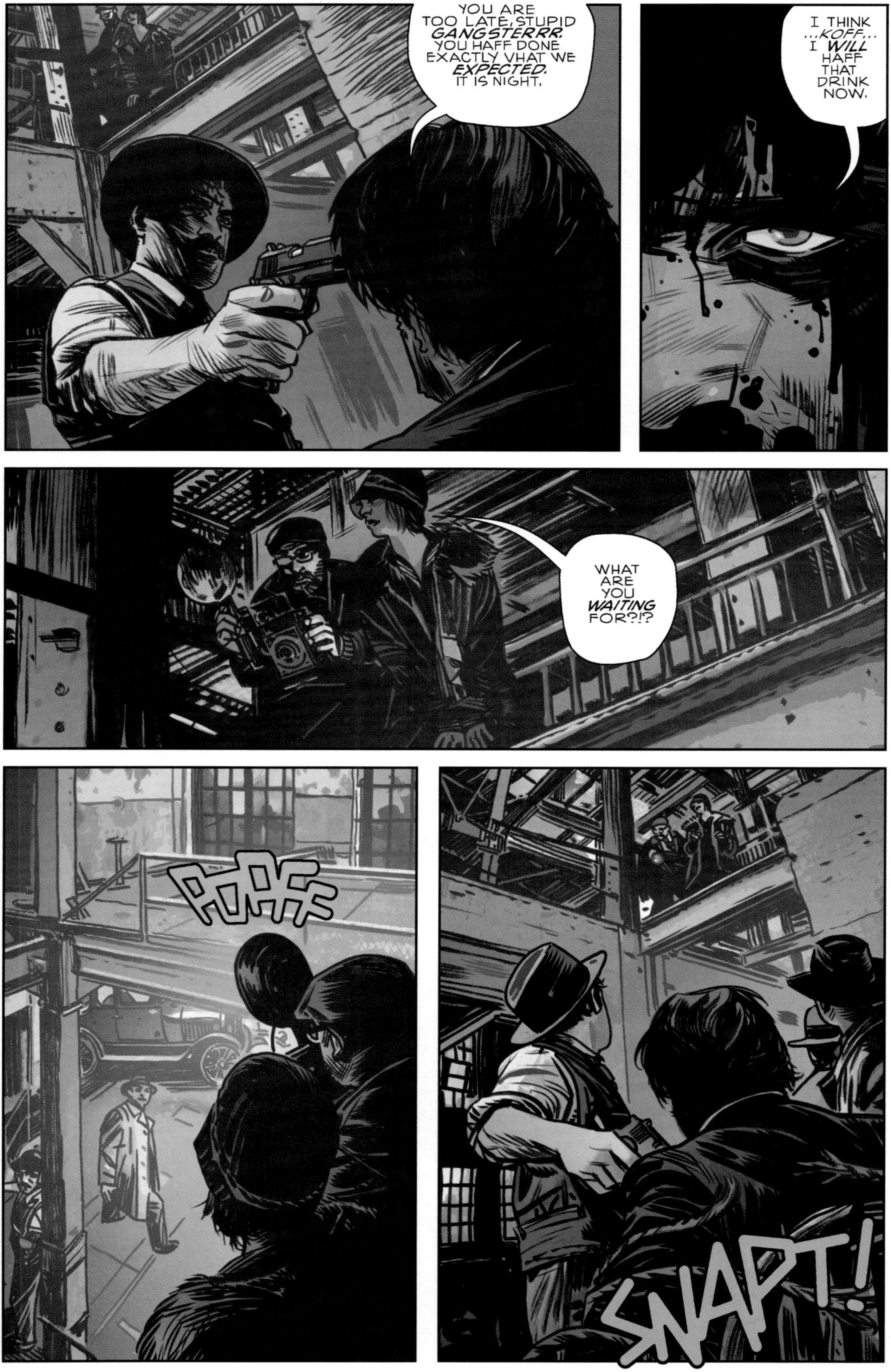
YOU ARE TOO LATE, STUPID GANGSTERRR. YOU HAFF DONE EXACTLY VHAT WE EXPECTED. IT IS NIGHT.
I THINK ...KOFF... I WILL HAFF THAT DRINK NOW.
WHAT ARE YOU WAITING FOR?!?
POFF
SNAPT!

DRAGONMIR MANSION...

FATHER. MOTHER. I HAVE TRIED.

I HAVE TRIED, BUT I HAVE FAILED. FAILED US ALL.

DO NOT *SKULK* IN THE HALLWAY LIKE A *RODENT*, VASELI. COME IN, AND BRING THE *COUNCIL* WITH YOU.

SLAM

YOU ARE NOT *SURPRISED* TO SEE US, I THINK, GREGORI.

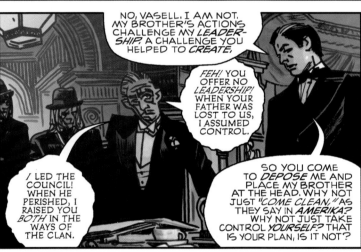

NO, VASELL. I AM NOT. MY BROTHER'S ACTIONS CHALLENGE MY *LEADER-SHIP*. A CHALLENGE YOU HELPED TO *CREATE*.

FEH! YOU OFFER NO *LEADERSHIP!* WHEN YOUR FATHER WAS LOST TO US, I ASSUMED CONTROL.

I LED THE COUNCIL! WHEN HE *PERISHED*, I RAISED YOU *BOTH* IN THE WAYS OF THE CLAN.

SO YOU COME TO *DEPOSE* ME AND PLACE MY BROTHER AT THE HEAD. WHY NOT JUST *"COME CLEAN,"* AS THEY SAY IN *AMERIKA?* WHY NOT JUST TAKE CONTROL *YOURSELF?* THAT IS YOUR PLAN, IS IT NOT?

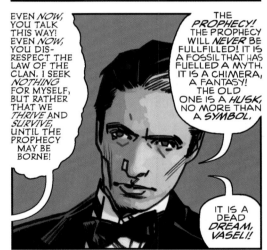

EVEN *NOW,* YOU TALK THIS WAY! EVEN *NOW,* YOU DIS-RESPECT THE LAW OF THE CLAN. I SEEK *NOTHING* FOR MYSELF, BUT RATHER THAT WE *THRIVE* AND *SURVIVE,* UNTIL THE PROPHECY MAY BE BORNE!

THE *PROPHECY!* THE PROPHECY WILL *NEVER* BE FULLFILLED! IT IS A FOSSIL THAT HAS FUELLED A MYTH. IT IS A CHIMERA, A FANTASY! THE OLD ONE IS A *HUSK,* NO MORE THAN A *SYMBOL.*

IT IS A DEAD *DREAM,* VASEL!!

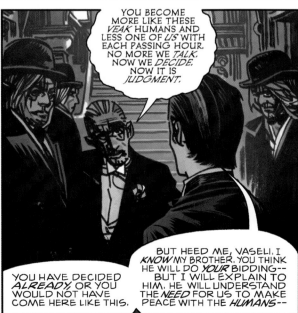

YOU BECOME MORE LIKE THESE *VEAK* HUMANS AND LESS ONE OF *US* WITH EACH PASSING HOUR. NO MORE WE *TALK.* NOW WE *DECIDE,* NOW IT IS *JUDGMENT.*

YOU HAVE DECIDED *ALREADY,* OR YOU WOULD NOT HAVE COME HERE LIKE THIS.

BUT HEED ME, VASELI. I *KNOW* MY BROTHER. YOU THINK HE WILL DO *YOUR* BIDDING-- BUT I WILL EXPLAIN TO HIM, HE WILL UNDERSTAND THE *NEED* FOR US TO MAKE PEACE WITH THE *HUMANS*--

THEN VE MUST *KEEP* YOU FROM *TALKING,* MUST VE NOT?

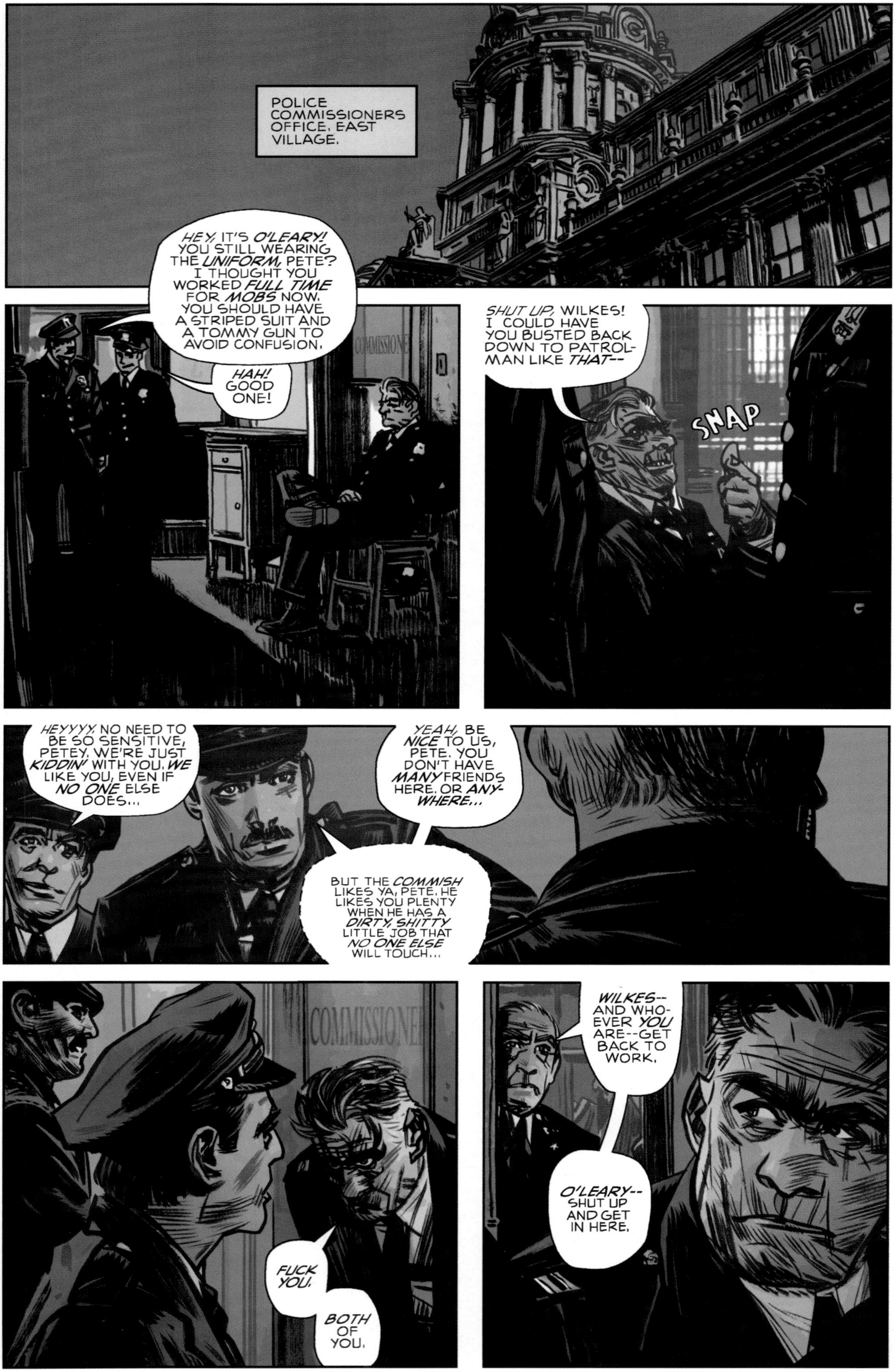
POLICE COMMISSIONERS OFFICE, EAST VILLAGE.
HEY, IT'S O'LEARY! YOU STILL WEARING THE UNIFORM, PETE? I THOUGHT YOU WORKED FULL TIME FOR MOBS NOW. YOU SHOULD HAVE A STRIPED SUIT AND A TOMMY GUN TO AVOID CONFUSION.
HAH! GOOD ONE!
COMMISSIONE
SHUT UP, WILKES! I COULD HAVE YOU BUSTED BACK DOWN TO PATROLMAN LIKE THAT--
SNAP
HEYYYY, NO NEED TO BE SO SENSITIVE, PETEY. WE'RE JUST KIDDIN' WITH YOU. WE LIKE YOU, EVEN IF NO ONE ELSE DOES...
YEAH, BE NICE TO US, PETE. YOU DON'T HAVE MANY FRIENDS HERE. OR ANYWHERE...
BUT THE COMMISH LIKES YA, PETE. HE LIKES YOU PLENTY WHEN HE HAS A DIRTY, SHITTY LITTLE JOB THAT NO ONE ELSE WILL TOUCH...
COMMISSIONER
FUCK YOU.
BOTH OF YOU.
WILKES-- AND WHOEVER YOU ARE--GET BACK TO WORK.
O'LEARY-- SHUT UP AND GET IN HERE.

YOU'RE IN CONTACT WITH THIS *DRAGONMIR* FAMILY, AREN'T YOU? YOU SET THEM UP WITH BAVA, DIDN'T YOU?

THEY NEEDED SOMEONE TO BRING SOME HOOCH AND *SUPPLIES* IN, SO I PUT THEM TOGETHER, *YEAH.*

FOR A NICE *FAT FEE,* I BET.

NEVER MIND THAT. TELL ME *STRAIGHT,* O'LEARY --ARE THESE DRAGONMIRS TAKING OVER THE GANGS? THEY GOT *PLANS* FOR THIS CITY?

WELL, IT'S *NEWS* TO ME IF THEY ARE SIR. THEY JUST BEEN PAYING ME TO LOOK THE OTHER WAY WHEN THEY GET DELIVERIES.

BUT I MADE SURE *YOU* GOT *YOUR* CUT, SIR, EVERY TIME--YOU *KNOW* THAT.

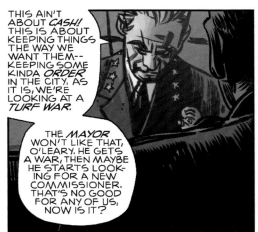

THIS AIN'T ABOUT *CASH!* THIS IS ABOUT KEEPING THINGS THE WAY WE WANT THEM-- KEEPING SOME KINDA *ORDER* IN THE CITY, AS IT IS, WE'RE LOOKING AT A *TURF WAR.*

THE *MAYOR* WON'T LIKE THAT, O'LEARY. HE GETS A WAR, THEN MAYBE HE STARTS LOOK- ING FOR A NEW COMMISSIONER. THAT'S NO GOOD FOR ANY OF US, NOW IS IT?

THIS IS *TOMPKINS,* HE'S FROM CHICAGO. HE HELPS KEEP *CAPONE* FROM GETTING OUT OF HAND, SO THINGS RUN NICE AND SMOOTH.

WE'RE GOING IN TO SHOW THOSE NEW BOYS THAT IT'S THE *COPS* WHO RUN THIS CITY.

I NEED YOU TO GO ALONG. HELP HIM GET IN TO THEIR PLACE WITHOUT TOO MUCH *EFFORT,* WITHOUT TOO MUCH *NOISE,* UNNERSTAN?

YES, SIR.

WE'RE GOING IN TOMORROW. JUST AFTER SUNRISE, *THREE TRUCKS, THIRTY MEN,* ALL TOGETHER, *NO SURPRISES,* O'LEARY. I DON'T LIKE *SURPRISES.*

OH, I CAN GET YOU IN THERE, NO TROUBLE. FAR AS I KNOW, THEY AIN'T EVEN *ARMED.*

WELL, *WE* WILL BE, JUST IN CASE THEY TURN *FEISTY.*

GOOD TO KNOW, SIR. GOOD TO KNOW.

BUT LET'S HIT THEM BEFORE DAWN, WHILE IT'S STILL DARK.

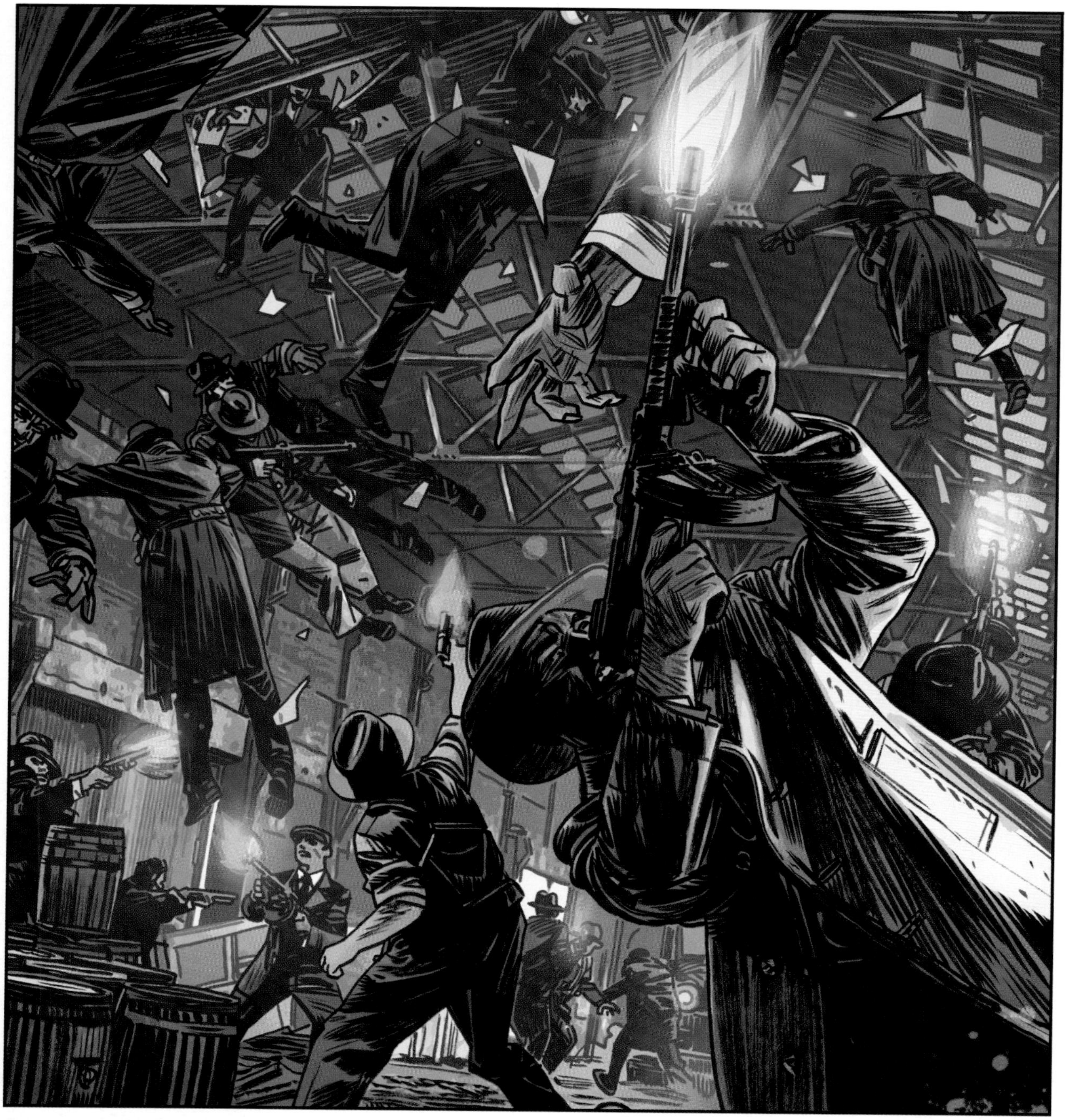

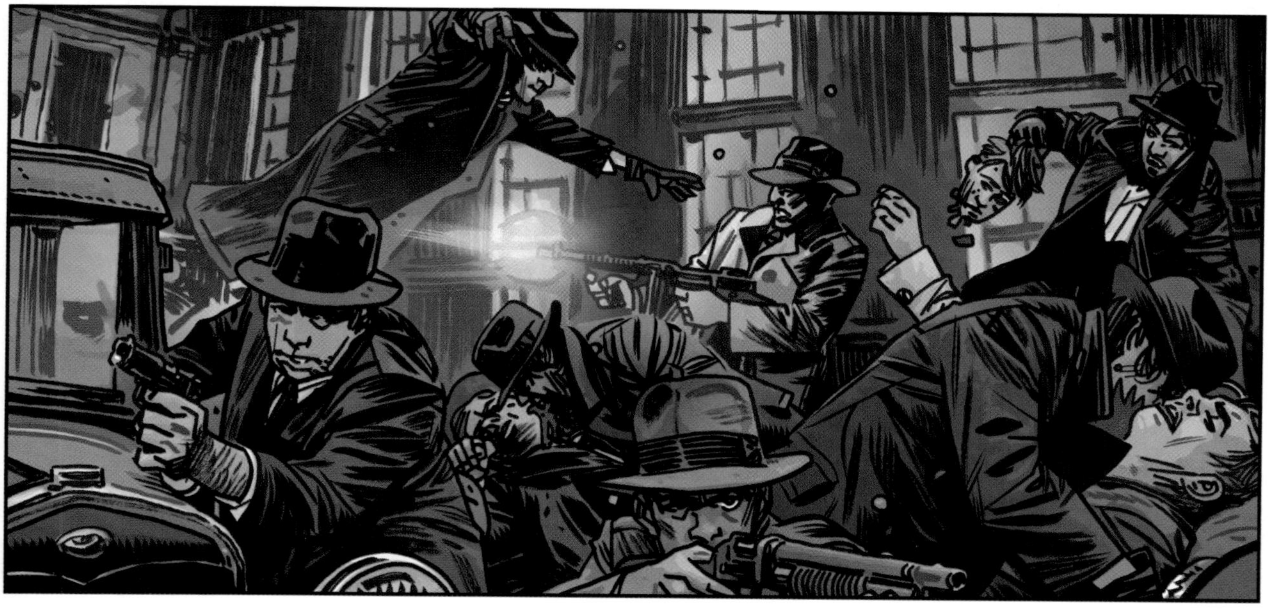

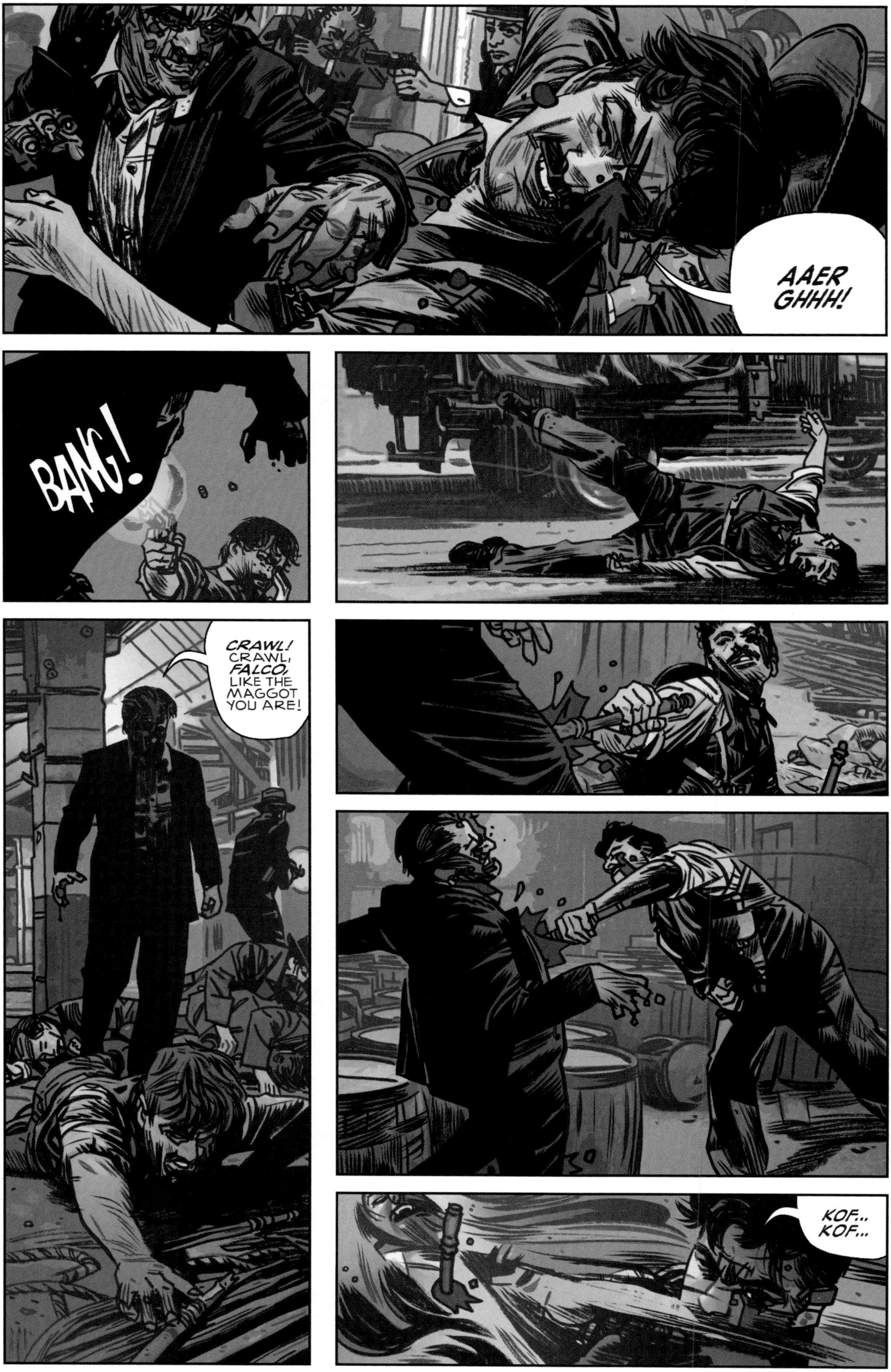
AAER GHHH!
BANG!
CRAWL! CRAWL, FALCO, LIKE THE MAGGOT YOU ARE!
KOF... KOF...

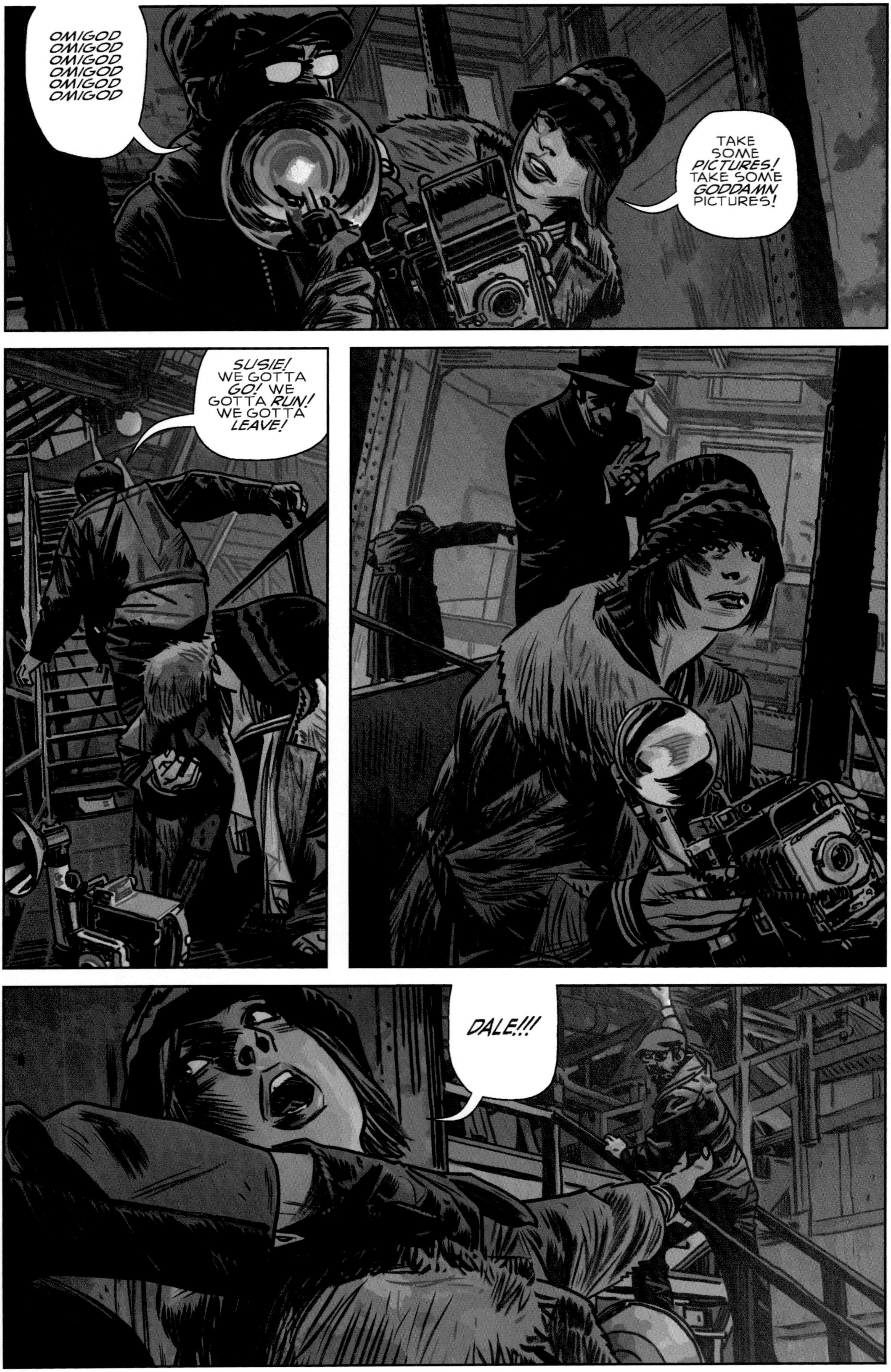

OMIGOD OMIGOD OMIGOD OMIGOD OMIGOD OMIGOD
TAKE SOME PICTURES! TAKE SOME GODDAMN PICTURES!
SUSIE! WE GOTTA GO! WE GOTTA RUN! WE GOTTA LEAVE!
DALE!!!

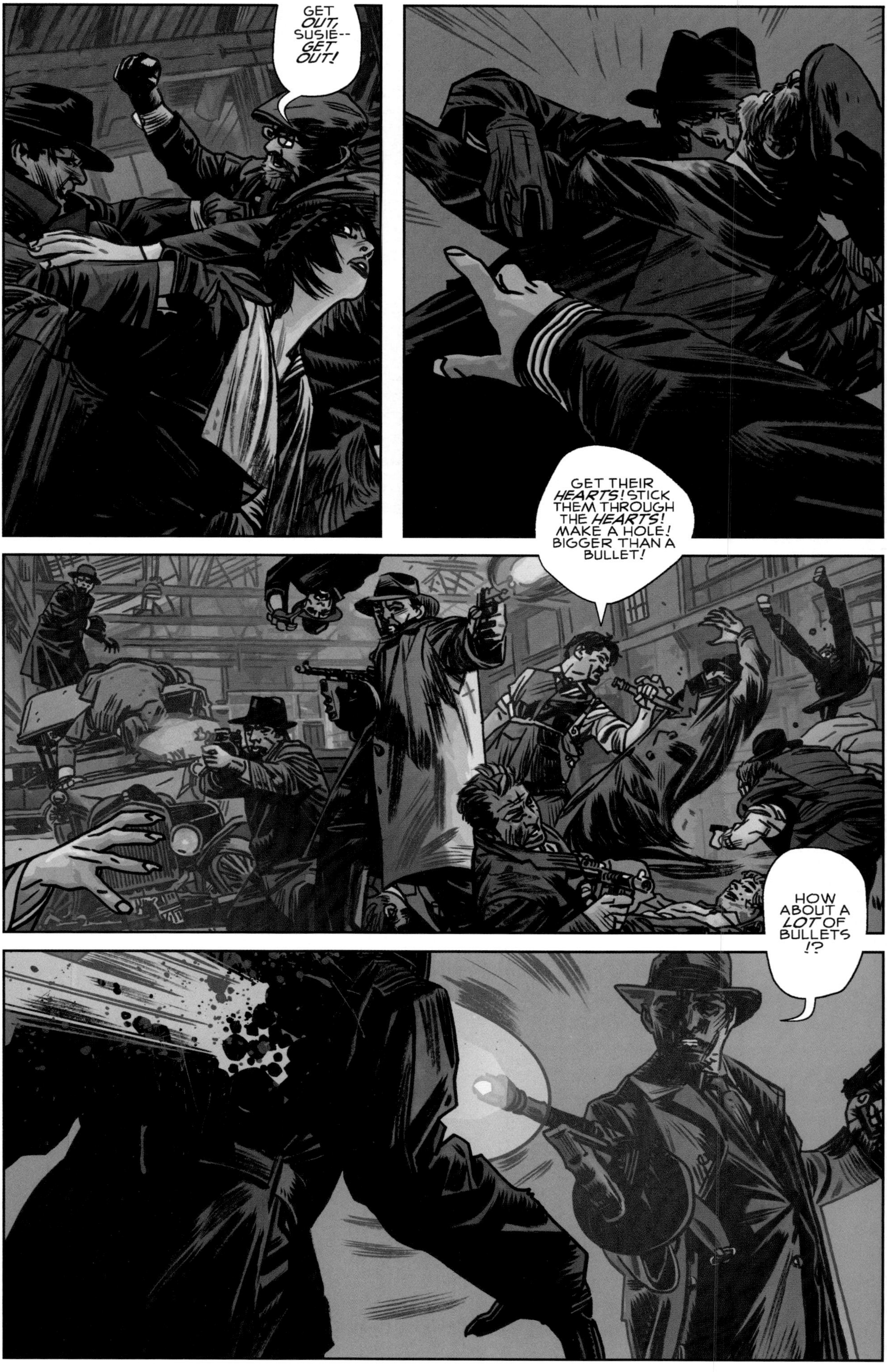
GET OUT, SUSIE-- GET OUT!
GET THEIR HEARTS! STICK THEM THROUGH THE HEARTS! MAKE A HOLE! BIGGER THAN A BULLET!
HOW ABOUT A LOT OF BULLETS!?

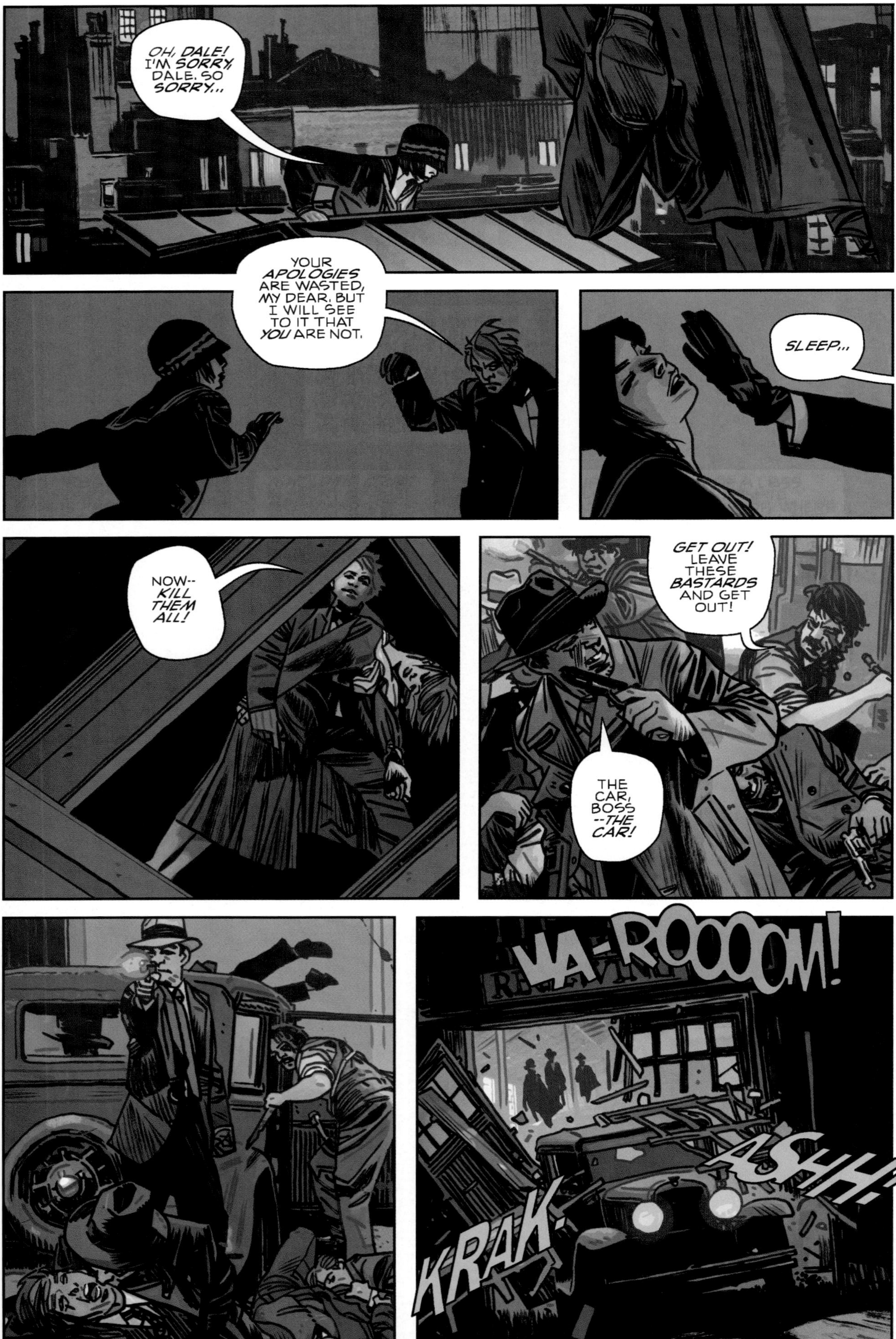
OH, DALE! I'M SORRY, DALE. SO SORRY...
YOUR APOLOGIES ARE WASTED, MY DEAR. BUT I WILL SEE TO IT THAT YOU ARE NOT.
SLEEP...
NOW-- KILL THEM ALL!
GET OUT! LEAVE THESE BASTARDS AND GET OUT!
THE CAR, BOSS --THE CAR!
VA-ROOOOM!
KRAK-ASH!!

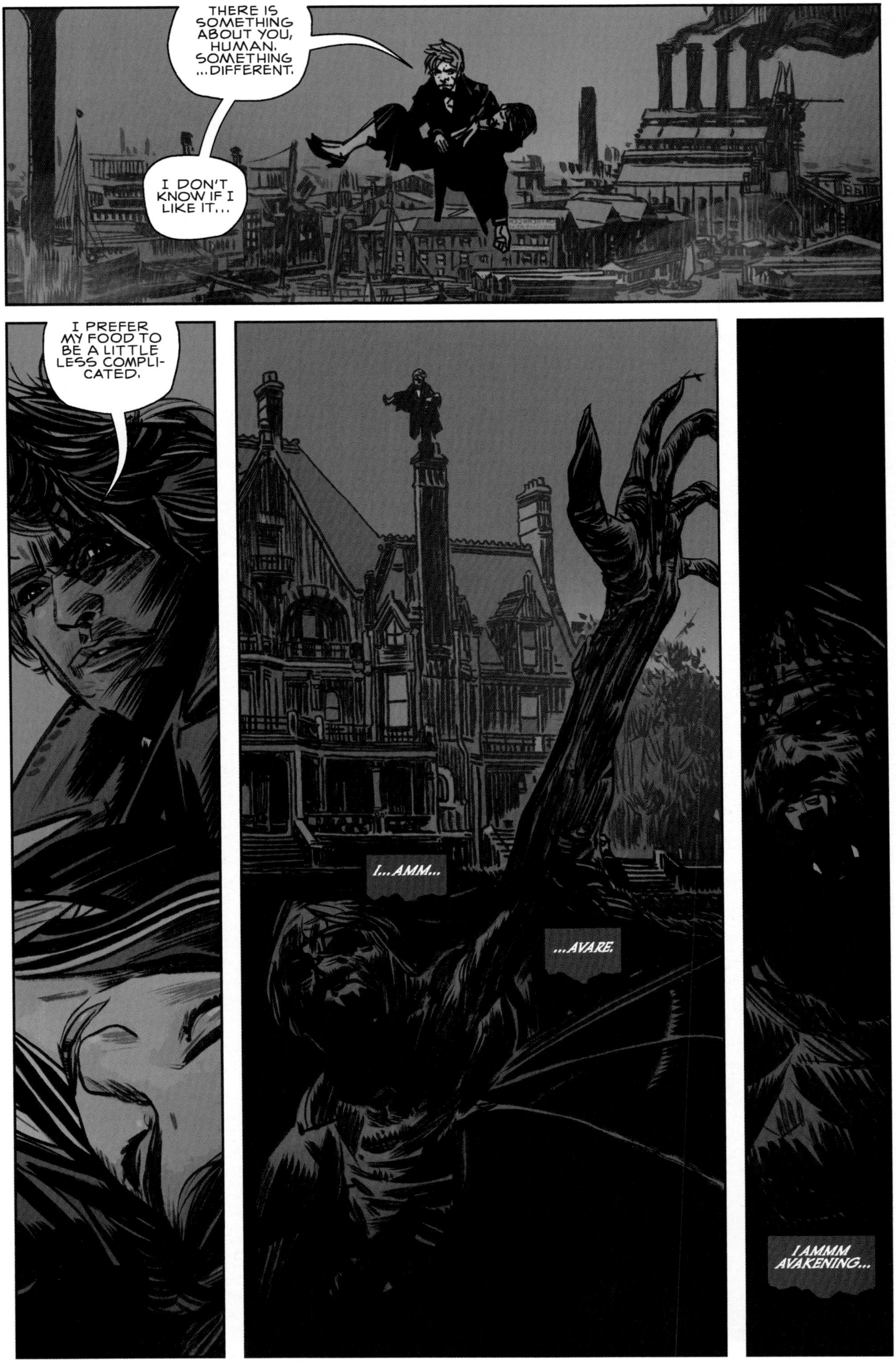
THERE IS SOMETHING ABOUT YOU, HUMAN. SOMETHING ...DIFFERENT.
I DON'T KNOW IF I LIKE IT...
I PREFER MY FOOD TO BE A LITTLE LESS COMPLI-CATED.
I...AMM...
...AVARE.
IAMMM AVAKENING...

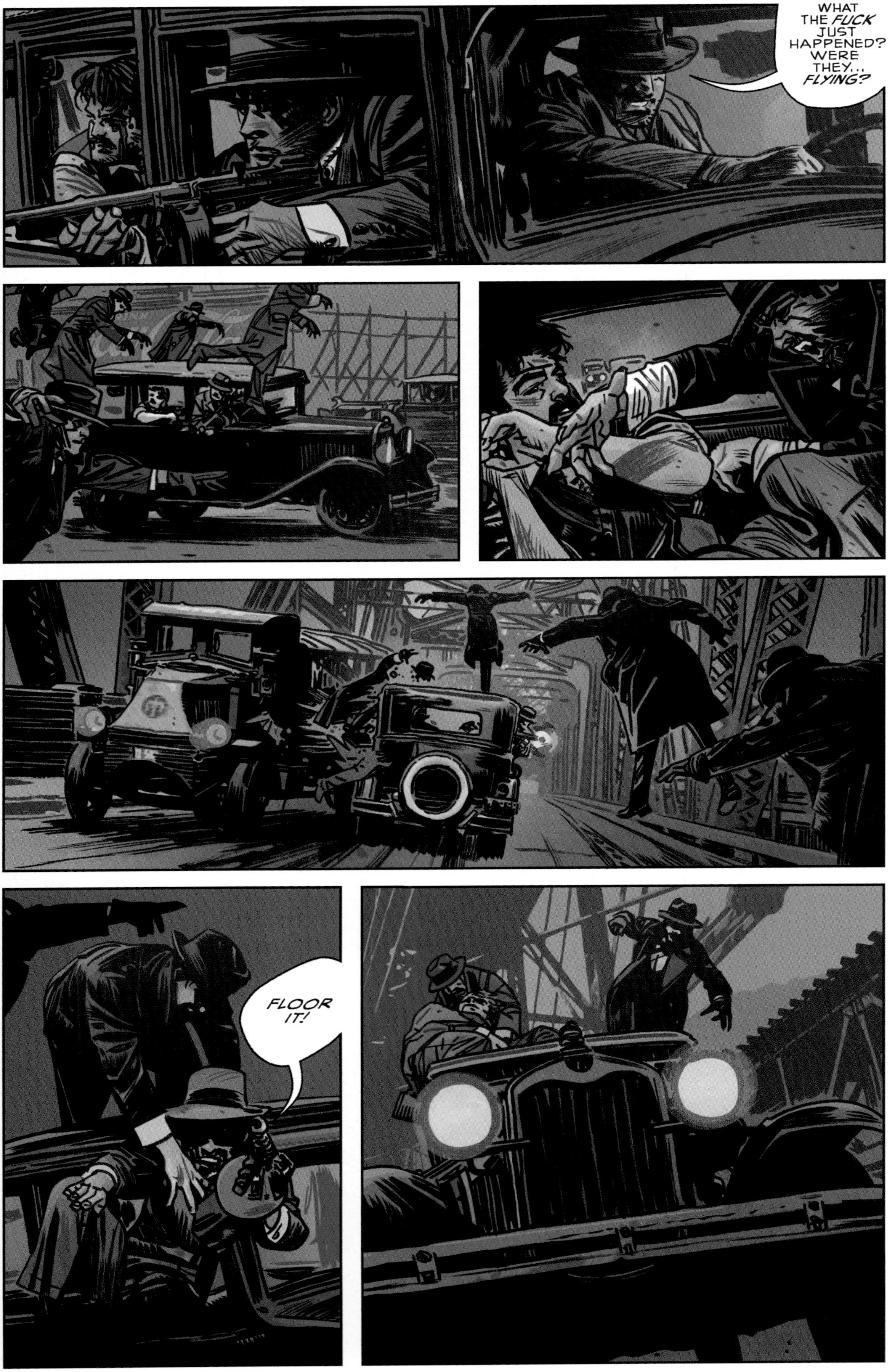
WHAT THE *FUCK* JUST HAPPENED? WERE THEY... *FLYING?*
FLOOR IT!

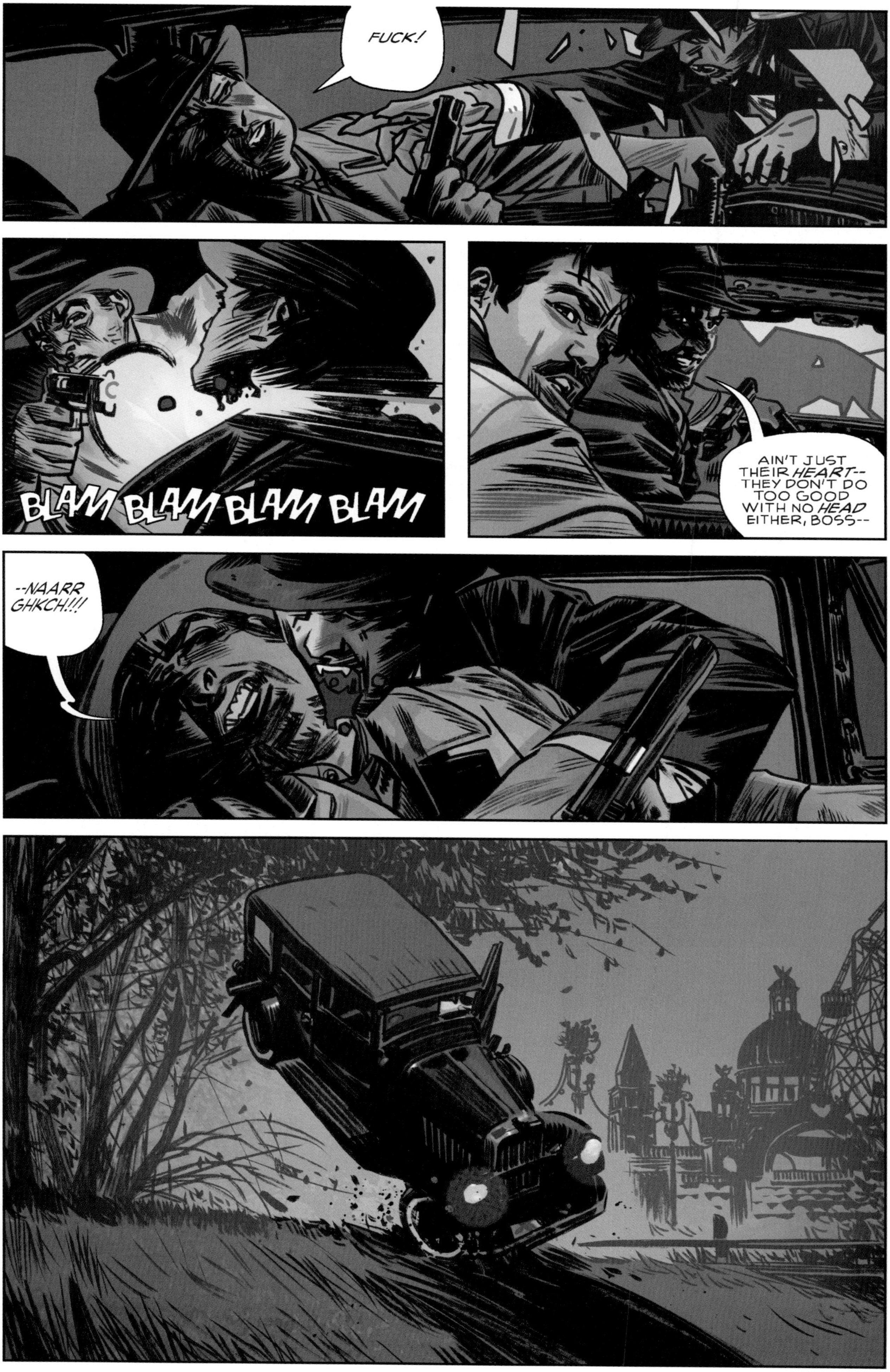

FUCK!
BLAM BLAM BLAM BLAM
AIN'T JUST THEIR *HEART*-- THEY DON'T DO TOO GOOD WITH NO *HEAD* EITHER, BOSS--
--NAARR GHKCH!!!

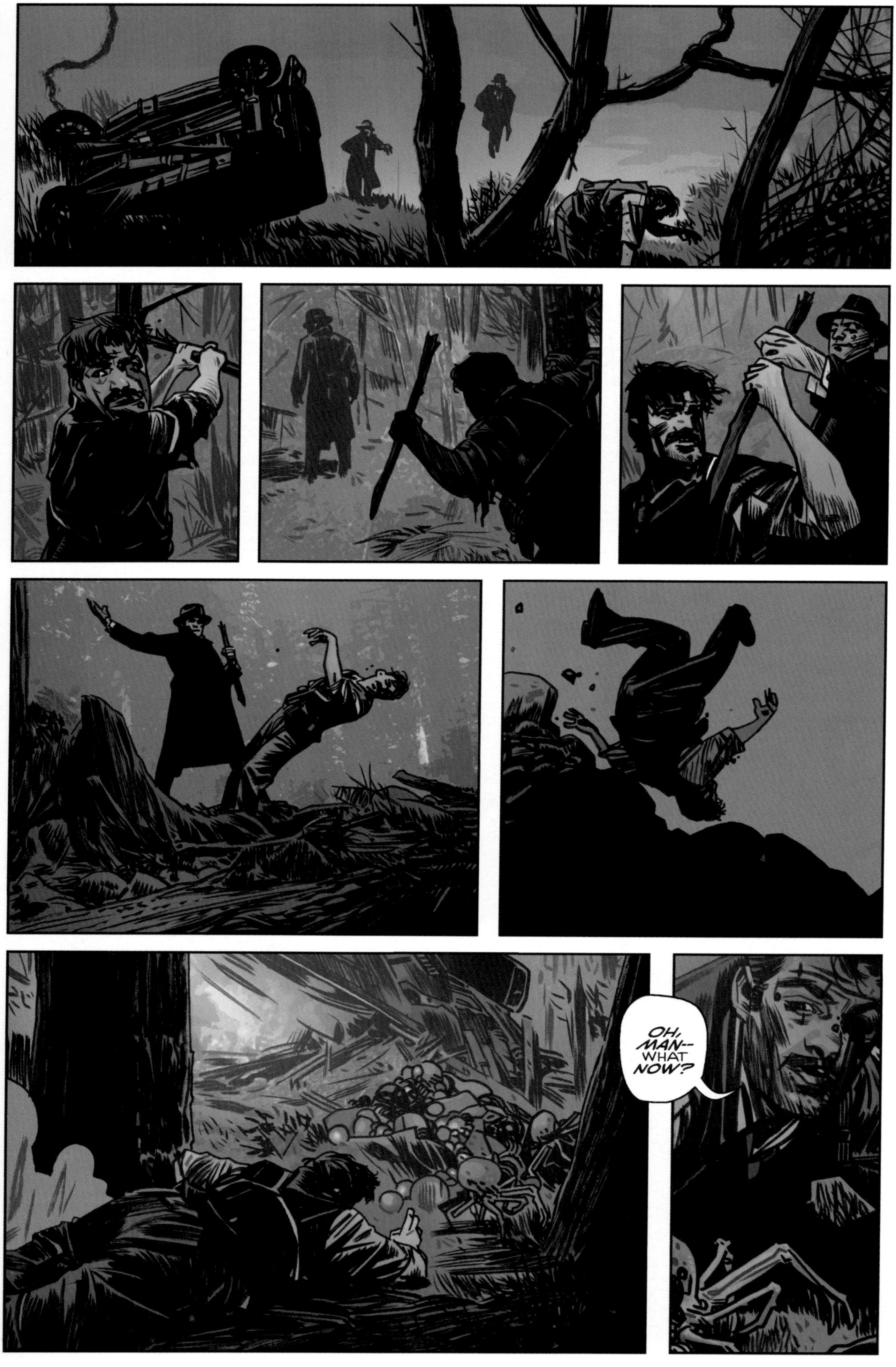
OH, MAN-- WHAT NOW?

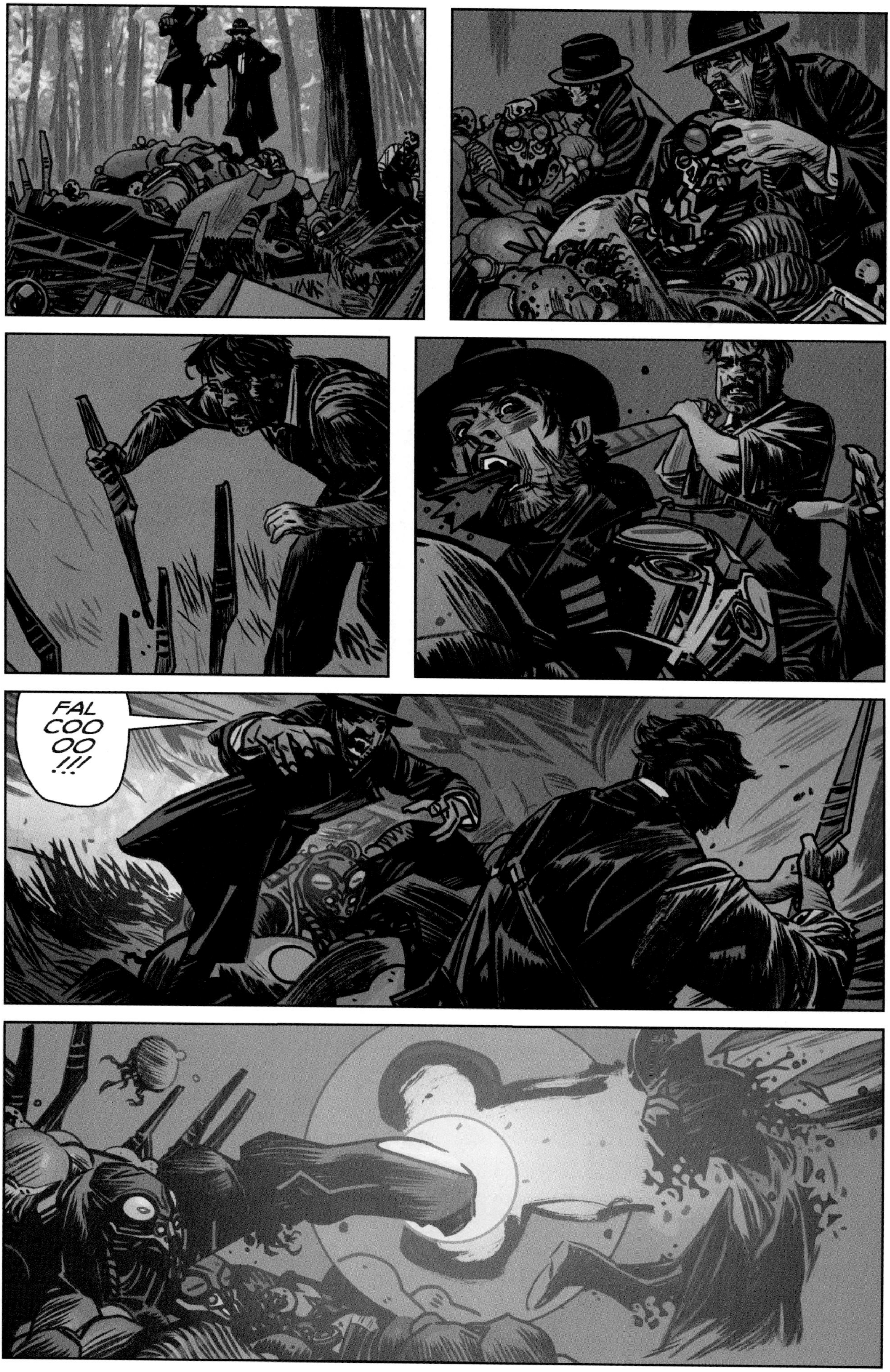
FAL COOOO !!!

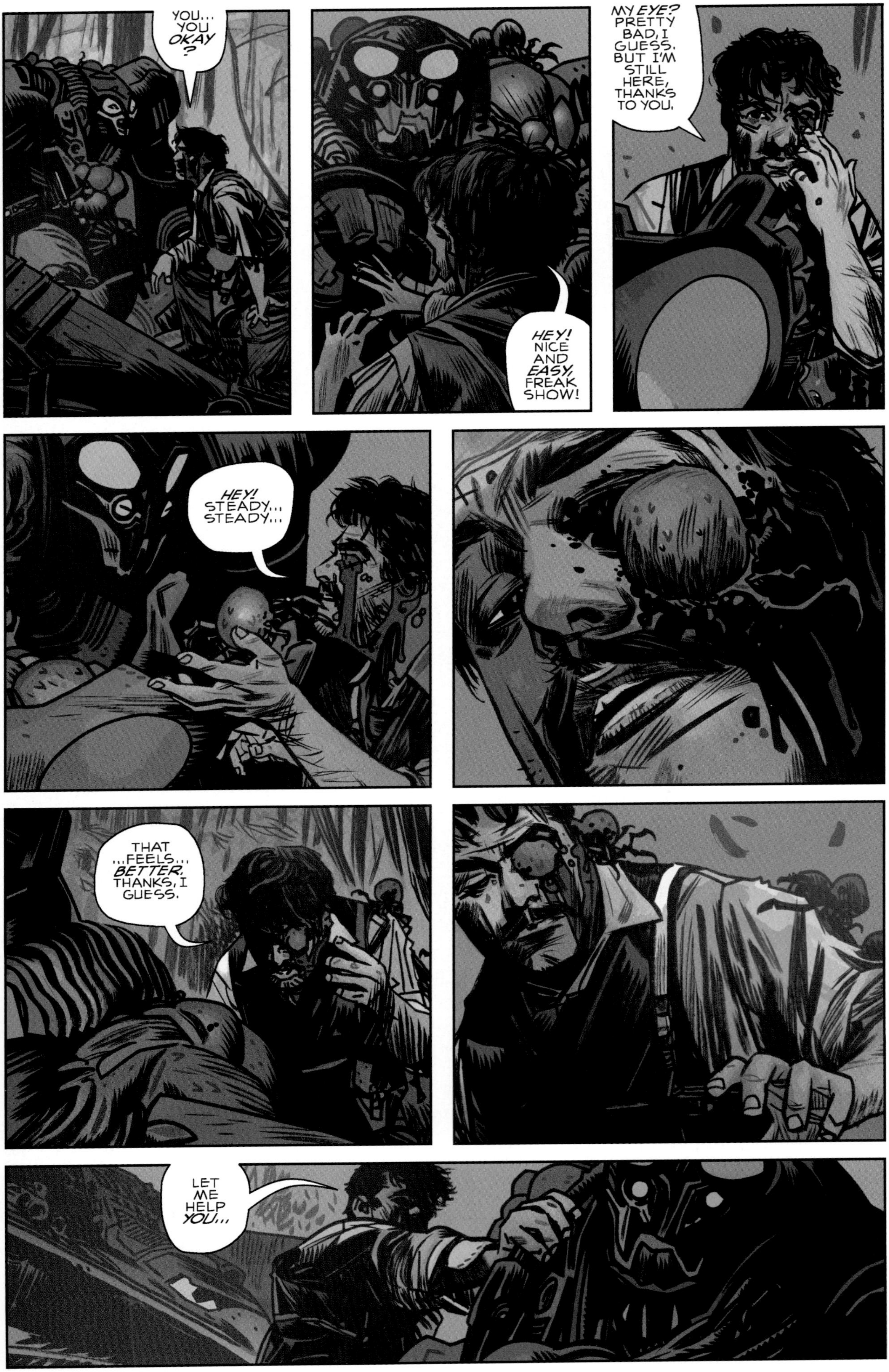
YOU... YOU OKAY?
HEY! NICE AND EASY, FREAK SHOW!
MY EYE? PRETTY BAD, I GUESS. BUT I'M STILL HERE, THANKS TO YOU.
HEY! STEADY... STEADY...
THAT ...FEELS... BETTER. THANKS, I GUESS.
LET ME HELP YOU...

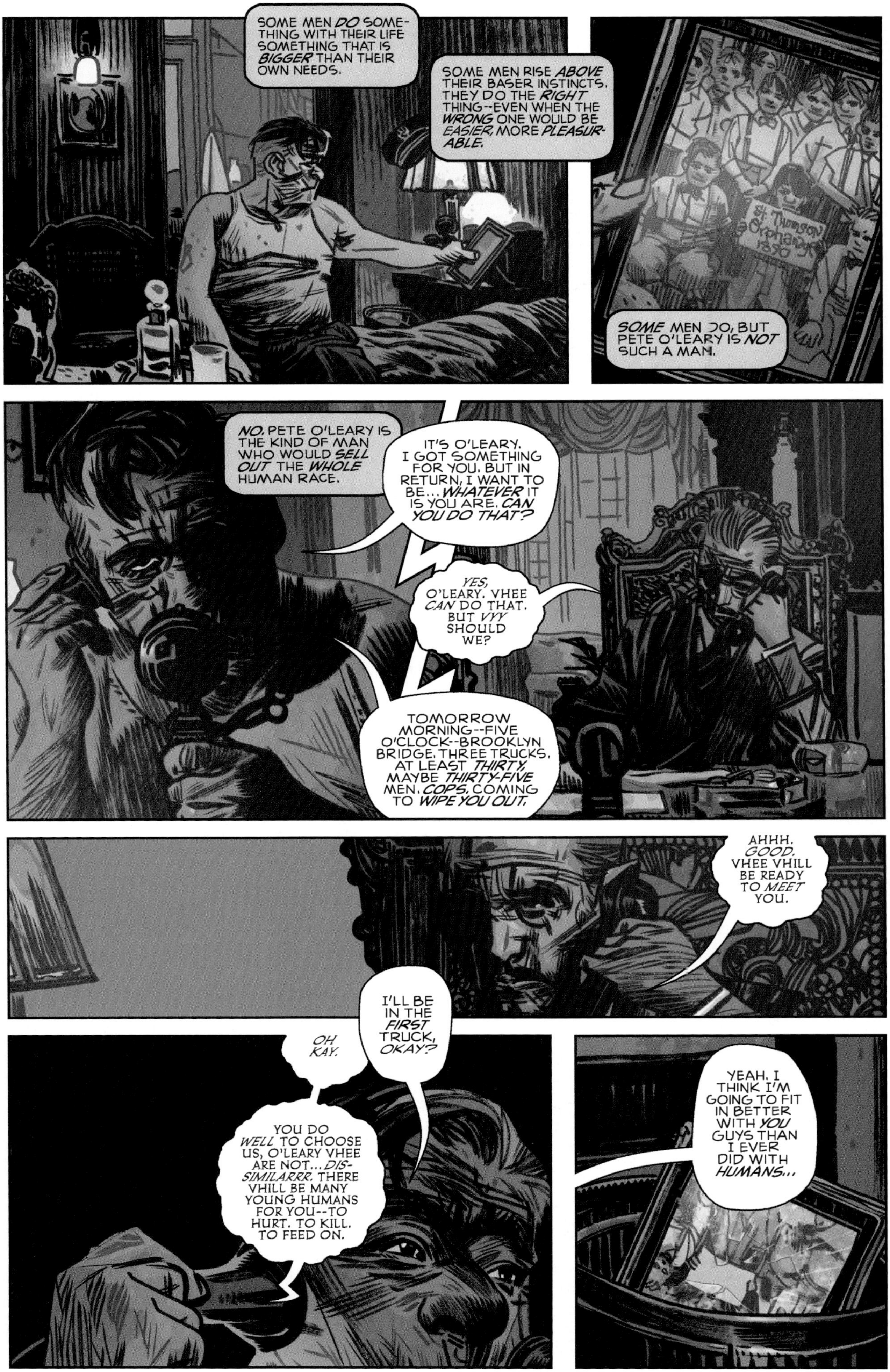
SOME MEN DO SOMETHING WITH THEIR LIFE SOMETHING THAT IS BIGGER THAN THEIR OWN NEEDS.
SOME MEN RISE ABOVE THEIR BASER INSTINCTS. THEY DO THE RIGHT THING--EVEN WHEN THE WRONG ONE WOULD BE EASIER, MORE PLEASURABLE.
St. Thomson Orphanage 1890
SOME MEN DO, BUT PETE O'LEARY IS NOT SUCH A MAN.
NO. PETE O'LEARY IS THE KIND OF MAN WHO WOULD SELL OUT THE WHOLE HUMAN RACE.
IT'S O'LEARY. I GOT SOMETHING FOR YOU. BUT IN RETURN, I WANT TO BE... WHATEVER IT IS YOU ARE. CAN YOU DO THAT?
YES, O'LEARY. VHEE CAN DO THAT. BUT VYY SHOULD WE?
TOMORROW MORNING--FIVE O'CLOCK--BROOKLYN BRIDGE. THREE TRUCKS. AT LEAST THIRTY. MAYBE THIRTY-FIVE MEN. COPS, COMING TO WIPE YOU OUT.
AHHH. GOOD. VHEE VHILL BE READY TO MEET YOU.
I'LL BE IN THE FIRST TRUCK, OKAY?
OH KAY.
YOU DO WELL TO CHOOSE US, O'LEARY VHEE ARE NOT... DISSIMILARRR. THERE VHILL BE MANY YOUNG HUMANS FOR YOU--TO HURT. TO KILL. TO FEED ON.
YEAH. I THINK I'M GOING TO FIT IN BETTER WITH YOU GUYS THAN I EVER DID WITH HUMANS...

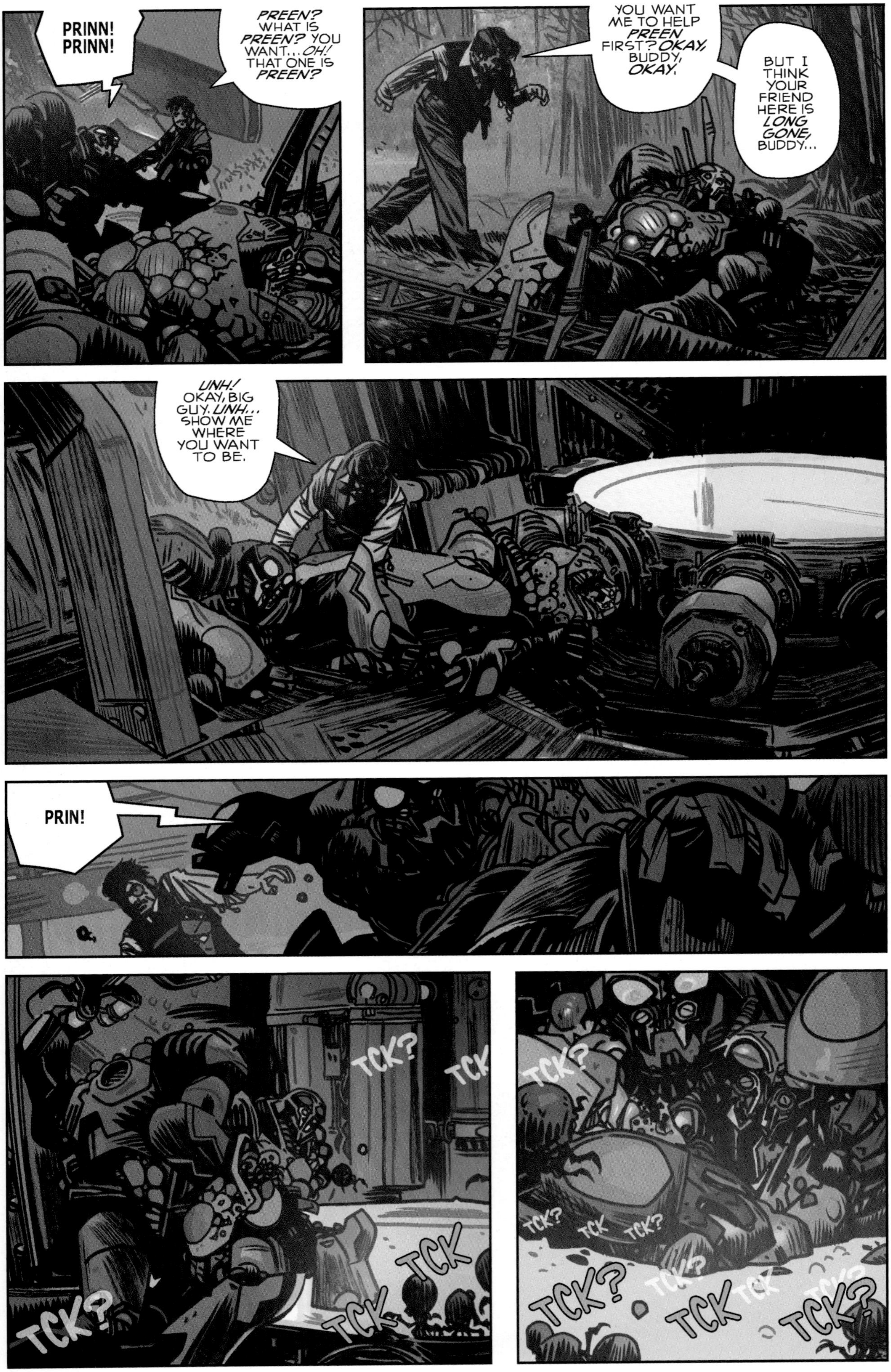
PRINN! PRINN!
PREEN? WHAT IS PREEN? YOU WANT... OH! THAT ONE IS PREEN?
YOU WANT ME TO HELP PREEN FIRST? OKAY, BUDDY, OKAY.
BUT I THINK YOUR FRIEND HERE IS LONG GONE, BUDDY...
UNH! OKAY, BIG GUY. UNH... SHOW ME WHERE YOU WANT TO BE.
PRIN!
TCK? TCK
TCK TCK? TCK
TCK? TCK TCK?
TCK? TCK TCK? TCK TCK TCK?

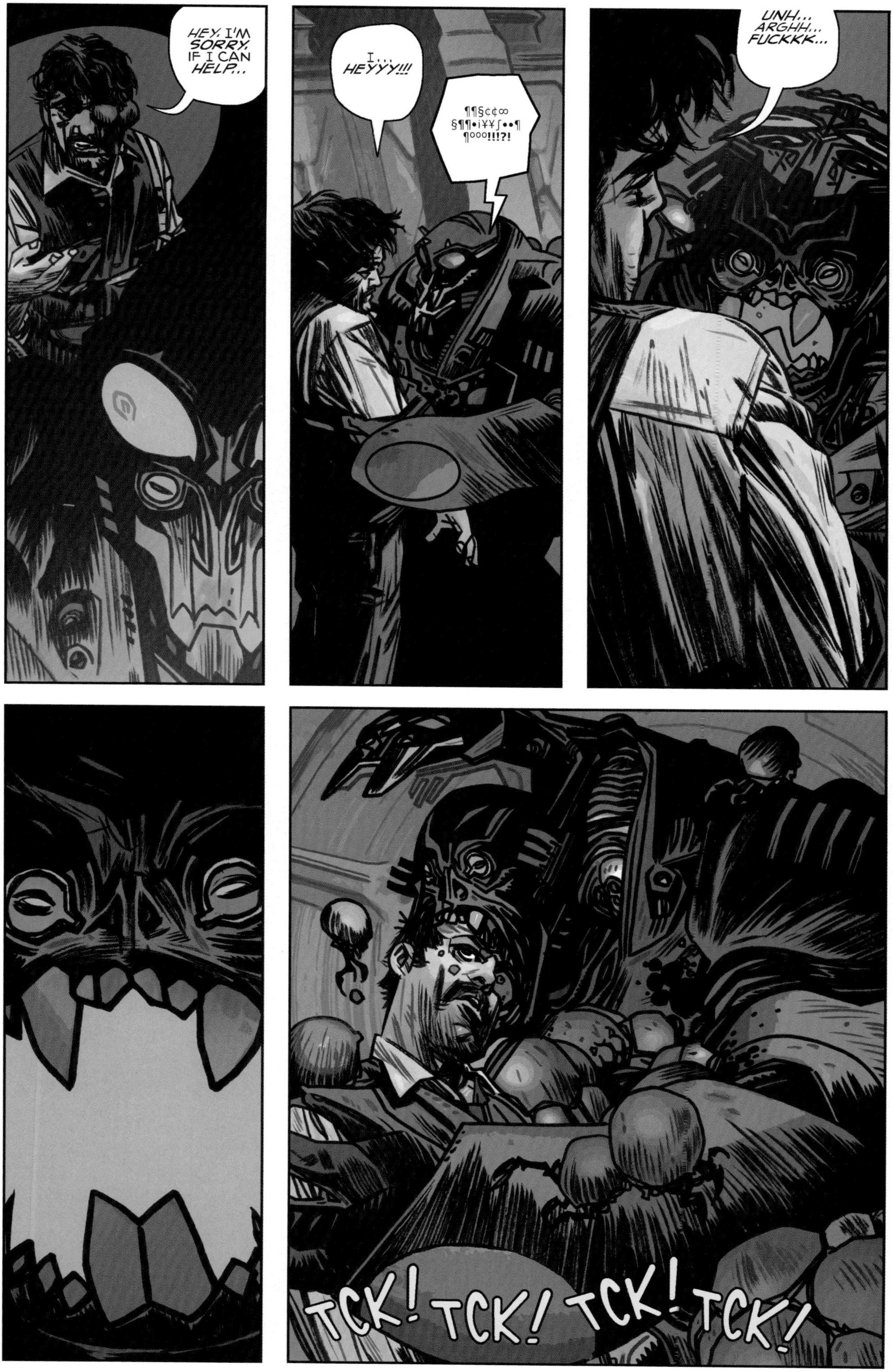
HEY, I'M SORRY. IF I CAN HELP...
I... HEYYY!!!
¶¶§¢¢∞ §¶¶•i¥¥∫••¶ ¶ºººº!!!?!
UNH... ARGHH... FUCKKK...
TCK! TCK! TCK! TCK!

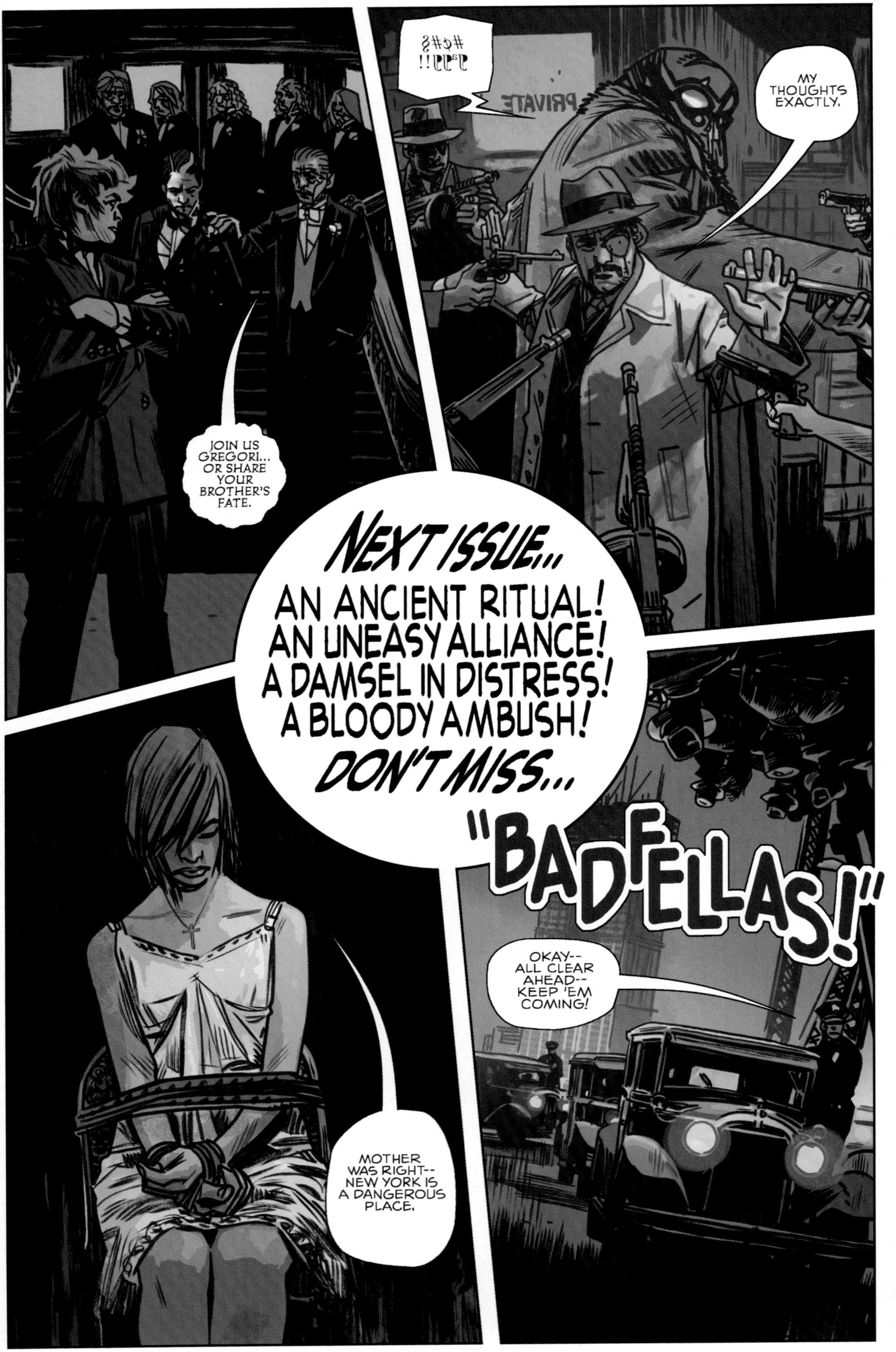
JOIN US GREGORI... OR SHARE YOUR BROTHER'S FATE.
MY THOUGHTS EXACTLY.
PRIVATE
NEXT ISSUE...
AN ANCIENT RITUAL!
AN UNEASY ALLIANCE!
A DAMSEL IN DISTRESS!
A BLOODY AMBUSH!
DON'T MISS...
"BADFELLAS!"
MOTHER WAS RIGHT-- NEW YORK IS A DANGEROUS PLACE.
OKAY-- ALL CLEAR AHEAD-- KEEP 'EM COMING!

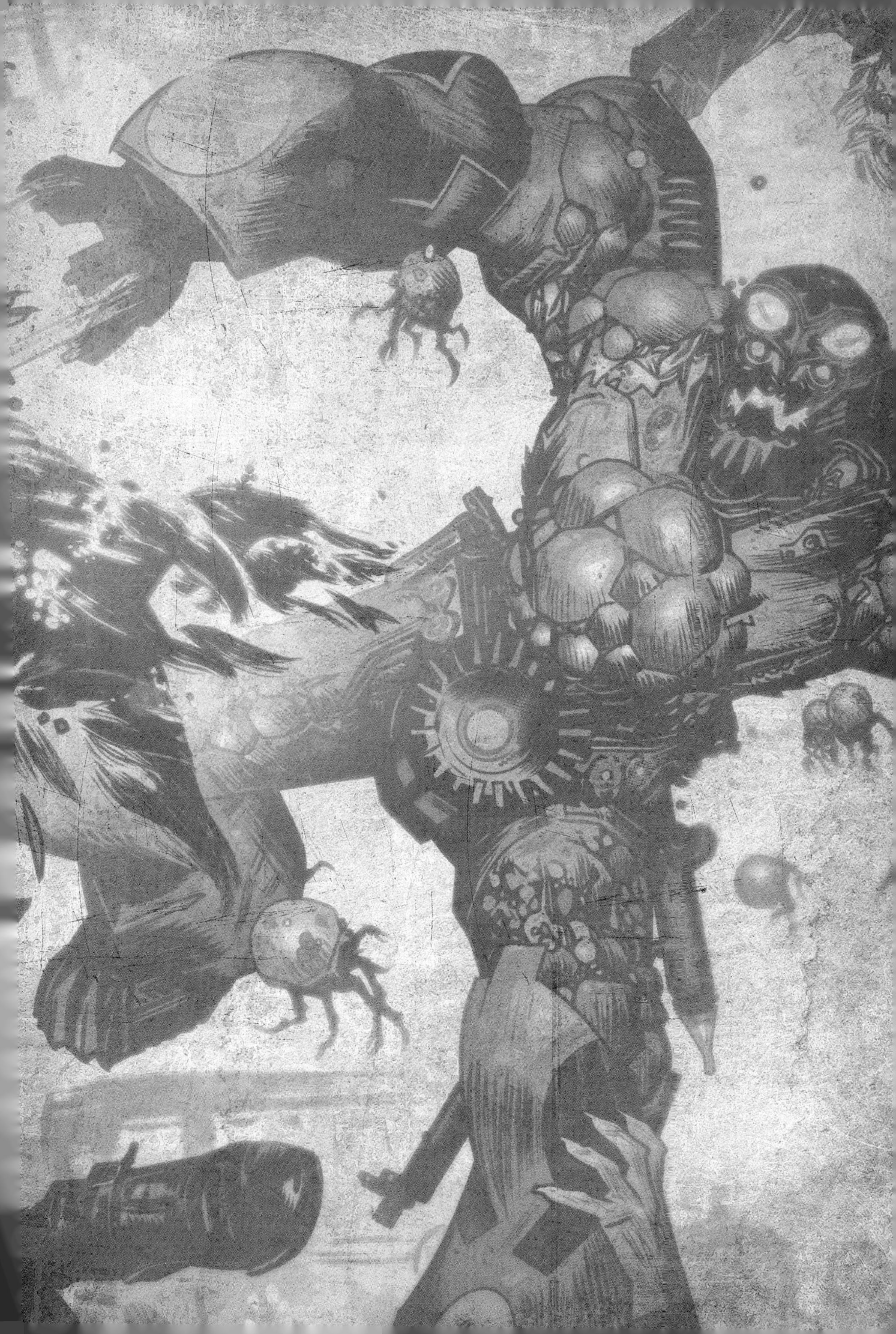

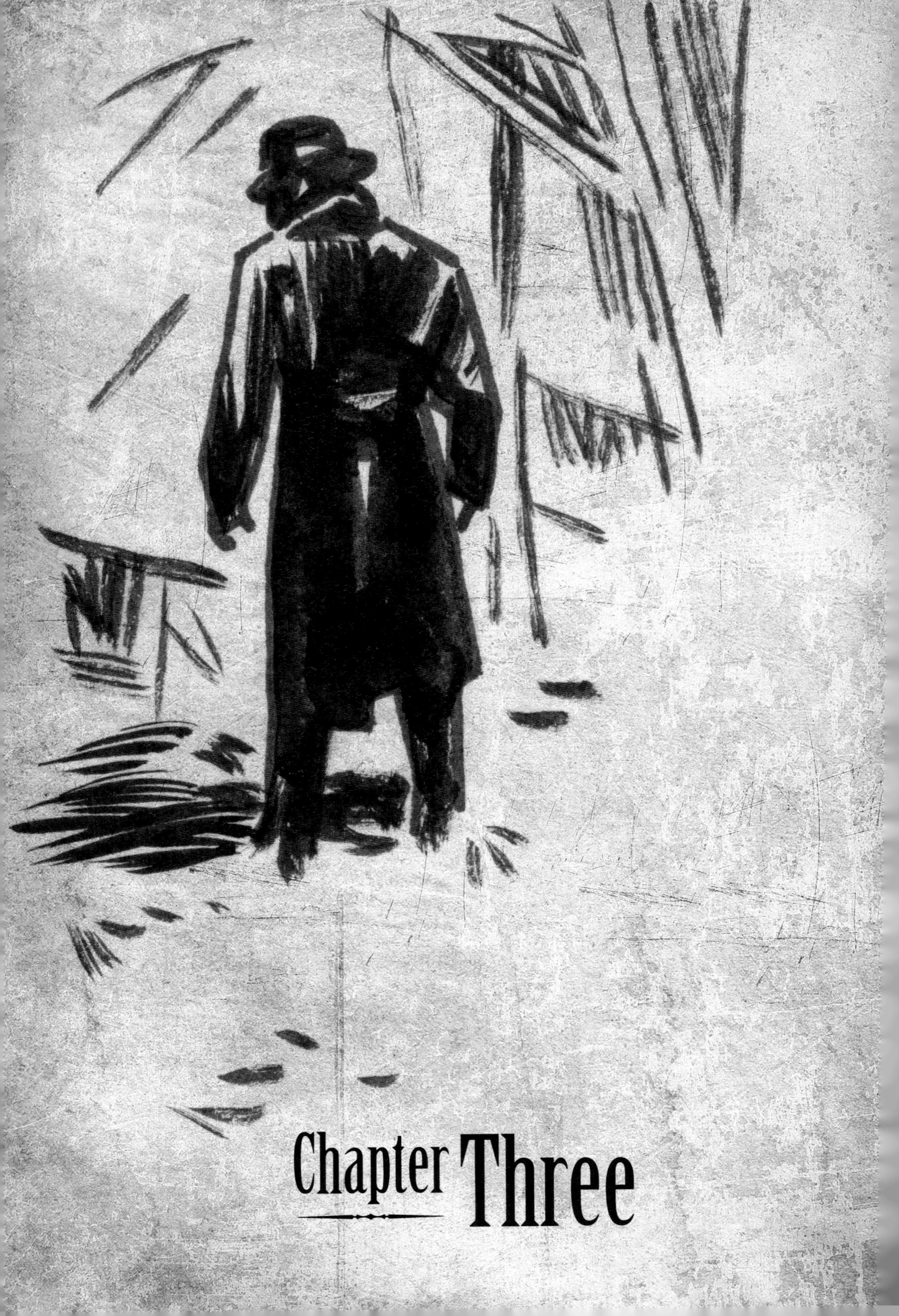

Chapter Three

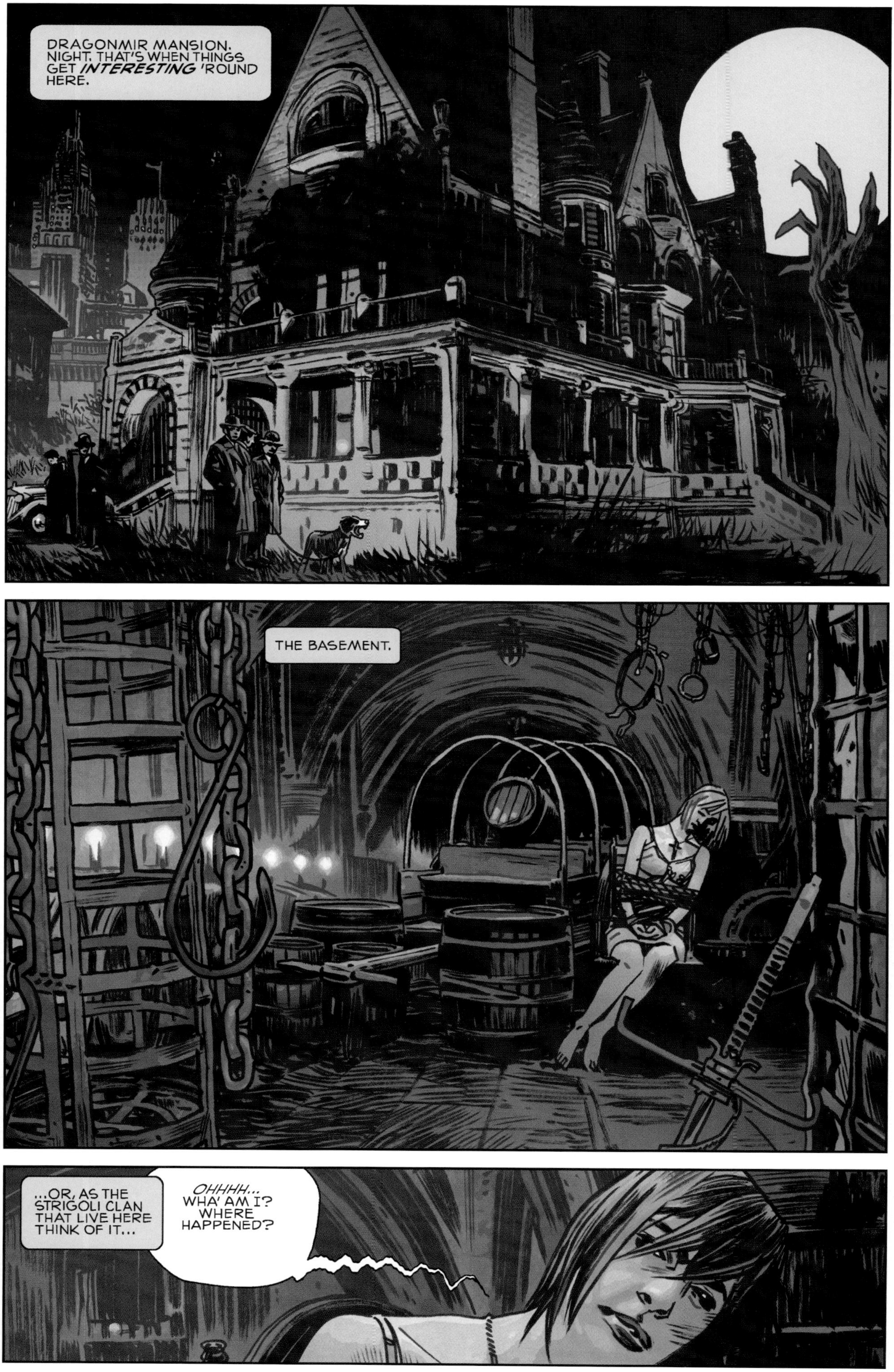
DRAGONMIR MANSION. NIGHT. THAT'S WHEN THINGS GET *INTERESTING* 'ROUND HERE.
THE BASEMENT.
...OR, AS THE STRIGOLI CLAN THAT LIVE HERE THINK OF IT...
OHHHH... WHA' AM I? WHERE HAPPENED?

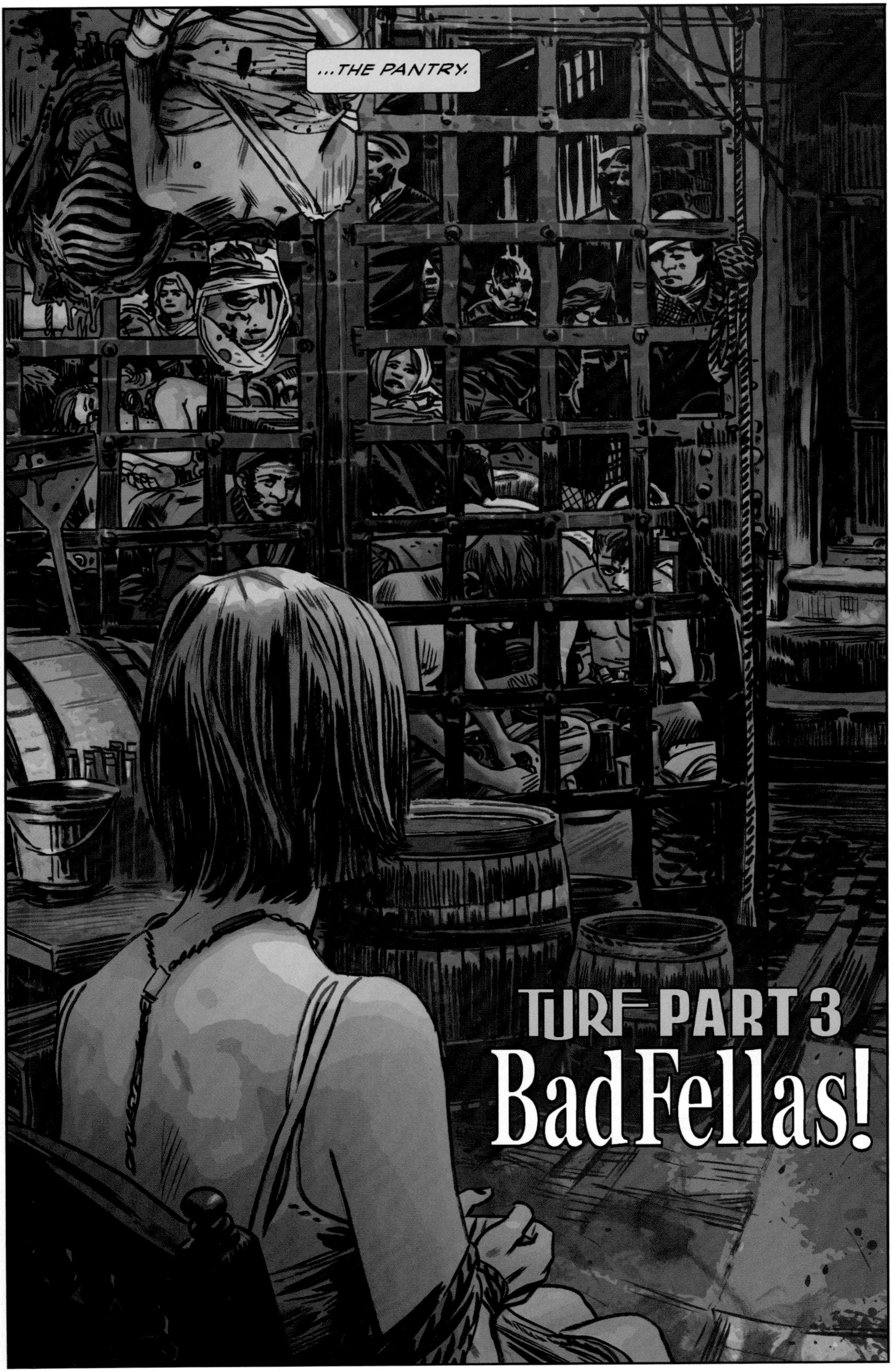
...THE PANTRY.
TURF PART 3
BadFellas!

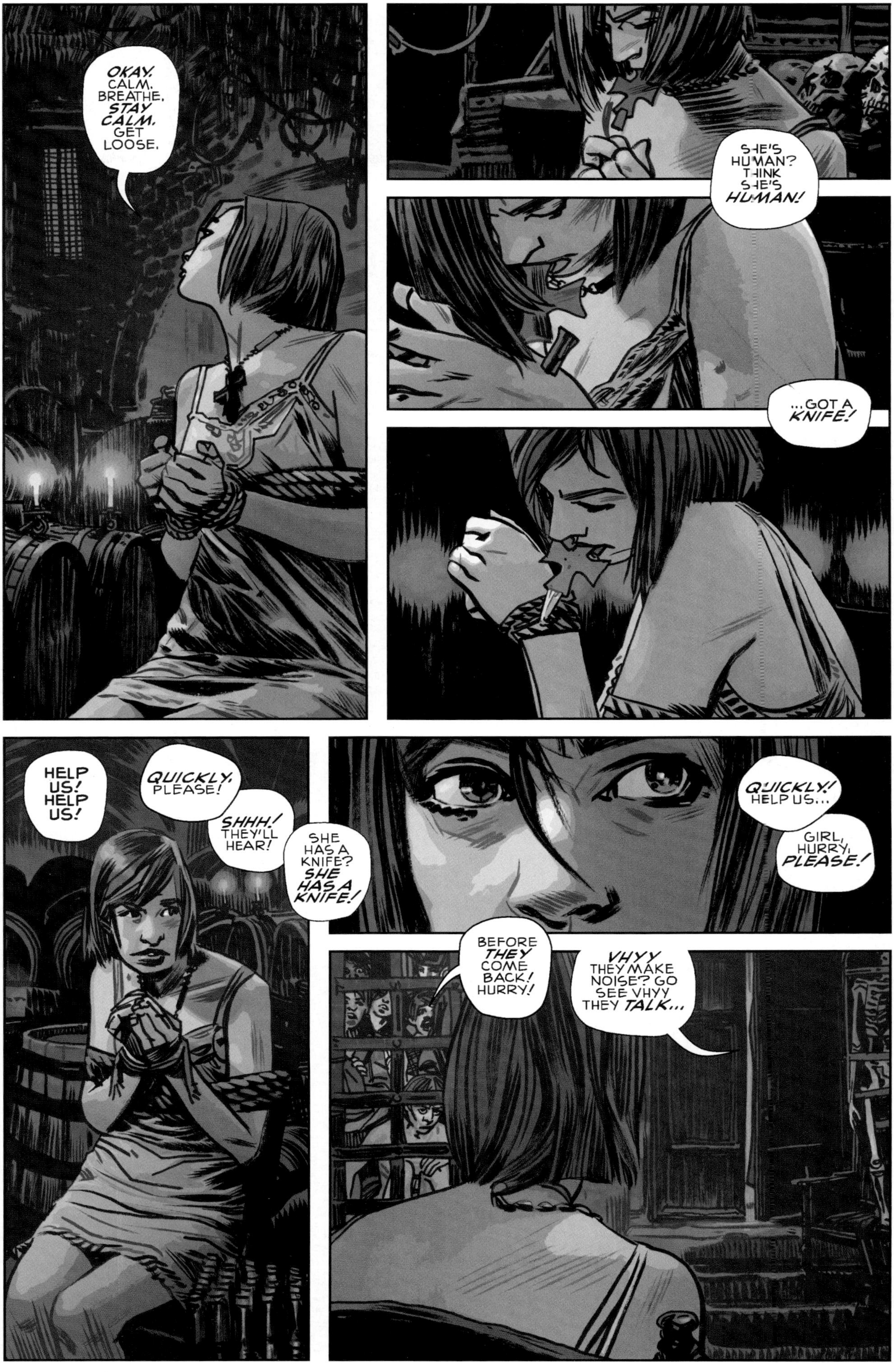
OKAY. CALM. BREATHE. STAY CALM. GET LOOSE.
SHE'S HUMAN? THINK SHE'S HUMAN!
...GOT A KNIFE!
HELP US! HELP US!
QUICKLY, PLEASE!
SHHH! THEY'LL HEAR!
SHE HAS A KNIFE? SHE HAS A KNIFE!
QUICKLY! HELP US...
GIRL, HURRY, PLEASE!
BEFORE THEY COME BACK! HURRY!
VHYY THEY MAKE NOISE? GO SEE VHYY THEY TALK...

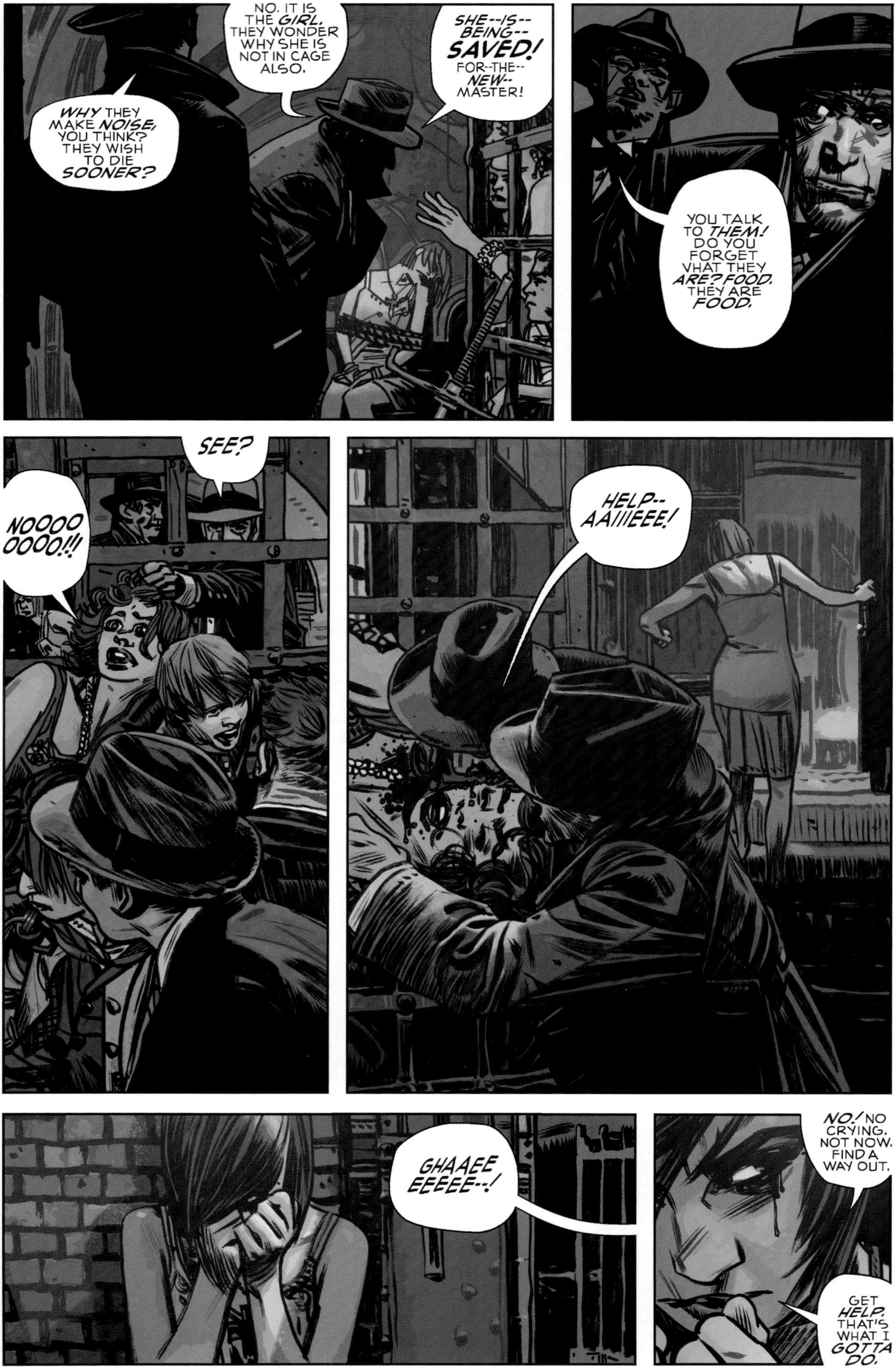
WHY THEY MAKE NOISE, YOU THINK? THEY WISH TO DIE SOONER?
NO. IT IS THE GIRL. THEY WONDER WHY SHE IS NOT IN CAGE ALSO.
SHE--IS--BEING--SAVED! FOR--THE--NEW--MASTER!
YOU TALK TO THEM! DO YOU FORGET VHAT THEY ARE? FOOD. THEY ARE FOOD.
SEE?
NOOOO OOOO!!!
HELP--AAIIIEEE!
GHAAEE EEEEE--!
NO! NO CRYING. NOT NOW. FIND A WAY OUT.
GET HELP. THAT'S WHAT I GOTTA DO.

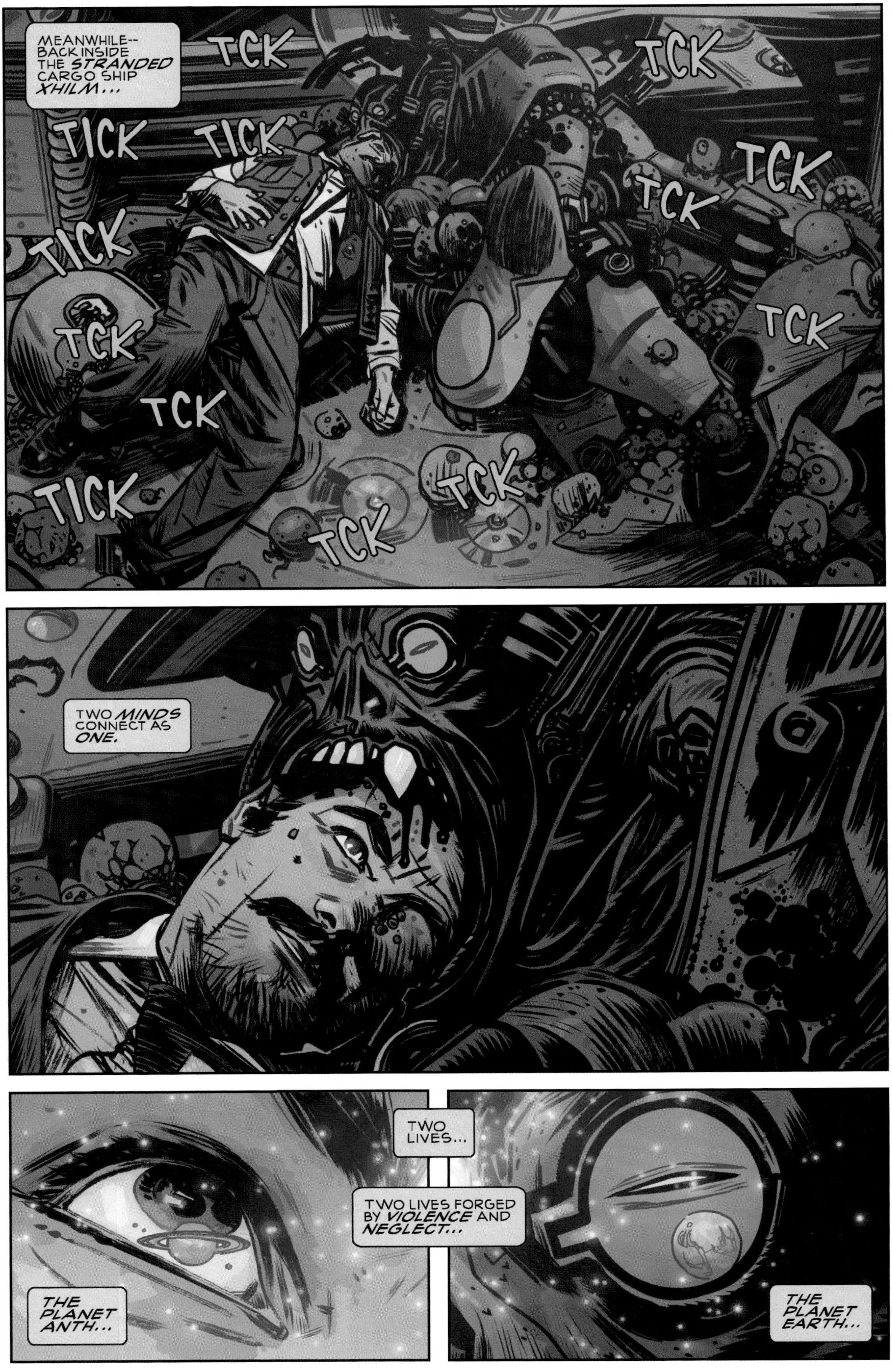
MEANWHILE-- BACK INSIDE THE STRANDED CARGO SHIP XHILM...
TCK
TCK
TICK
TICK
TCK
TCK
TICK
TCK
TCK
TCK
TICK
TCK
TCK
TWO MINDS CONNECT AS ONE.
TWO LIVES...
TWO LIVES FORGED BY VIOLENCE AND NEGLECT...
THE PLANET ANTH...
THE PLANET EARTH...

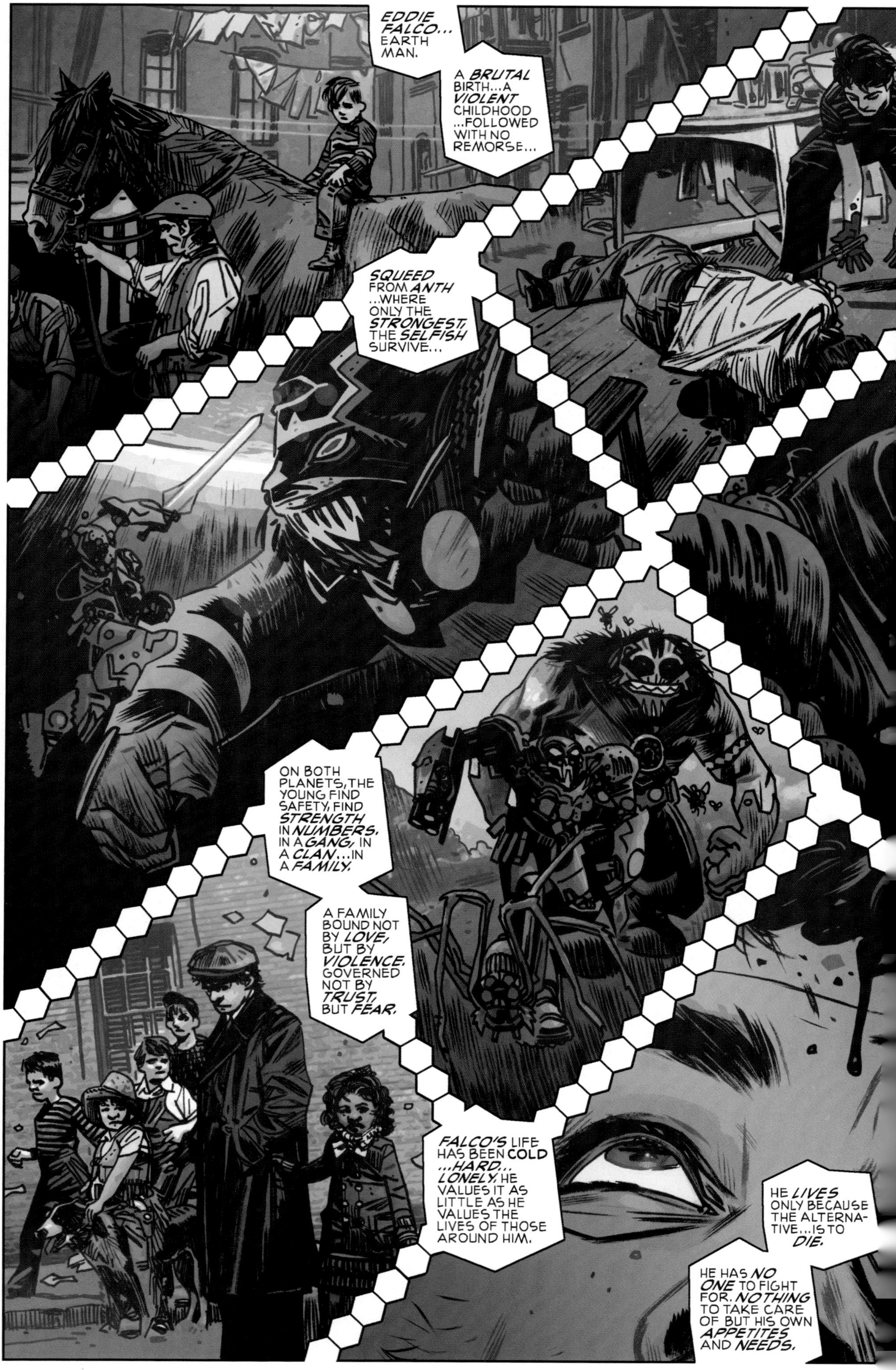

EDDIE FALCO... EARTH MAN.
A BRUTAL BIRTH...A VIOLENT CHILDHOOD ...FOLLOWED WITH NO REMORSE...
SQUEED FROM ANTH ...WHERE ONLY THE STRONGEST, THE SELFISH SURVIVE...
ON BOTH PLANETS, THE YOUNG FIND SAFETY, FIND STRENGTH IN NUMBERS. IN A GANG, IN A CLAN...IN A FAMILY.
A FAMILY BOUND NOT BY LOVE, BUT BY VIOLENCE. GOVERNED NOT BY TRUST, BUT FEAR.
FALCO'S LIFE HAS BEEN COLD ...HARD... LONELY. HE VALUES IT AS LITTLE AS HE VALUES THE LIVES OF THOSE AROUND HIM.
HE LIVES ONLY BECAUSE THE ALTERNATIVE...IS TO DIE.
HE HAS NO ONE TO FIGHT FOR. NOTHING TO TAKE CARE OF BUT HIS OWN APPETITES AND NEEDS.

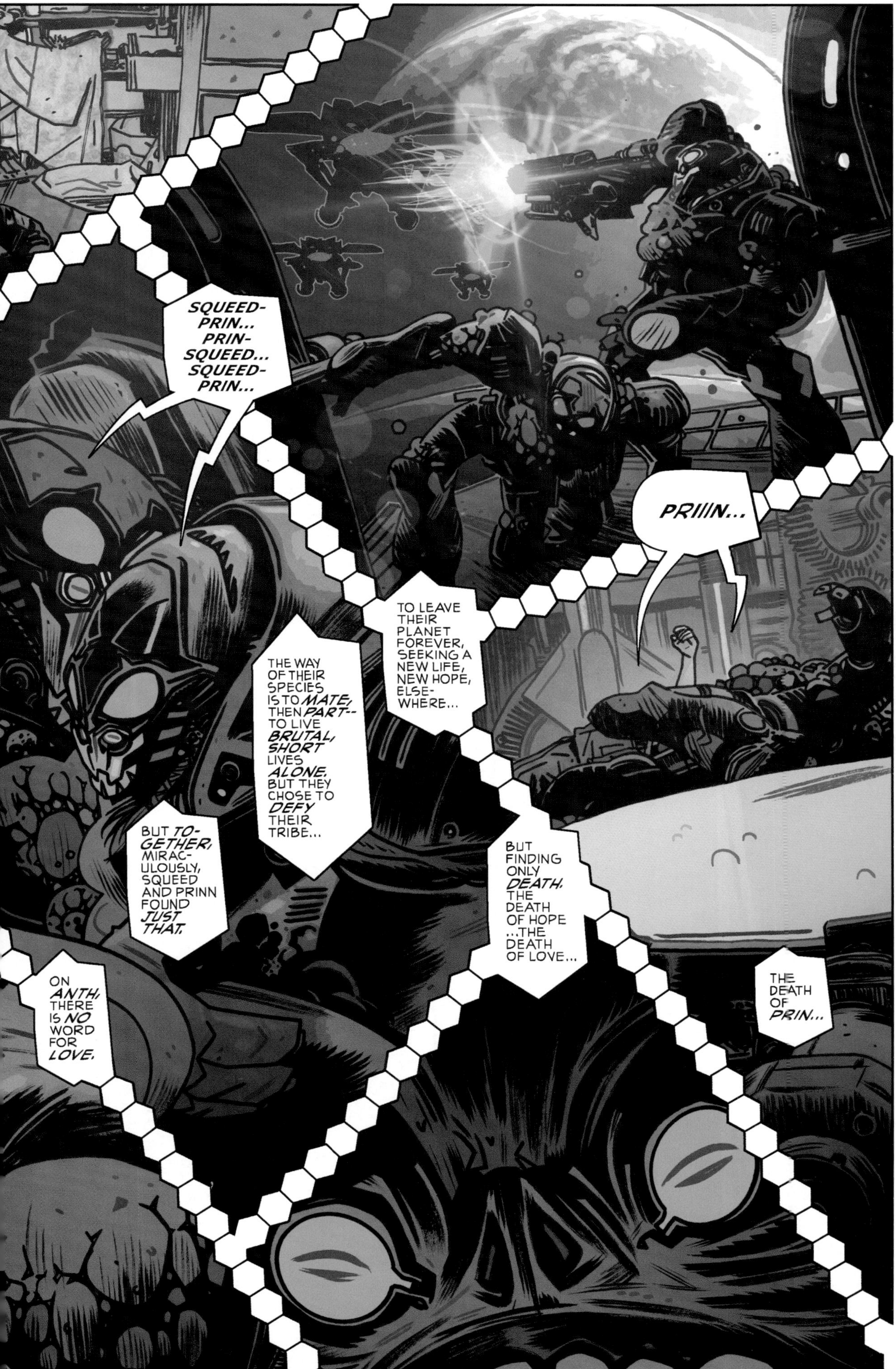
SQUEED-PRIN... PRIN-SQUEED... SQUEED-PRIN...
PRIIIN...
TO LEAVE THEIR PLANET FOREVER, SEEKING A NEW LIFE, NEW HOPE, ELSE-WHERE...
THE WAY OF THEIR SPECIES IS TO *MATE*, THEN *PART*-- TO LIVE *BRUTAL, SHORT* LIVES *ALONE*. BUT THEY CHOSE TO *DEFY* THEIR TRIBE...
BUT *TO-GETHER*, MIRAC-ULOUSLY, SQUEED AND PRINN FOUND *JUST THAT*.
BUT FINDING ONLY *DEATH*. THE DEATH OF HOPE ...THE DEATH OF LOVE...
ON *ANTH*, THERE IS *NO* WORD FOR *LOVE*.
THE DEATH OF *PRIN*...

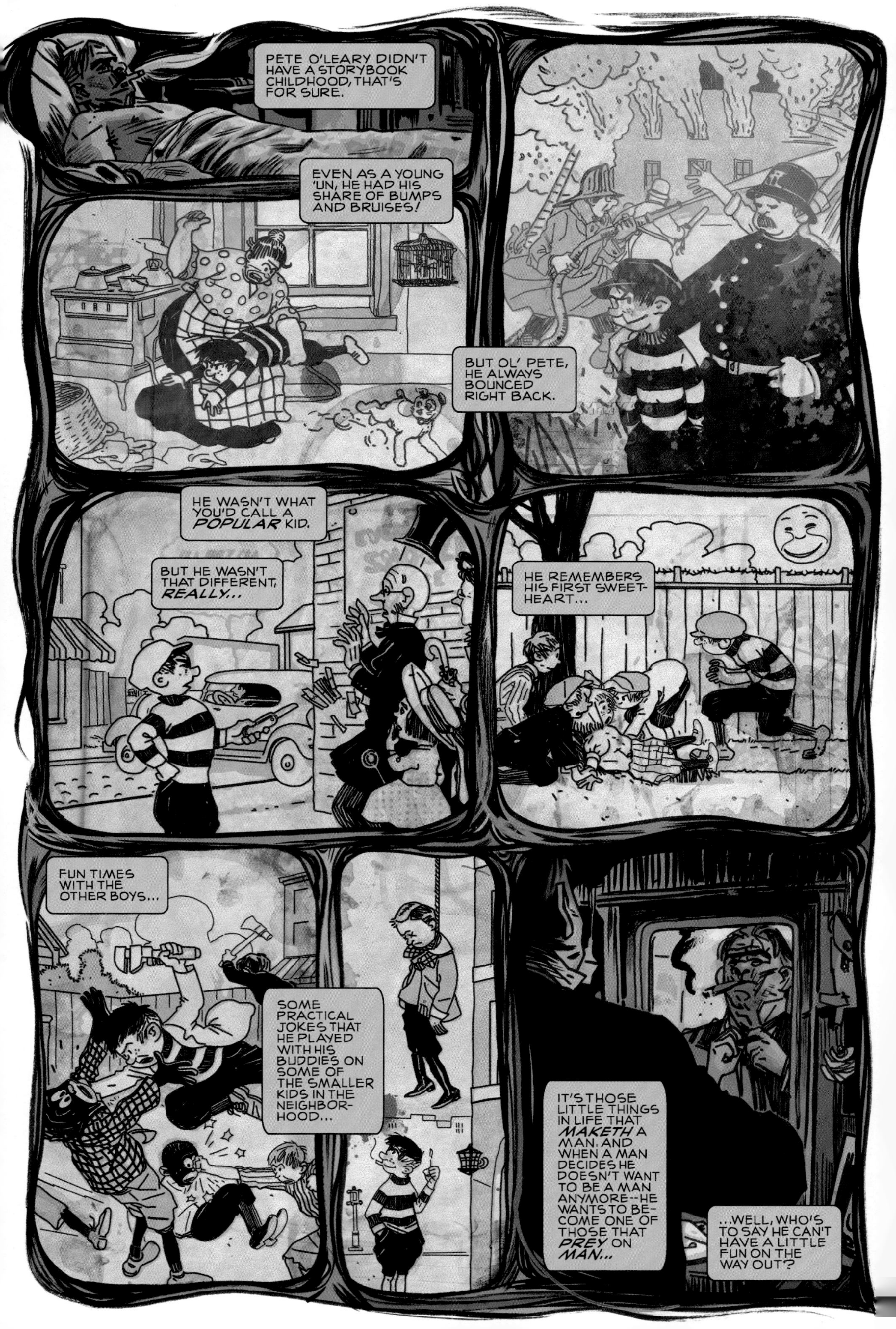
PETE O'LEARY DIDN'T HAVE A STORYBOOK CHILDHOOD, THAT'S FOR SURE.
EVEN AS A YOUNG 'UN, HE HAD HIS SHARE OF BUMPS AND BRUISES!
BUT OL' PETE, HE ALWAYS BOUNCED RIGHT BACK.
HE WASN'T WHAT YOU'D CALL A *POPULAR* KID.
BUT HE WASN'T THAT DIFFERENT, *REALLY...*
HE REMEMBERS HIS FIRST SWEET-HEART...
FUN TIMES WITH THE OTHER BOYS...
SOME PRACTICAL JOKES THAT HE PLAYED WITH HIS BUDDIES ON SOME OF THE SMALLER KIDS IN THE NEIGHBOR-HOOD...
IT'S THOSE LITTLE THINGS IN LIFE THAT *MAKETH* A MAN. AND WHEN A MAN DECIDES HE DOESN'T WANT TO BE A MAN ANYMORE--HE WANTS TO BE-COME ONE OF THOSE THAT *PREY* ON *MAN...*
...WELL, WHO'S TO SAY HE CAN'T HAVE A LITTLE FUN ON THE WAY OUT?

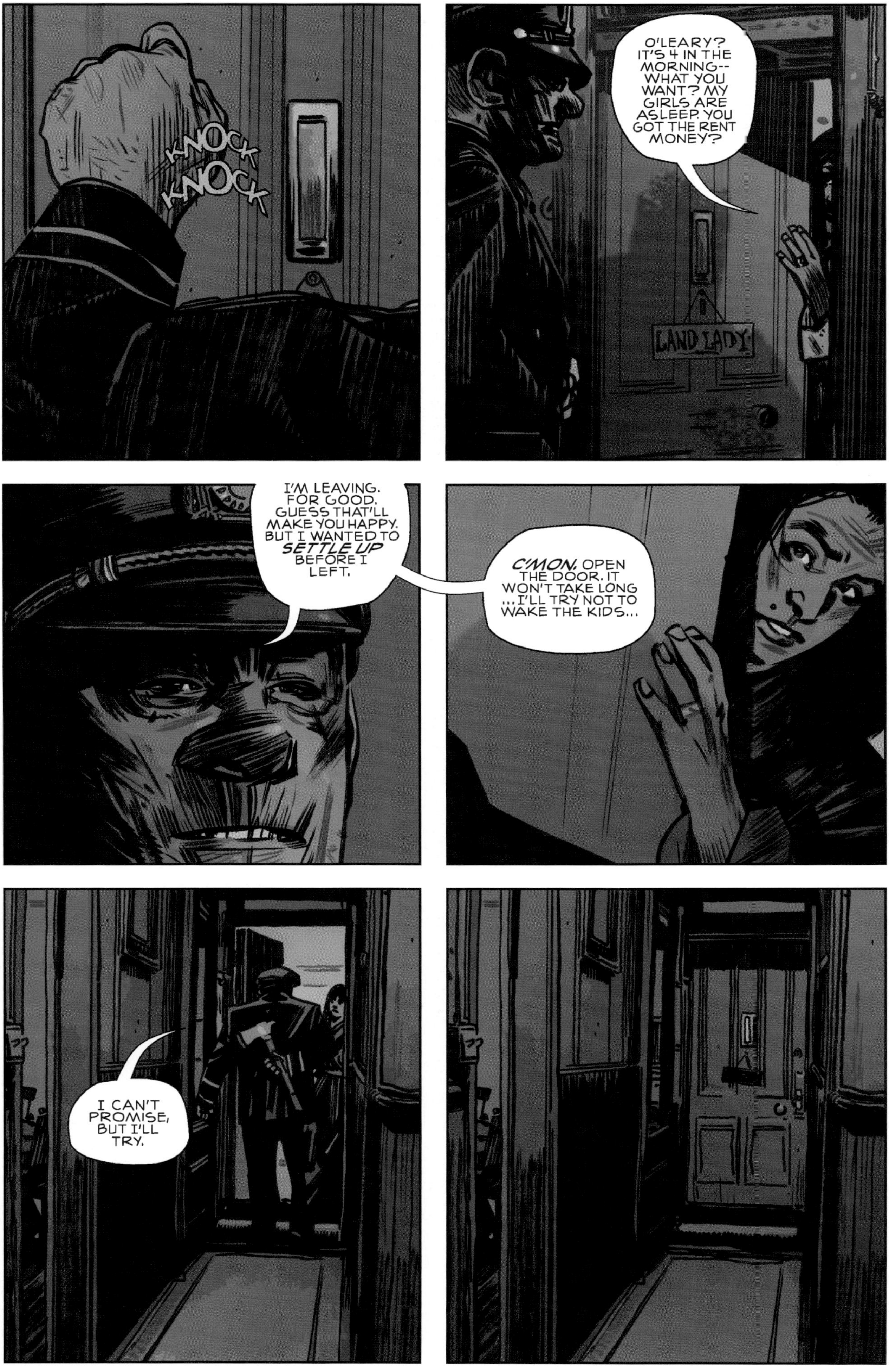
KNOCK KNOCK
O'LEARY? IT'S 4 IN THE MORNING-- WHAT YOU WANT? MY GIRLS ARE ASLEEP. YOU GOT THE RENT MONEY?
LAND LADY
I'M LEAVING. FOR GOOD. GUESS THAT'LL MAKE YOU HAPPY. BUT I WANTED TO SETTLE UP BEFORE I LEFT.
C'MON. OPEN THE DOOR. IT WON'T TAKE LONG ...I'LL TRY NOT TO WAKE THE KIDS...
I CAN'T PROMISE, BUT I'LL TRY.

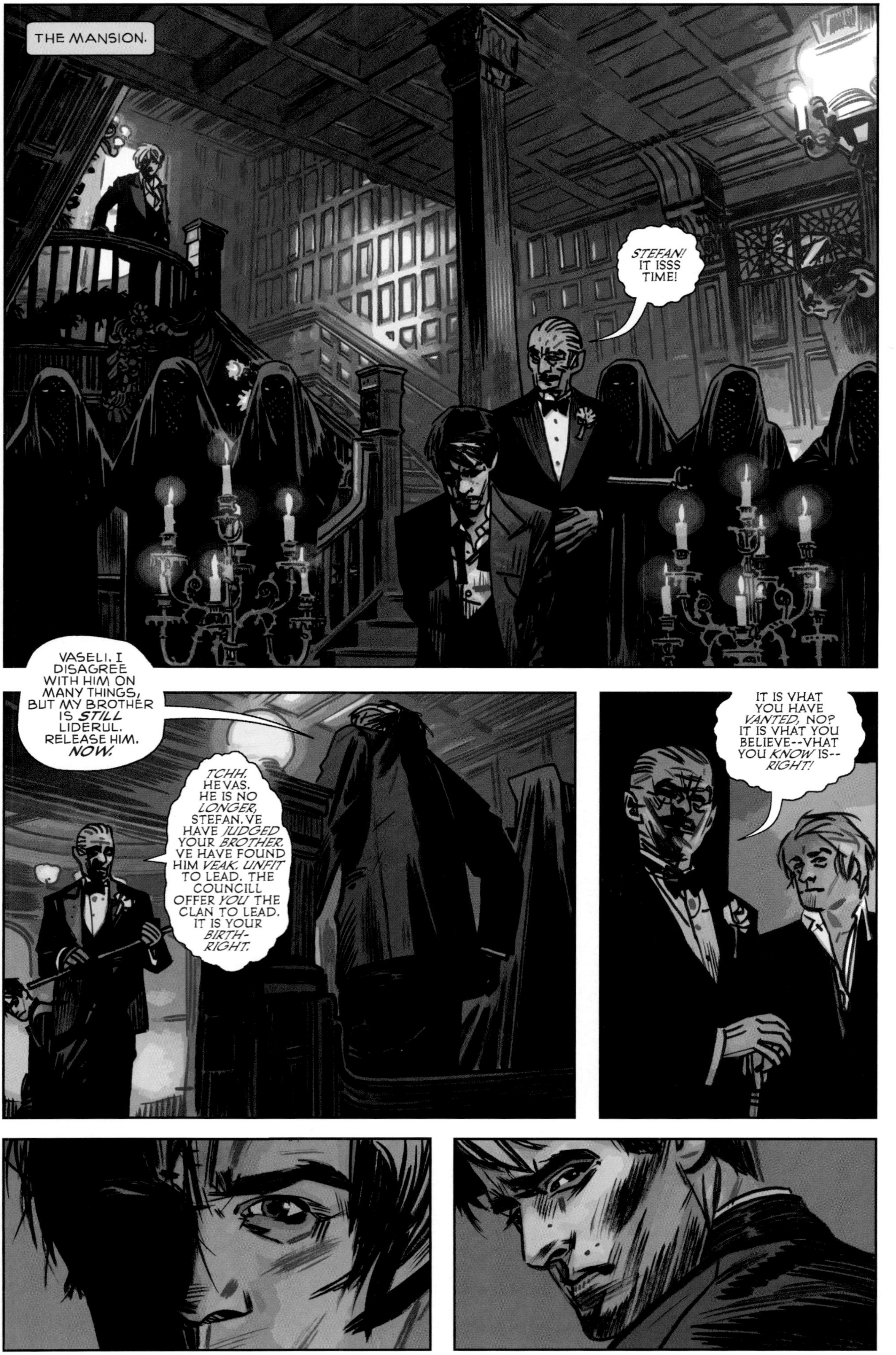
THE MANSION.
STEFAN! IT ISSS TIME!
VASELI. I DISAGREE WITH HIM ON MANY THINGS, BUT MY BROTHER IS STILL LIDERUL. RELEASE HIM. NOW.
TCHH. HE VAS. HE IS NO LONGER, STEFAN. VE HAVE JUDGED YOUR BROTHER. VE HAVE FOUND HIM VEAK. UNFIT TO LEAD. THE COUNCILL OFFER YOU THE CLAN TO LEAD. IT IS YOUR BIRTH-RIGHT.
IT IS VHAT YOU HAVE VANTED, NO? IT IS VHAT YOU BELIEVE--VHAT YOU KNOW IS--RIGHT!

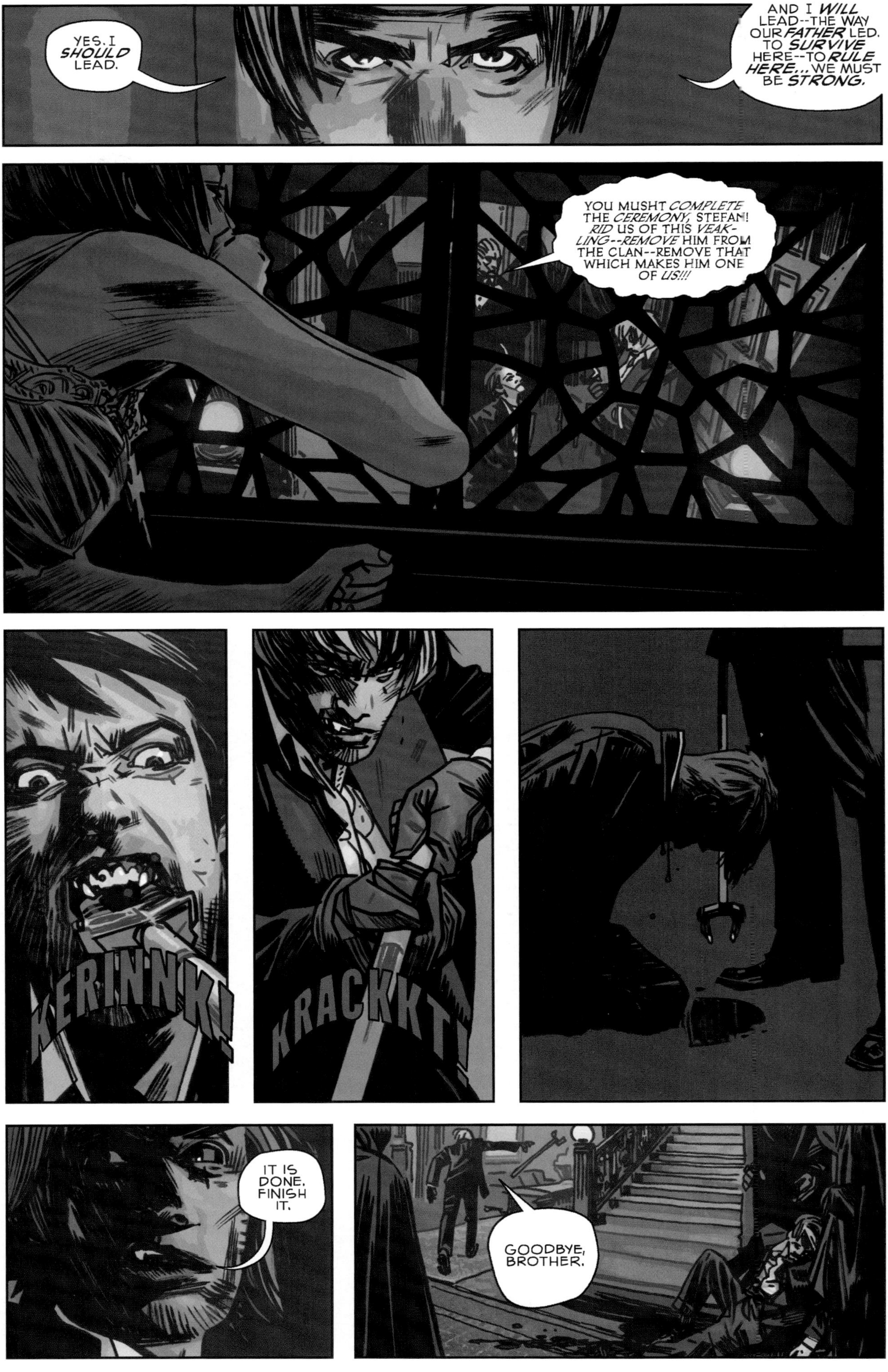
YES. I SHOULD LEAD.
AND I WILL LEAD--THE WAY OUR FATHER LED. TO SURVIVE HERE--TO RULE HERE... WE MUST BE STRONG.
YOU MUSHT COMPLETE THE CEREMONY, STEFAN! RID US OF THIS VEAK-LING--REMOVE HIM FROM THE CLAN--REMOVE THAT WHICH MAKES HIM ONE OF US!!!
KERINNK!!
KRACKKT!!
IT IS DONE. FINISH IT.
GOODBYE, BROTHER.

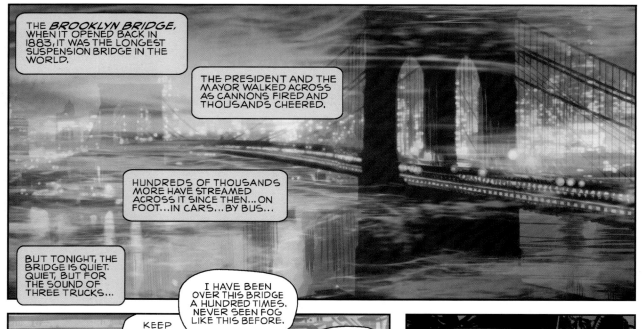

THE *BROOKLYN BRIDGE*, WHEN IT OPENED BACK IN 1883, IT WAS THE LONGEST SUSPENSION BRIDGE IN THE WORLD.

THE PRESIDENT AND THE MAYOR WALKED ACROSS AS CANNONS FIRED AND THOUSANDS CHEERED.

HUNDREDS OF THOUSANDS MORE HAVE STREAMED ACROSS IT SINCE THEN... ON FOOT...IN CARS...BY BUS...

BUT TONIGHT, THE BRIDGE IS QUIET. QUIET, BUT FOR THE SOUND OF THREE TRUCKS...

I HAVE BEEN OVER THIS BRIDGE A HUNDRED TIMES. NEVER SEEN FOG LIKE THIS BEFORE.

KEEP DRIVING...

WHY'D WE HAVE TO GO SO LATE--OR EARLY--OR WHATEVER TIME THIS? IF THEY AIN'T ARMED AND WE *ARE*, WHAT'S THE PROBLEM?

O'LEARY SAYS WE HIT THEM BEFORE THE SUN COMES UP, AND HE KNOWS THEM BEST. QUIT FUSSIN' AND DRIVE.

SLOW DOWN. THERE'S SOME- THING UP AHEAD...IN THE MIST...

LOOKS LIKE BIRDS ...OR BATS... OR... *JESUS!*

JESUS CAN'T HELP YOU HERE!

BLAMM!

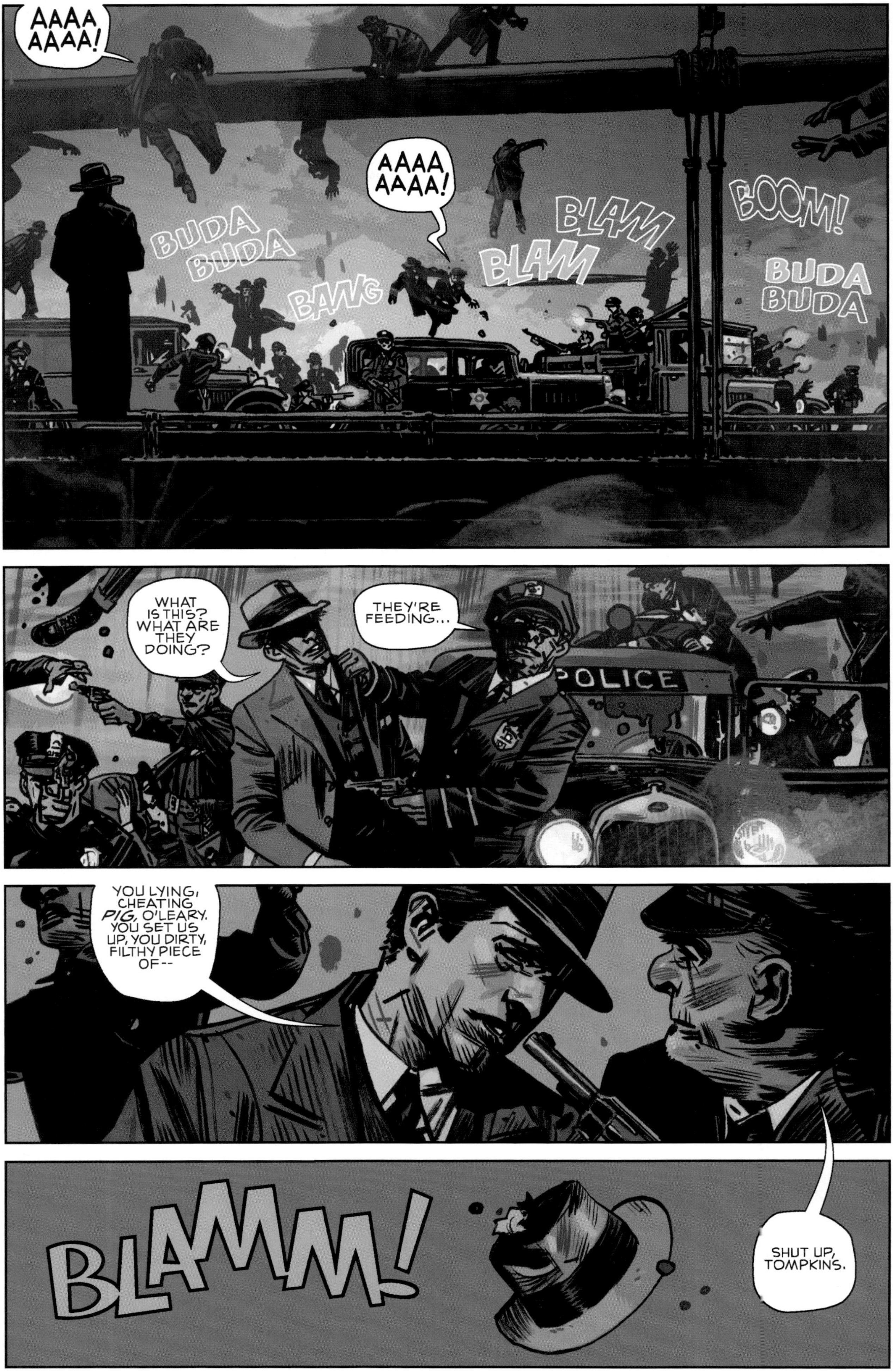
AAAA AAAA!
AAAA AAAA!
BUDA BUDA
BANG
BLAM
BLAM
BOOM!
BUDA BUDA
WHAT IS THIS? WHAT ARE THEY DOING?
THEY'RE FEEDING...
POLICE
YOU LYING, CHEATING PIG, O'LEARY. YOU SET US UP, YOU DIRTY, FILTHY PIECE OF--
BLAMM!
SHUT UP, TOMPKINS.

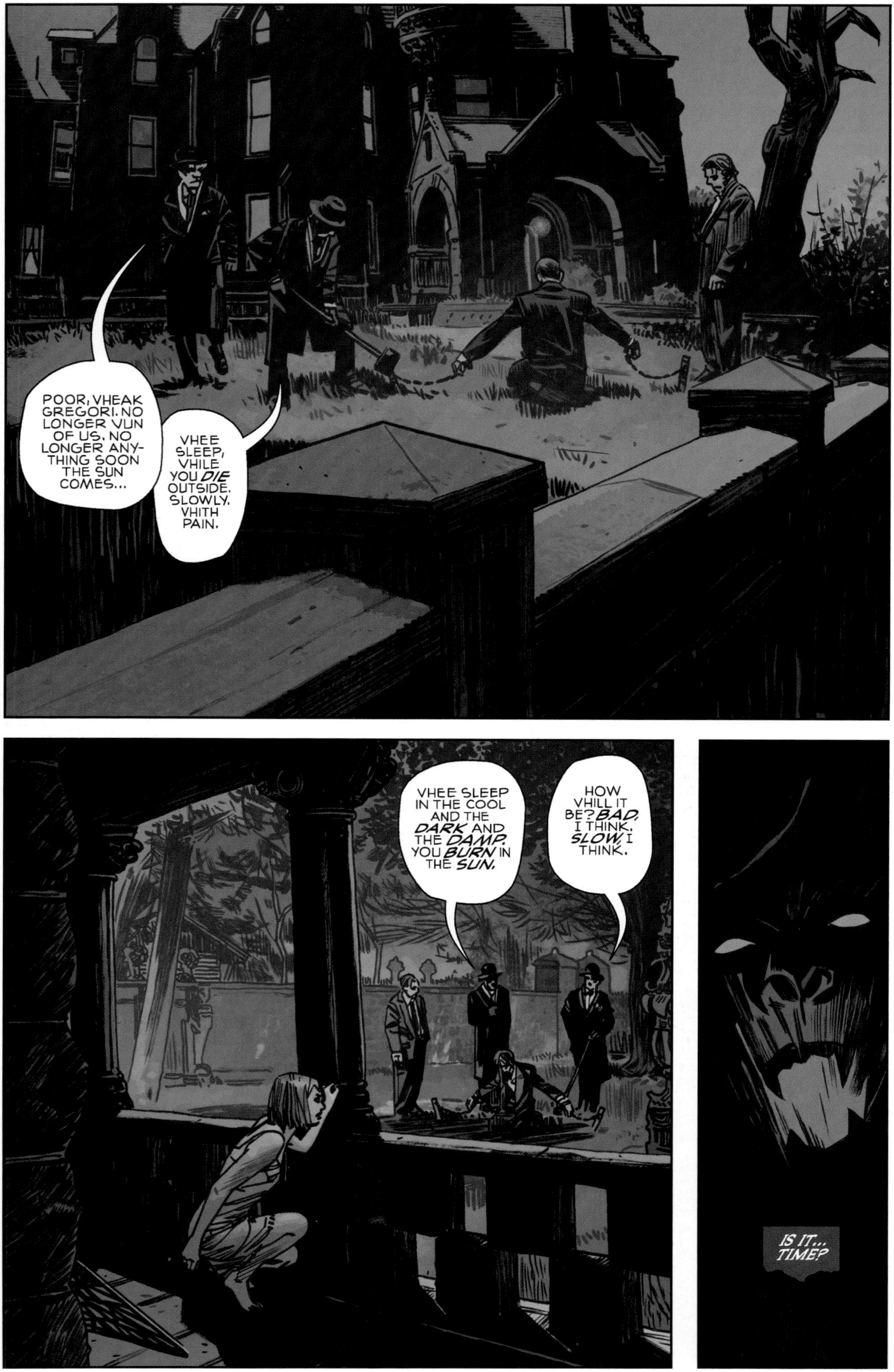
POOR, VHEAK GREGORI. NO LONGER VUN OF US. NO LONGER ANY-THING SOON THE SUN COMES...
VHEE SLEEP, VHILE YOU *DIE* OUTSIDE. SLOWLY. VHITH PAIN.
VHEE SLEEP IN THE COOL AND THE *DARK* AND THE *DAMP.* YOU *BURN* IN THE *SUN.*
HOW VHILL IT BE? *BAD,* I THINK. *SLOW,* I THINK.
IS IT... TIME?

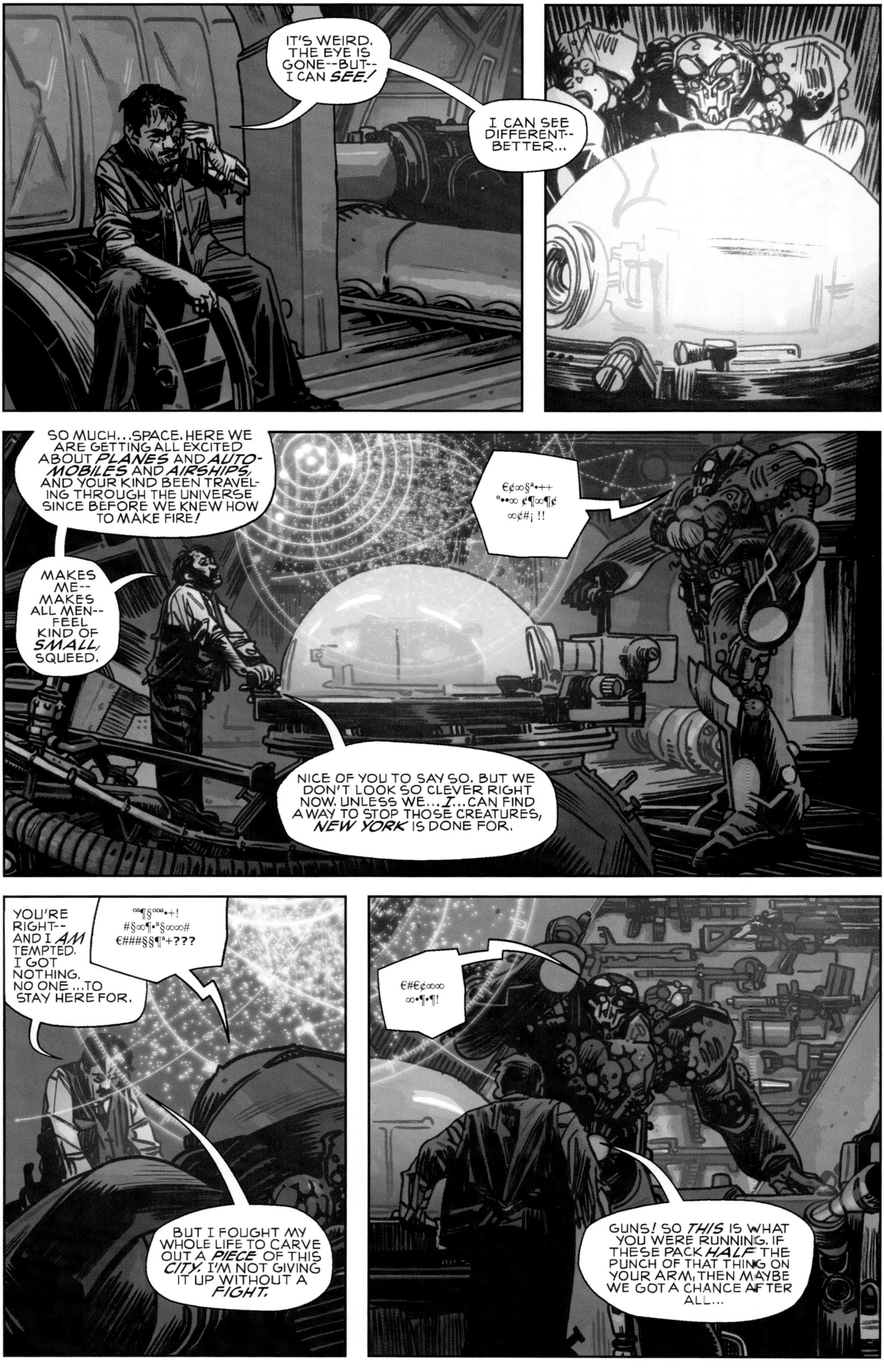

IT'S WEIRD. THE EYE IS GONE--BUT-- I CAN SEE!
I CAN SEE DIFFERENT-- BETTER...
SO MUCH...SPACE. HERE WE ARE GETTING ALL EXCITED ABOUT PLANES AND AUTOMOBILES AND AIRSHIPS, AND YOUR KIND BEEN TRAVELING THROUGH THE UNIVERSE SINCE BEFORE WE KNEW HOW TO MAKE FIRE!
MAKES ME-- MAKES ALL MEN-- FEEL KIND OF SMALL, SQUEED.
€¢∞§ª•++ º••∞ ¢¶∞¶¢ ∞¢#¡ !!
NICE OF YOU TO SAY SO. BUT WE DON'T LOOK SO CLEVER RIGHT NOW. UNLESS WE...I...CAN FIND A WAY TO STOP THOSE CREATURES, NEW YORK IS DONE FOR.
YOU'RE RIGHT-- AND I AM TEMPTED. I GOT NOTHING. NO ONE ...TO STAY HERE FOR.
ºª¶§ººª•+! #§∞¶•ª§∞∞# €###§§¶ª+???
BUT I FOUGHT MY WHOLE LIFE TO CARVE OUT A PIECE OF THIS CITY. I'M NOT GIVING IT UP WITHOUT A FIGHT.
€#€¢∞∞ ∞•¶•¶!
GUNS! SO THIS IS WHAT YOU WERE RUNNING. IF THESE PACK HALF THE PUNCH OF THAT THING ON YOUR ARM, THEN MAYBE WE GOT A CHANCE AFTER ALL...

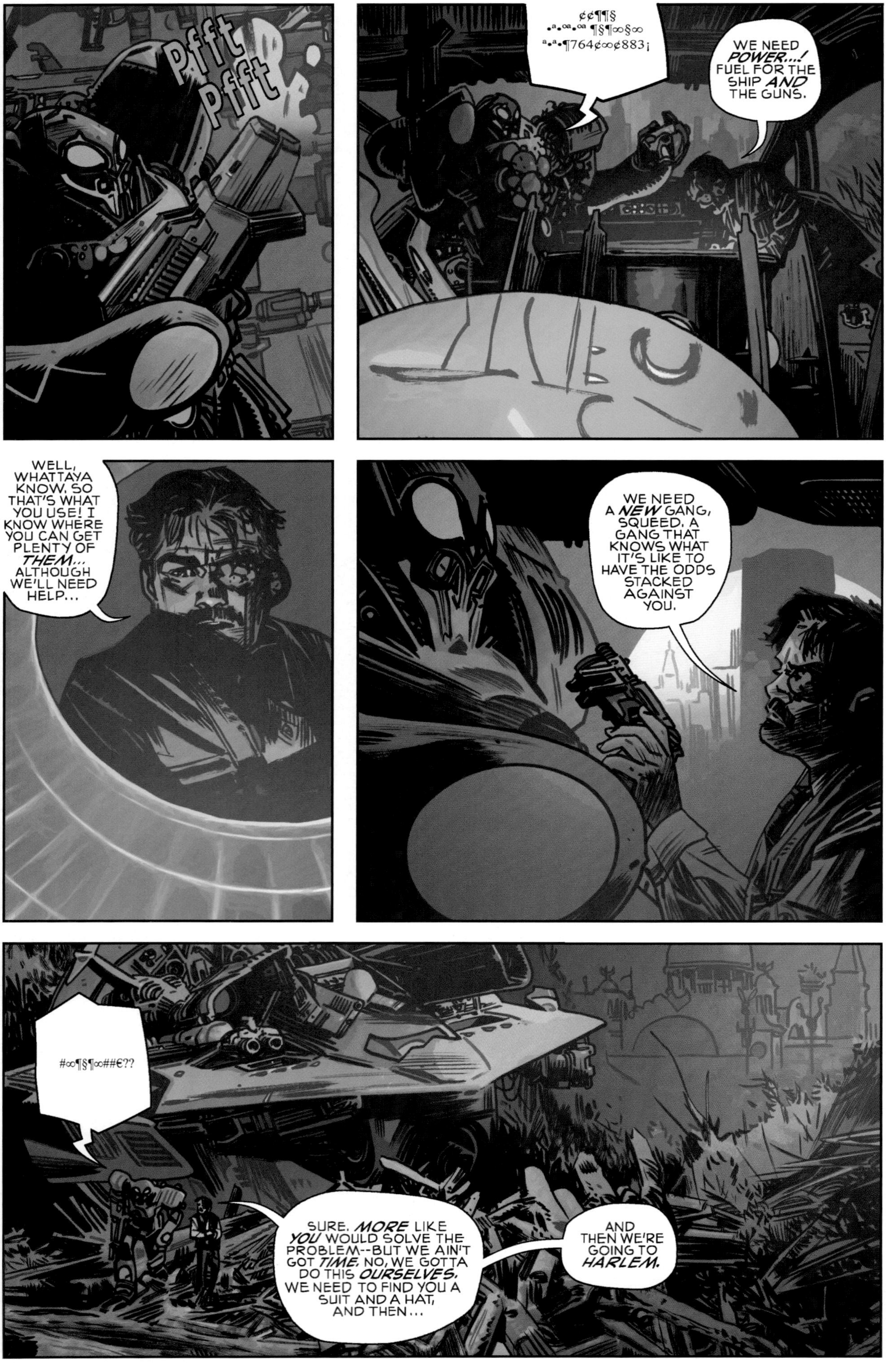
Pfft
Pfft
¢¢¶¶§ •ª•ºª•ºª ¶§¶∞§∞ ª•ª•¶764¢∞¢883¡
WE NEED POWER...! FUEL FOR THE SHIP AND THE GUNS.
WELL, WHATTAYA KNOW. SO THAT'S WHAT YOU USE! I KNOW WHERE YOU CAN GET PLENTY OF THEM... ALTHOUGH WE'LL NEED HELP...
WE NEED A NEW GANG, SQUEED. A GANG THAT KNOWS WHAT IT'S LIKE TO HAVE THE ODDS STACKED AGAINST YOU.
#∞¶§¶∞##€??
SURE. MORE LIKE YOU WOULD SOLVE THE PROBLEM--BUT WE AIN'T GOT TIME. NO, WE GOTTA DO THIS OURSELVES. WE NEED TO FIND YOU A SUIT AND A HAT, AND THEN...
AND THEN WE'RE GOING TO HARLEM.

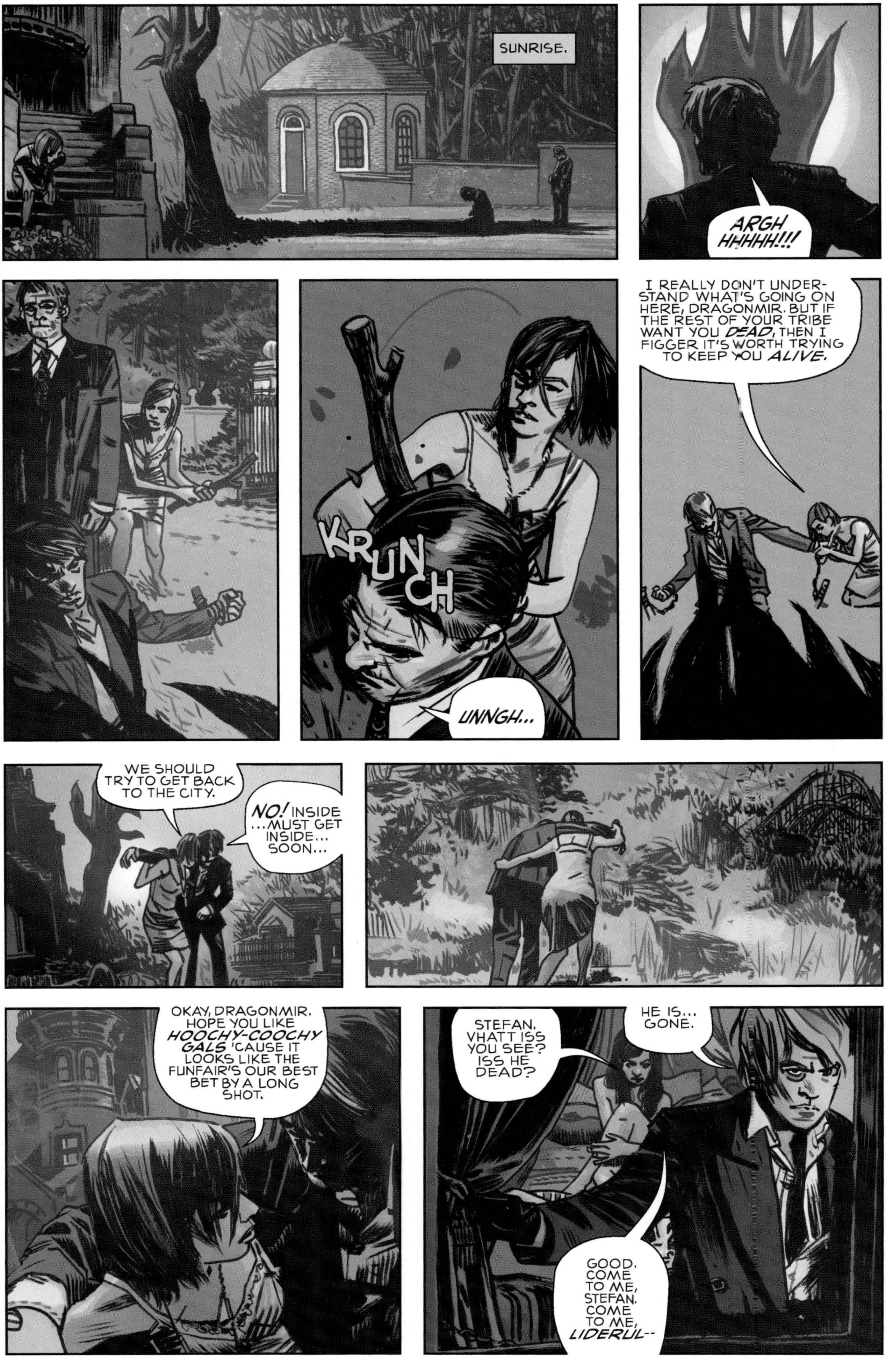
SUNRISE.
ARGH HHHHH!!!
KRUNCH
UNNGH...
I REALLY DON'T UNDERSTAND WHAT'S GOING ON HERE, DRAGONMIR. BUT IF THE REST OF YOUR TRIBE WANT YOU DEAD, THEN I FIGGER IT'S WORTH TRYING TO KEEP YOU ALIVE.
WE SHOULD TRY TO GET BACK TO THE CITY.
NO! INSIDE ...MUST GET INSIDE... SOON...
OKAY, DRAGONMIR. HOPE YOU LIKE HOOCHY-COOCHY GALS 'CAUSE IT LOOKS LIKE THE FUNFAIR'S OUR BEST BET BY A LONG SHOT.
STEFAN. VHATT ISS YOU SEE? ISS HE DEAD?
HE IS... GONE.
GOOD. COME TO ME, STEFAN. COME TO ME, LIDERUL--

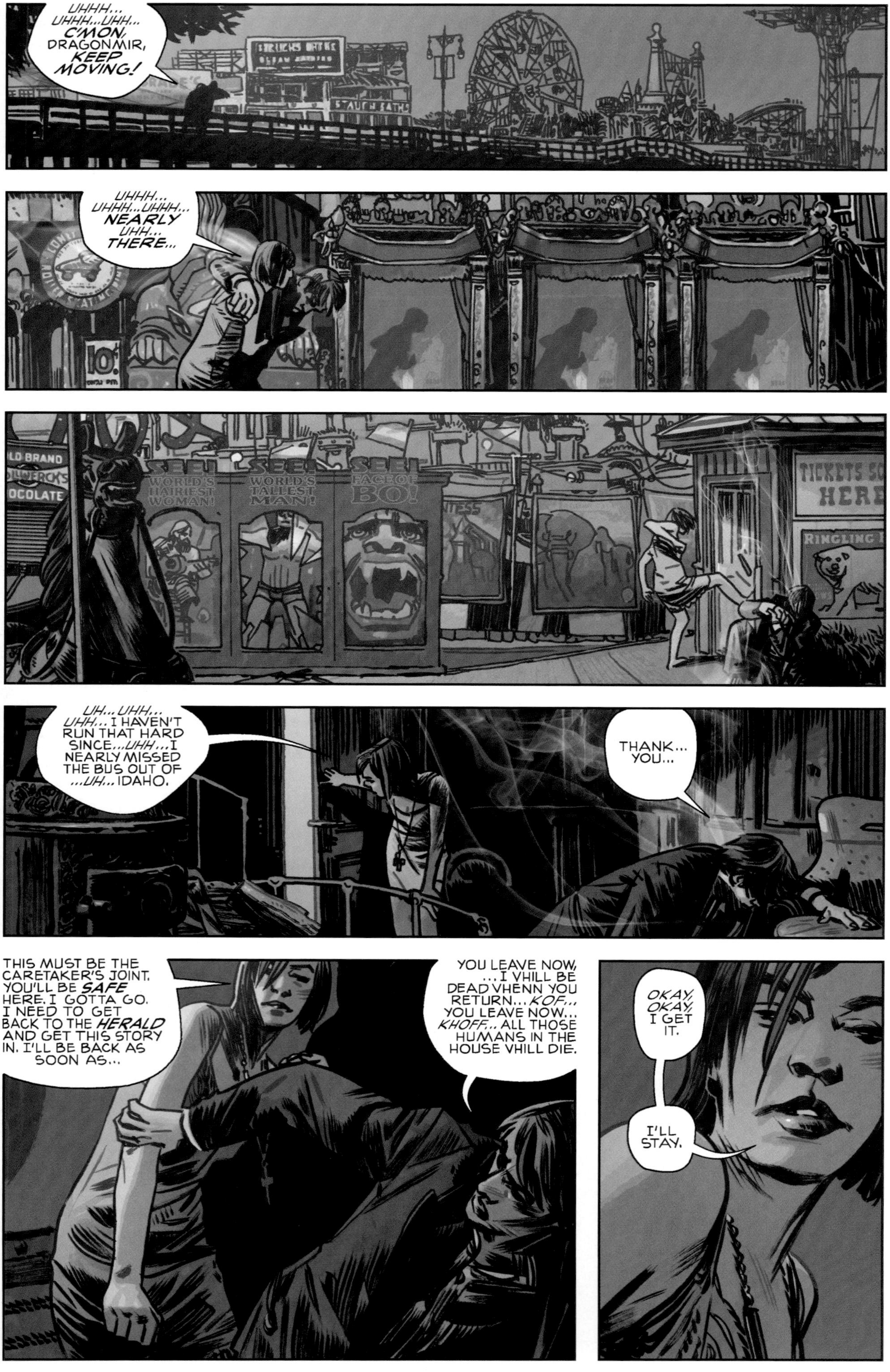

UHHH... UHHH...UHH... C'MON, DRAGONMIR, KEEP MOVING!
UHHH... UHHH...UHHH... NEARLY UHH... THERE...
SEE! WORLD'S HAIRIEST WOMAN!
SEE! WORLD'S TALLEST MAN!
SEE! FACE OF BO!
TICKETS SO HERE
UH...UHH... UHH... I HAVEN'T RUN THAT HARD SINCE...UHH...I NEARLY MISSED THE BUS OUT OF ...UH... IDAHO.
THANK... YOU...
THIS MUST BE THE CARETAKER'S JOINT. YOU'LL BE SAFE HERE. I GOTTA GO. I NEED TO GET BACK TO THE HERALD AND GET THIS STORY IN. I'LL BE BACK AS SOON AS...
YOU LEAVE NOW, ...I VHILL BE DEAD VHENN YOU RETURN... KOF... YOU LEAVE NOW... KHOFF... ALL THOSE HUMANS IN THE HOUSE VHILL DIE.
OKAY, OKAY, I GET IT.
I'LL STAY.

SOME THINK IT BEGINS AT 96TH STREET.

OTHERS INSIST YOU REALLY NEED TO BE AS HIGH AS 105TH.

BUT THE TRUTH IS, MOST WHITE FOLK SAY THAT WHER-EVER NEGROES LIVE IN NEW YORK, THAT'S *HARLEM*.

•¶•¶ºaa ∞#€ # €¢∞—≠!!

THE *HAT* IS *FINE*. STOP GOING ON ABOUT THE *HAT*. AT LEAST YOU DIDN'T HAVE A STRANGER SUCK MOST OF YOUR HAIR OFF.

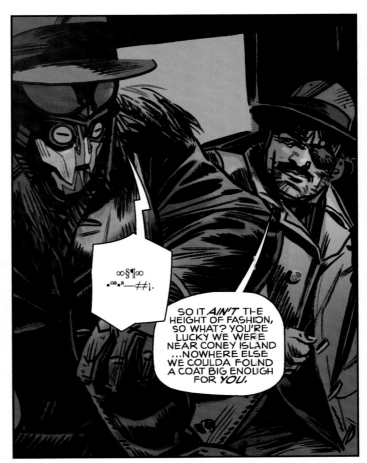

∞§¶∞ •ºa•a—#¡.

SO IT *AIN'T* THE HEIGHT OF FASHION, SO WHAT? YOU'RE LUCKY WE WERE NEAR CONEY ISLAND ...NOWHERE ELSE WE COULDA FOUND A COAT BIG ENOUGH FOR *YOU*.

NOW STICK CLOSE AND DON'T MAKE ANY MOVES.

£$$% @@^* ?

IT'S CALLED A TIP.

125TH STREET AND LEXING-TON AVENUE. THE PALATIAL RESIDENCE OF THE SELF-APPOINTED **REVEREND** SAMUEL KANE, ESQ.

THIS **WON'T** BE EASY. KANE AIN'T ONE FOR VISITORS. BAVA SENT A BUNCH OF **GOONS** UP TO SEE HIM A YEAR BACK. NEVER SAW THEM AGAIN. WORD IS, HE FED THEM TO HIS *CAT*.

$% €∞¢ •• €#∞¢§•€€€# ¢∞??

IT'S A **BIG** CAT.

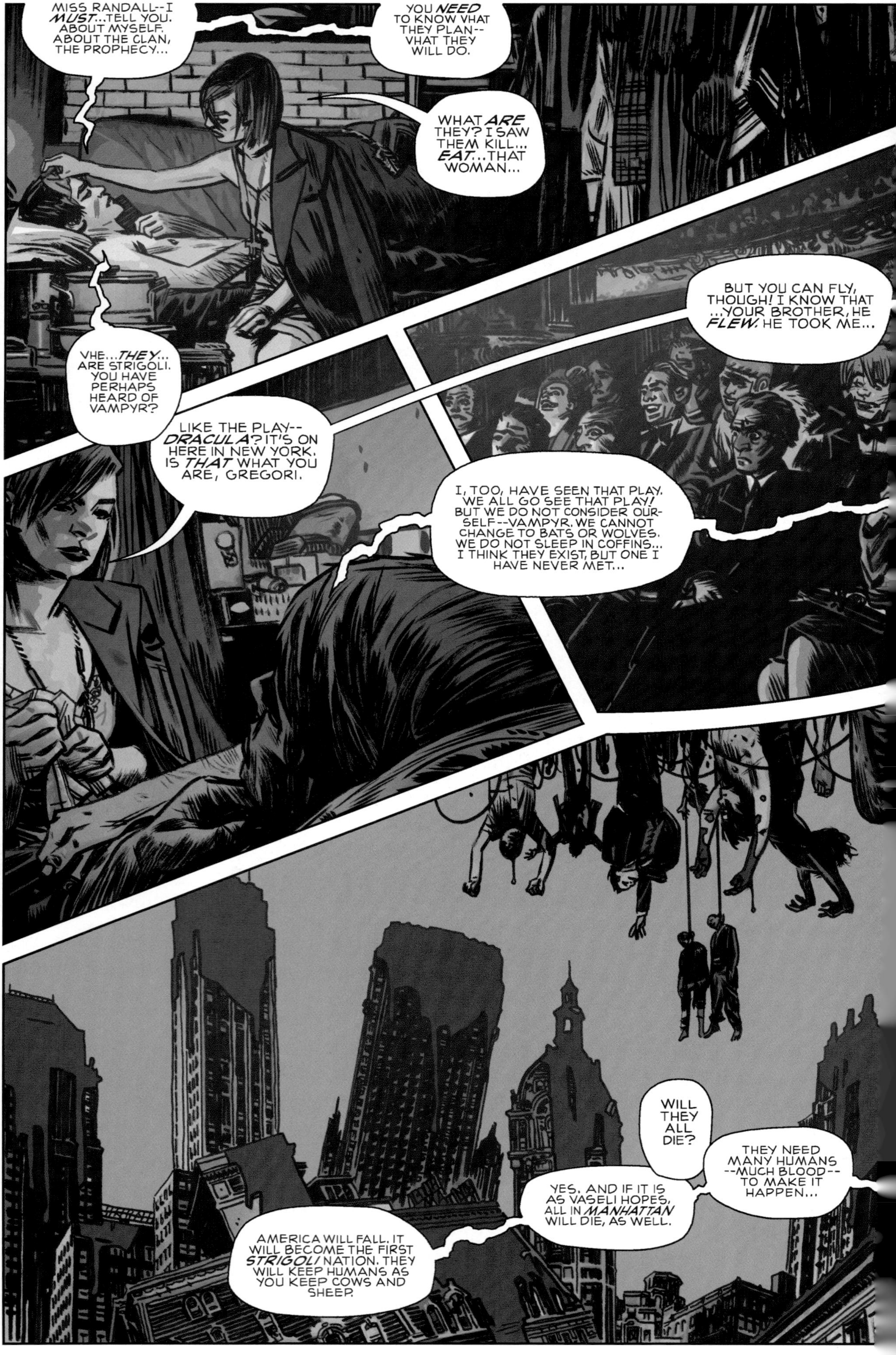
MISS RANDALL--I MUST...TELL YOU. ABOUT MYSELF. ABOUT THE CLAN, THE PROPHECY...
YOU NEED TO KNOW VHAT THEY PLAN--VHAT THEY WILL DO.
WHAT ARE THEY? I SAW THEM KILL... EAT...THAT WOMAN...
VHE...THEY... ARE STRIGOLI. YOU HAVE PERHAPS HEARD OF VAMPYR?
LIKE THE PLAY--DRACULA? IT'S ON HERE IN NEW YORK. IS THAT WHAT YOU ARE, GREGORI.
BUT YOU CAN FLY, THOUGH! I KNOW THAT ...YOUR BROTHER, HE FLEW. HE TOOK ME...
I, TOO, HAVE SEEN THAT PLAY. WE ALL GO SEE THAT PLAY! BUT WE DO NOT CONSIDER OUR-SELF--VAMPYR. WE CANNOT CHANGE TO BATS OR WOLVES. WE DO NOT SLEEP IN COFFINS... I THINK THEY EXIST, BUT ONE I HAVE NEVER MET...
WILL THEY ALL DIE?
THEY NEED MANY HUMANS --MUCH BLOOD-- TO MAKE IT HAPPEN...
YES. AND IF IT IS AS VASELI HOPES, ALL IN MANHATTAN WILL DIE, AS WELL.
AMERICA WILL FALL. IT WILL BECOME THE FIRST STRIGOLI NATION. THEY WILL KEEP HUMANS AS YOU KEEP COWS AND SHEEP.

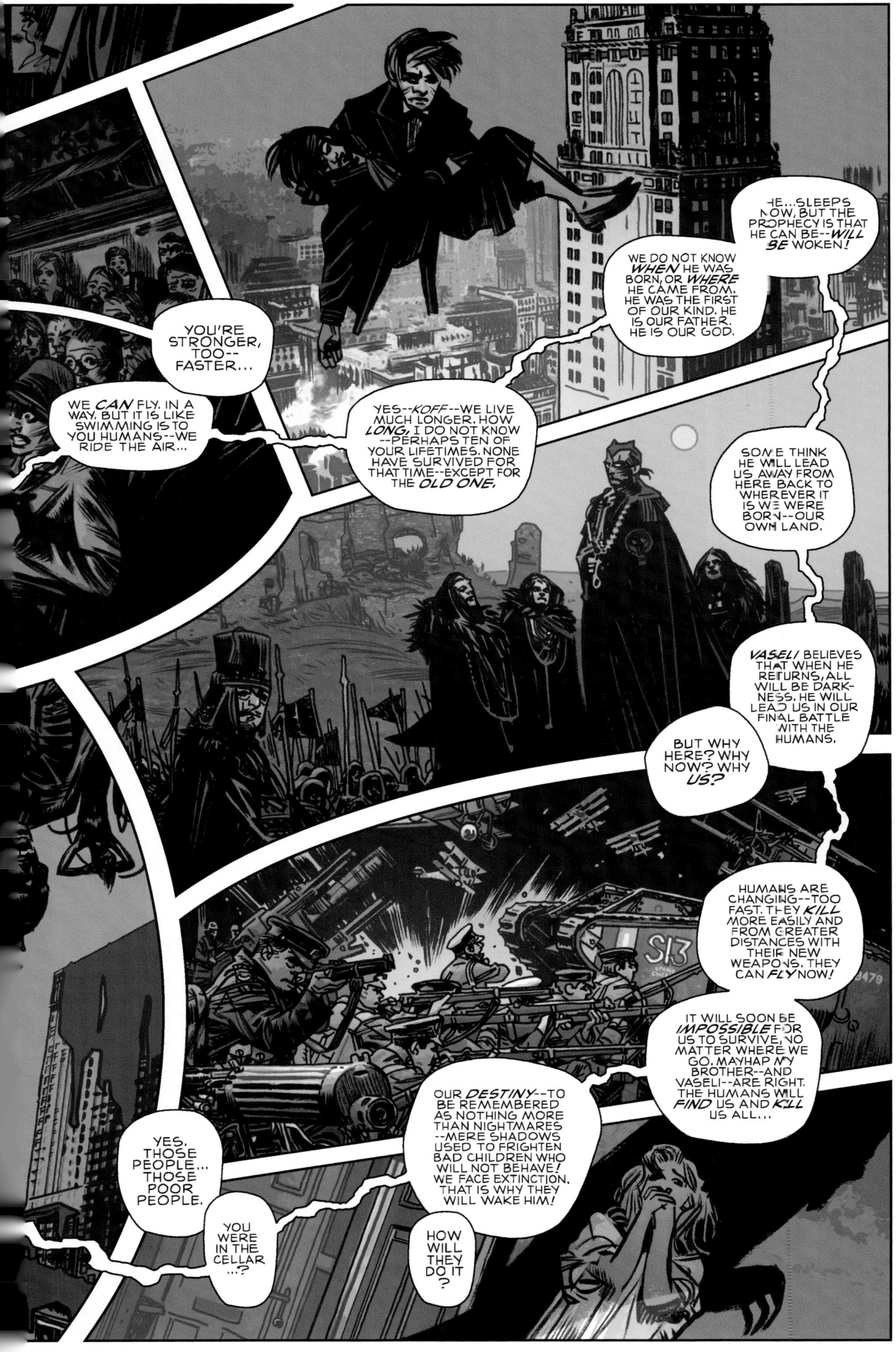
YOU'RE STRONGER, TOO-- FASTER...
WE DO NOT KNOW WHEN HE WAS BORN, OR WHERE HE CAME FROM. HE WAS THE FIRST OF OUR KIND. HE IS OUR FATHER. HE IS OUR GOD.
HE...SLEEPS NOW, BUT THE PROPHECY IS THAT HE CAN BE--WILL BE WOKEN!
WE CAN FLY, IN A WAY, BUT IT IS LIKE SWIMMING IS TO YOU HUMANS--WE RIDE THE AIR...
YES--KOFF--WE LIVE MUCH LONGER. HOW LONG, I DO NOT KNOW --PERHAPS TEN OF YOUR LIFETIMES. NONE HAVE SURVIVED FOR THAT TIME--EXCEPT FOR THE OLD ONE.
SOME THINK HE WILL LEAD US AWAY FROM HERE BACK TO WHEREVER IT IS WE WERE BORN--OUR OWN LAND.
VASELI BELIEVES THAT WHEN HE RETURNS, ALL WILL BE DARKNESS. HE WILL LEAD US IN OUR FINAL BATTLE WITH THE HUMANS.
BUT WHY HERE? WHY NOW? WHY US?
HUMANS ARE CHANGING--TOO FAST. THEY KILL MORE EASILY AND FROM GREATER DISTANCES WITH THEIR NEW WEAPONS. THEY CAN FLY NOW!
S13
IT WILL SOON BE IMPOSSIBLE FOR US TO SURVIVE, NO MATTER WHERE WE GO. MAYHAP MY BROTHER--AND VASELI--ARE RIGHT. THE HUMANS WILL FIND US AND KILL US ALL...
OUR DESTINY--TO BE REMEMBERED AS NOTHING MORE THAN NIGHTMARES --MERE SHADOWS USED TO FRIGHTEN BAD CHILDREN WHO WILL NOT BEHAVE! WE FACE EXTINCTION. THAT IS WHY THEY WILL WAKE HIM!
YES. THOSE PEOPLE... THOSE POOR PEOPLE.
YOU WERE IN THE CELLAR ...?
HOW WILL THEY DO IT ?

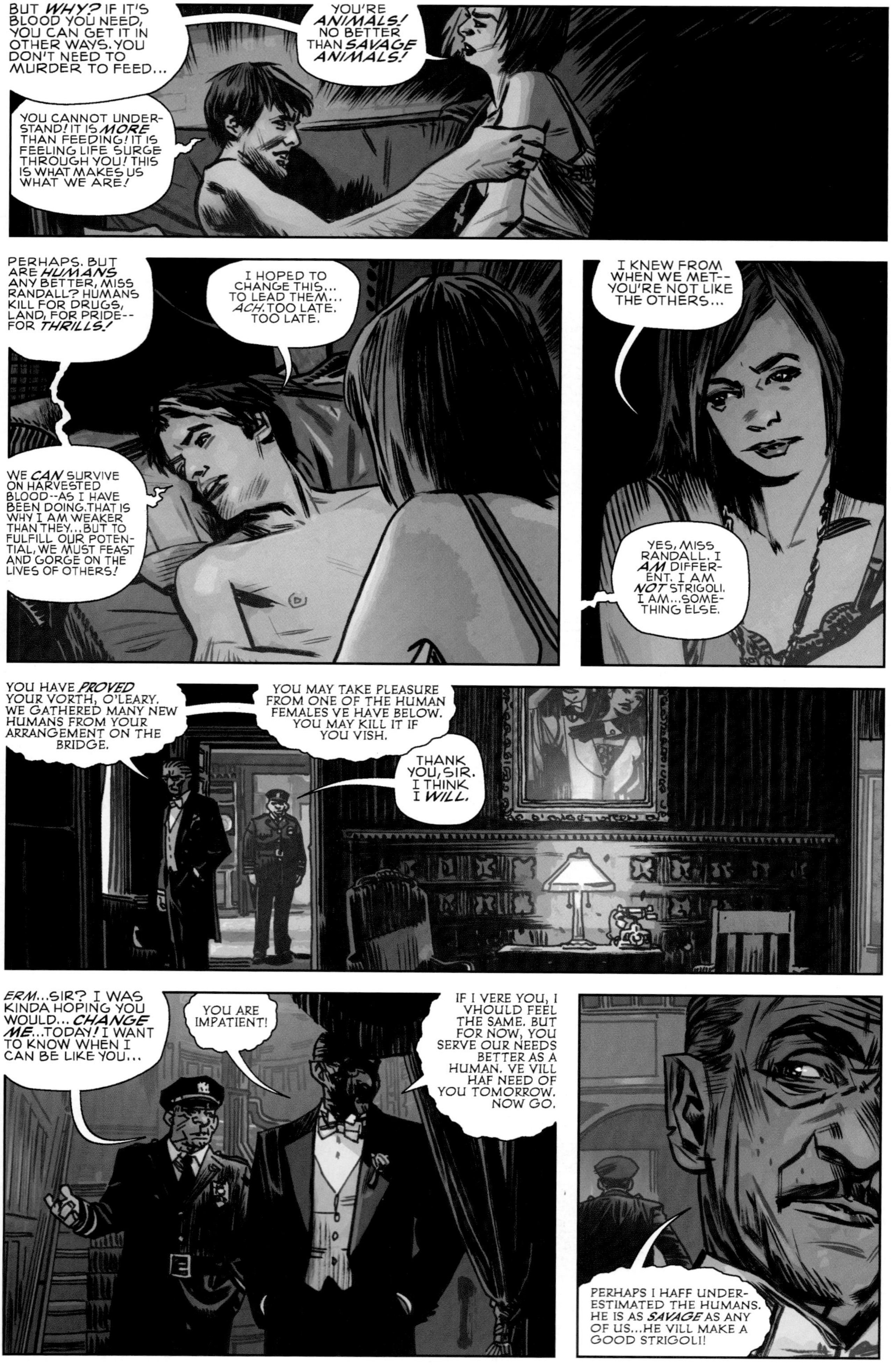
BUT WHY? IF IT'S BLOOD YOU NEED, YOU CAN GET IT IN OTHER WAYS. YOU DON'T NEED TO MURDER TO FEED...
YOU'RE ANIMALS! NO BETTER THAN SAVAGE ANIMALS!
YOU CANNOT UNDER-STAND! IT IS MORE THAN FEEDING! IT IS FEELING LIFE SURGE THROUGH YOU! THIS IS WHAT MAKES US WHAT WE ARE!
PERHAPS. BUT ARE HUMANS ANY BETTER, MISS RANDALL? HUMANS KILL FOR DRUGS, LAND, FOR PRIDE--FOR THRILLS!
I HOPED TO CHANGE THIS... TO LEAD THEM... ACH. TOO LATE. TOO LATE.
WE CAN SURVIVE ON HARVESTED BLOOD--AS I HAVE BEEN DOING. THAT IS WHY I AM WEAKER THAN THEY... BUT TO FULFILL OUR POTEN-TIAL, WE MUST FEAST AND GORGE ON THE LIVES OF OTHERS!
I KNEW FROM WHEN WE MET--YOU'RE NOT LIKE THE OTHERS...
YES, MISS RANDALL. I AM DIFFER-ENT. I AM NOT STRIGOLI. I AM... SOME-THING ELSE.
YOU HAVE PROVED YOUR VORTH, O'LEARY. WE GATHERED MANY NEW HUMANS FROM YOUR ARRANGEMENT ON THE BRIDGE.
YOU MAY TAKE PLEASURE FROM ONE OF THE HUMAN FEMALES VE HAVE BELOW. YOU MAY KILL IT IF YOU VISH.
THANK YOU, SIR. I THINK I WILL.
ERM... SIR? I WAS KINDA HOPING YOU WOULD... CHANGE ME... TODAY! I WANT TO KNOW WHEN I CAN BE LIKE YOU...
YOU ARE IMPATIENT!
IF I VERE YOU, I VHOULD FEEL THE SAME. BUT FOR NOW, YOU SERVE OUR NEEDS BETTER AS A HUMAN. VE VILL HAF NEED OF YOU TOMORROW. NOW GO.
PERHAPS I HAFF UNDER-ESTIMATED THE HUMANS. HE IS AS SAVAGE AS ANY OF US... HE VILL MAKE A GOOD STRIGOLI!

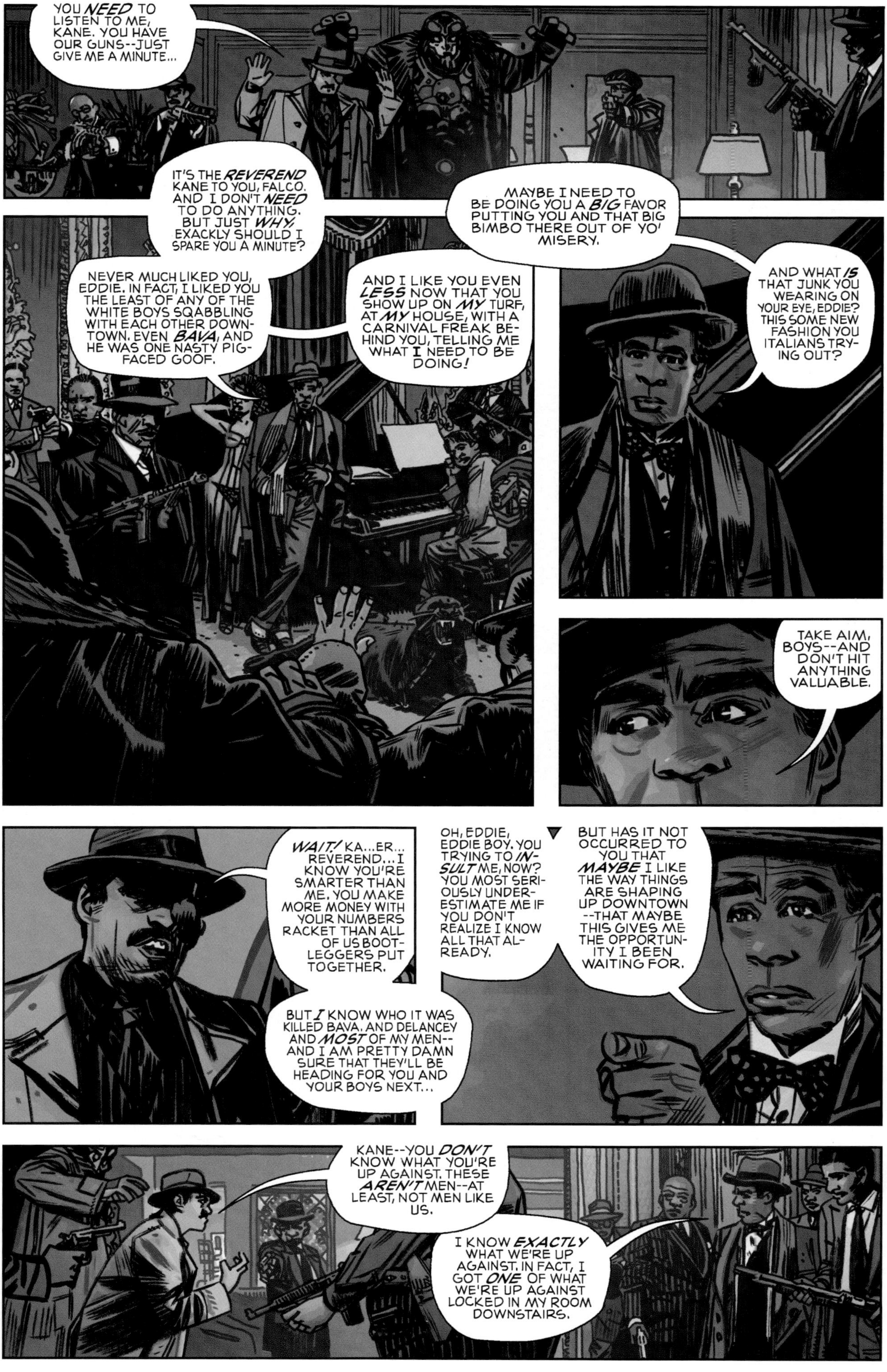

YOU NEED TO LISTEN TO ME, KANE. YOU HAVE OUR GUNS--JUST GIVE ME A MINUTE...
IT'S THE REVEREND KANE TO YOU, FALCO. AND I DON'T NEED TO DO ANYTHING. BUT JUST WHY, EXACKLY SHOULD I SPARE YOU A MINUTE?
MAYBE I NEED TO BE DOING YOU A BIG FAVOR PUTTING YOU AND THAT BIG BIMBO THERE OUT OF YO' MISERY.
NEVER MUCH LIKED YOU, EDDIE. IN FACT, I LIKED YOU THE LEAST OF ANY OF THE WHITE BOYS SQABBLING WITH EACH OTHER DOWN-TOWN. EVEN BAVA, AND HE WAS ONE NASTY PIG-FACED GOOF.
AND I LIKE YOU EVEN LESS NOW THAT YOU SHOW UP ON MY TURF, AT MY HOUSE, WITH A CARNIVAL FREAK BE-HIND YOU, TELLING ME WHAT I NEED TO BE DOING!
AND WHAT IS THAT JUNK YOU WEARING ON YOUR EYE, EDDIE? THIS SOME NEW FASHION YOU ITALIANS TRY-ING OUT?
TAKE AIM, BOYS--AND DON'T HIT ANYTHING VALUABLE.
WAIT! KA...ER... REVEREND...I KNOW YOU'RE SMARTER THAN ME. YOU MAKE MORE MONEY WITH YOUR NUMBERS RACKET THAN ALL OF US BOOT-LEGGERS PUT TOGETHER.
BUT I KNOW WHO IT WAS KILLED BAVA. AND DELANCEY AND MOST OF MY MEN-- AND I AM PRETTY DAMN SURE THAT THEY'LL BE HEADING FOR YOU AND YOUR BOYS NEXT...
OH, EDDIE, EDDIE BOY. YOU TRYING TO IN-SULT ME, NOW? YOU MOST SERI-OUSLY UNDER-ESTIMATE ME IF YOU DON'T REALIZE I KNOW ALL THAT AL-READY.
BUT HAS IT NOT OCCURRED TO YOU THAT MAYBE I LIKE THE WAY THINGS ARE SHAPING UP DOWNTOWN --THAT MAYBE THIS GIVES ME THE OPPORTUN-ITY I BEEN WAITING FOR.
KANE--YOU DON'T KNOW WHAT YOU'RE UP AGAINST. THESE AREN'T MEN--AT LEAST, NOT MEN LIKE US.
I KNOW EXACTLY WHAT WE'RE UP AGAINST. IN FACT, I GOT ONE OF WHAT WE'RE UP AGAINST LOCKED IN MY ROOM DOWNSTAIRS.

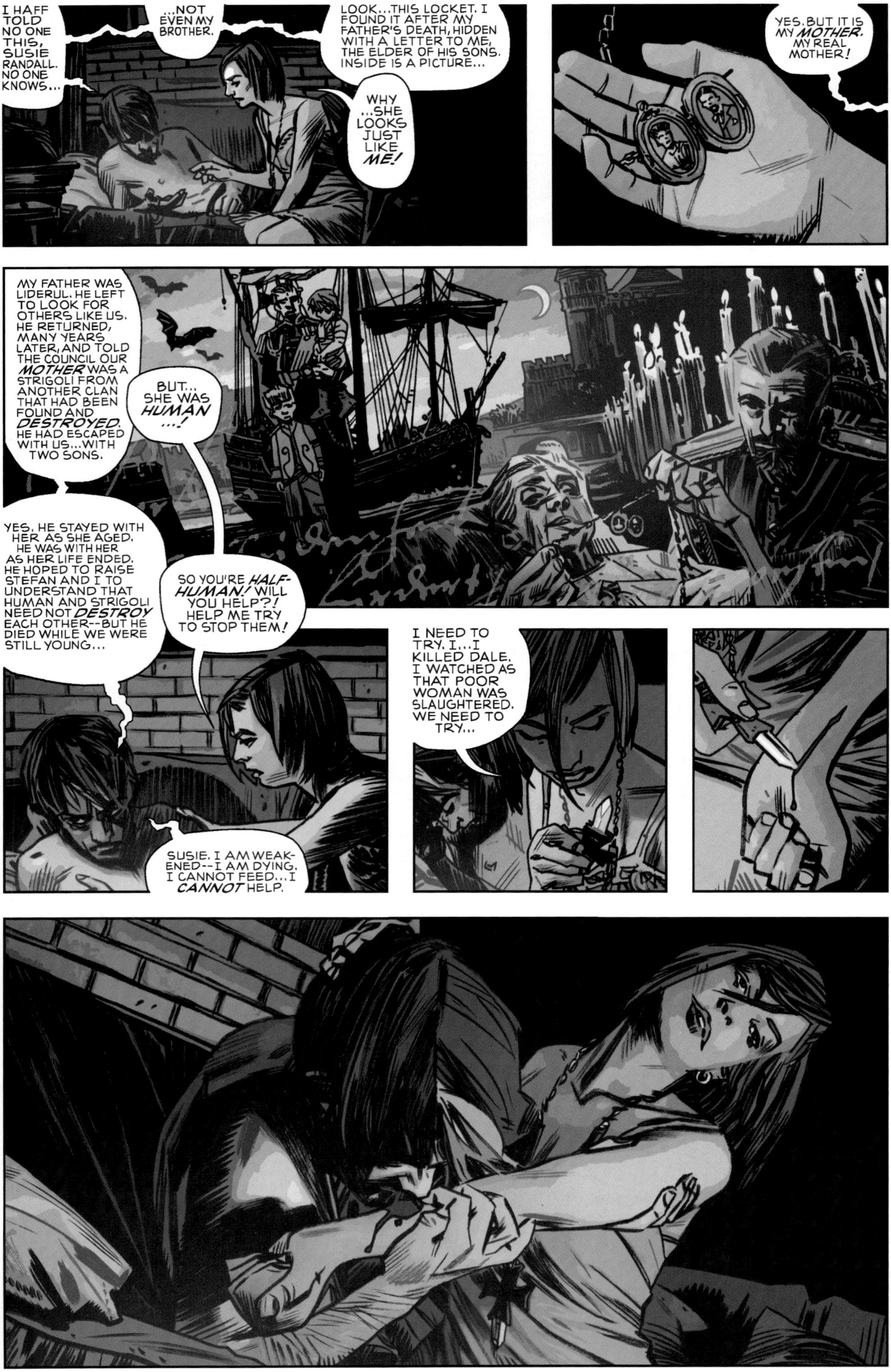
I HAFF TOLD NO ONE THIS, SUSIE RANDALL. NO ONE KNOWS...
...NOT EVEN MY BROTHER.
LOOK...THIS LOCKET. I FOUND IT AFTER MY FATHER'S DEATH, HIDDEN WITH A LETTER TO ME, THE ELDER OF HIS SONS. INSIDE IS A PICTURE...
WHY ...SHE LOOKS JUST LIKE ME!
YES. BUT IT IS MY MOTHER. MY REAL MOTHER!
MY FATHER WAS LIDERUL. HE LEFT TO LOOK FOR OTHERS LIKE US. HE RETURNED, MANY YEARS LATER, AND TOLD THE COUNCIL OUR MOTHER WAS A STRIGOLI FROM ANOTHER CLAN THAT HAD BEEN FOUND AND DESTROYED. HE HAD ESCAPED WITH US...WITH TWO SONS.
BUT... SHE WAS HUMAN ...!
YES. HE STAYED WITH HER AS SHE AGED. HE WAS WITH HER AS HER LIFE ENDED. HE HOPED TO RAISE STEFAN AND I TO UNDERSTAND THAT HUMAN AND STRIGOLI NEED NOT DESTROY EACH OTHER--BUT HE DIED WHILE WE WERE STILL YOUNG...
SO YOU'RE HALF-HUMAN! WILL YOU HELP?! HELP ME TRY TO STOP THEM!
SUSIE. I AM WEAKENED--I AM DYING. I CANNOT FEED...I CANNOT HELP.
I NEED TO TRY. I...I KILLED DALE. I WATCHED AS THAT POOR WOMAN WAS SLAUGHTERED. WE NEED TO TRY...

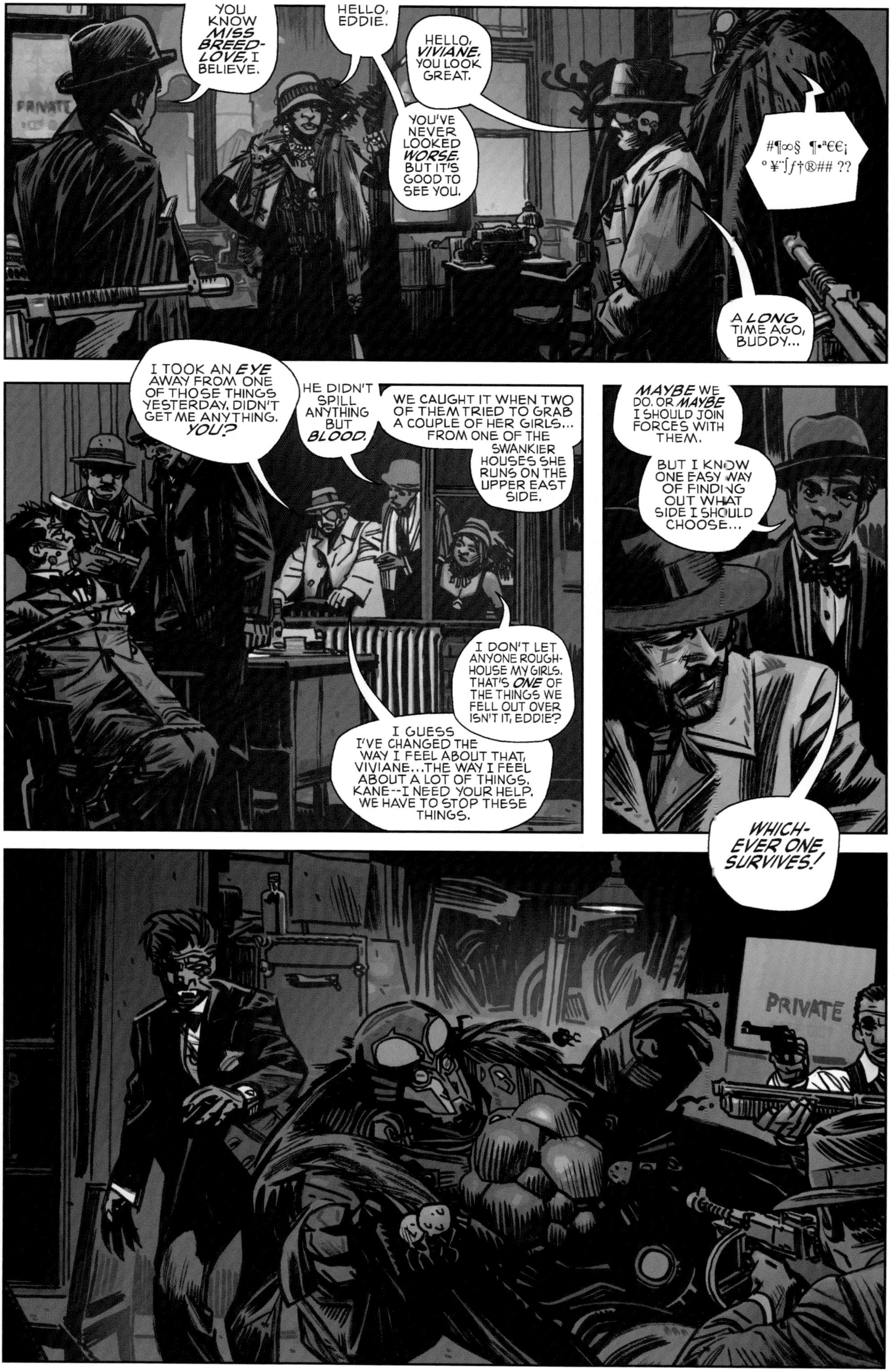
YOU KNOW MISS BREED-LOVE, I BELIEVE.
HELLO, EDDIE.
HELLO, VIVIANE. YOU LOOK GREAT.
YOU'VE NEVER LOOKED WORSE. BUT IT'S GOOD TO SEE YOU.
#¶∞§ ¶•ª€€¡ º¥¨∫ƒ†®## ??
A LONG TIME AGO, BUDDY...
I TOOK AN EYE AWAY FROM ONE OF THOSE THINGS YESTERDAY. DIDN'T GET ME ANYTHING. YOU?
HE DIDN'T SPILL ANYTHING BUT BLOOD.
WE CAUGHT IT WHEN TWO OF THEM TRIED TO GRAB A COUPLE OF HER GIRLS... FROM ONE OF THE SWANKIER HOUSES SHE RUNS ON THE UPPER EAST SIDE.
I DON'T LET ANYONE ROUGH-HOUSE MY GIRLS. THAT'S ONE OF THE THINGS WE FELL OUT OVER ISN'T IT, EDDIE?
I GUESS I'VE CHANGED THE WAY I FEEL ABOUT THAT, VIVIANE...THE WAY I FEEL ABOUT A LOT OF THINGS. KANE--I NEED YOUR HELP. WE HAVE TO STOP THESE THINGS.
MAYBE WE DO. OR MAYBE I SHOULD JOIN FORCES WITH THEM.
BUT I KNOW ONE EASY WAY OF FINDING OUT WHAT SIDE I SHOULD CHOOSE...
WHICH-EVER ONE SURVIVES!
PRIVATE

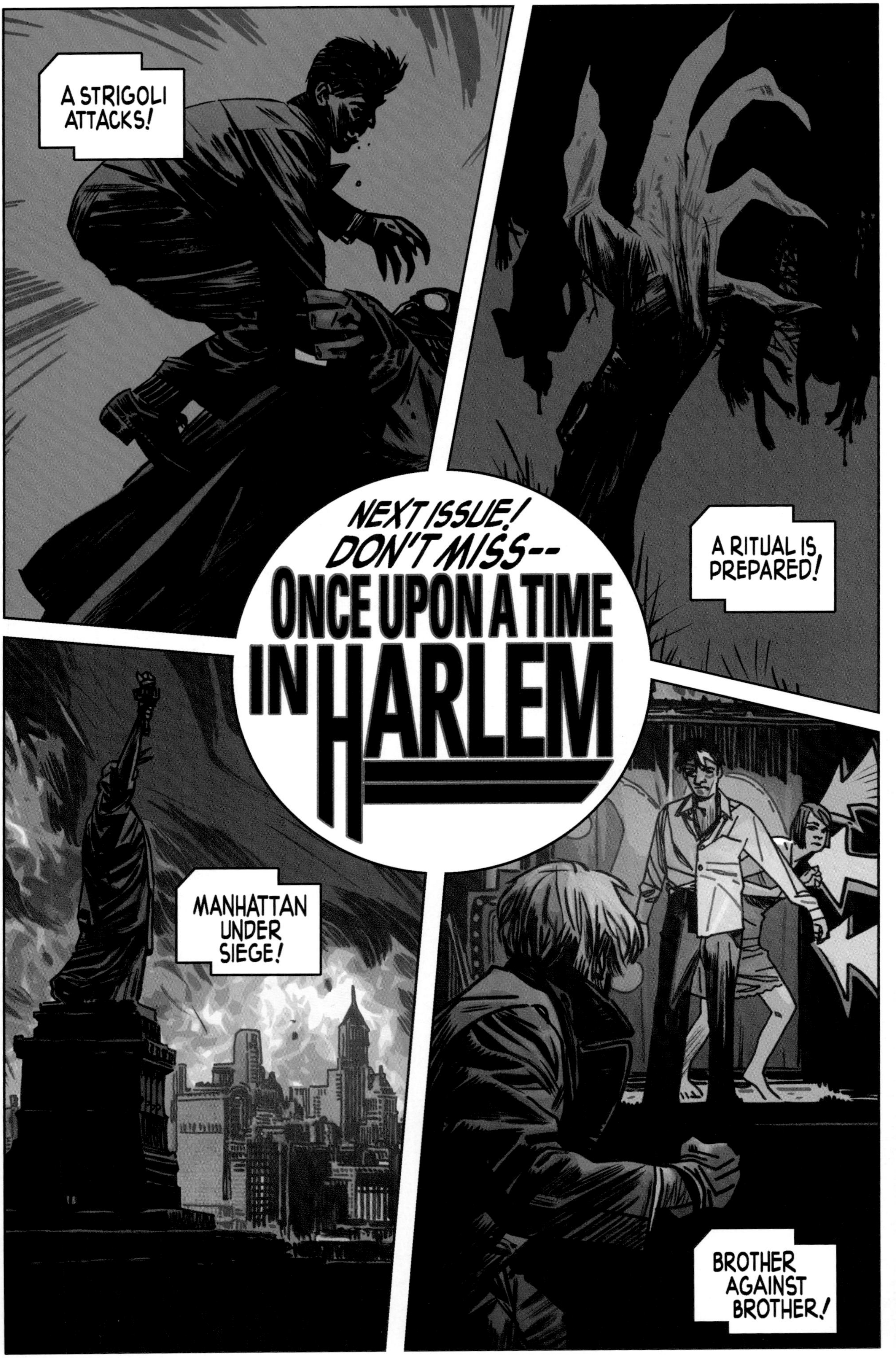
A STRIGOLI ATTACKS!
A RITUAL IS PREPARED!
NEXT ISSUE! DON'T MISS--
ONCE UPON A TIME IN HARLEM
MANHATTAN UNDER SIEGE!
BROTHER AGAINST BROTHER!

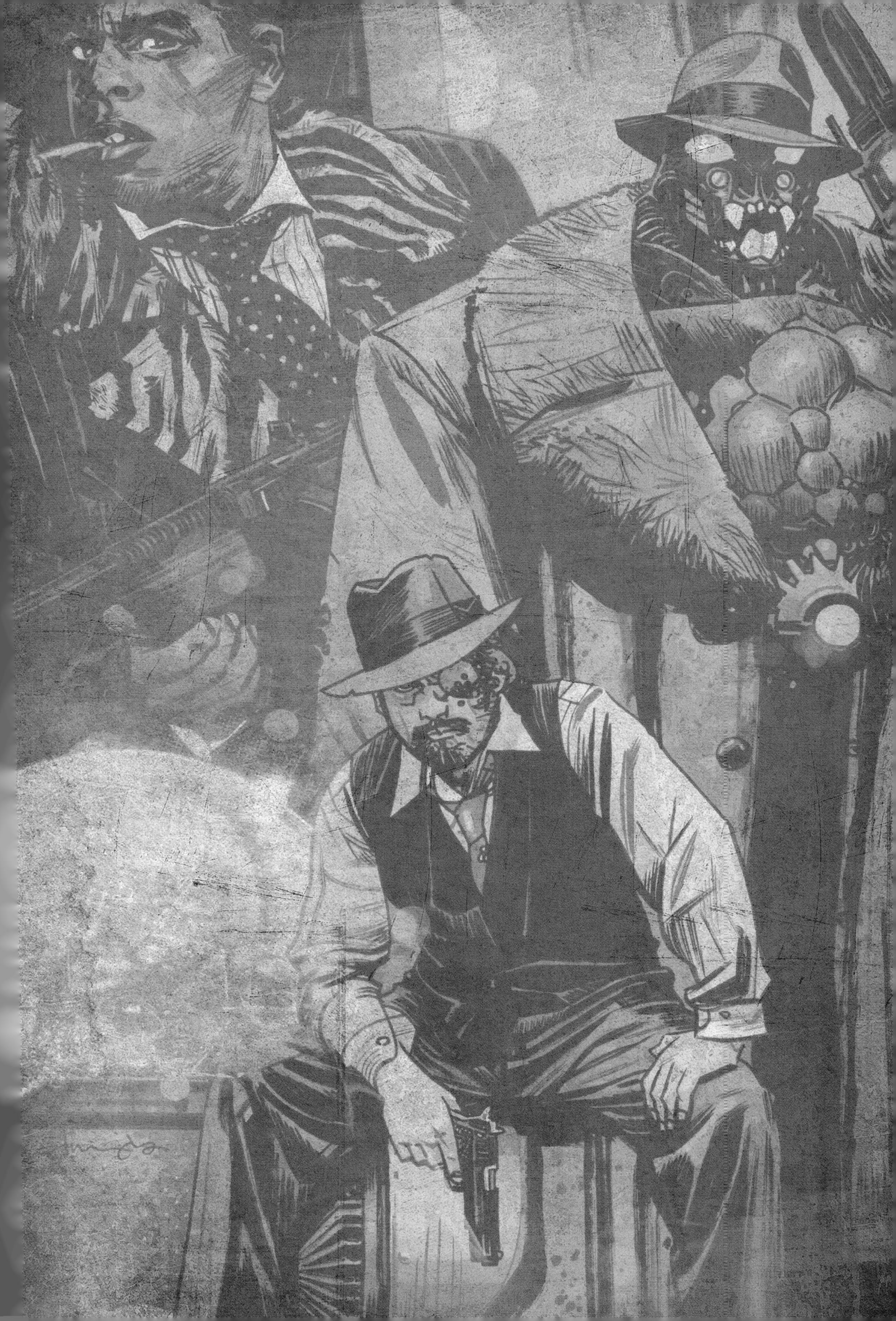

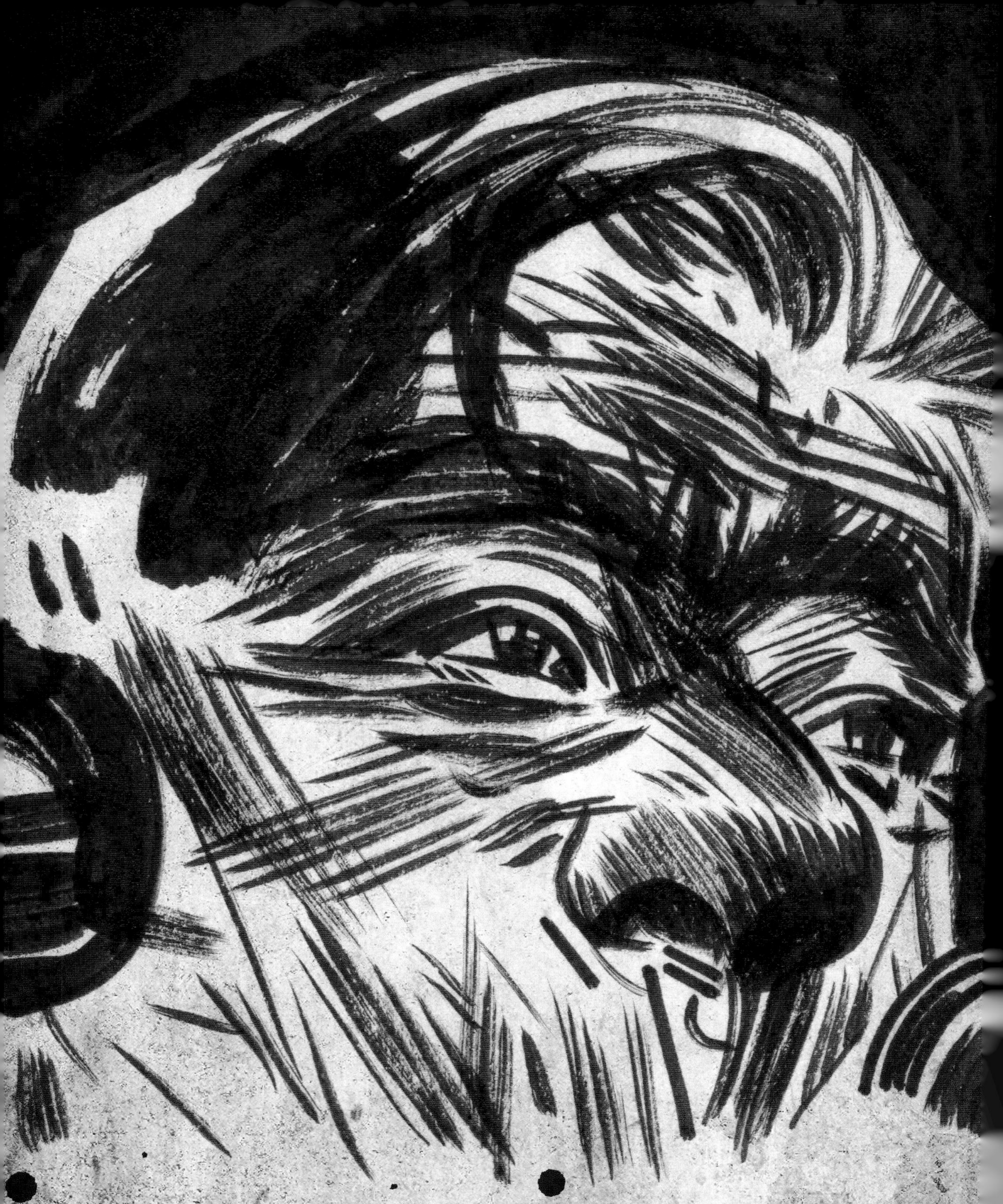

Chapter Four

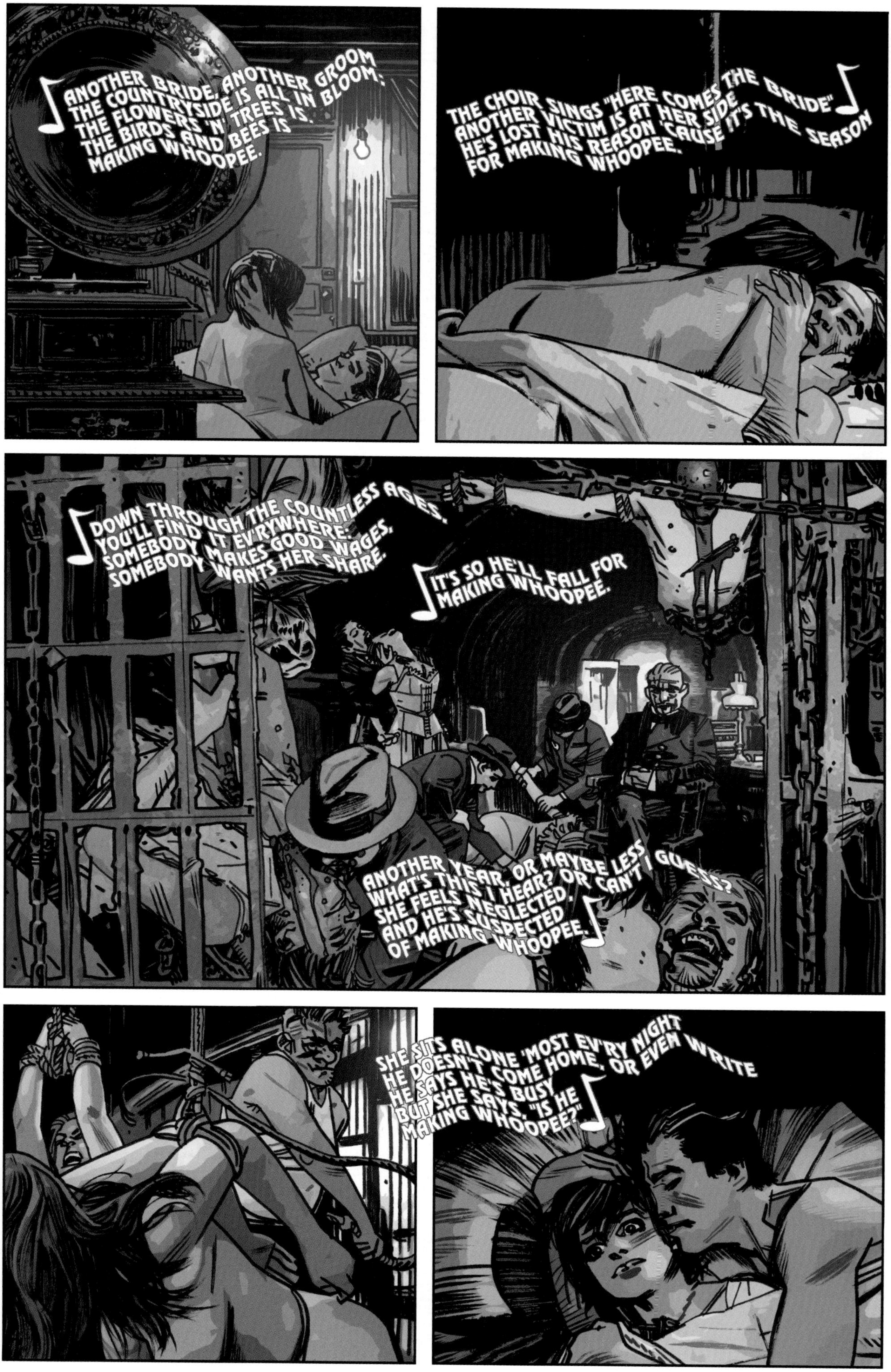
ANOTHER BRIDE, ANOTHER GROOM
THE COUNTRYSIDE IS ALL IN BLOOM.
THE FLOWERS 'N' TREES IS,
THE BIRDS AND BEES IS
MAKING WHOOPEE.
THE CHOIR SINGS "HERE COMES THE BRIDE"
ANOTHER VICTIM IS AT HER SIDE
HE'S LOST HIS REASON 'CAUSE IT'S THE SEASON
FOR MAKING WHOOPEE.
DOWN THROUGH THE COUNTLESS AGES,
YOU'LL FIND IT EV'RYWHERE.
SOMEBODY MAKES GOOD WAGES,
SOMEBODY WANTS HER SHARE.
IT'S SO HE'LL FALL FOR
MAKING WHOOPEE.
ANOTHER YEAR, OR MAYBE LESS
WHAT'S THIS I HEAR? OR CAN'T I GUESS?
SHE FEELS NEGLECTED,
AND HE'S SUSPECTED
OF MAKING WHOOPEE.
SHE SITS ALONE 'MOST EV'RY NIGHT
HE DOESN'T COME HOME, OR EVEN WRITE
HE SAYS HE'S BUSY
BUT SHE SAYS, "IS HE
MAKING WHOOPEE?"

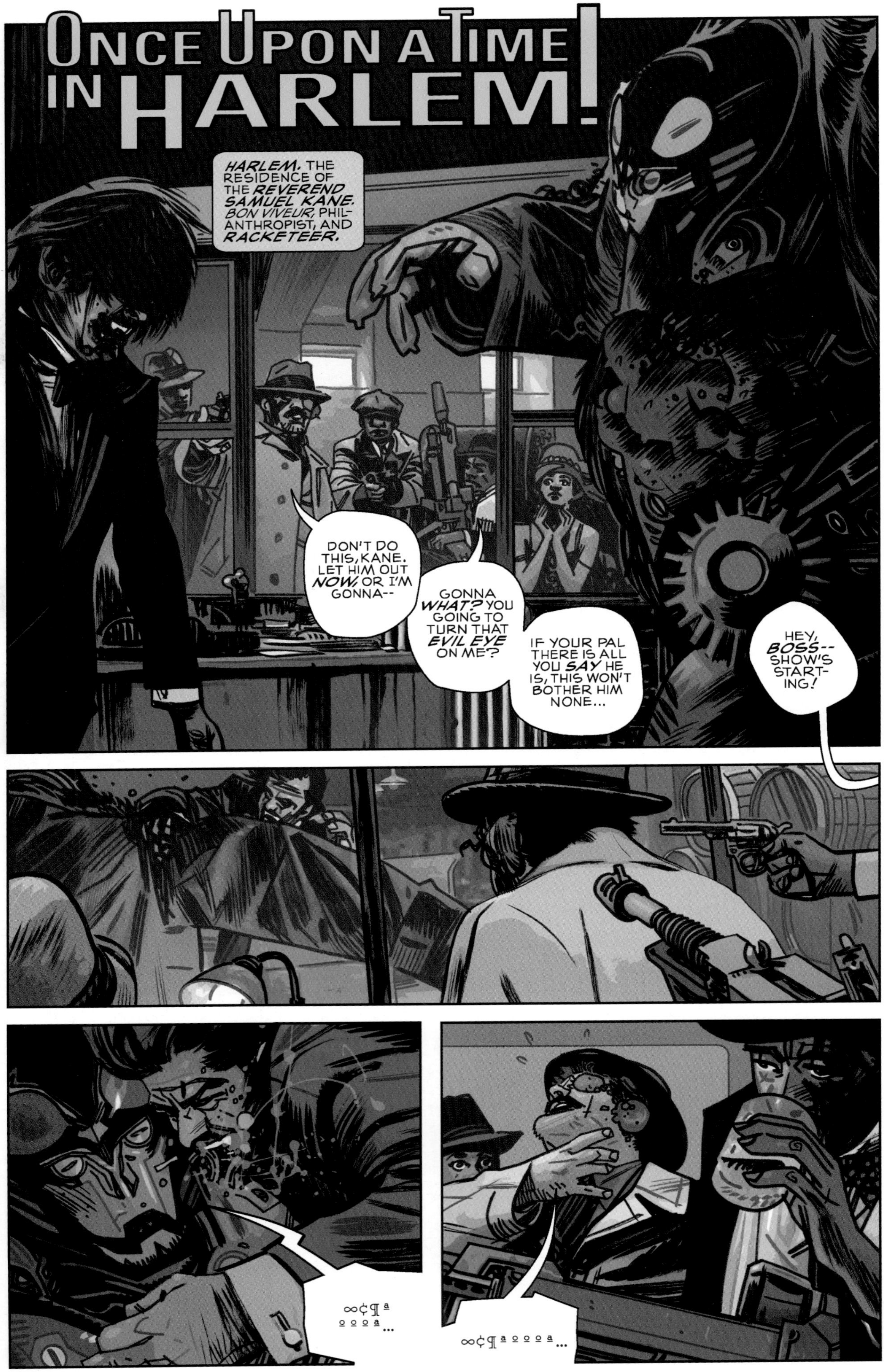
ONCE UPON A TIME IN HARLEM!
HARLEM. THE RESIDENCE OF THE REVEREND SAMUEL KANE. BON VIVEUR, PHILANTHROPIST, AND RACKETEER.
DON'T DO THIS, KANE. LET HIM OUT NOW, OR I'M GONNA--
GONNA WHAT? YOU GOING TO TURN THAT EVIL EYE ON ME?
IF YOUR PAL THERE IS ALL YOU SAY HE IS, THIS WON'T BOTHER HIM NONE...
HEY, BOSS-- SHOW'S STARTING!
∞¢¶ª ºººª...
∞¢¶ª ºººª...

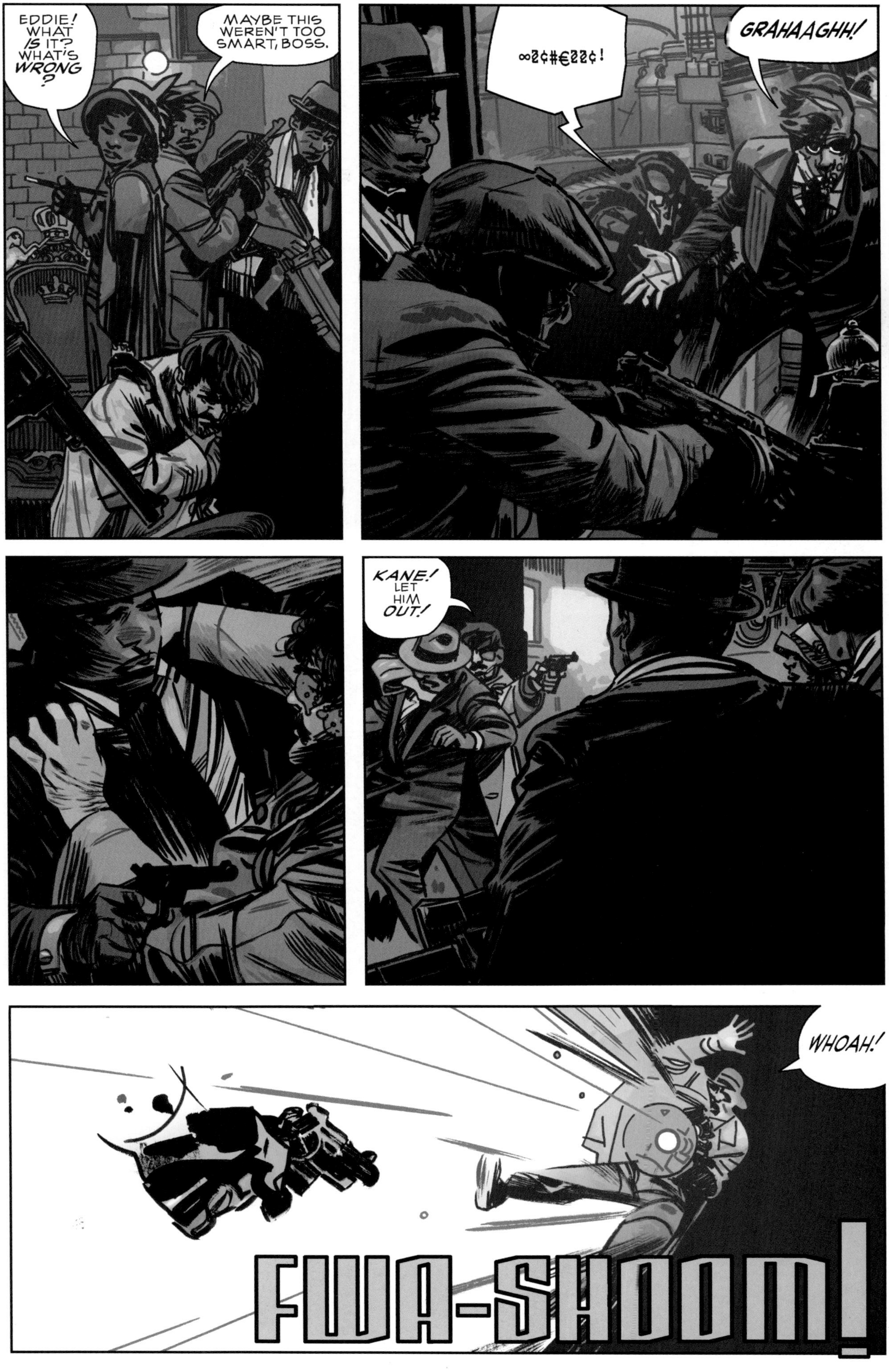
EDDIE! WHAT *IS* IT? WHAT'S *WRONG*?
MAYBE THIS WEREN'T TOO SMART, BOSS.
∞ƻ¢#€ƻƻ¢!
GRAHAAGHH!
KANE! LET HIM OUT!
WHOAH!
FWA-SHOOM!

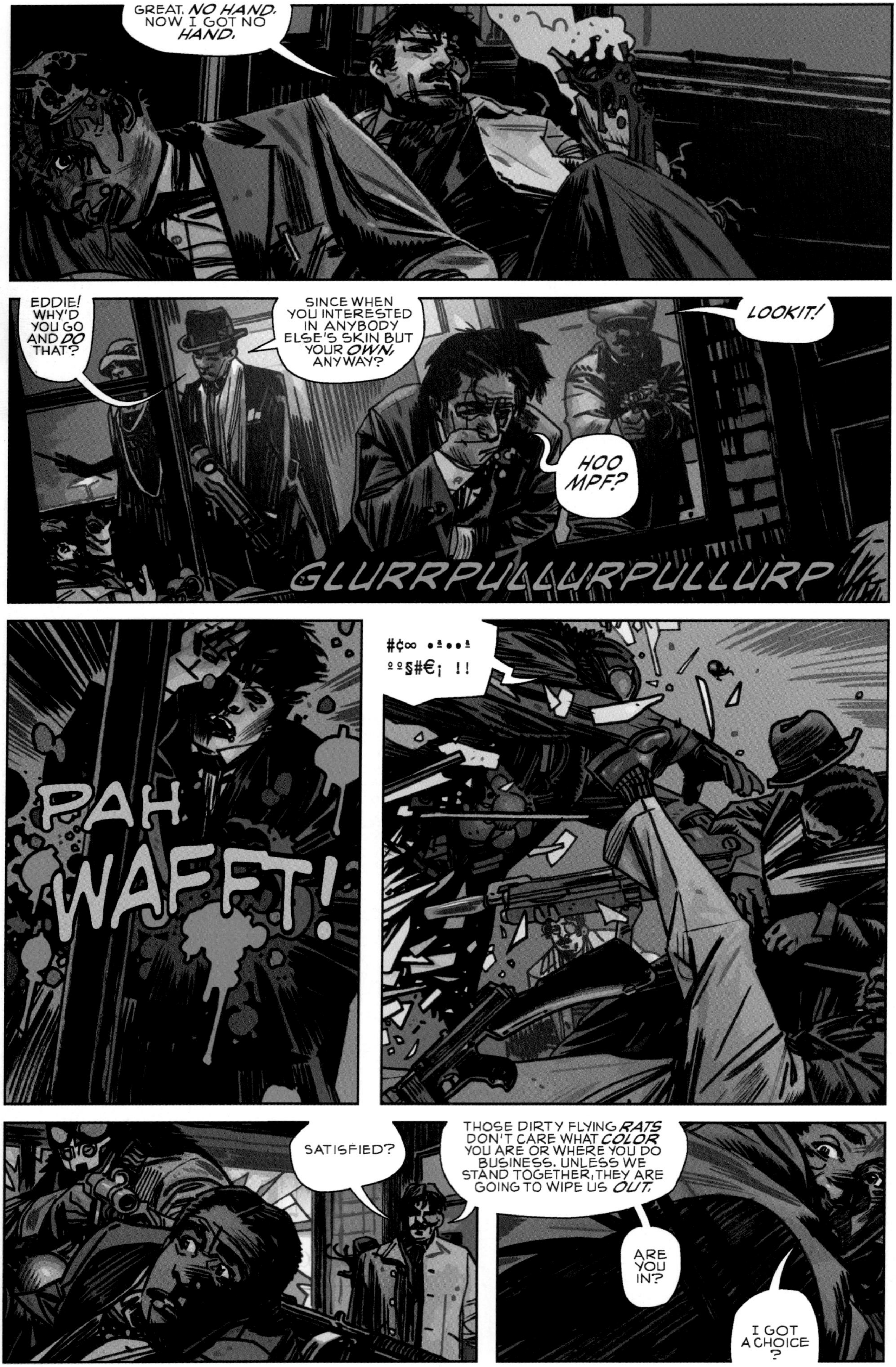

GREAT. NO HAND. NOW I GOT NO HAND.
EDDIE! WHY'D YOU GO AND DO THAT?
SINCE WHEN YOU INTERESTED IN ANYBODY ELSE'S SKIN BUT YOUR OWN, ANYWAY?
LOOKIT!
HOO MPF?
GLURRPULLURPULLURP
PAH WAFFT!
#¢∞ •ª••ª ºº§#€¡ !!
SATISFIED?
THOSE DIRTY FLYING RATS DON'T CARE WHAT COLOR YOU ARE OR WHERE YOU DO BUSINESS. UNLESS WE STAND TOGETHER, THEY ARE GOING TO WIPE US OUT.
ARE YOU IN?
I GOT A CHOICE?

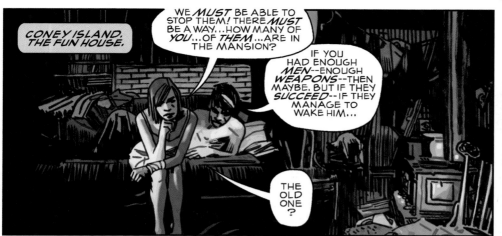

CONEY ISLAND.
THE FUN HOUSE.

WE *MUST* BE ABLE TO STOP THEM! THERE *MUST* BE A WAY...HOW MANY OF *YOU*...OF *THEM*...ARE IN THE MANSION?

IF YOU HAD ENOUGH *MEN*--ENOUGH *WEAPONS*--THEN MAYBE. BUT IF THEY *SUCCEED*--IF THEY MANAGE TO WAKE HIM...

THE OLD ONE?

YES. IF IT *IS* AS THE PROPHECY FORETELLS...IF THEY WAKE THE MANKILLER...THEN *NO*, THEY WILL NOT BE STOPPED.

WE WILL NOT BE STOPPED.

OKAY. *SORRY*. I KNOW *YOU'RE* DIFFERENT ...BUT IF WE *CAN* GET THE MEN--AND IF WE ATTACK *SOON*--THERE CAN'T BE THAT MANY OF...

OF THE *ORIGINAL CLAN*? LESS THAN *FORTY*, BUT SOON THERE WILL BE MORE.

WE *CAN* TURN A HUMAN INTO STRIGOLI...

BY BITING THEM? LIKE *DRACULA*?!

PLEASE. FORGET ABOUT THAT *SILLY* PLAY. IT IS MORE COMPLEX THAN THAT...IT IS NOT A GIFT WE GIVE LIGHTLY--WE DO IT *RARELY*...ONLY WHEN WE *MUST*!

MOST COMMONLY TO TAKE A MATE, BUT SOMETIMES...

...SOMETIMES TO MAKE OUR CLAN STRONGER FOR BATTLE.

THAT IS WHAT VASELI WILL PERSUADE MY BROTHER TO DO. WITH *MORE* STRIGOLI, AND IF THE *OLD ONE* RISES, THEN I FEAR IT IS INEVITABLE.

JUST AS NIGHT MUST *ALWAYS* FOLLOW DAY, YOU AND YOUR KIND ARE DOOMED.

I *AM* SORRY, SUSIE RANDALL.

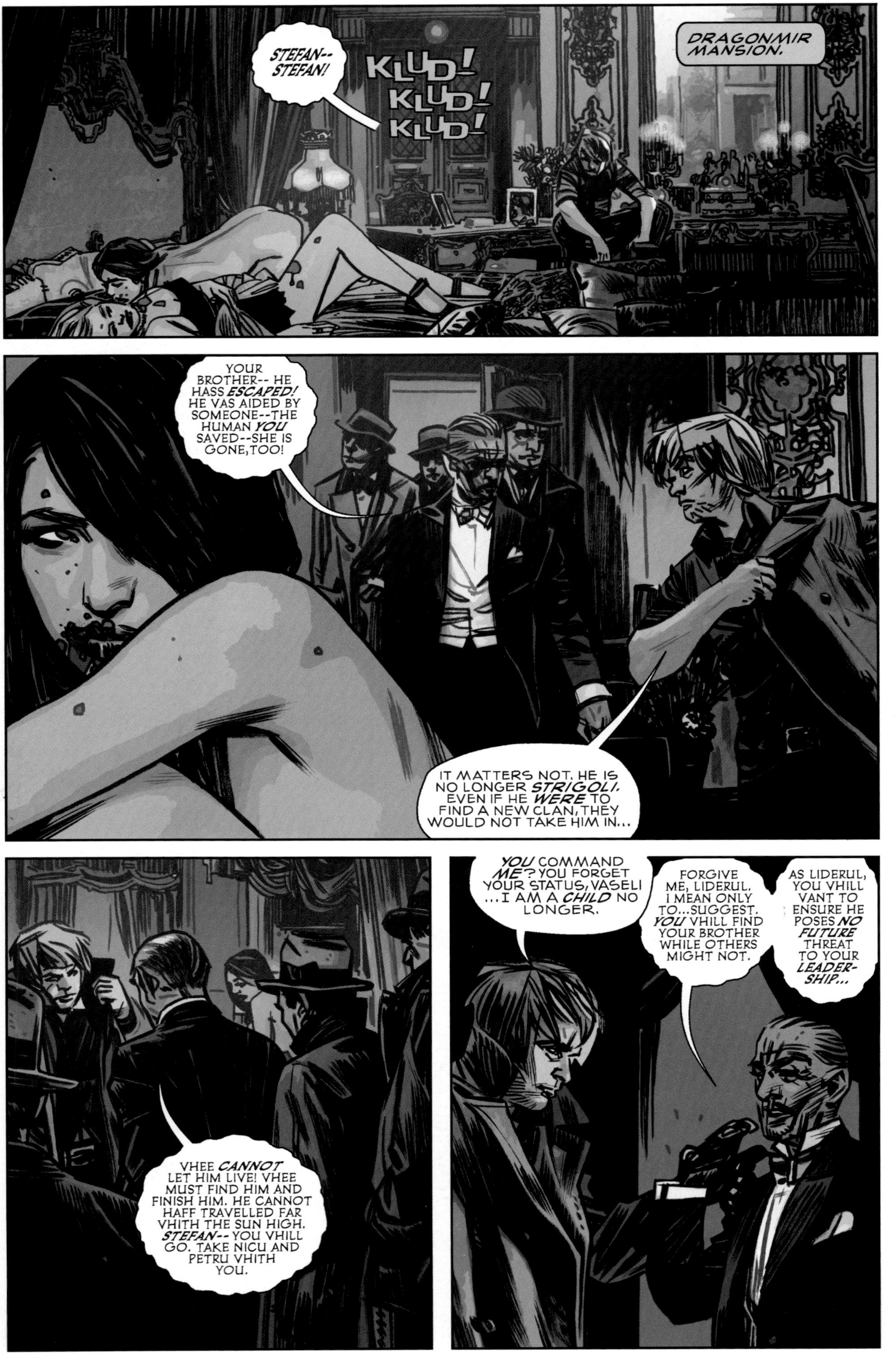
DRAGONMIR MANSION.
STEFAN--STEFAN!
KLUD! KLUD! KLUD!
YOUR BROTHER-- HE HASS ESCAPED! HE VAS AIDED BY SOMEONE--THE HUMAN YOU SAVED--SHE IS GONE, TOO!
IT MATTERS NOT. HE IS NO LONGER STRIGOLI. EVEN IF HE WERE TO FIND A NEW CLAN, THEY WOULD NOT TAKE HIM IN...
VHEE CANNOT LET HIM LIVE! VHEE MUST FIND HIM AND FINISH HIM. HE CANNOT HAFF TRAVELLED FAR VHITH THE SUN HIGH. STEFAN-- YOU VHILL GO. TAKE NICU AND PETRU VHITH YOU.
YOU COMMAND ME? YOU FORGET YOUR STATUS, VASELI ...I AM A CHILD NO LONGER.
FORGIVE ME, LIDERUL. I MEAN ONLY TO...SUGGEST. YOU VHILL FIND YOUR BROTHER WHILE OTHERS MIGHT NOT.
AS LIDERUL, YOU VHILL VANT TO ENSURE HE POSES NO FUTURE THREAT TO YOUR LEADER-SHIP...

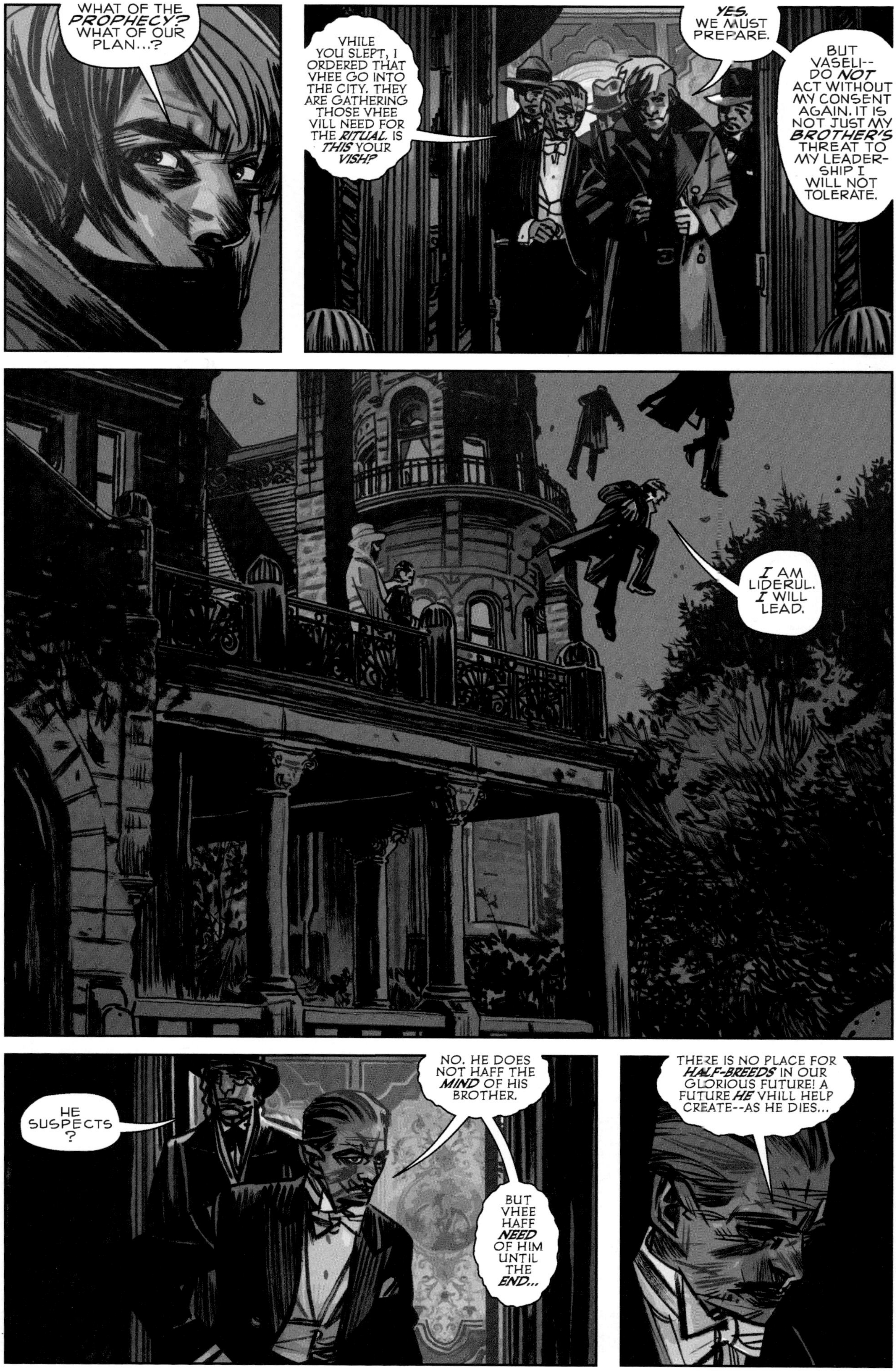
WHAT OF THE PROPHECY? WHAT OF OUR PLAN...?
VHILE YOU SLEPT, I ORDERED THAT VHEE GO INTO THE CITY. THEY ARE GATHERING THOSE VHEE VILL NEED FOR THE RITUAL. IS THIS YOUR VISH?
YES. WE MUST PREPARE.
BUT VASELI--DO NOT ACT WITHOUT MY CONSENT AGAIN. IT IS NOT JUST MY BROTHER'S THREAT TO MY LEADERSHIP I WILL NOT TOLERATE.
I AM LIDERUL. I WILL LEAD.
HE SUSPECTS?
NO. HE DOES NOT HAFF THE MIND OF HIS BROTHER.
BUT VHEE HAFF NEED OF HIM UNTIL THE END...
THERE IS NO PLACE FOR HALF-BREEDS IN OUR GLORIOUS FUTURE! A FUTURE HE VHILL HELP CREATE--AS HE DIES...

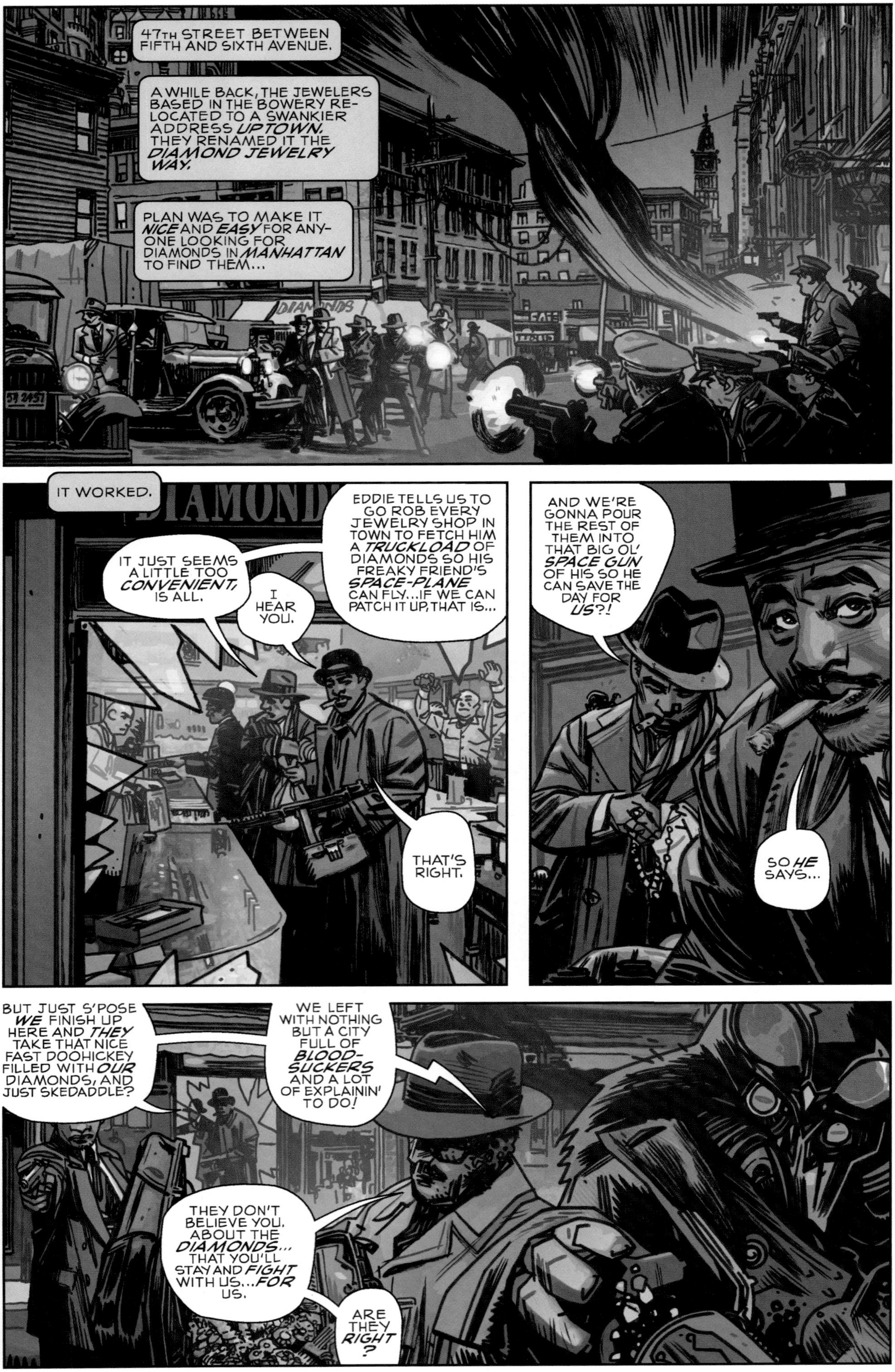
47th STREET BETWEEN FIFTH AND SIXTH AVENUE.
A WHILE BACK, THE JEWELERS BASED IN THE BOWERY RELOCATED TO A SWANKIER ADDRESS UPTOWN. THEY RENAMED IT THE DIAMOND JEWELRY WAY.
PLAN WAS TO MAKE IT NICE AND EASY FOR ANYONE LOOKING FOR DIAMONDS IN MANHATTAN TO FIND THEM...
DIAMONDS
CAFE
IT WORKED.
DIAMOND
IT JUST SEEMS A LITTLE TOO CONVENIENT, IS ALL.
I HEAR YOU.
EDDIE TELLS US TO GO ROB EVERY JEWELRY SHOP IN TOWN TO FETCH HIM A TRUCKLOAD OF DIAMONDS SO HIS FREAKY FRIEND'S SPACE-PLANE CAN FLY...IF WE CAN PATCH IT UP, THAT IS...
THAT'S RIGHT.
AND WE'RE GONNA POUR THE REST OF THEM INTO THAT BIG OL' SPACE GUN OF HIS SO HE CAN SAVE THE DAY FOR US?!
SO HE SAYS...
BUT JUST S'POSE WE FINISH UP HERE AND THEY TAKE THAT NICE FAST DOOHICKEY FILLED WITH OUR DIAMONDS, AND JUST SKEDADDLE?
WE LEFT WITH NOTHING BUT A CITY FULL OF BLOOD-SUCKERS AND A LOT OF EXPLAININ' TO DO!
THEY DON'T BELIEVE YOU. ABOUT THE DIAMONDS... THAT YOU'LL STAY AND FIGHT WITH US...FOR US.
ARE THEY RIGHT?

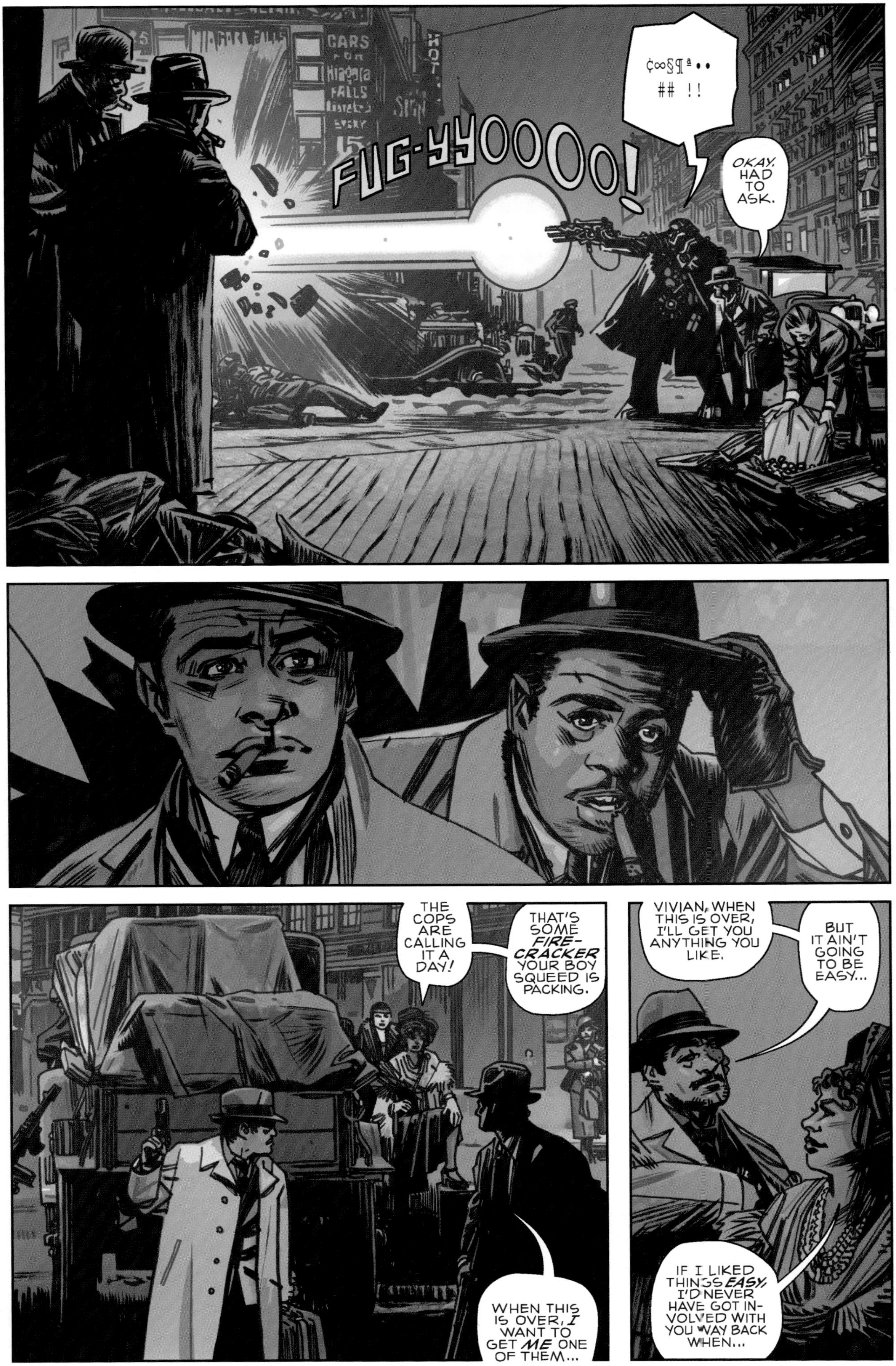
FUG-YYOOOOO!
¢∞§¶ª•• ## !!
OKAY, HAD TO ASK.
THE COPS ARE CALLING IT A DAY!
THAT'S SOME FIRE-CRACKER YOUR BOY SQUEED IS PACKING.
WHEN THIS IS OVER, I WANT TO GET ME ONE OF THEM...
VIVIAN, WHEN THIS IS OVER, I'LL GET YOU ANYTHING YOU LIKE.
BUT IT AIN'T GOING TO BE EASY...
IF I LIKED THINGS EASY, I'D NEVER HAVE GOT IN-VOLVED WITH YOU WAY BACK WHEN...

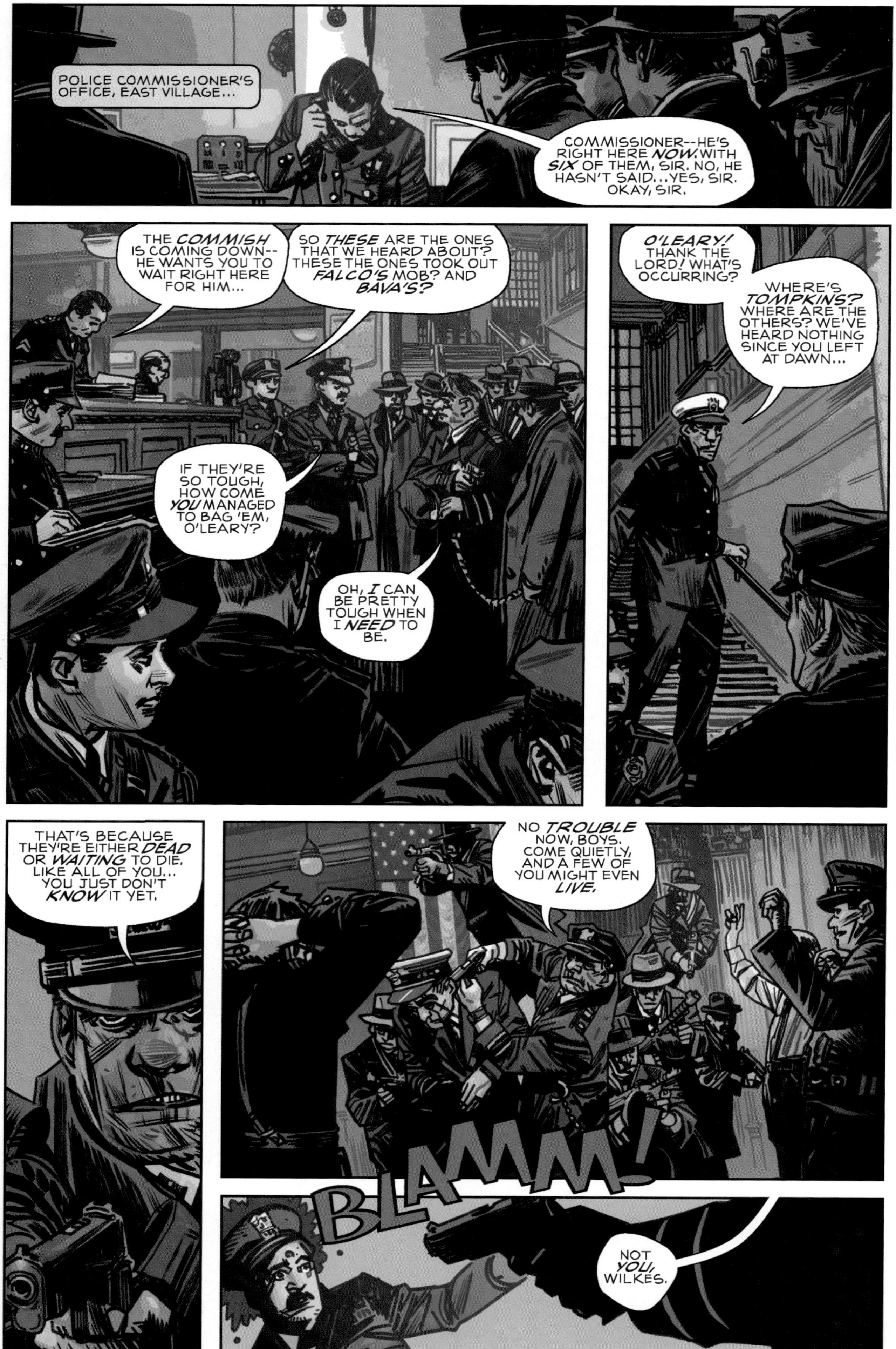

POLICE COMMISSIONER'S OFFICE, EAST VILLAGE...
COMMISSIONER--HE'S RIGHT HERE *NOW*. WITH *SIX* OF THEM, SIR. NO, HE HASN'T SAID...YES, SIR. OKAY, SIR.
THE *COMMISH* IS COMING DOWN-- HE WANTS YOU TO WAIT RIGHT HERE FOR HIM...
SO *THESE* ARE THE ONES THAT WE HEARD ABOUT? THESE THE ONES TOOK OUT *FALCO'S* MOB? AND *BAVA'S?*
IF THEY'RE SO TOUGH, HOW COME *YOU* MANAGED TO BAG 'EM, O'LEARY?
OH, *I* CAN BE PRETTY TOUGH WHEN I *NEED* TO BE.
O'LEARY! THANK THE LORD! WHAT'S OCCURRING?
WHERE'S *TOMPKINS?* WHERE ARE THE OTHERS? WE'VE HEARD NOTHING SINCE YOU LEFT AT DAWN...
THAT'S BECAUSE THEY'RE EITHER *DEAD* OR *WAITING* TO DIE, LIKE ALL OF YOU... YOU JUST DON'T *KNOW* IT YET.
NO *TROUBLE* NOW, BOYS. COME QUIETLY, AND A FEW OF YOU MIGHT EVEN *LIVE.*
BLAMM!
NOT *YOU*, WILKES.

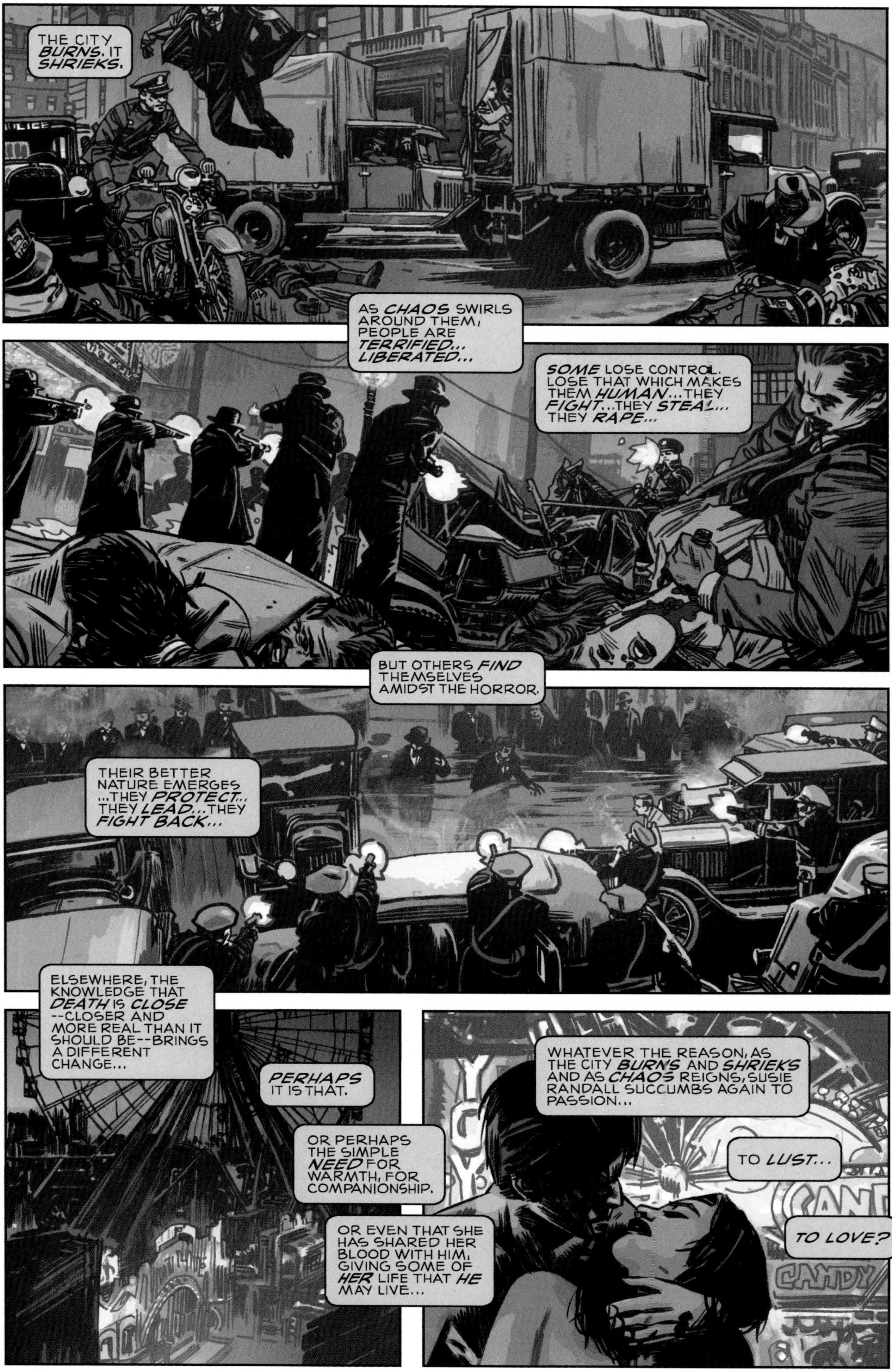
THE CITY BURNS. IT SHRIEKS.
AS CHAOS SWIRLS AROUND THEM, PEOPLE ARE TERRIFIED... LIBERATED...
SOME LOSE CONTROL. LOSE THAT WHICH MAKES THEM HUMAN...THEY FIGHT...THEY STEAL... THEY RAPE...
BUT OTHERS FIND THEMSELVES AMIDST THE HORROR.
THEIR BETTER NATURE EMERGES ...THEY PROTECT... THEY LEAD...THEY FIGHT BACK...
ELSEWHERE, THE KNOWLEDGE THAT DEATH IS CLOSE --CLOSER AND MORE REAL THAN IT SHOULD BE--BRINGS A DIFFERENT CHANGE...
PERHAPS IT IS THAT.
OR PERHAPS THE SIMPLE NEED FOR WARMTH, FOR COMPANIONSHIP.
OR EVEN THAT SHE HAS SHARED HER BLOOD WITH HIM, GIVING SOME OF HER LIFE THAT HE MAY LIVE...
WHATEVER THE REASON, AS THE CITY BURNS AND SHRIEKS AND AS CHAOS REIGNS, SUSIE RANDALL SUCCUMBS AGAIN TO PASSION...
TO LUST...
TO LOVE?

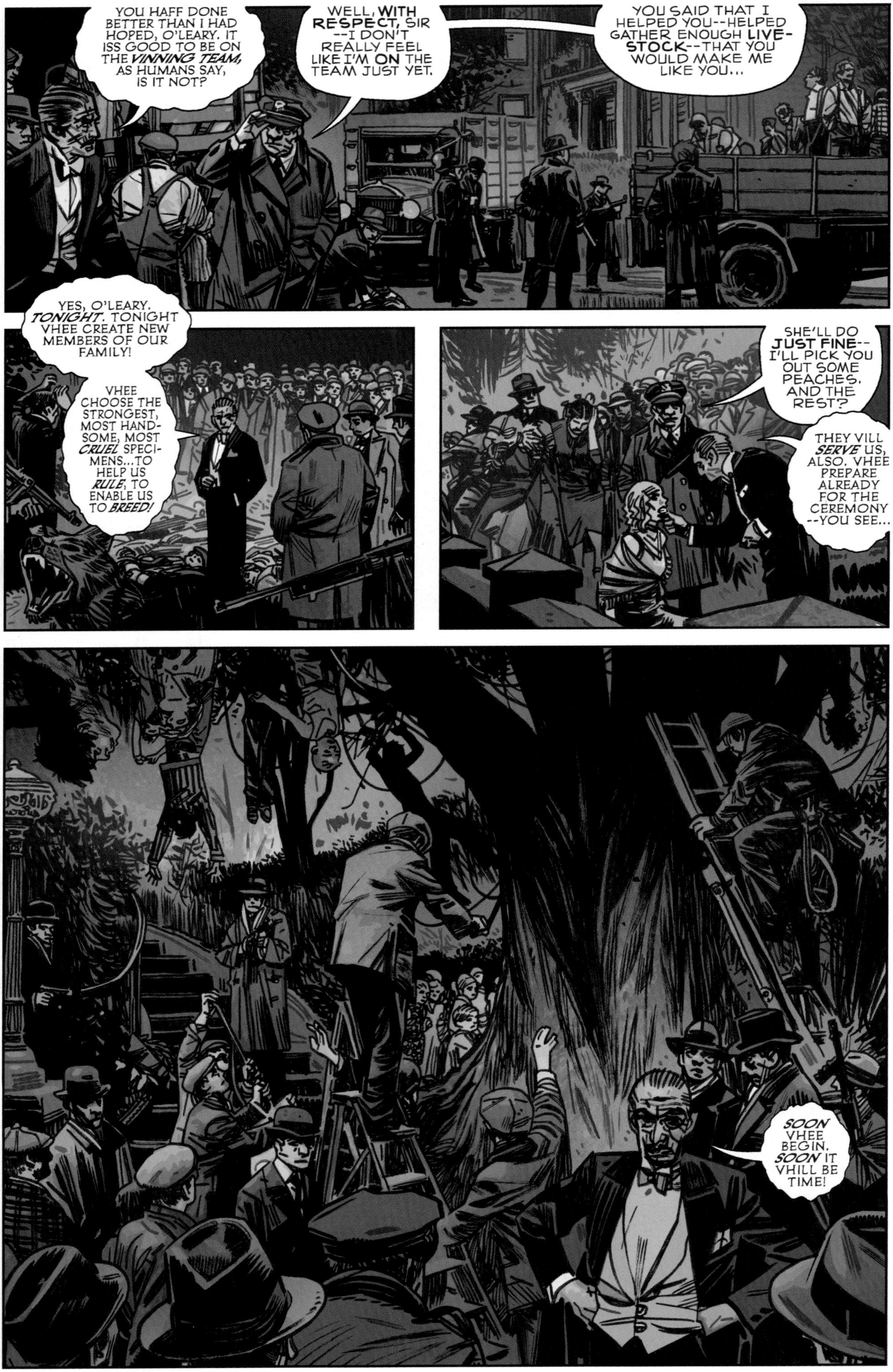
YOU HAFF DONE BETTER THAN I HAD HOPED, O'LEARY. IT ISS GOOD TO BE ON THE *VINNING TEAM,* AS HUMANS SAY, IS IT NOT?
WELL, **WITH RESPECT,** SIR --I DON'T REALLY FEEL LIKE I'M **ON** THE TEAM JUST YET.
YOU SAID THAT I HELPED YOU--HELPED GATHER ENOUGH **LIVE-STOCK**--THAT YOU WOULD MAKE ME LIKE YOU...
YES, O'LEARY. ***TONIGHT***. TONIGHT VHEE CREATE NEW MEMBERS OF OUR FAMILY!
VHEE CHOOSE THE STRONGEST, MOST HAND-SOME, MOST *CRUEL* SPECI-MENS...TO HELP US *RULE*, TO ENABLE US TO *BREED!*
SHE'LL DO **JUST FINE**-- I'LL PICK YOU OUT SOME PEACHES. AND THE REST?
THEY VILL *SERVE* US, ALSO. VHEE PREPARE ALREADY FOR THE CEREMONY --YOU SEE...
SOON VHEE BEGIN. *SOON* IT VHILL BE TIME!

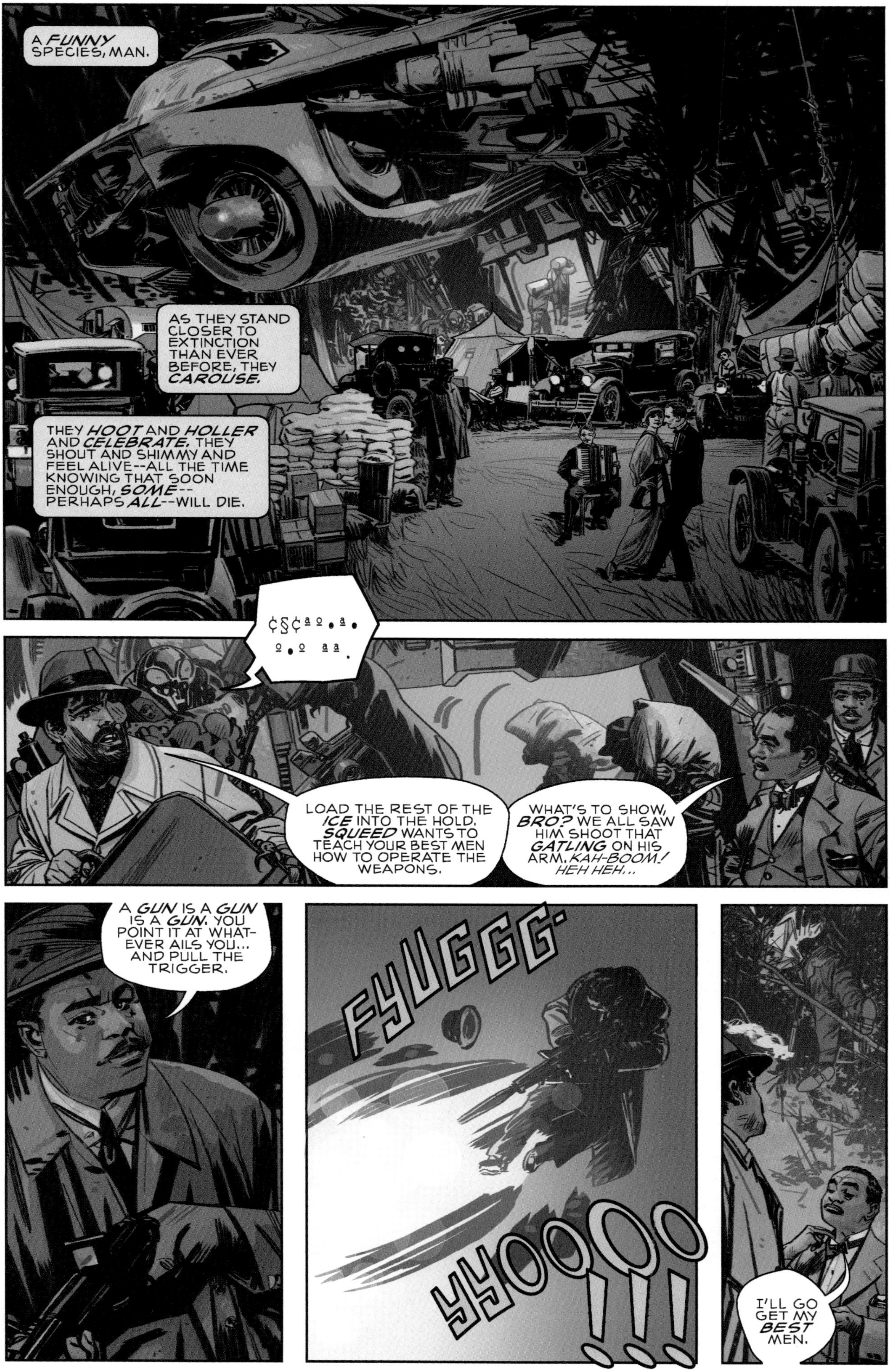
A FUNNY SPECIES, MAN.
AS THEY STAND CLOSER TO EXTINCTION THAN EVER BEFORE, THEY CAROUSE.
THEY HOOT AND HOLLER AND CELEBRATE. THEY SHOUT AND SHIMMY AND FEEL ALIVE--ALL THE TIME KNOWING THAT SOON ENOUGH, SOME--PERHAPS ALL--WILL DIE.
¢§¢ª º • ª • º • º ª ª .
LOAD THE REST OF THE ICE INTO THE HOLD. SQUEED WANTS TO TEACH YOUR BEST MEN HOW TO OPERATE THE WEAPONS.
WHAT'S TO SHOW, BRO? WE ALL SAW HIM SHOOT THAT GATLING ON HIS ARM. KAH-BOOM! HEH HEH...
A GUN IS A GUN IS A GUN. YOU POINT IT AT WHAT-EVER AILS YOU... AND PULL THE TRIGGER.
FYUGGG-
YYOOOO!!!!
I'LL GO GET MY BEST MEN.

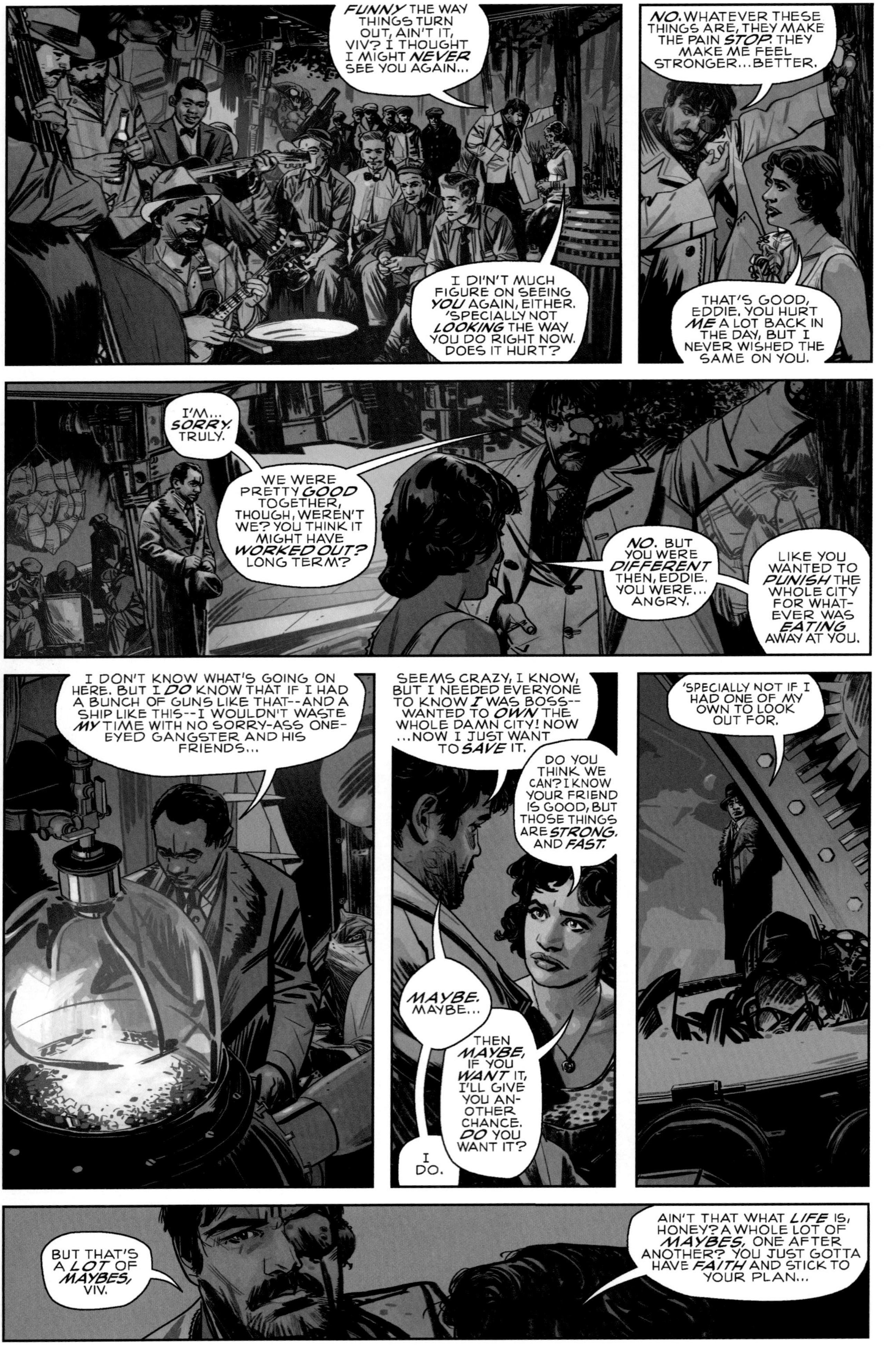
FUNNY THE WAY THINGS TURN OUT, AIN'T IT, VIV? I THOUGHT I MIGHT NEVER SEE YOU AGAIN...
I DIN'T MUCH FIGURE ON SEEING YOU AGAIN, EITHER. 'SPECIALLY NOT LOOKING THE WAY YOU DO RIGHT NOW. DOES IT HURT?
NO. WHATEVER THESE THINGS ARE, THEY MAKE THE PAIN STOP. THEY MAKE ME FEEL STRONGER... BETTER.
THAT'S GOOD, EDDIE. YOU HURT ME A LOT BACK IN THE DAY, BUT I NEVER WISHED THE SAME ON YOU.
I'M... SORRY. TRULY.
WE WERE PRETTY GOOD TOGETHER, THOUGH, WEREN'T WE? YOU THINK IT MIGHT HAVE WORKED OUT? LONG TERM?
NO. BUT YOU WERE DIFFERENT THEN, EDDIE. YOU WERE... ANGRY.
LIKE YOU WANTED TO PUNISH THE WHOLE CITY FOR WHAT-EVER WAS EATING AWAY AT YOU.
I DON'T KNOW WHAT'S GOING ON HERE. BUT I DO KNOW THAT IF I HAD A BUNCH OF GUNS LIKE THAT--AND A SHIP LIKE THIS--I WOULDN'T WASTE MY TIME WITH NO SORRY-ASS ONE-EYED GANGSTER AND HIS FRIENDS...
SEEMS CRAZY, I KNOW, BUT I NEEDED EVERYONE TO KNOW I WAS BOSS--WANTED TO OWN THE WHOLE DAMN CITY! NOW ...NOW I JUST WANT TO SAVE IT.
DO YOU THINK WE CAN? I KNOW YOUR FRIEND IS GOOD, BUT THOSE THINGS ARE STRONG. AND FAST.
MAYBE. MAYBE...
THEN MAYBE, IF YOU WANT IT, I'LL GIVE YOU AN-OTHER CHANCE. DO YOU WANT IT?
I DO.
'SPECIALLY NOT IF I HAD ONE OF MY OWN TO LOOK OUT FOR.
BUT THAT'S A LOT OF MAYBES, VIV.
AIN'T THAT WHAT LIFE IS, HONEY? A WHOLE LOT OF MAYBES, ONE AFTER ANOTHER? YOU JUST GOTTA HAVE FAITH AND STICK TO YOUR PLAN...

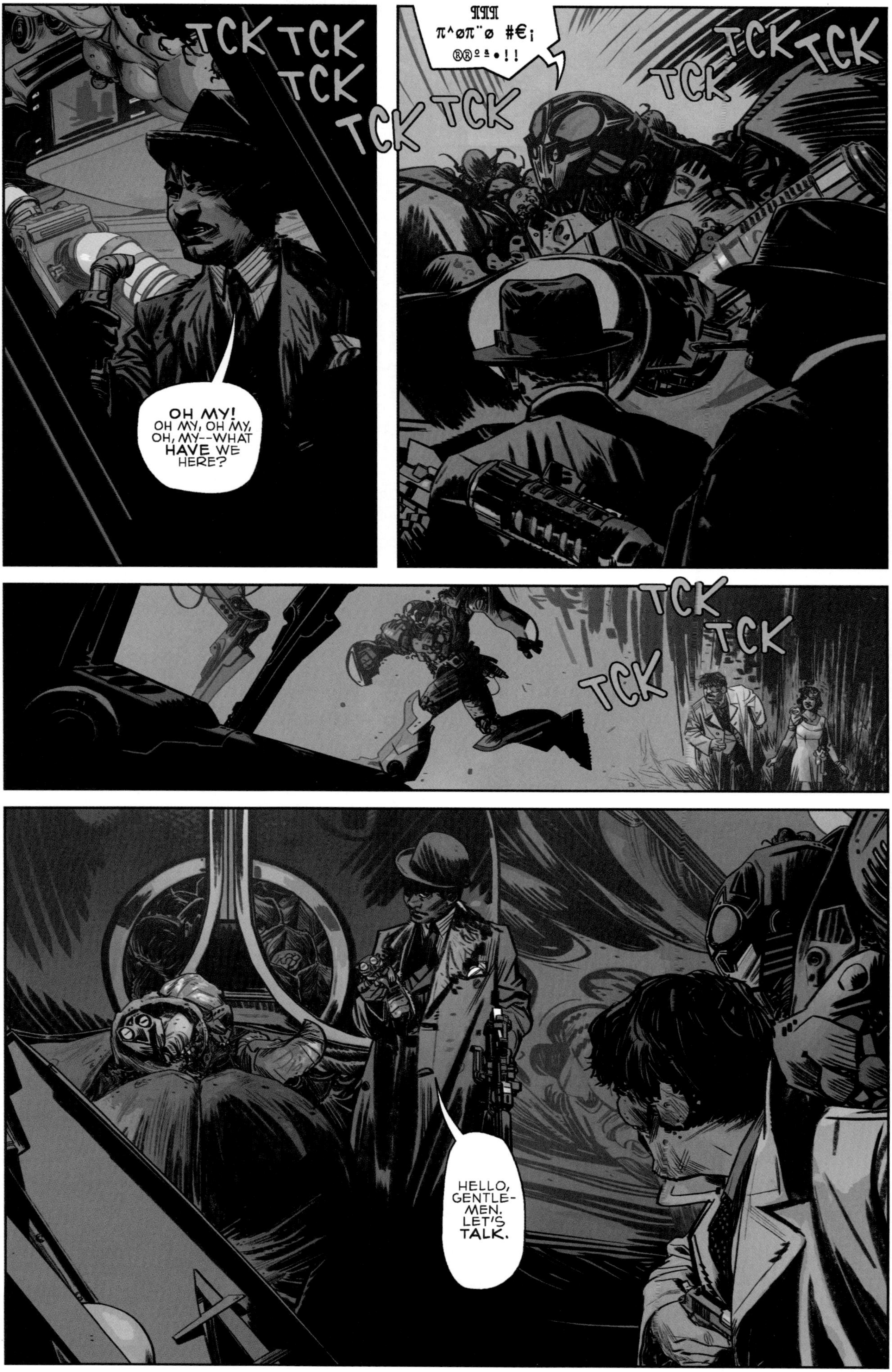
TCK TCK TCK TCK TCK
OH MY! OH MY, OH MY, OH, MY--WHAT HAVE WE HERE?
¶¶¶ π^øπ¨ø #€¡ ®®ºª•!!
TCK TCK TCK TCK
TCK TCK TCK
HELLO, GENTLE-MEN. LET'S TALK.

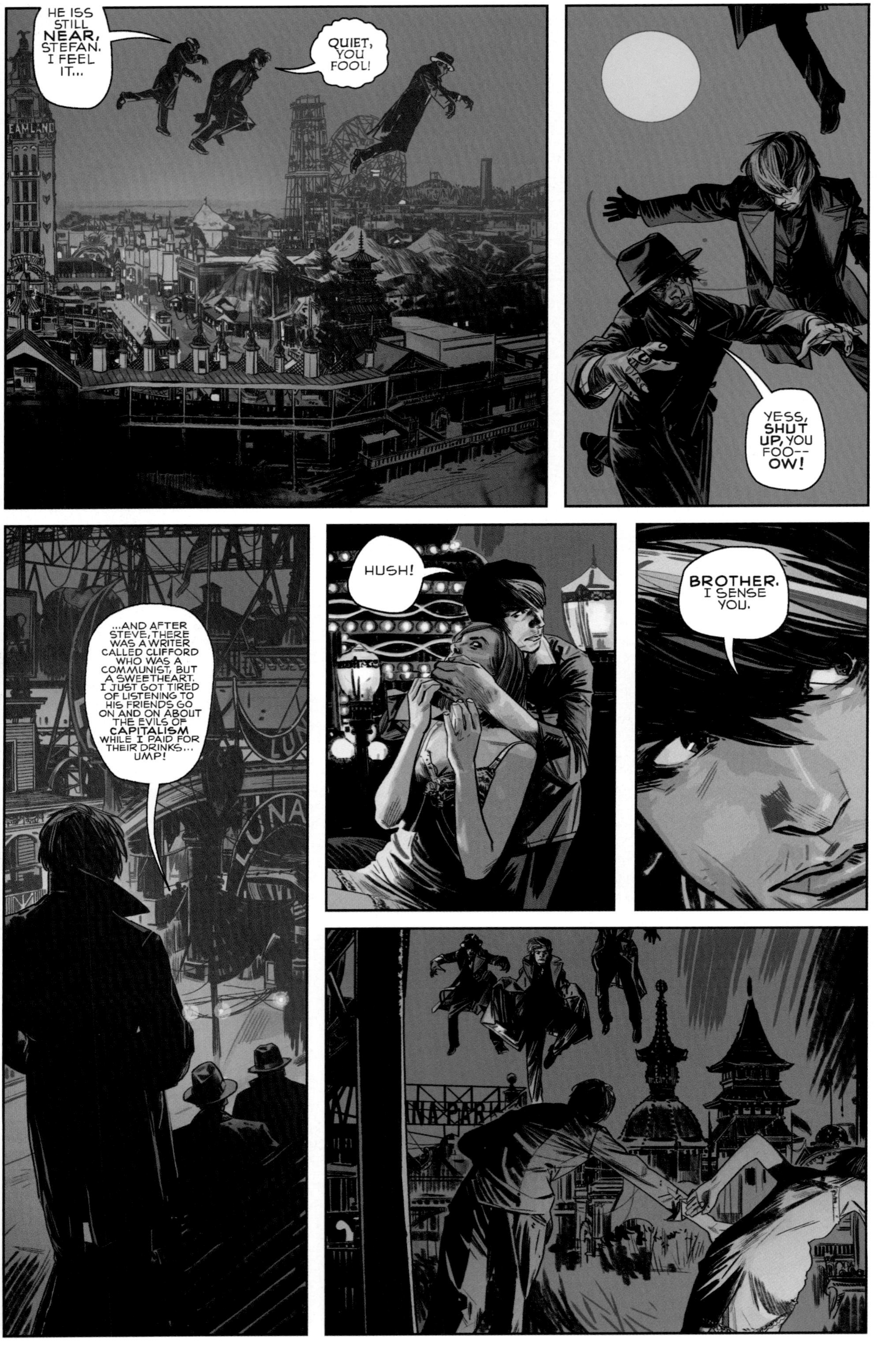
HE ISS STILL NEAR, STEFAN. I FEEL IT...
QUIET, YOU FOOL!
YESS, SHUT UP, YOU FOO-- OW!
...AND AFTER STEVE, THERE WAS A WRITER CALLED CLIFFORD WHO WAS A COMMUNIST, BUT A SWEETHEART. I JUST GOT TIRED OF LISTENING TO HIS FRIENDS GO ON AND ON ABOUT THE EVILS OF CAPITALISM WHILE I PAID FOR THEIR DRINKS... UMP!
HUSH!
BROTHER. I SENSE YOU.

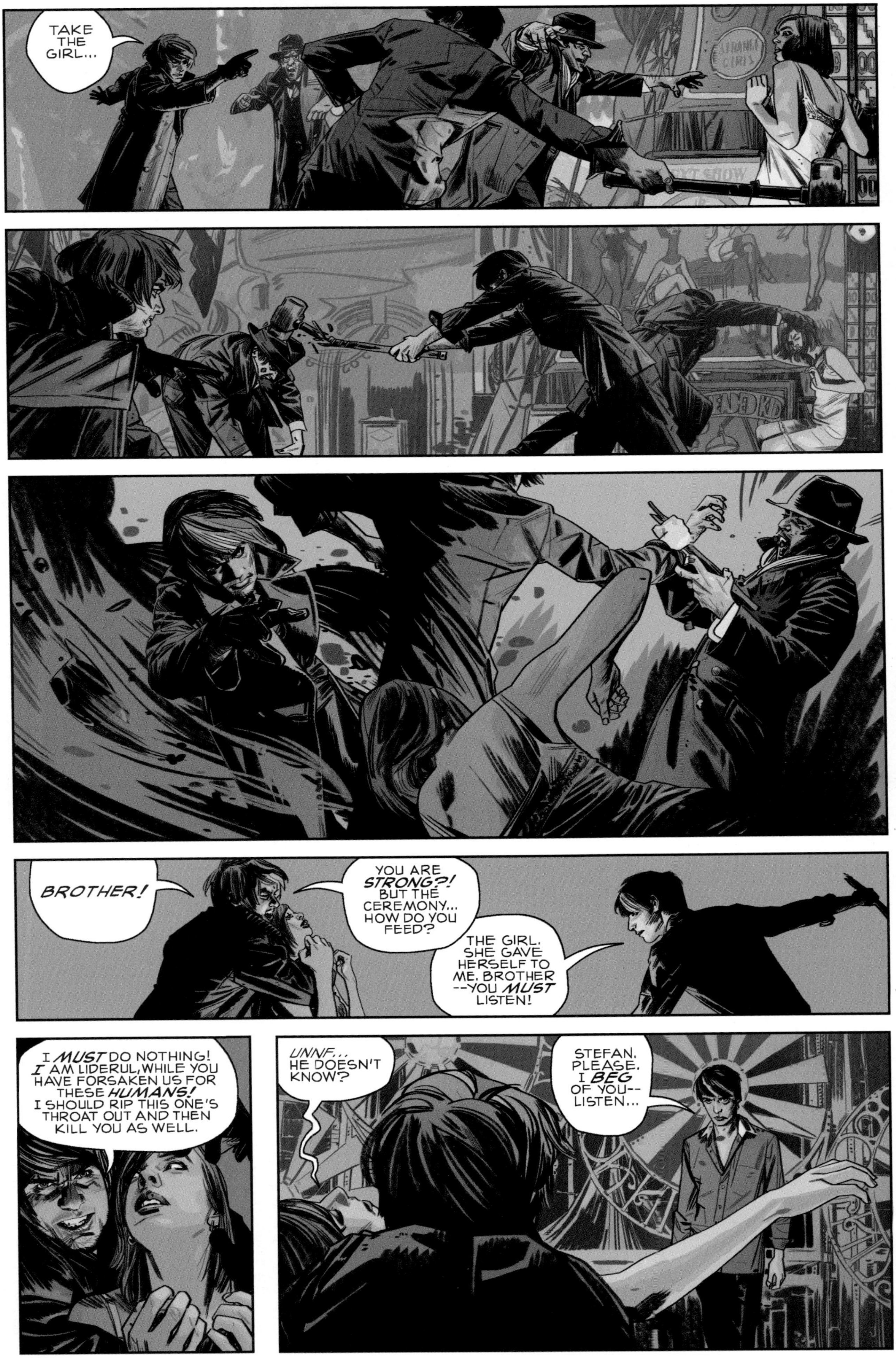
TAKE THE GIRL...
BROTHER!
YOU ARE *STRONG?!* BUT THE CEREMONY... HOW DO YOU FEED?
THE GIRL. SHE GAVE HERSELF TO ME. BROTHER --YOU *MUST* LISTEN!
I *MUST* DO NOTHING! *I* AM LIDERUL, WHILE YOU HAVE FORSAKEN US FOR THESE *HUMANS!* I SHOULD RIP THIS ONE'S THROAT OUT AND THEN KILL YOU AS WELL.
UNNF... *HE DOESN'T KNOW?*
STEFAN. PLEASE. I *BEG* OF YOU-- LISTEN...

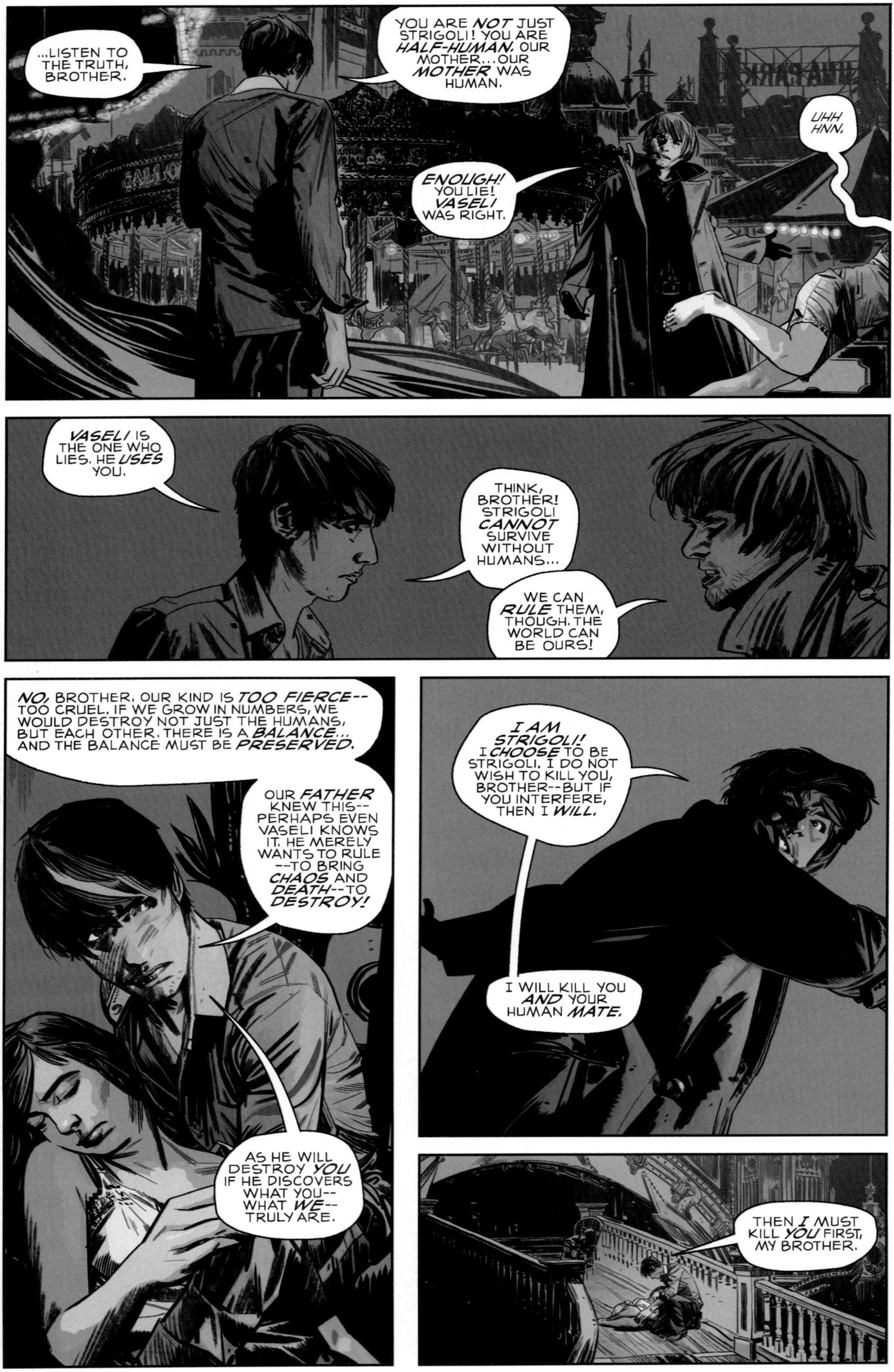
...LISTEN TO THE TRUTH, BROTHER.
YOU ARE NOT JUST STRIGOLI! YOU ARE HALF-HUMAN. OUR MOTHER... OUR MOTHER WAS HUMAN.
UHH HNN.
ENOUGH! YOU LIE! VASELI WAS RIGHT.
VASELI IS THE ONE WHO LIES. HE USES YOU.
THINK, BROTHER! STRIGOLI CANNOT SURVIVE WITHOUT HUMANS...
WE CAN RULE THEM, THOUGH. THE WORLD CAN BE OURS!
NO, BROTHER. OUR KIND IS TOO FIERCE--TOO CRUEL. IF WE GROW IN NUMBERS, WE WOULD DESTROY NOT JUST THE HUMANS, BUT EACH OTHER. THERE IS A BALANCE... AND THE BALANCE MUST BE PRESERVED.
OUR FATHER KNEW THIS--PERHAPS EVEN VASELI KNOWS IT. HE MERELY WANTS TO RULE--TO BRING CHAOS AND DEATH--TO DESTROY!
AS HE WILL DESTROY YOU IF HE DISCOVERS WHAT YOU--WHAT WE--TRULY ARE.
I AM STRIGOLI! I CHOOSE TO BE STRIGOLI. I DO NOT WISH TO KILL YOU, BROTHER--BUT IF YOU INTERFERE, THEN I WILL.
I WILL KILL YOU AND YOUR HUMAN MATE.
THEN I MUST KILL YOU FIRST, MY BROTHER.

YOU THREATEN SOMEONE'S *FAMILY,* YOU KNOW IT AIN'T GOING TO END WELL.

DID *HE* TELL YOU 'BOUT THIS *NURSERY* OF HIS?

NO. BUT THAT *DON'T* MEAN WE CAN'T *TRUST* HIM.

THE *HELL* IT DON'T! HE BEEN PLAY-ING YOU, EDDIE.

USING US TO GRAB ENOUGH ICE TO POWER THIS *SPACE-PLANE* OF HIS SO HE CAN FLY BACK TO WHEREVER HE CAME FROM AND LEAVE *US* AS GOOD AS DEAD...

¢ # ∞

• ª • o

_ ª ª!

NO! ꟻꟻꟻ S •§ ªªªª•ª–#! I CAN HANDLE THIS...

WHICH SIDE *YOU* ON, NOW, EDDIE?

YOU DON'T EXACKLY LOOK *HUMAN* NO MORE...YOU EVEN SPEAK THAT SPACE-TALK--SURE *YOU* AIN'T PLANNING ON LEAV-ING US ALL BEHIND AND HEAD-ING OFF WITH YOUR NEW BEST FRIEND?

MAYBE I *DON'T* LOOK IT...

...BUT I'M MORE HUMAN THAN YOU RIGHT NOW...PUT THE GUN DOWN, KANE. I DON'T *WANT* TO KILL YOU--

--BUT UNLESS YOU TAKE YOUR FINGER *OFF* THAT TRIGGER, YOU'RE A DEAD MAN...

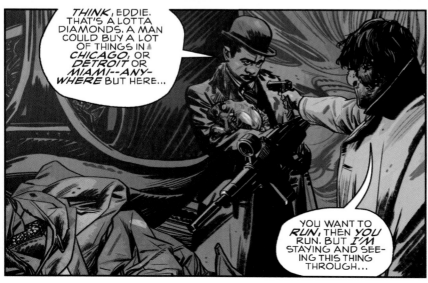

THINK, EDDIE. THAT'S A LOTTA DIAMONDS. A MAN COULD BUY A LOT OF THINGS IN *CHICAGO,* OR *DETROIT* OR *MIAMI*--ANY-WHERE BUT HERE...

YOU WANT TO *RUN,* THEN *YOU* RUN. BUT *I'M* STAYING AND SEE-ING THIS THING THROUGH...

SO PUT DOWN THAT GUN, OR I *WILL* KILL YOU, KANE.

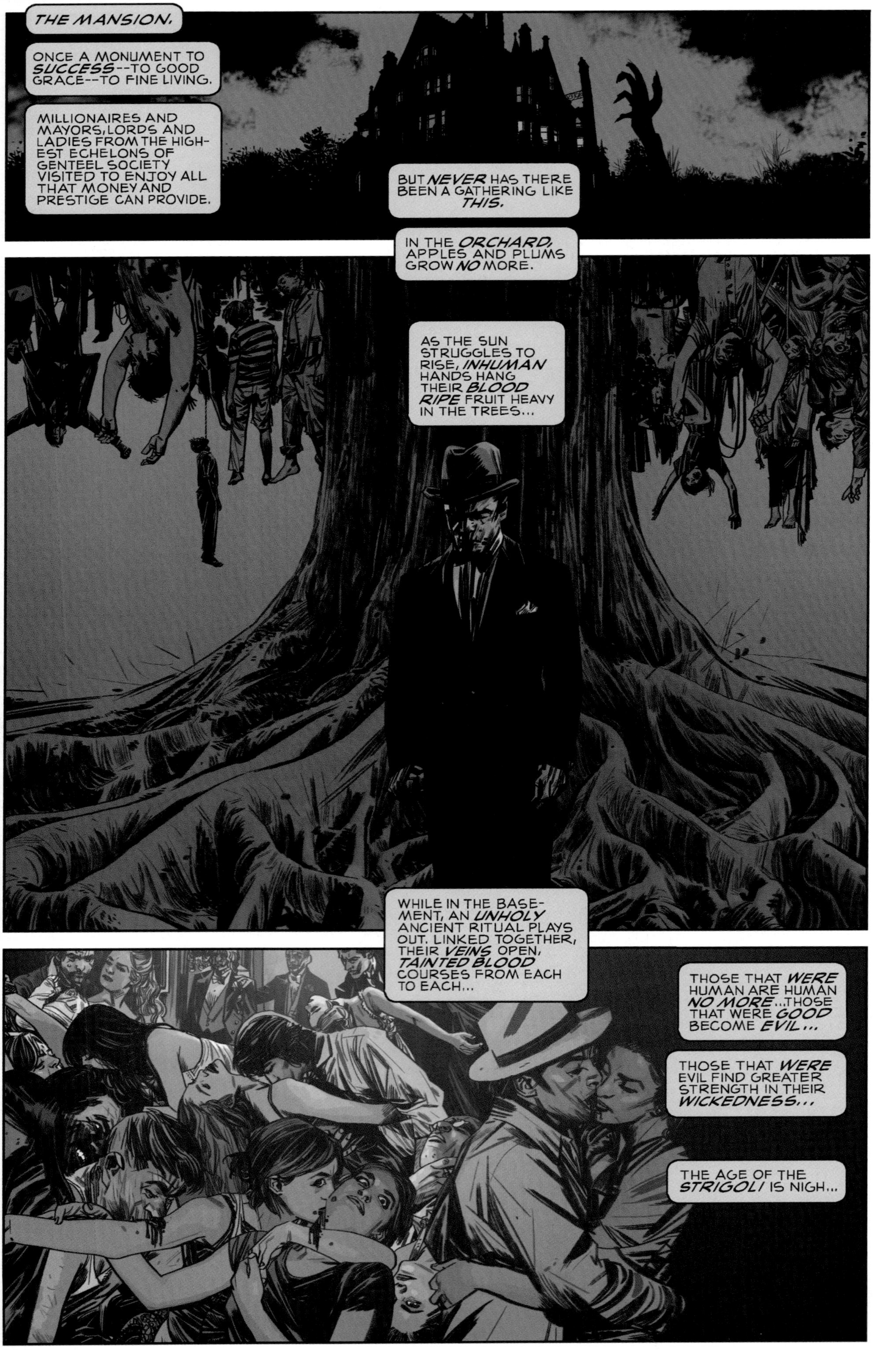
THE MANSION.
ONCE A MONUMENT TO SUCCESS--TO GOOD GRACE--TO FINE LIVING.
MILLIONAIRES AND MAYORS, LORDS AND LADIES FROM THE HIGHEST ECHELONS OF GENTEEL SOCIETY VISITED TO ENJOY ALL THAT MONEY AND PRESTIGE CAN PROVIDE.
BUT NEVER HAS THERE BEEN A GATHERING LIKE THIS.
IN THE ORCHARD, APPLES AND PLUMS GROW NO MORE.
AS THE SUN STRUGGLES TO RISE, INHUMAN HANDS HANG THEIR BLOOD RIPE FRUIT HEAVY IN THE TREES...
WHILE IN THE BASEMENT, AN UNHOLY ANCIENT RITUAL PLAYS OUT. LINKED TOGETHER, THEIR VEINS OPEN, TAINTED BLOOD COURSES FROM EACH TO EACH...
THOSE THAT WERE HUMAN ARE HUMAN NO MORE...THOSE THAT WERE GOOD BECOME EVIL...
THOSE THAT WERE EVIL FIND GREATER STRENGTH IN THEIR WICKEDNESS...
THE AGE OF THE STRIGOI IS NIGH...

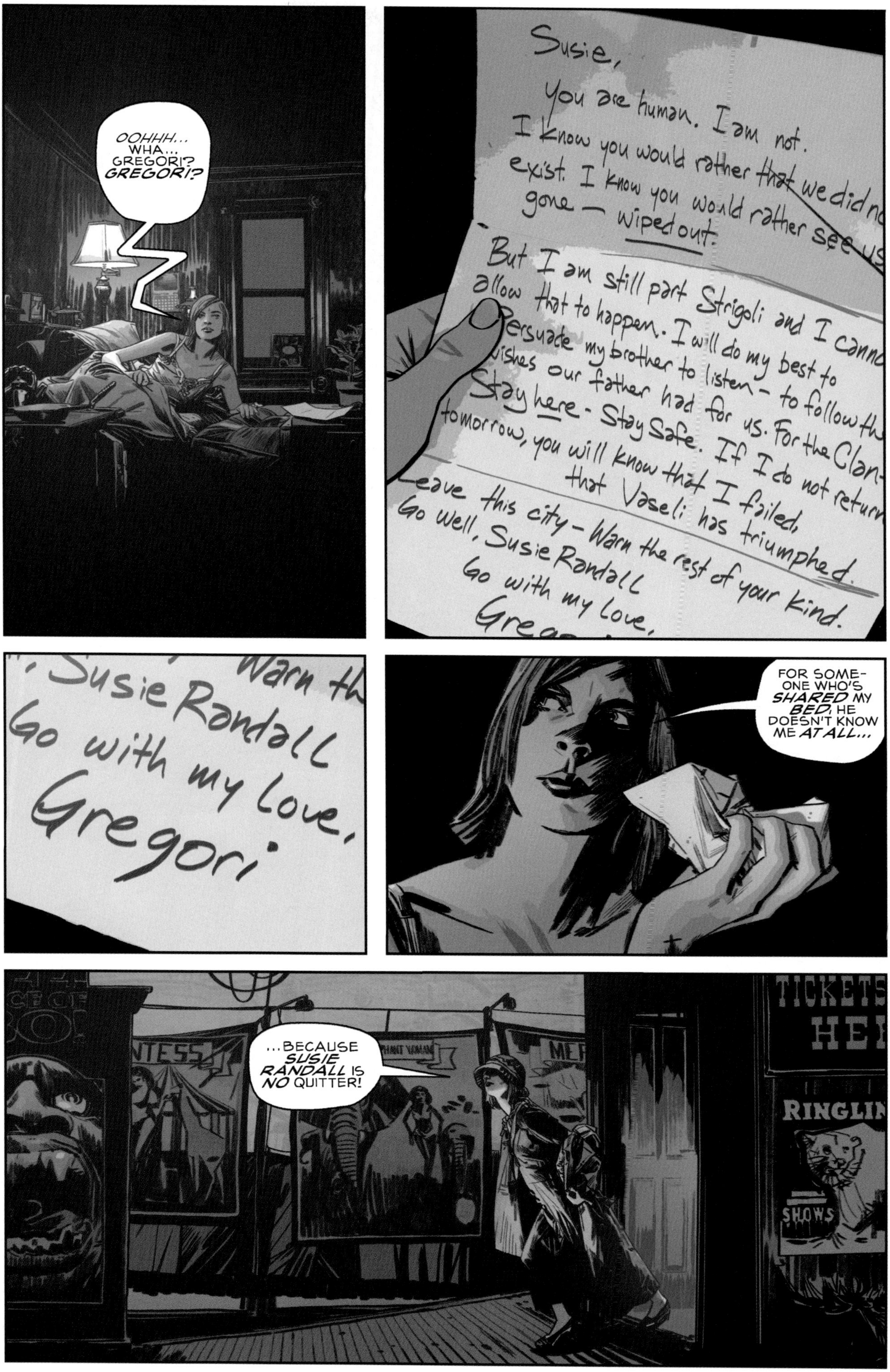
OOHHH... WHA... GREGORI? GREGORI?
Susie,
You are human. I am not.
I know you would rather that we did
exist. I know you would rather see us
gone — wiped out.
But I am still part Strigoli and I can
allow that to happen. I will do my best to
persuade my brother to listen – to follow th
wishes our father had for us. For the Clan –
Stay here - Stay Safe. If I do not return
tomorrow, you will know that I failed,
that Vaseli has triumphed.
Leave this city – Warn the rest of your kind.
Go well, Susie Randall
Go with my Love,
Susie Randall
Go with my Love,
Gregori
FOR SOMEONE WHO'S SHARED MY BED, HE DOESN'T KNOW ME AT ALL...
...BECAUSE SUSIE RANDALL IS NO QUITTER!
TICKETS
RINGLIN
SHOWS

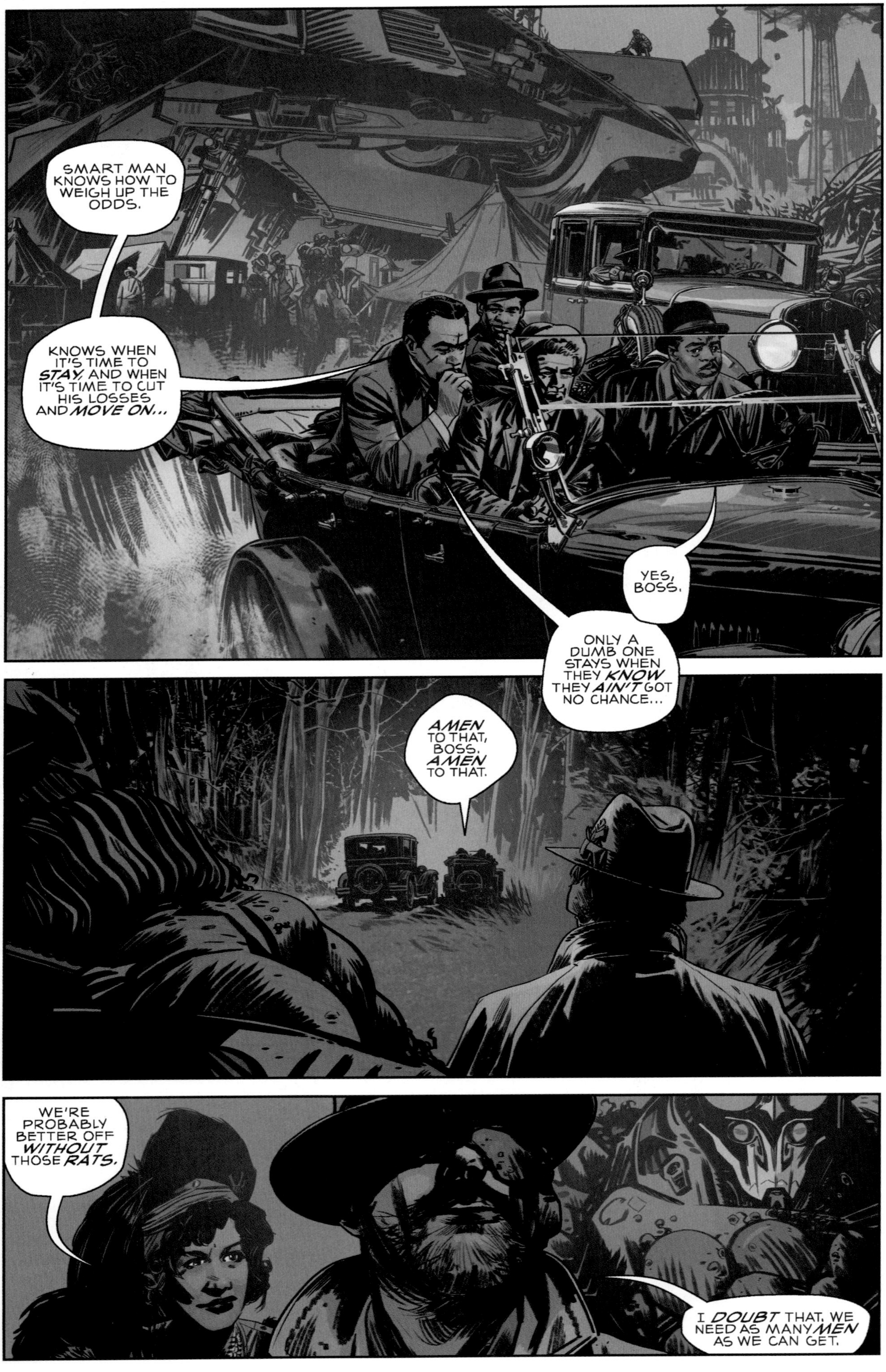
SMART MAN KNOWS HOW TO WEIGH UP THE ODDS.
KNOWS WHEN IT'S TIME TO STAY, AND WHEN IT'S TIME TO CUT HIS LOSSES AND MOVE ON...
YES, BOSS.
ONLY A DUMB ONE STAYS WHEN THEY KNOW THEY AIN'T GOT NO CHANCE...
AMEN TO THAT, BOSS. AMEN TO THAT.
WE'RE PROBABLY BETTER OFF WITHOUT THOSE RATS.
I DOUBT THAT. WE NEED AS MANY MEN AS WE CAN GET.

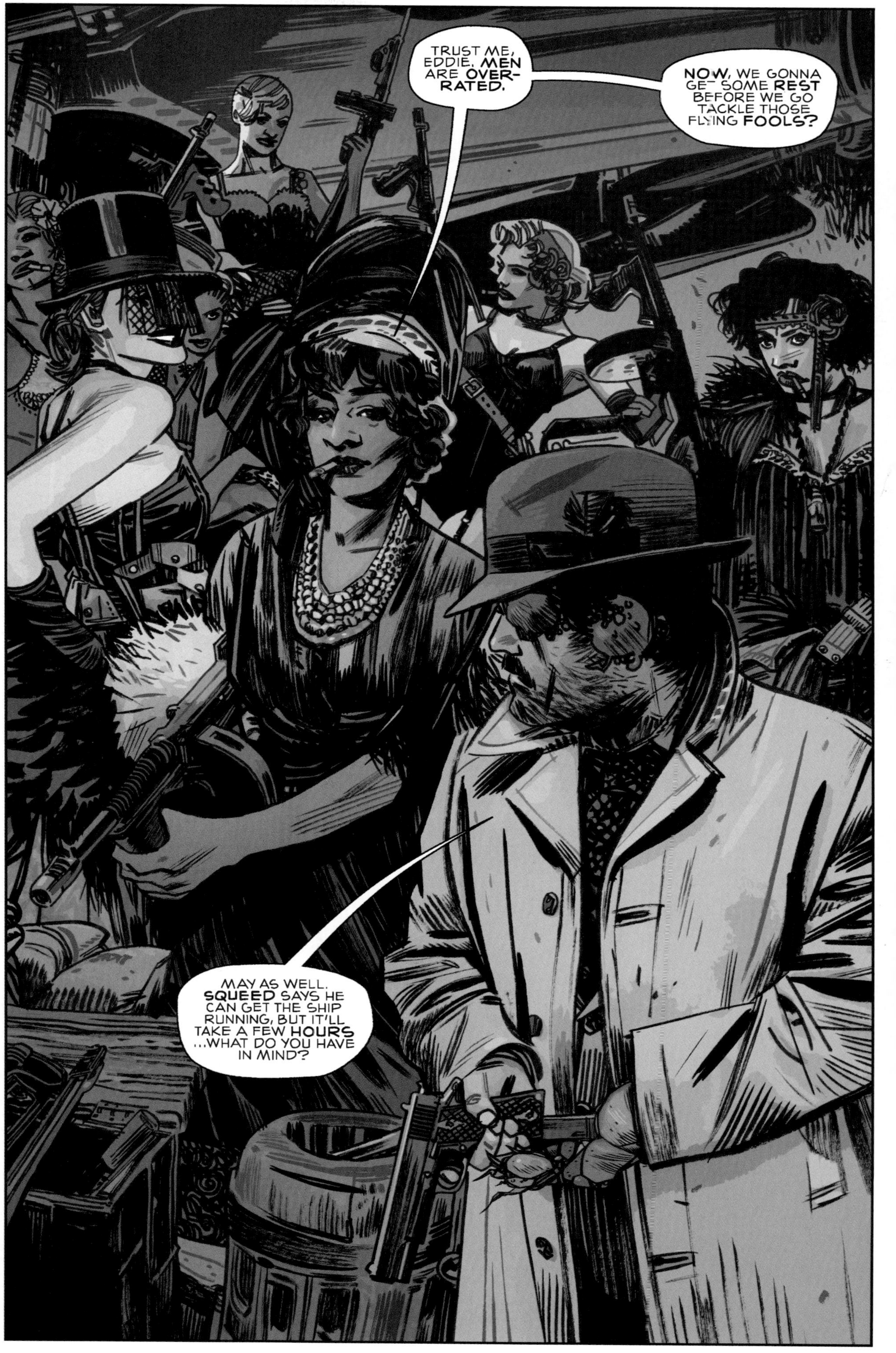
TRUST ME, EDDIE. MEN ARE OVER-RATED.
NOW, WE GONNA GET SOME REST BEFORE WE GO TACKLE THOSE FLYING FOOLS?
MAY AS WELL. SQUEED SAYS HE CAN GET THE SHIP RUNNING, BUT IT'LL TAKE A FEW HOURS ...WHAT DO YOU HAVE IN MIND?

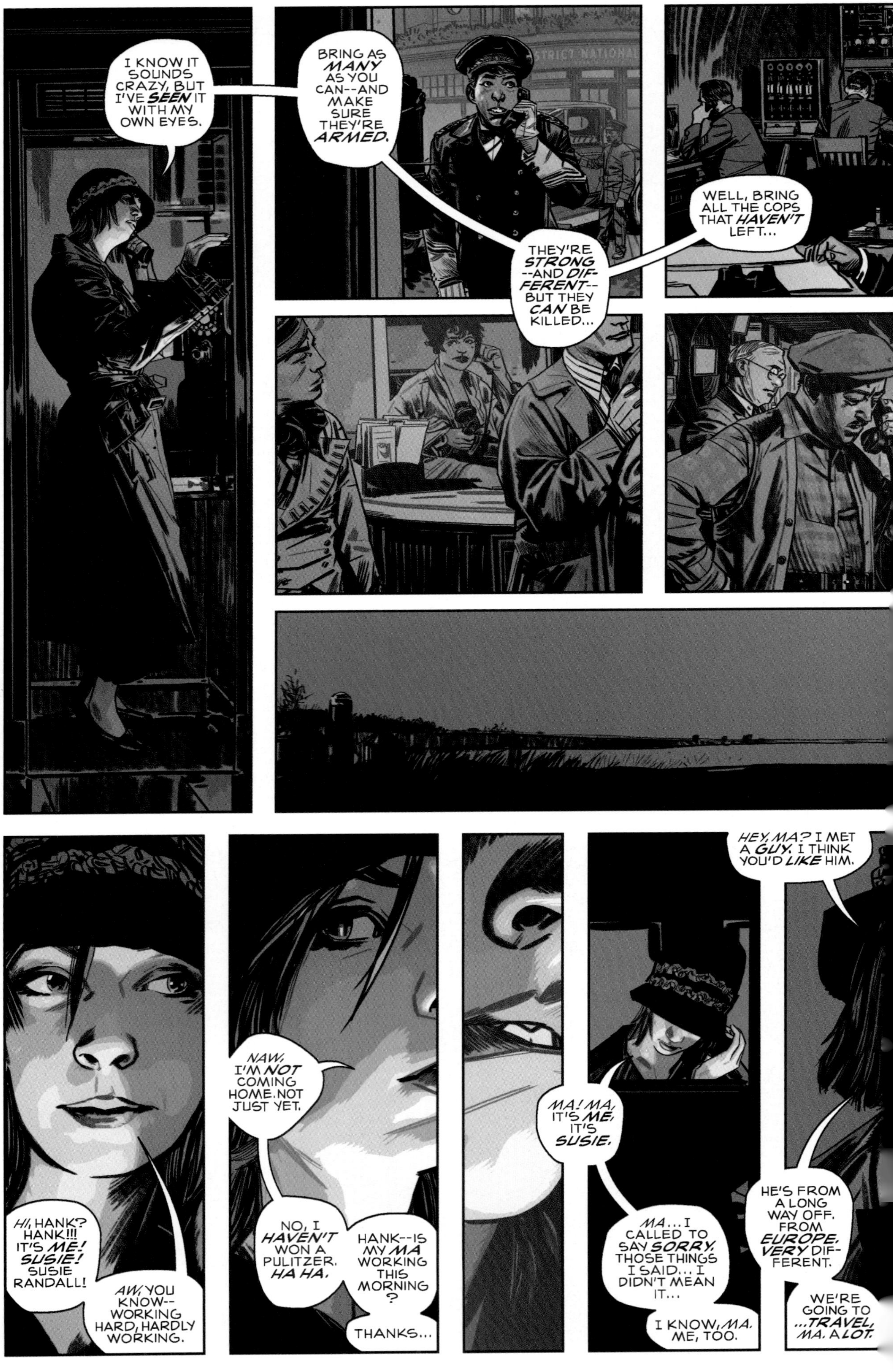
I KNOW IT SOUNDS CRAZY, BUT I'VE SEEN IT WITH MY OWN EYES.
BRING AS MANY AS YOU CAN--AND MAKE SURE THEY'RE ARMED.
THEY'RE STRONG --AND DIFFERENT-- BUT THEY CAN BE KILLED...
WELL, BRING ALL THE COPS THAT HAVEN'T LEFT...
HI, HANK? HANK!!! IT'S ME! SUSIE! SUSIE RANDALL!
AW, YOU KNOW-- WORKING HARD, HARDLY WORKING.
NAW, I'M NOT COMING HOME. NOT JUST YET.
NO, I HAVEN'T WON A PULITZER. HA HA.
HANK--IS MY MA WORKING THIS MORNING?
THANKS...
MA! MA, IT'S ME, IT'S SUSIE.
MA... I CALLED TO SAY SORRY. THOSE THINGS I SAID... I DIDN'T MEAN IT...
I KNOW, MA. ME, TOO.
HEY, MA? I MET A GUY. I THINK YOU'D LIKE HIM.
HE'S FROM A LONG WAY OFF. FROM EUROPE. VERY DIFFERENT.
WE'RE GOING TO ...TRAVEL, MA. A LOT.

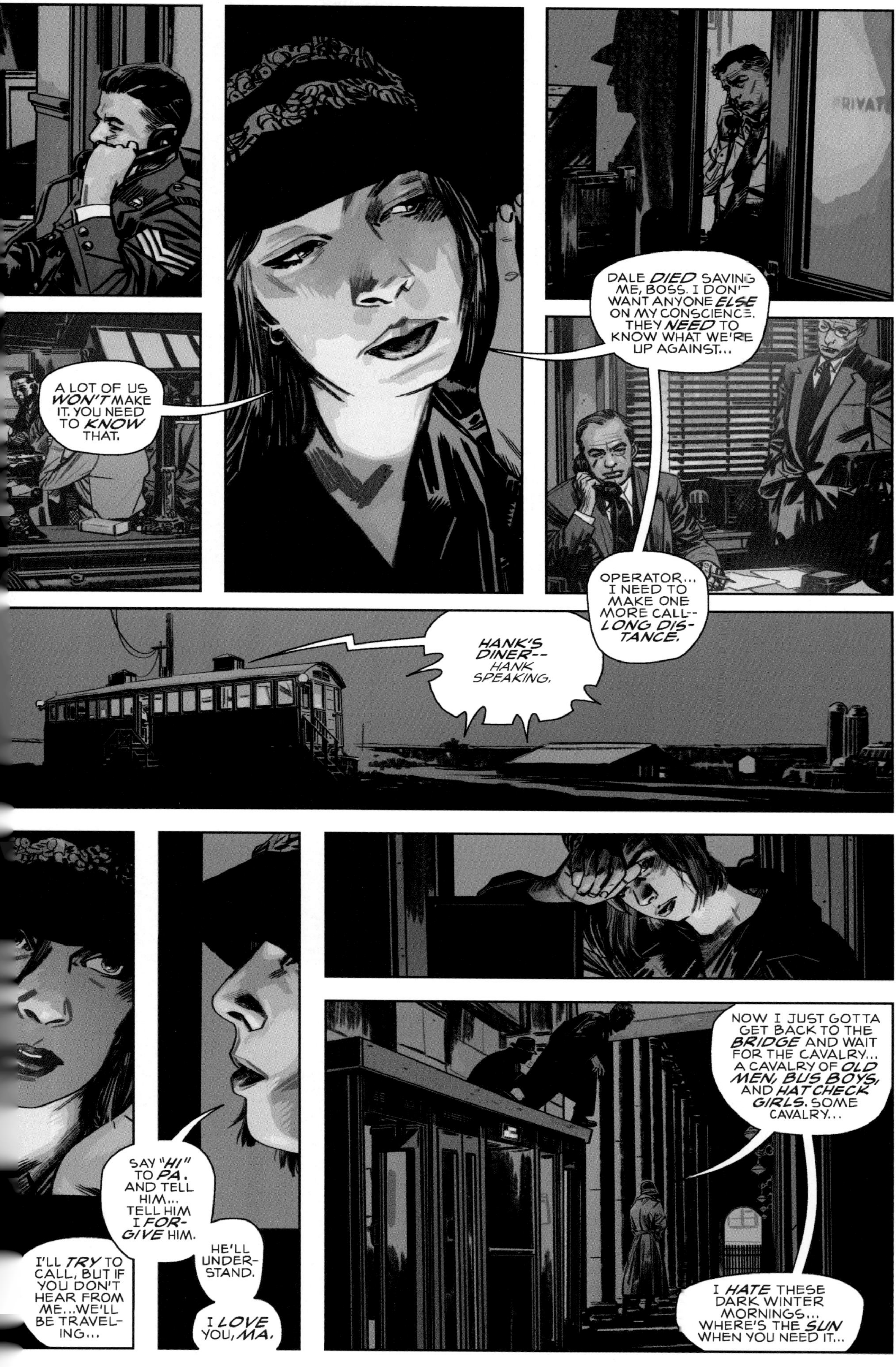
A LOT OF US WON'T MAKE IT. YOU NEED TO KNOW THAT.
DALE DIED SAVING ME, BOSS. I DON'T WANT ANYONE ELSE ON MY CONSCIENCE. THEY NEED TO KNOW WHAT WE'RE UP AGAINST...
PRIVATE
OPERATOR... I NEED TO MAKE ONE MORE CALL-- LONG DISTANCE.
HANK'S DINER-- HANK SPEAKING.
SAY "HI" TO PA. AND TELL HIM... TELL HIM I FORGIVE HIM.
I'LL TRY TO CALL, BUT IF YOU DON'T HEAR FROM ME...WE'LL BE TRAVELING...
HE'LL UNDERSTAND.
I LOVE YOU, MA.
NOW I JUST GOTTA GET BACK TO THE BRIDGE AND WAIT FOR THE CAVALRY... A CAVALRY OF OLD MEN, BUS BOYS, AND HAT CHECK GIRLS. SOME CAVALRY...
I HATE THESE DARK WINTER MORNINGS... WHERE'S THE SUN WHEN YOU NEED IT...

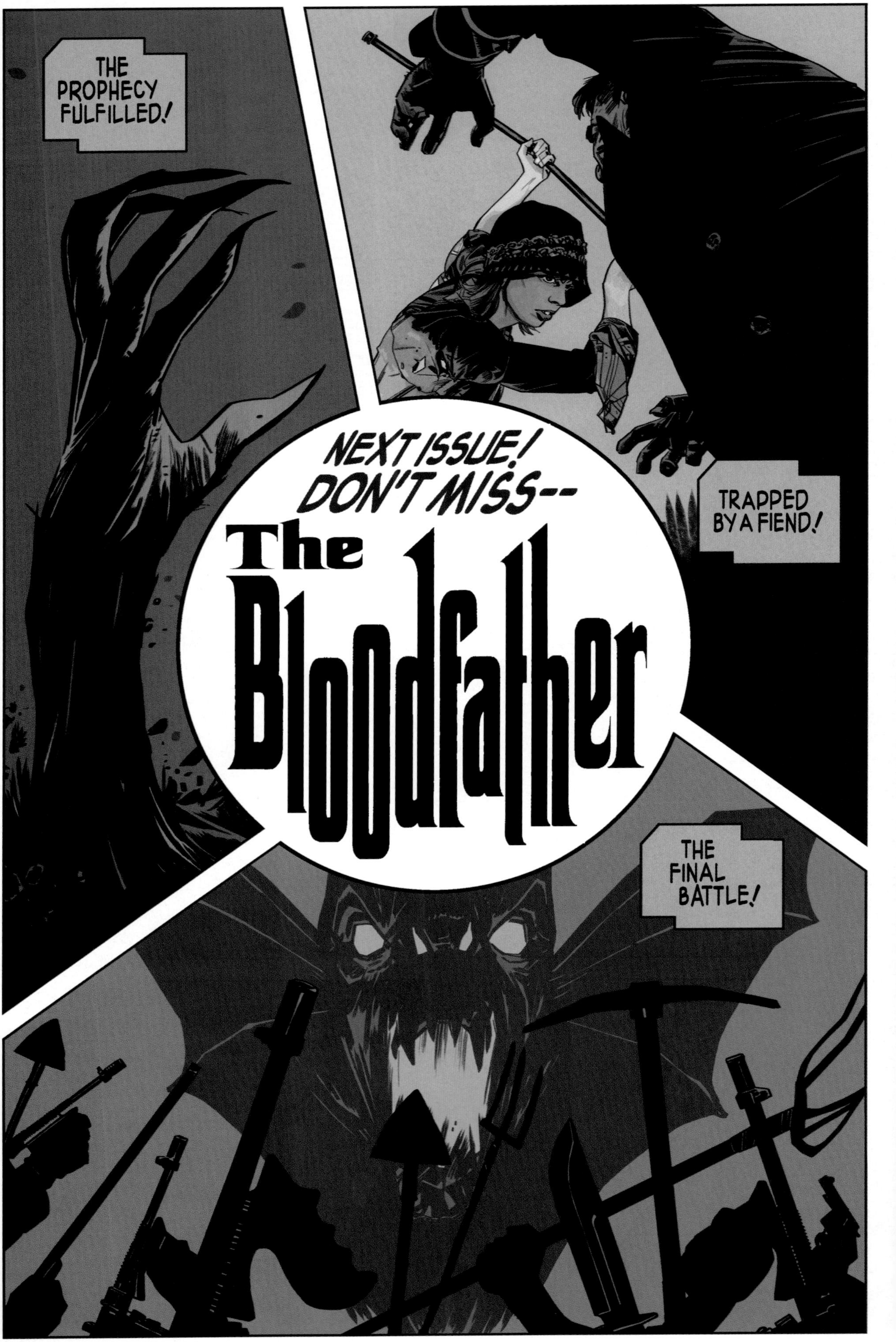

THE PROPHECY FULFILLED!
NEXT ISSUE! DON'T MISS--
The Bloodfather
TRAPPED BY A FIEND!
THE FINAL BATTLE!

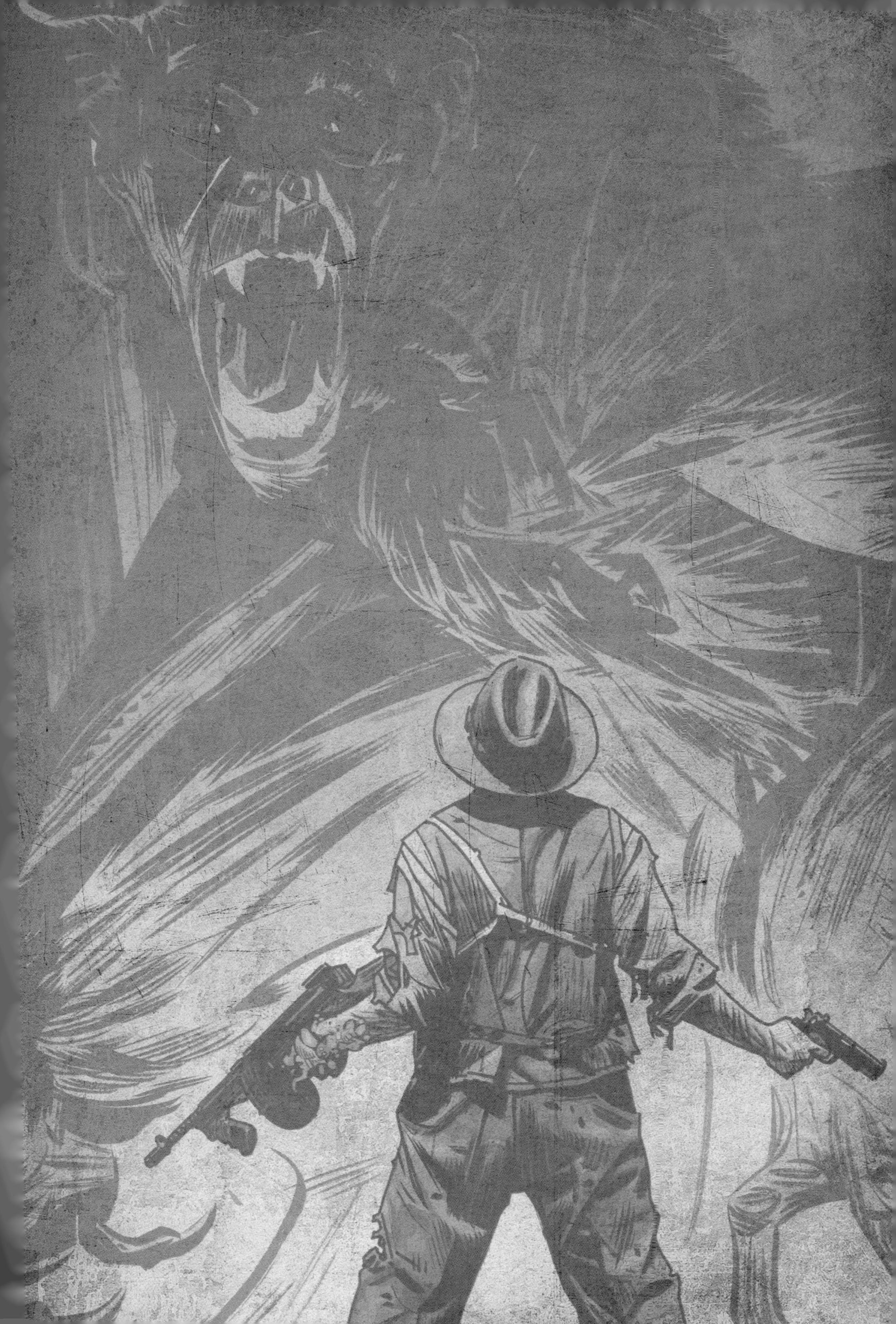

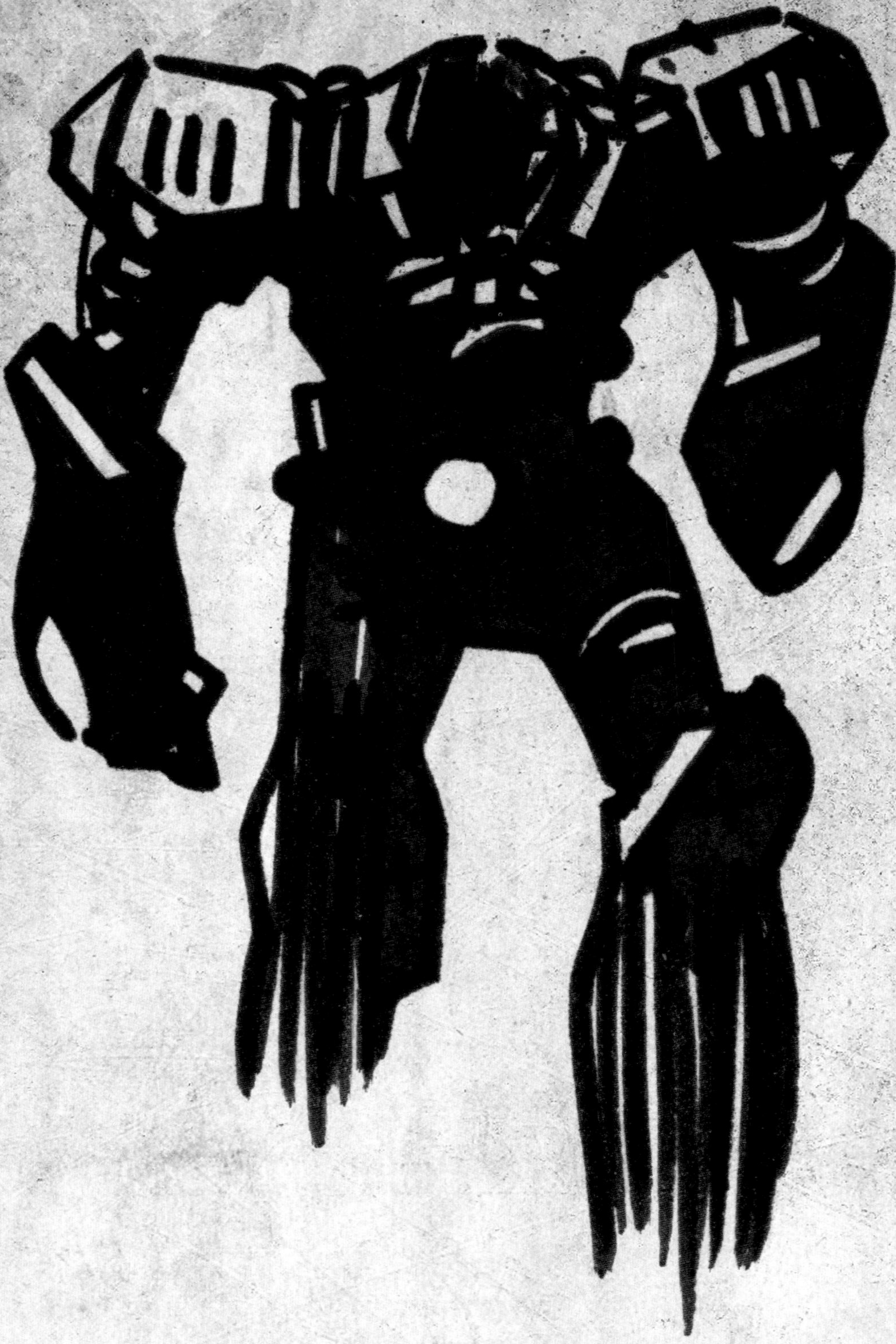

Chapter Five

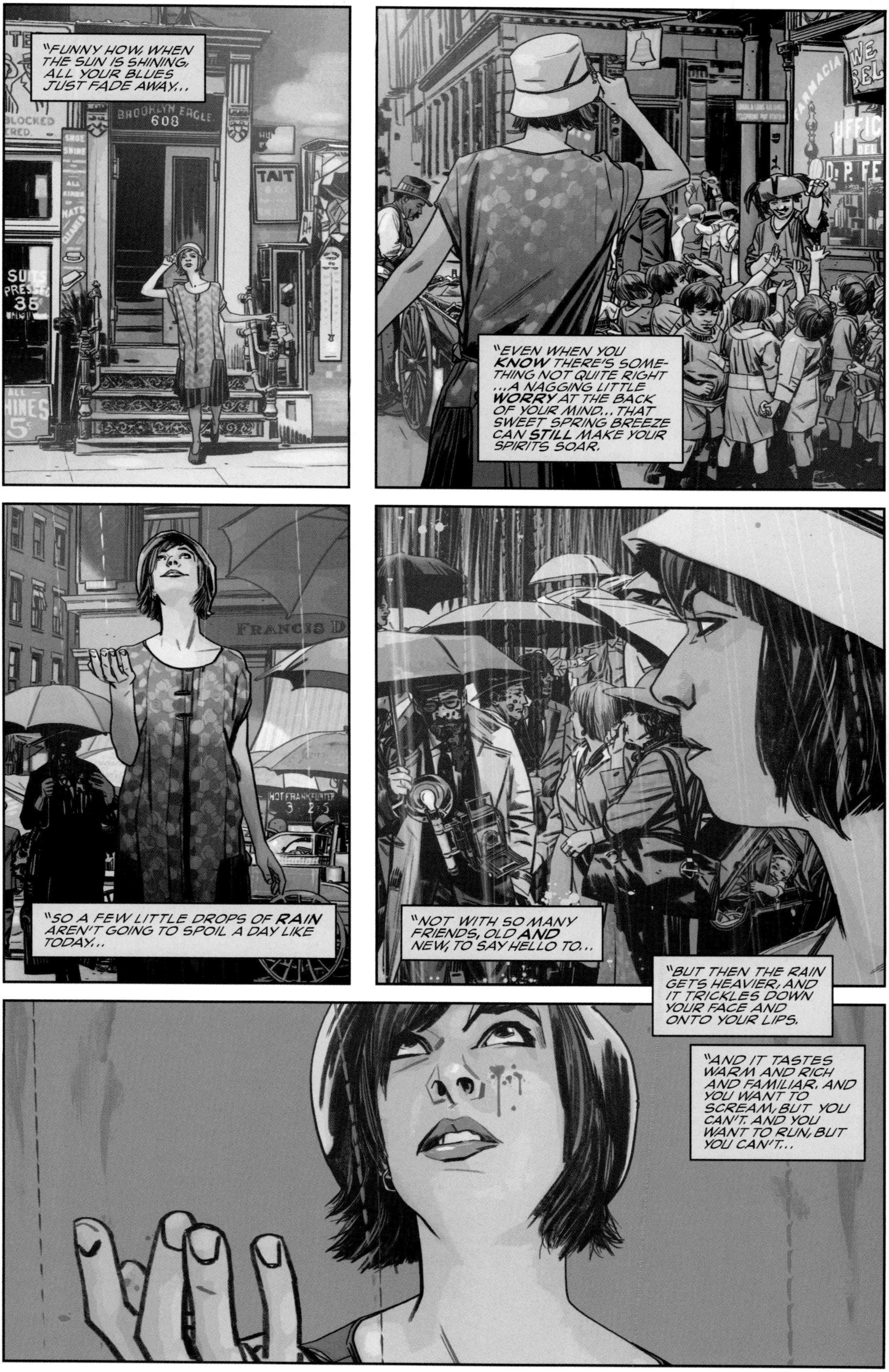
"FUNNY HOW, WHEN THE SUN IS SHINING, ALL YOUR BLUES JUST FADE AWAY...
BROOKLYN EAGLE 608
TAIT
"EVEN WHEN YOU **KNOW** THERE'S SOMETHING NOT QUITE RIGHT ...A NAGGING LITTLE **WORRY** AT THE BACK OF YOUR MIND... THAT SWEET SPRING BREEZE CAN **STILL** MAKE YOUR SPIRITS SOAR.
FARMACIA
"SO A FEW LITTLE DROPS OF **RAIN** AREN'T GOING TO SPOIL A DAY LIKE TODAY...
"NOT WITH SO MANY FRIENDS, OLD **AND** NEW, TO SAY HELLO TO...
"BUT THEN THE RAIN GETS HEAVIER, AND IT TRICKLES DOWN YOUR FACE AND ONTO YOUR LIPS.
"AND IT TASTES WARM AND RICH AND FAMILIAR. AND YOU WANT TO SCREAM, BUT YOU CAN'T. AND YOU WANT TO RUN, BUT YOU CAN'T...

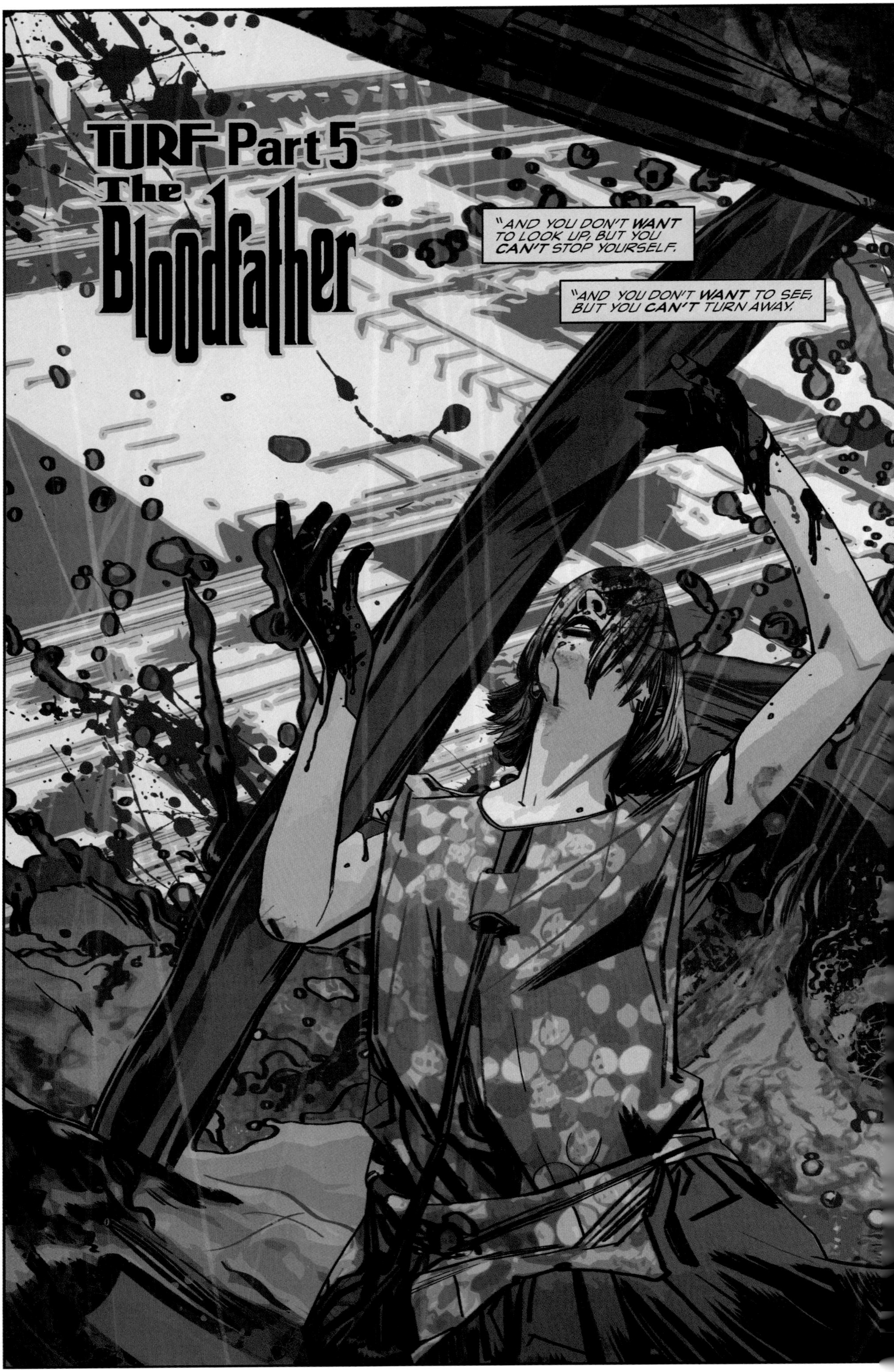

TURF Part 5
The Bloodfather
"AND YOU DON'T WANT TO LOOK UP, BUT YOU CAN'T STOP YOURSELF.
"AND YOU DON'T WANT TO SEE, BUT YOU CAN'T TURN AWAY.

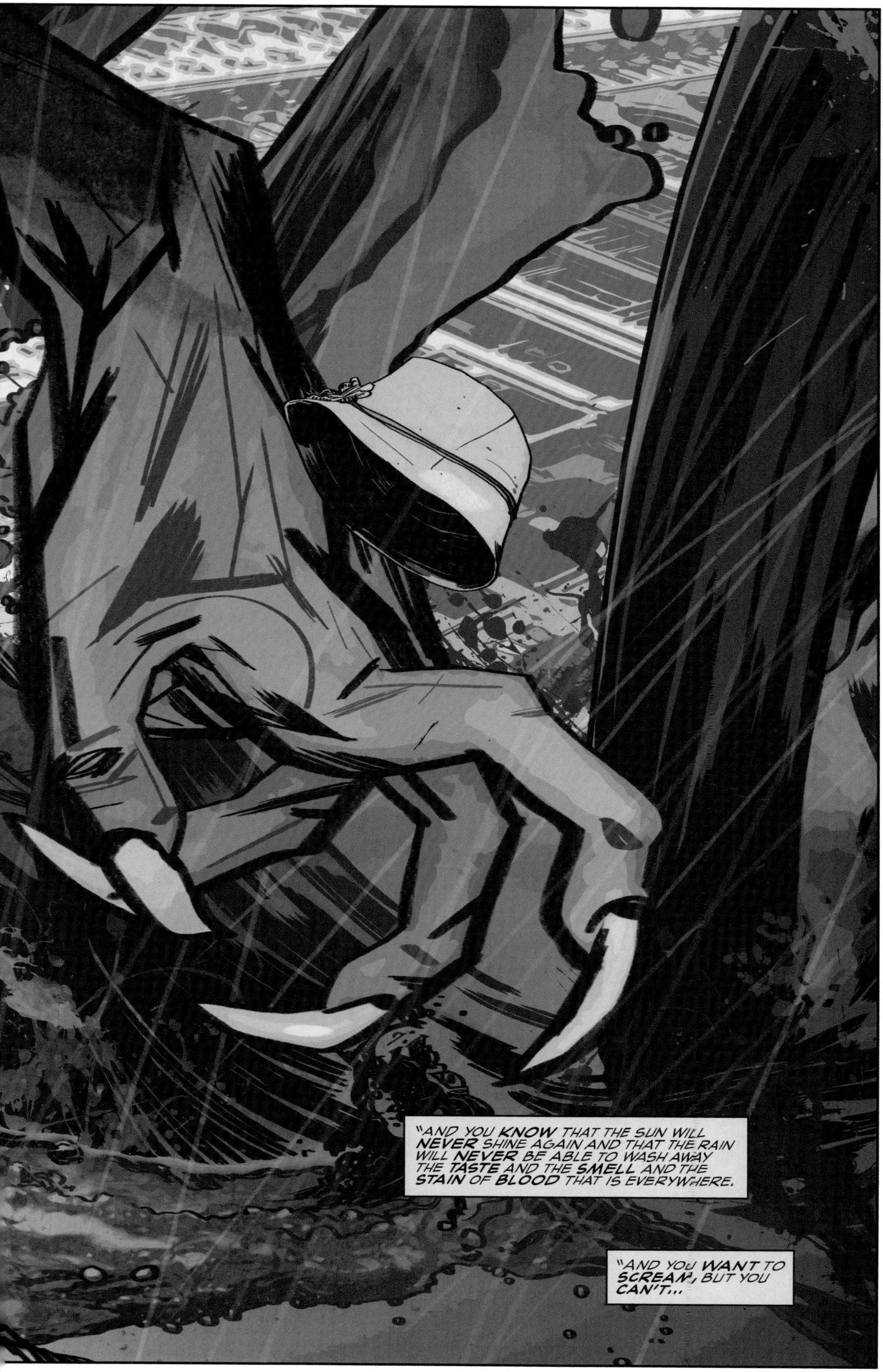
"AND YOU **KNOW** THAT THE SUN WILL **NEVER** SHINE AGAIN AND THAT THE RAIN WILL **NEVER** BE ABLE TO WASH AWAY THE **TASTE** AND THE **SMELL** AND THE **STAIN** OF **BLOOD** THAT IS EVERYWHERE.
"AND YOU **WANT** TO **SCREAM**, BUT YOU **CAN'T**...

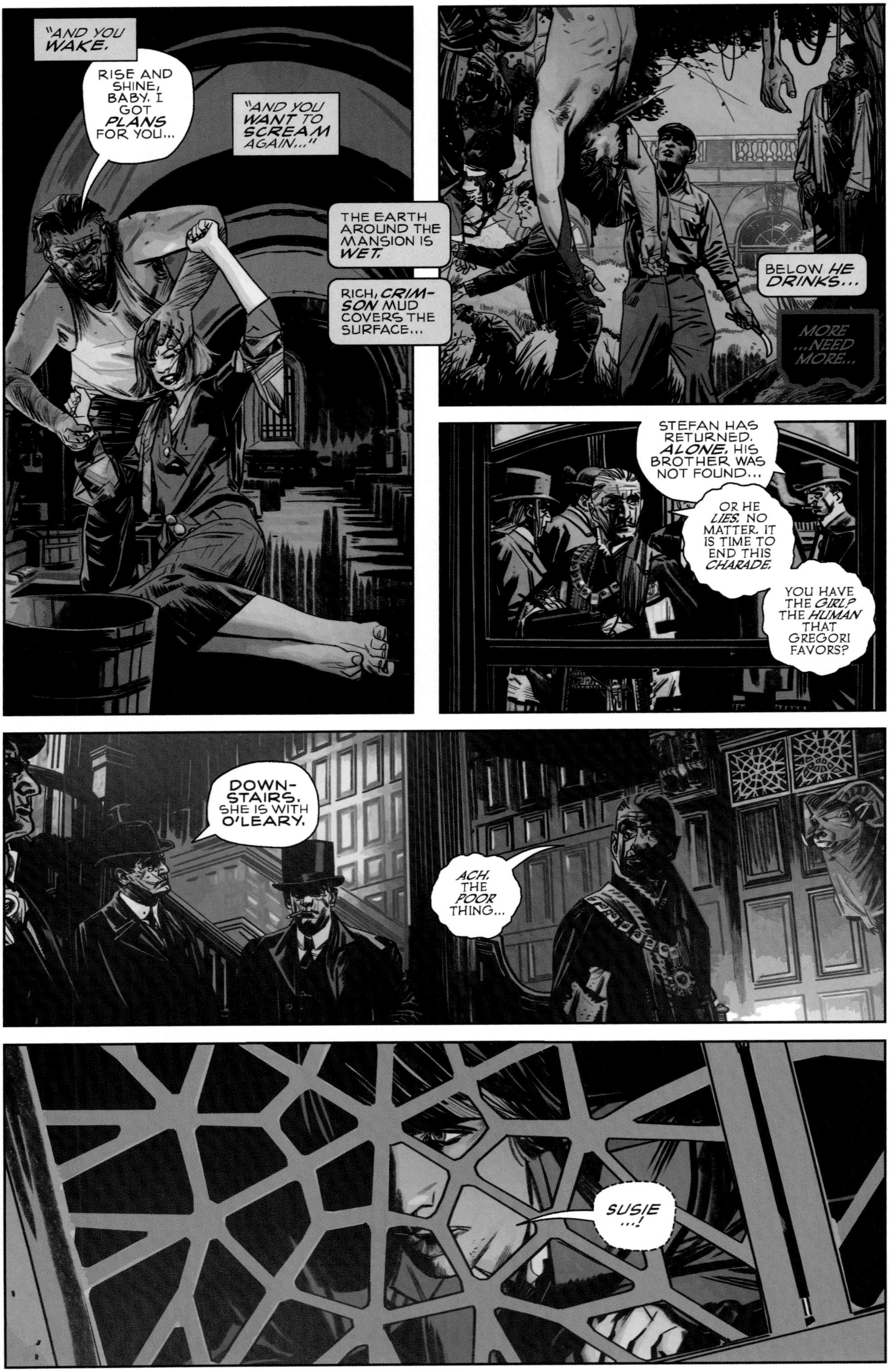

"AND YOU WAKE.
RISE AND SHINE, BABY. I GOT PLANS FOR YOU...
"AND YOU WANT TO SCREAM AGAIN..."
THE EARTH AROUND THE MANSION IS WET.
RICH, CRIMSON MUD COVERS THE SURFACE...
BELOW HE DRINKS...
MORE ...NEED MORE...
STEFAN HAS RETURNED. ALONE. HIS BROTHER WAS NOT FOUND...
OR HE LIES. NO MATTER. IT IS TIME TO END THIS CHARADE.
YOU HAVE THE GIRL? THE HUMAN THAT GREGORI FAVORS?
DOWNSTAIRS. SHE IS WITH O'LEARY.
ACH, THE POOR THING...
SUSIE ...!

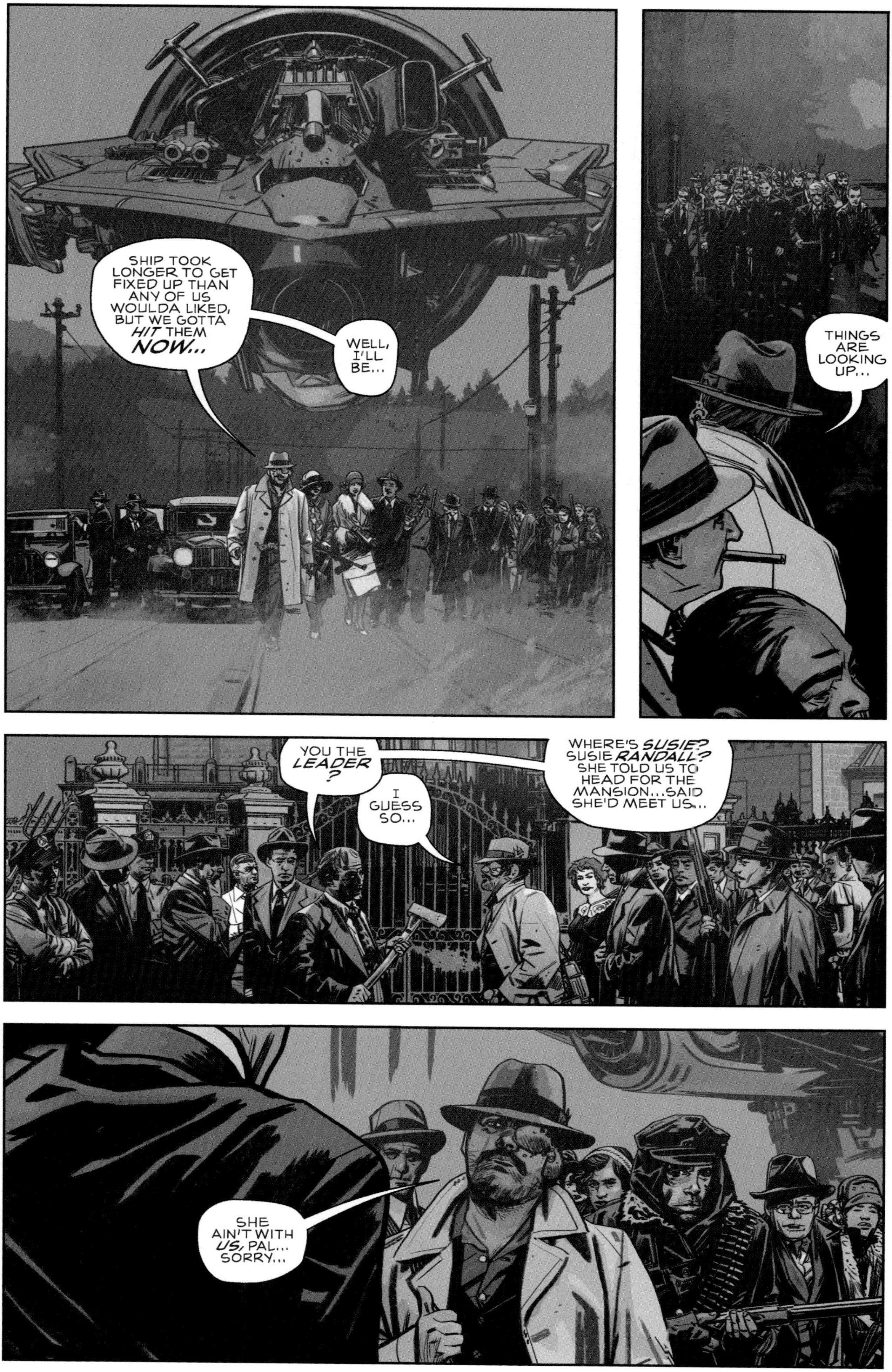
SHIP TOOK LONGER TO GET FIXED UP THAN ANY OF US WOULDA LIKED, BUT WE GOTTA HIT THEM NOW...
WELL, I'LL BE...
THINGS ARE LOOKING UP...
YOU THE LEADER?
I GUESS SO...
WHERE'S SUSIE? SUSIE RANDALL? SHE TOLD US TO HEAD FOR THE MANSION...SAID SHE'D MEET US...
SHE AIN'T WITH US, PAL... SORRY...

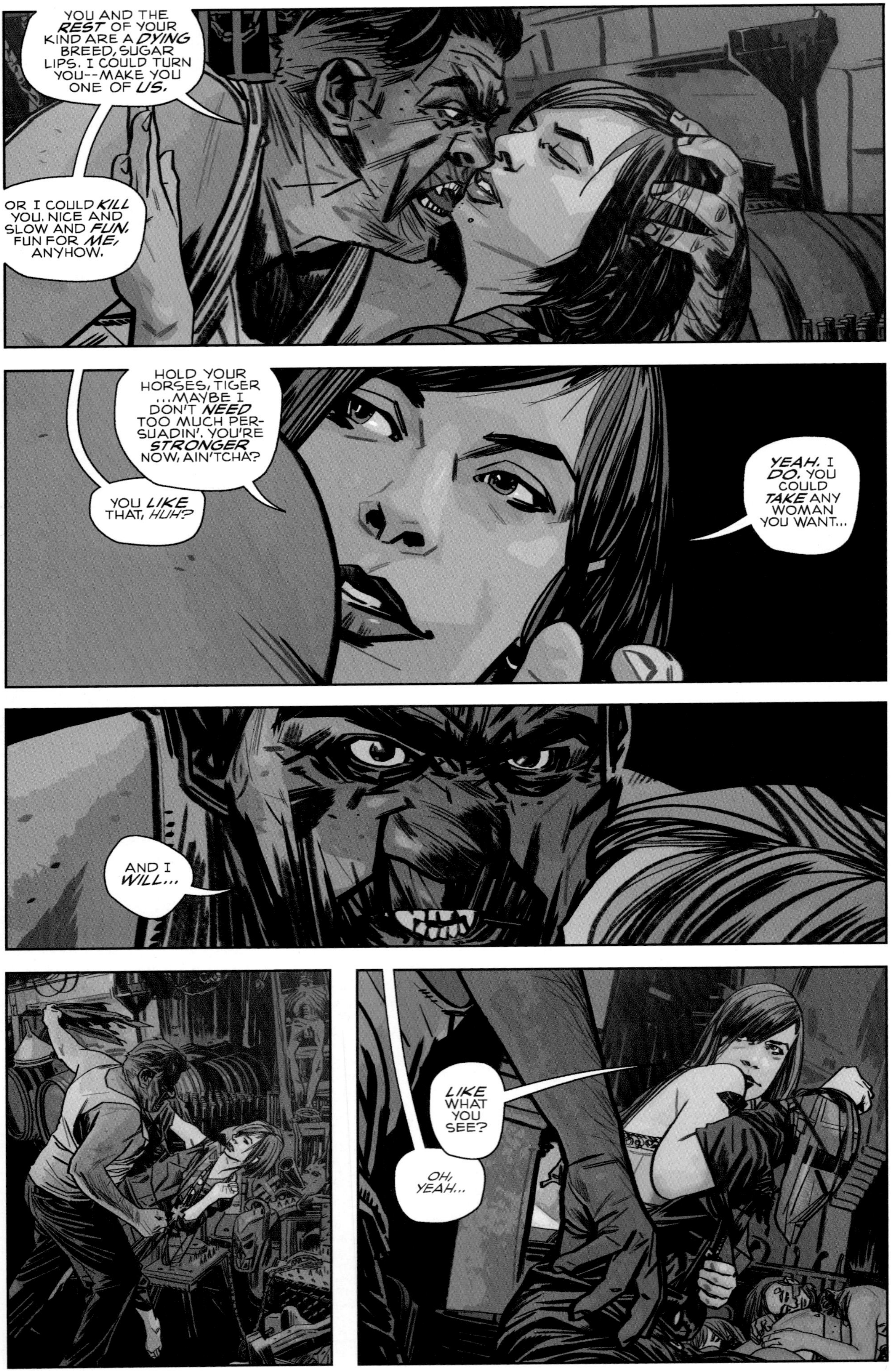
YOU AND THE REST OF YOUR KIND ARE A DYING BREED, SUGAR LIPS. I COULD TURN YOU--MAKE YOU ONE OF US.
OR I COULD KILL YOU, NICE AND SLOW AND FUN. FUN FOR ME, ANYHOW.
HOLD YOUR HORSES, TIGER ...MAYBE I DON'T NEED TOO MUCH PERSUADIN'. YOU'RE STRONGER NOW, AIN'TCHA?
YOU LIKE THAT, HUH?
YEAH. I DO. YOU COULD TAKE ANY WOMAN YOU WANT...
AND I WILL...
LIKE WHAT YOU SEE?
OH, YEAH...

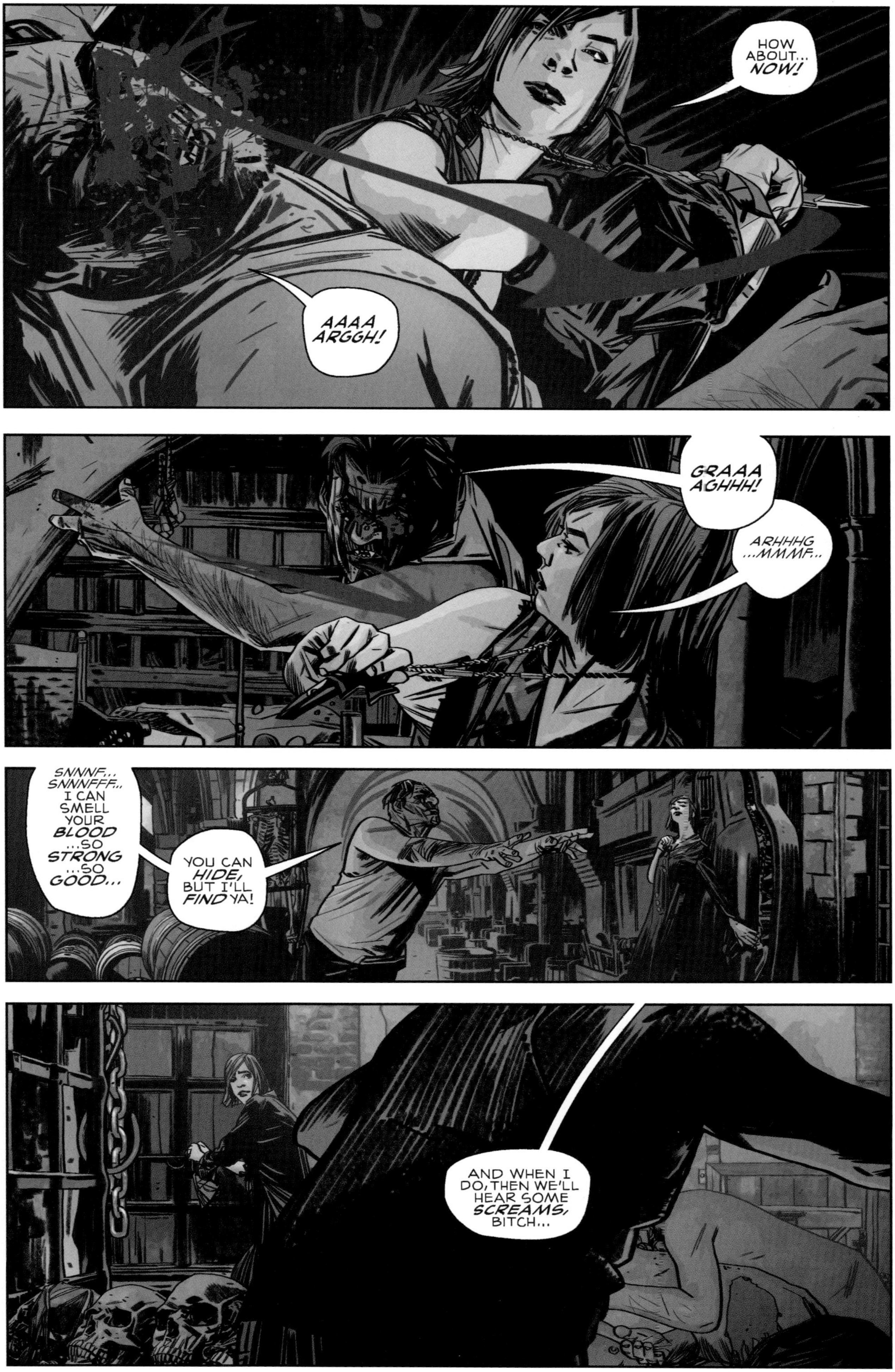
HOW ABOUT... NOW!
AAAA ARGGH!
GRAAA AGHHH!
ARHHHG ...MMMF...
SNNNF... SNNNFFF... I CAN SMELL YOUR BLOOD ...SO STRONG ...SO GOOD...
YOU CAN HIDE, BUT I'LL FIND YA!
AND WHEN I DO, THEN WE'LL HEAR SOME SCREAMS, BITCH...

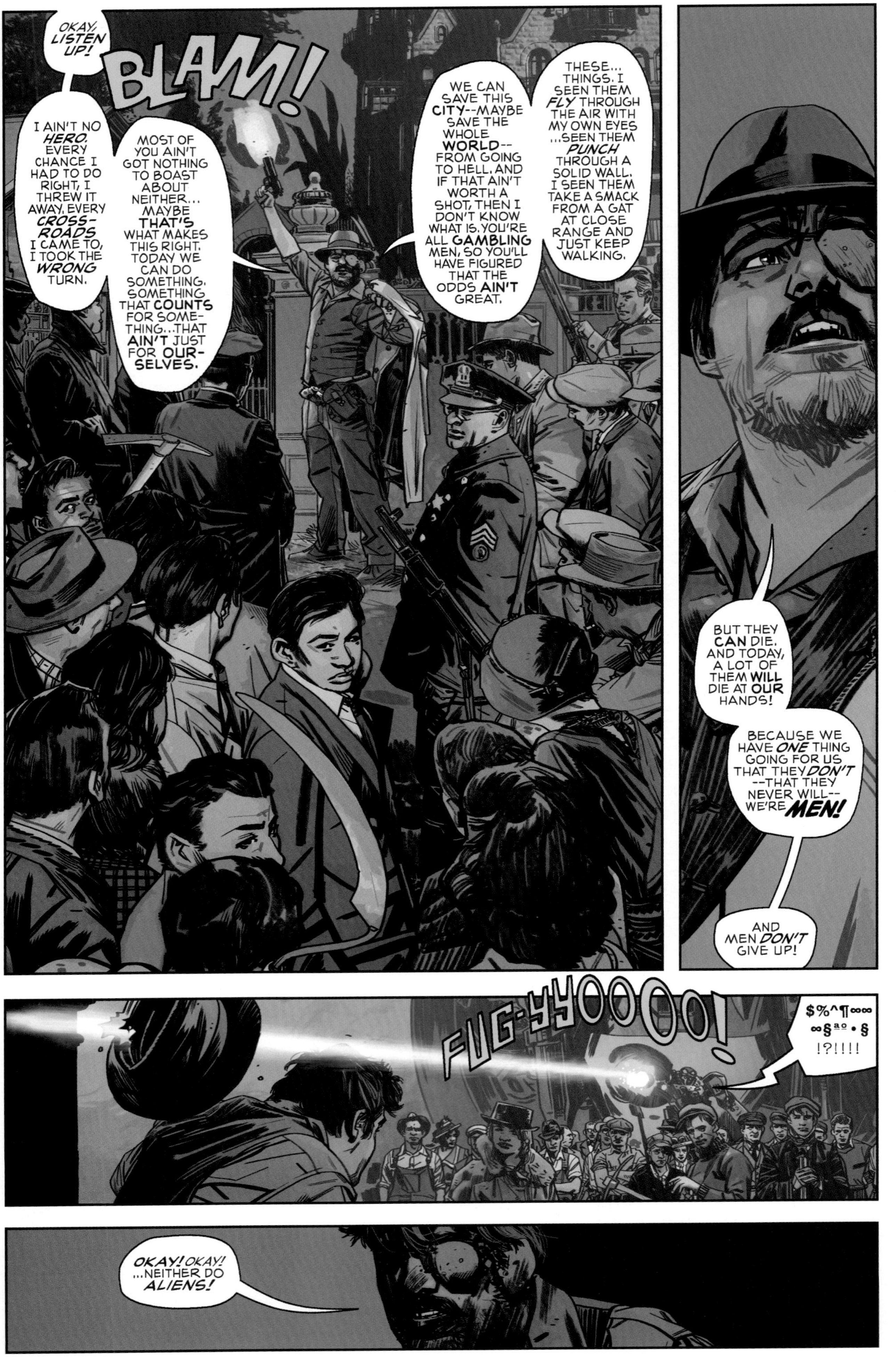

OKAY, LISTEN UP!
BLAM!
I AIN'T NO HERO. EVERY CHANCE I HAD TO DO RIGHT, I THREW IT AWAY. EVERY CROSS-ROADS I CAME TO, I TOOK THE WRONG TURN.
MOST OF YOU AIN'T GOT NOTHING TO BOAST ABOUT NEITHER... MAYBE THAT'S WHAT MAKES THIS RIGHT. TODAY WE CAN DO SOMETHING. SOMETHING THAT COUNTS FOR SOME-THING...THAT AIN'T JUST FOR OUR-SELVES.
WE CAN SAVE THIS CITY--MAYBE SAVE THE WHOLE WORLD--FROM GOING TO HELL. AND IF THAT AIN'T WORTH A SHOT, THEN I DON'T KNOW WHAT IS. YOU'RE ALL GAMBLING MEN, SO YOU'LL HAVE FIGURED THAT THE ODDS AIN'T GREAT.
THESE... THINGS. I SEEN THEM FLY THROUGH THE AIR WITH MY OWN EYES ...SEEN THEM PUNCH THROUGH A SOLID WALL. I SEEN THEM TAKE A SMACK FROM A GAT AT CLOSE RANGE AND JUST KEEP WALKING.
BUT THEY CAN DIE. AND TODAY, A LOT OF THEM WILL DIE AT OUR HANDS!
BECAUSE WE HAVE ONE THING GOING FOR US THAT THEY DON'T --THAT THEY NEVER WILL--WE'RE MEN!
AND MEN DON'T GIVE UP!
FUG-YYOOOO!
$%^¶∞∞ ∞§ªº•§ !?!!!!
OKAY! OKAY! ...NEITHER DO ALIENS!

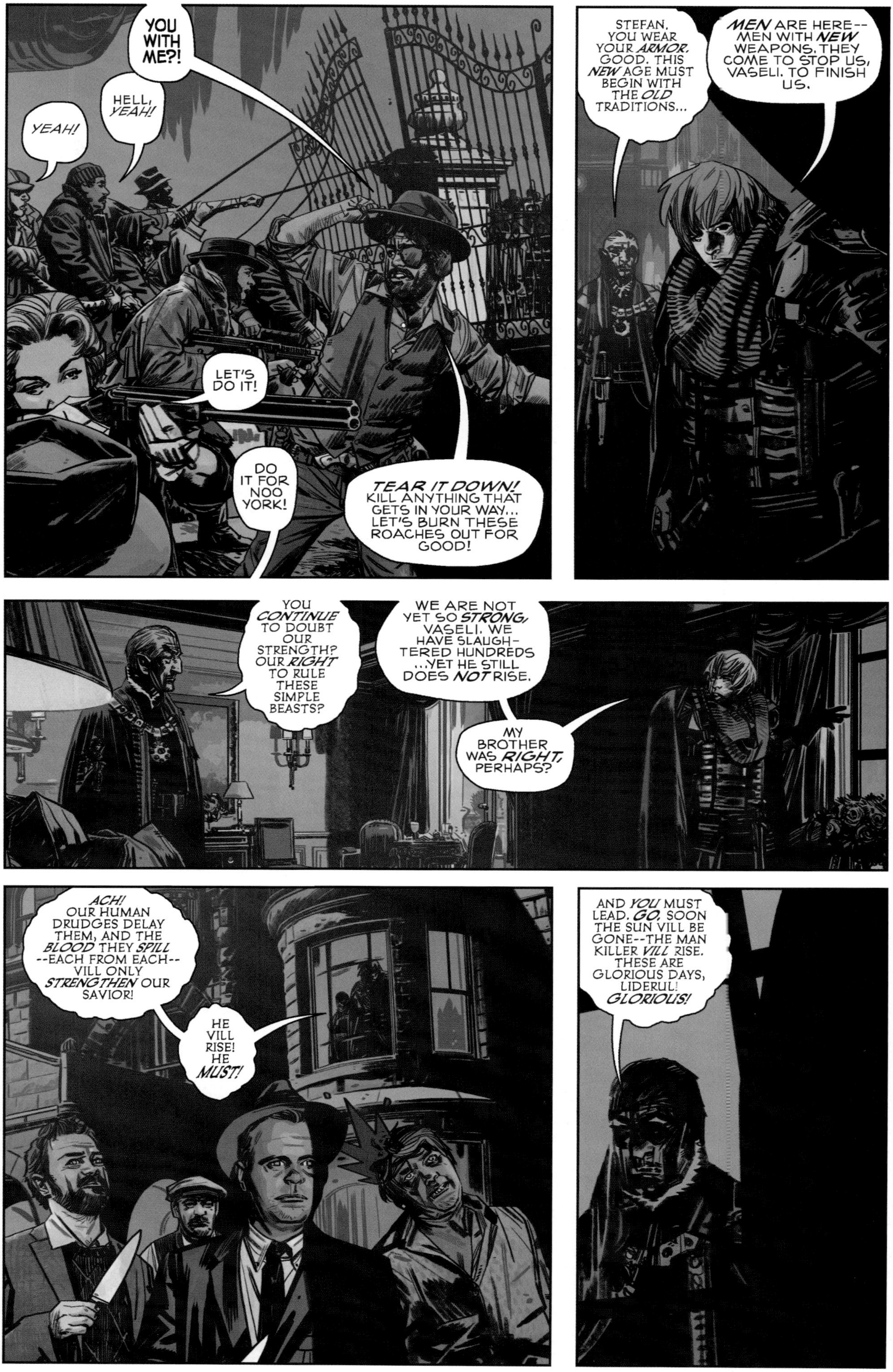
YOU WITH ME?!
HELL, YEAH!
YEAH!
LET'S DO IT!
DO IT FOR NOO YORK!
TEAR IT DOWN! KILL ANYTHING THAT GETS IN YOUR WAY... LET'S BURN THESE ROACHES OUT FOR GOOD!
STEFAN. YOU WEAR YOUR ARMOR. GOOD. THIS NEW AGE MUST BEGIN WITH THE OLD TRADITIONS...
MEN ARE HERE-- MEN WITH NEW WEAPONS. THEY COME TO STOP US, VASELI. TO FINISH US.
YOU CONTINUE TO DOUBT OUR STRENGTH? OUR RIGHT TO RULE THESE SIMPLE BEASTS?
WE ARE NOT YET SO STRONG, VASELI. WE HAVE SLAUGH-TERED HUNDREDS ...YET HE STILL DOES NOT RISE.
MY BROTHER WAS RIGHT, PERHAPS?
ACH! OUR HUMAN DRUDGES DELAY THEM, AND THE BLOOD THEY SPILL --EACH FROM EACH-- VILL ONLY STRENGTHEN OUR SAVIOR!
HE VILL RISE! HE MUST!
AND YOU MUST LEAD. GO. SOON THE SUN VILL BE GONE--THE MAN KILLER VILL RISE. THESE ARE GLORIOUS DAYS, LIDERUL! GLORIOUS!

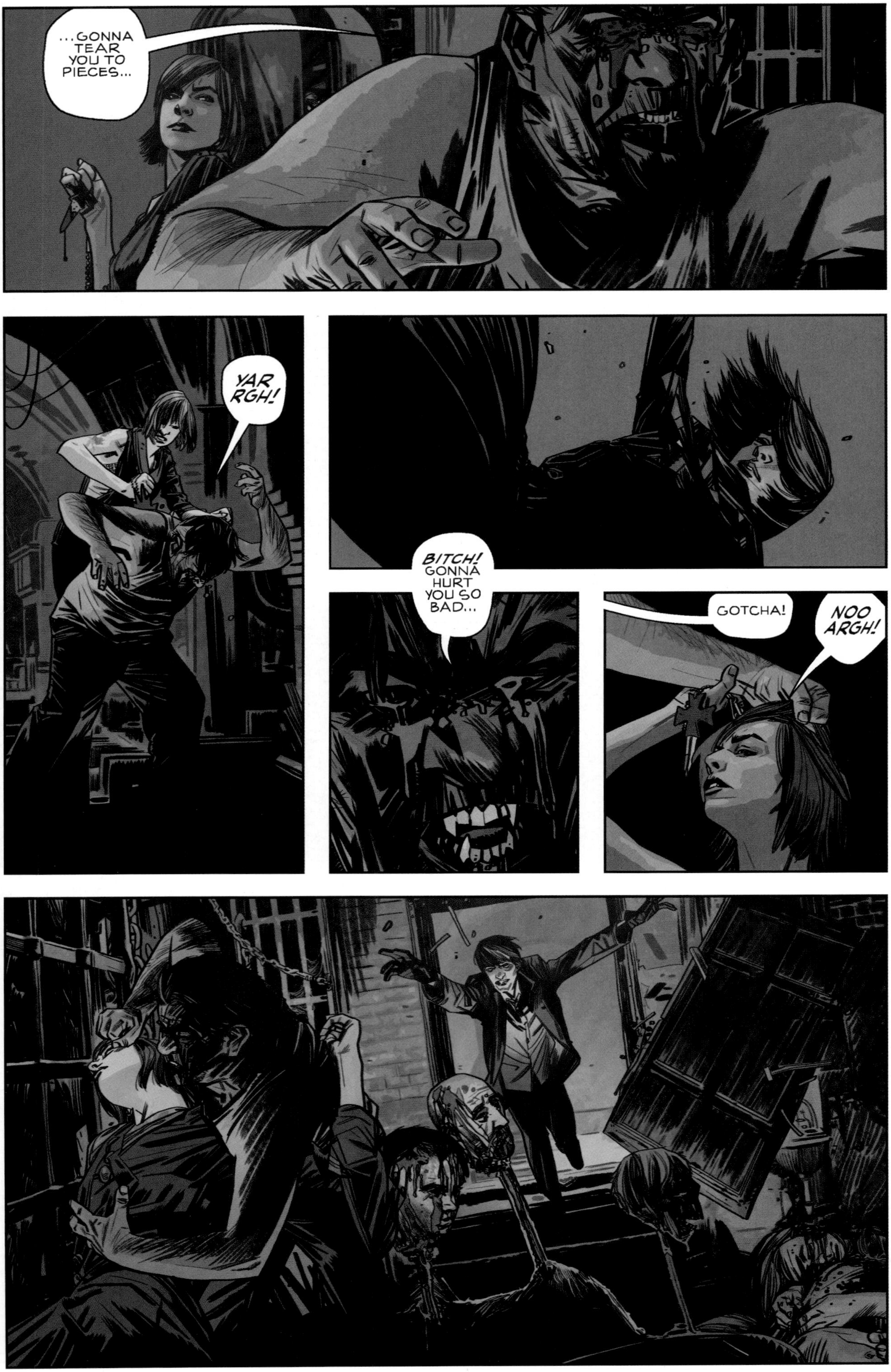
...GONNA TEAR YOU TO PIECES...
YAR RGH!
BITCH! GONNA HURT YOU SO BAD...
GOTCHA!
NOO ARGH!

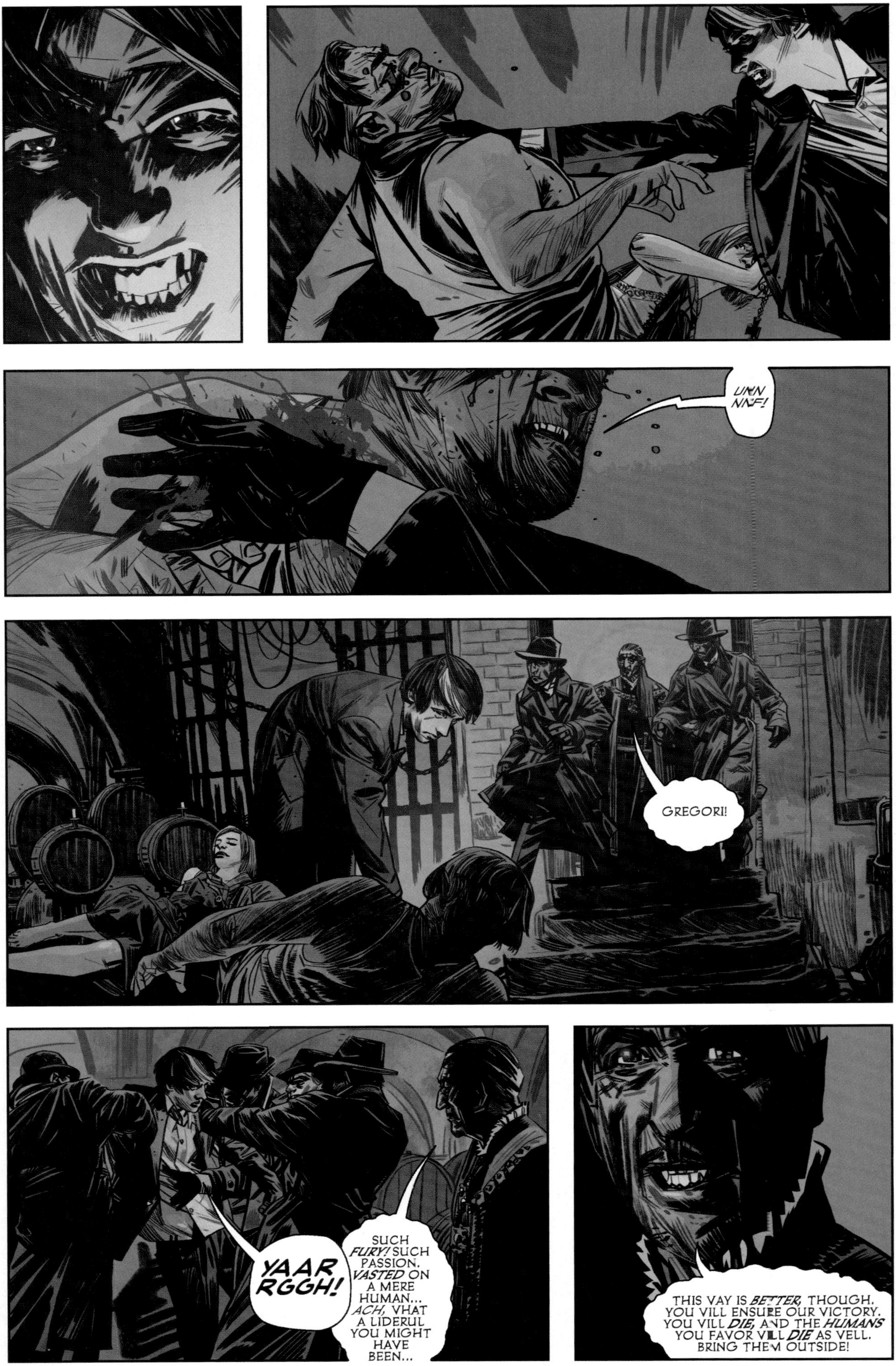
UNN NNF!
GREGORI!
YAAR RGGH!
SUCH FURY! SUCH PASSION. VASTED ON A MERE HUMAN... ACH, VHAT A LIDERUL YOU MIGHT HAVE BEEN...
THIS VAY IS BETTER, THOUGH. YOU VILL ENSURE OUR VICTORY. YOU VILL DIE, AND THE HUMANS YOU FAVOR VILL DIE AS VELL. BRING THEM OUTSIDE!

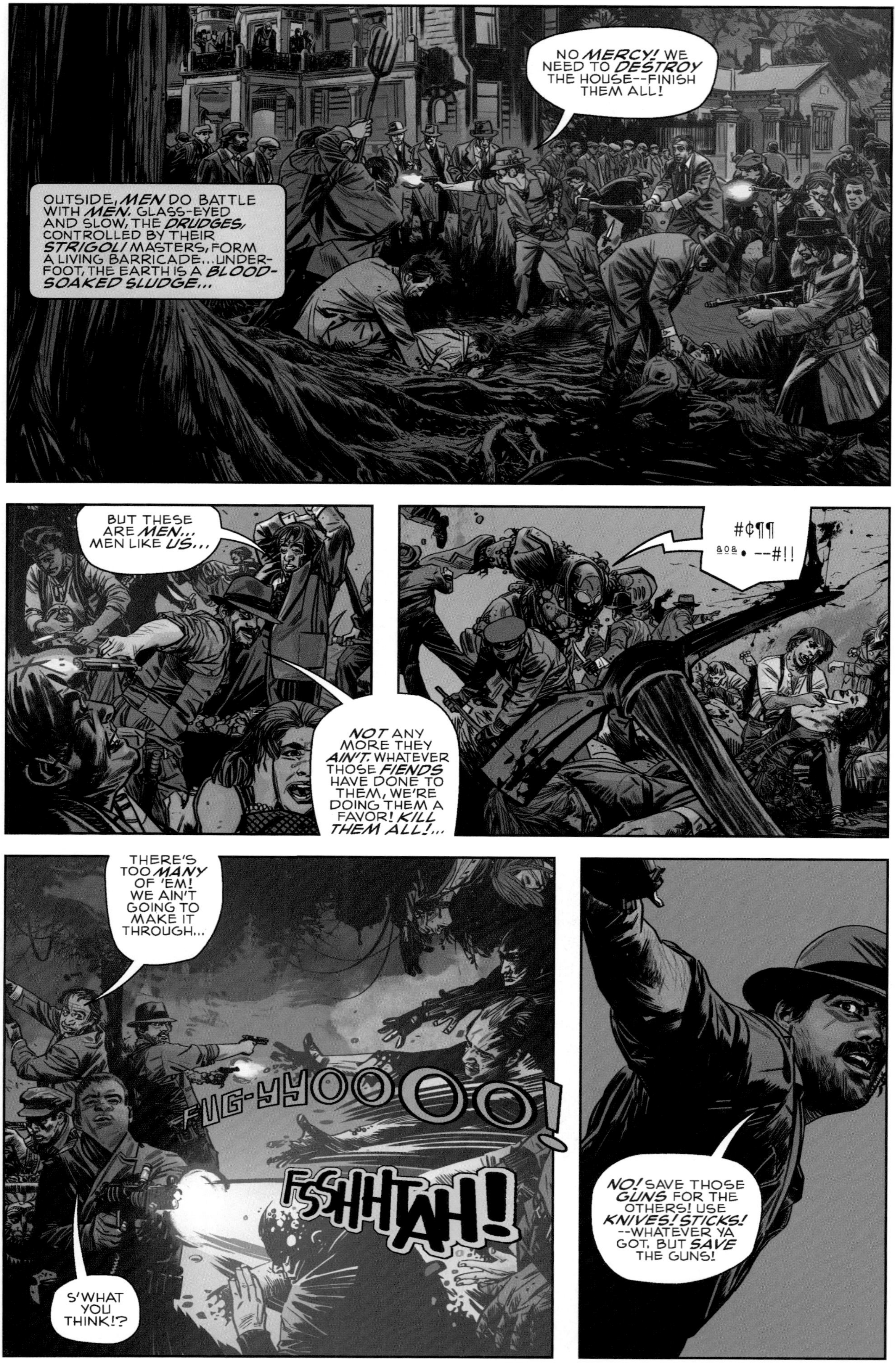

NO MERCY! WE NEED TO DESTROY THE HOUSE--FINISH THEM ALL!
OUTSIDE, MEN DO BATTLE WITH MEN. GLASS-EYED AND SLOW, THE DRUDGES, CONTROLLED BY THEIR STRIGOLI MASTERS, FORM A LIVING BARRICADE...UNDERFOOT, THE EARTH IS A BLOOD-SOAKED SLUDGE...
BUT THESE ARE MEN... MEN LIKE US...
NOT ANY MORE THEY AIN'T. WHATEVER THOSE FIENDS HAVE DONE TO THEM, WE'RE DOING THEM A FAVOR! KILL THEM ALL!...
#¢¶¶ ---#!!
THERE'S TOO MANY OF 'EM! WE AIN'T GOING TO MAKE IT THROUGH...
FUG-YYOOOOO!
FSHHTAH!
S'WHAT YOU THINK!?
NO! SAVE THOSE GUNS FOR THE OTHERS! USE KNIVES! STICKS! --WHATEVER YA GOT, BUT SAVE THE GUNS!

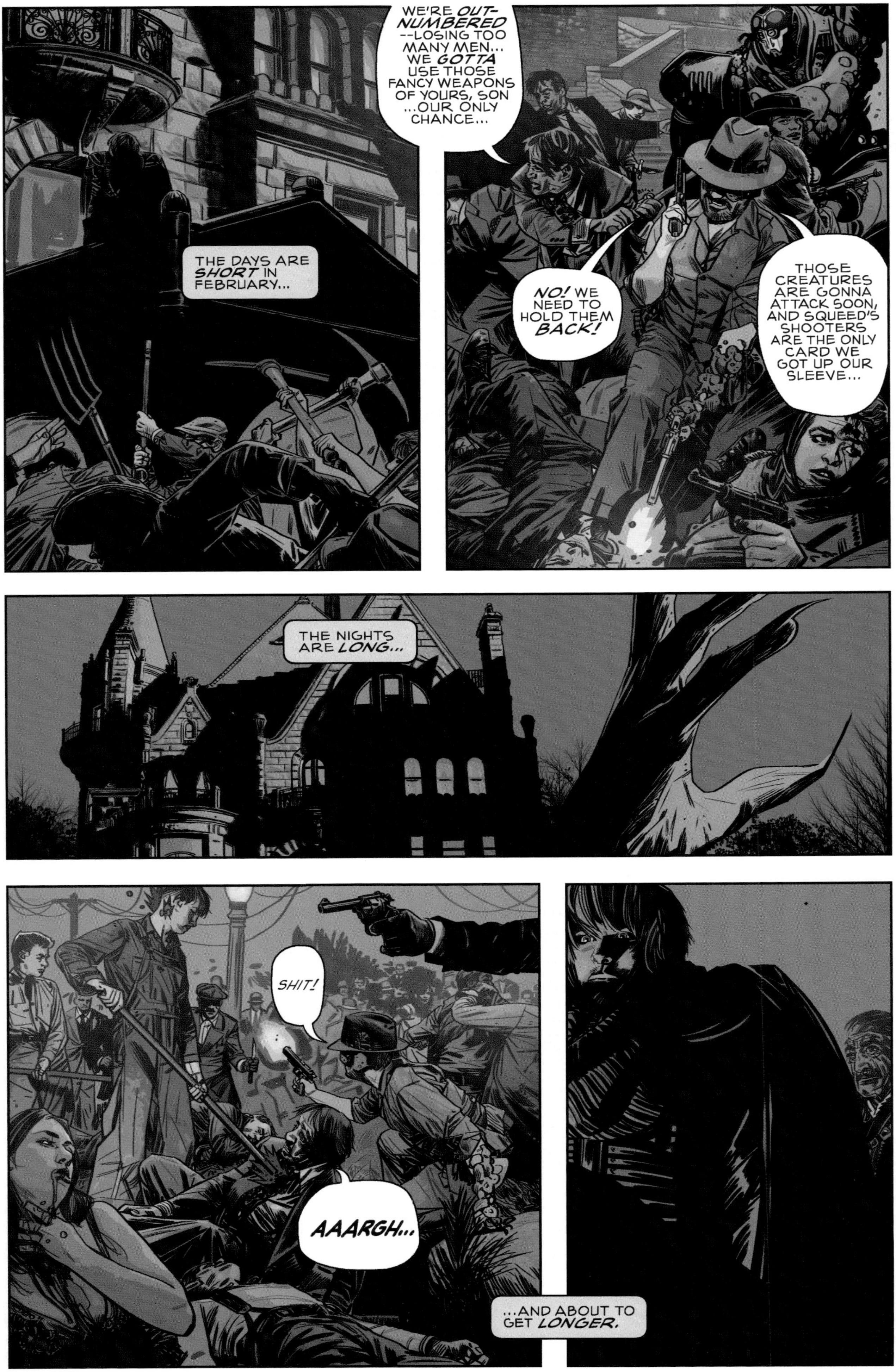
THE DAYS ARE SHORT IN FEBRUARY...
WE'RE OUT-NUMBERED --LOSING TOO MANY MEN... WE GOTTA USE THOSE FANCY WEAPONS OF YOURS, SON ...OUR ONLY CHANCE...
NO! WE NEED TO HOLD THEM BACK!
THOSE CREATURES ARE GONNA ATTACK SOON, AND SQUEED'S SHOOTERS ARE THE ONLY CARD WE GOT UP OUR SLEEVE...
THE NIGHTS ARE LONG...
SHIT!
AAARGH...
...AND ABOUT TO GET LONGER.

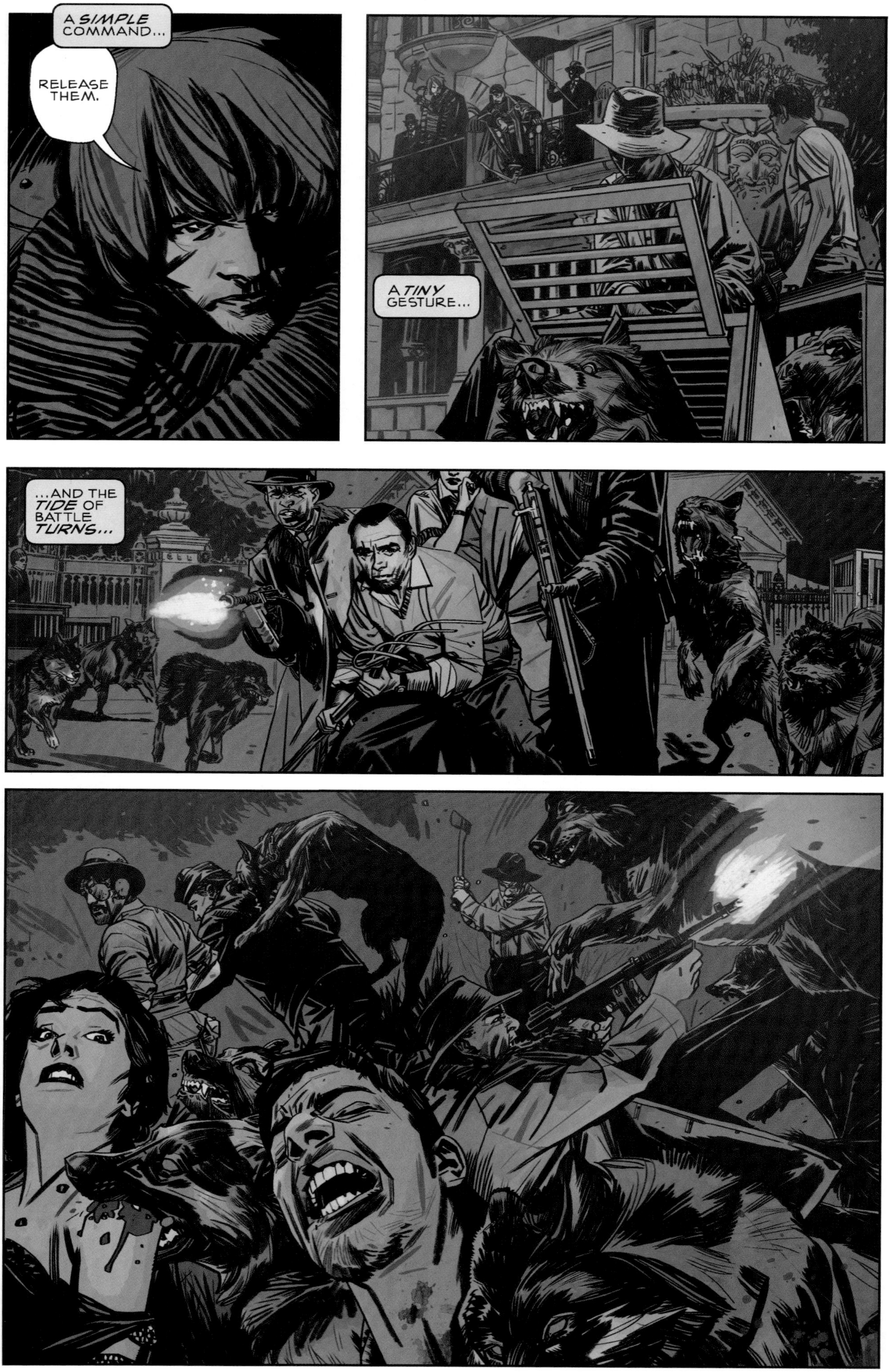
A SIMPLE COMMAND...
RELEASE THEM.
A TINY GESTURE...
...AND THE TIDE OF BATTLE TURNS...

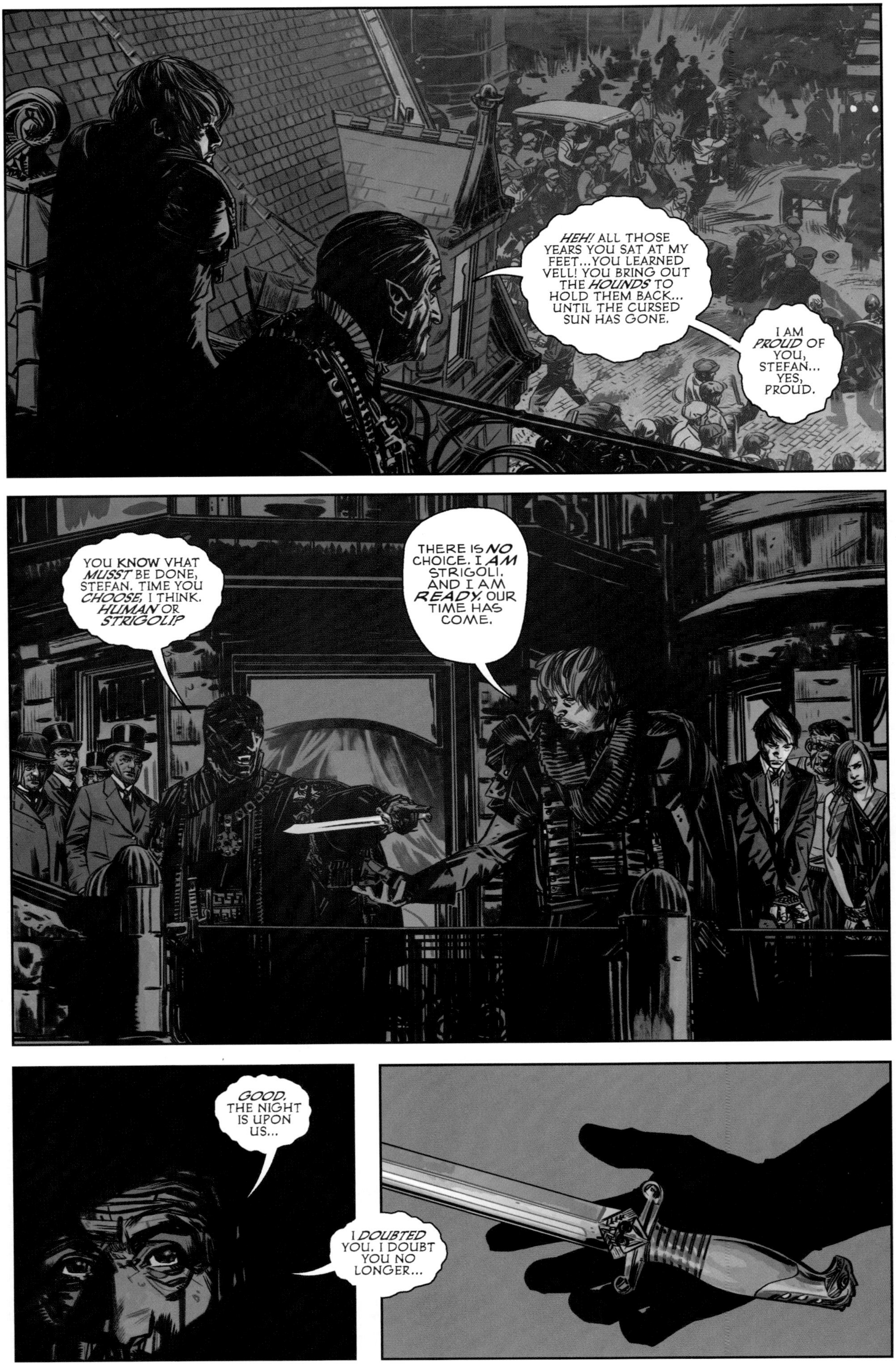
HEH! ALL THOSE YEARS YOU SAT AT MY FEET...YOU LEARNED VELL! YOU BRING OUT THE HOUNDS TO HOLD THEM BACK... UNTIL THE CURSED SUN HAS GONE.
I AM PROUD OF YOU, STEFAN... YES, PROUD.
YOU KNOW VHAT MUSST BE DONE, STEFAN. TIME YOU CHOOSE, I THINK. HUMAN OR STRIGOLI?
THERE IS NO CHOICE. I AM STRIGOLI. AND I AM READY. OUR TIME HAS COME.
GOOD. THE NIGHT IS UPON US...
I DOUBTED YOU. I DOUBT YOU NO LONGER...

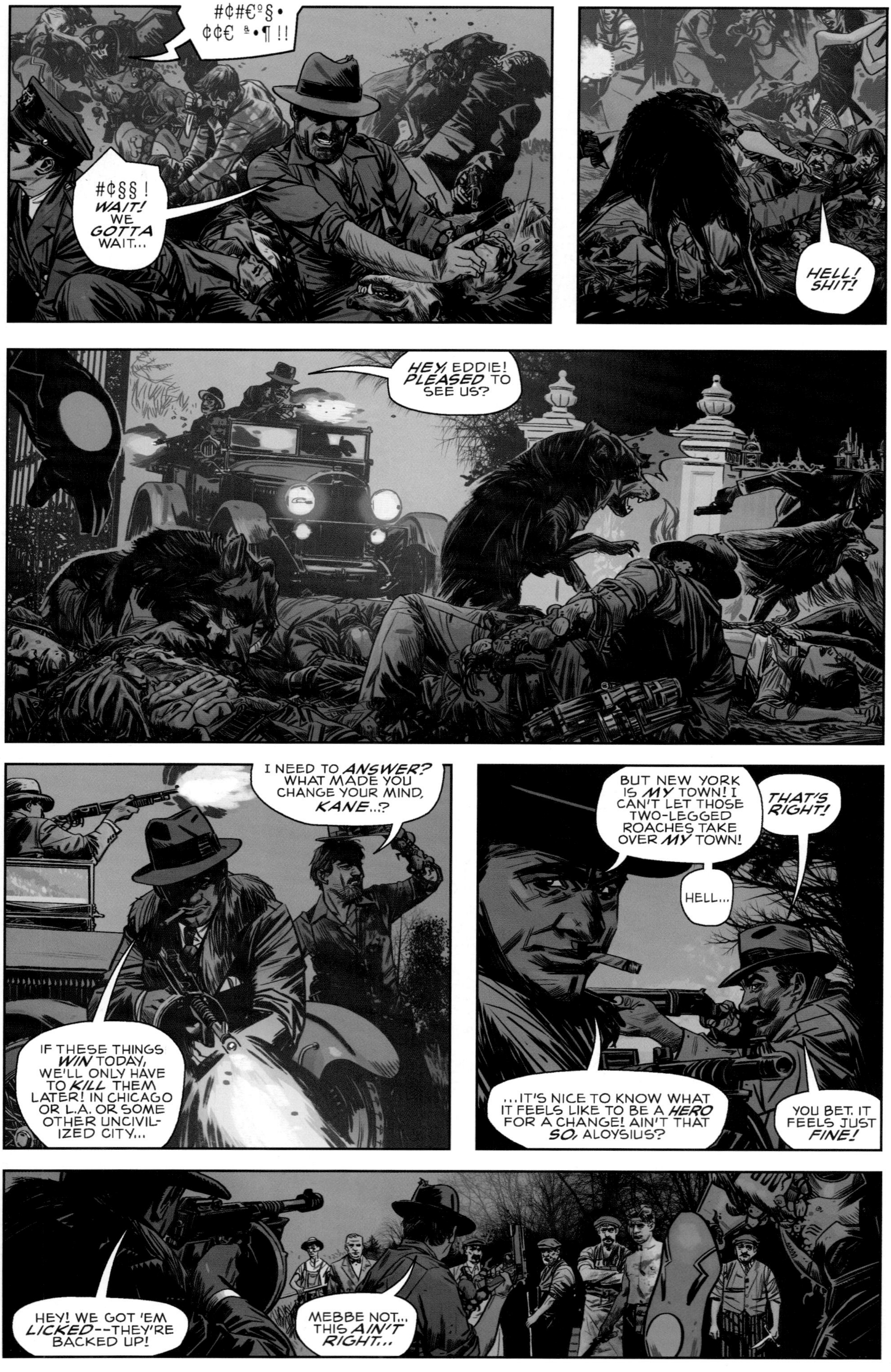
#¢#€º§• ¢¢€ ª•¶!!
#¢§§! WAIT! WE GOTTA WAIT...
HELL! SHIT!
HEY, EDDIE! PLEASED TO SEE US?
I NEED TO ANSWER? WHAT MADE YOU CHANGE YOUR MIND, KANE...?
IF THESE THINGS WIN TODAY, WE'LL ONLY HAVE TO KILL THEM LATER! IN CHICAGO OR L.A. OR SOME OTHER UNCIVIL-IZED CITY...
BUT NEW YORK IS MY TOWN! I CAN'T LET THOSE TWO-LEGGED ROACHES TAKE OVER MY TOWN!
THAT'S RIGHT!
HELL...
...IT'S NICE TO KNOW WHAT IT FEELS LIKE TO BE A HERO FOR A CHANGE! AIN'T THAT SO, ALOYSIUS?
YOU BET. IT FEELS JUST FINE!
HEY! WE GOT 'EM LICKED--THEY'RE BACKED UP!
MEBBE NOT... THIS AIN'T RIGHT...

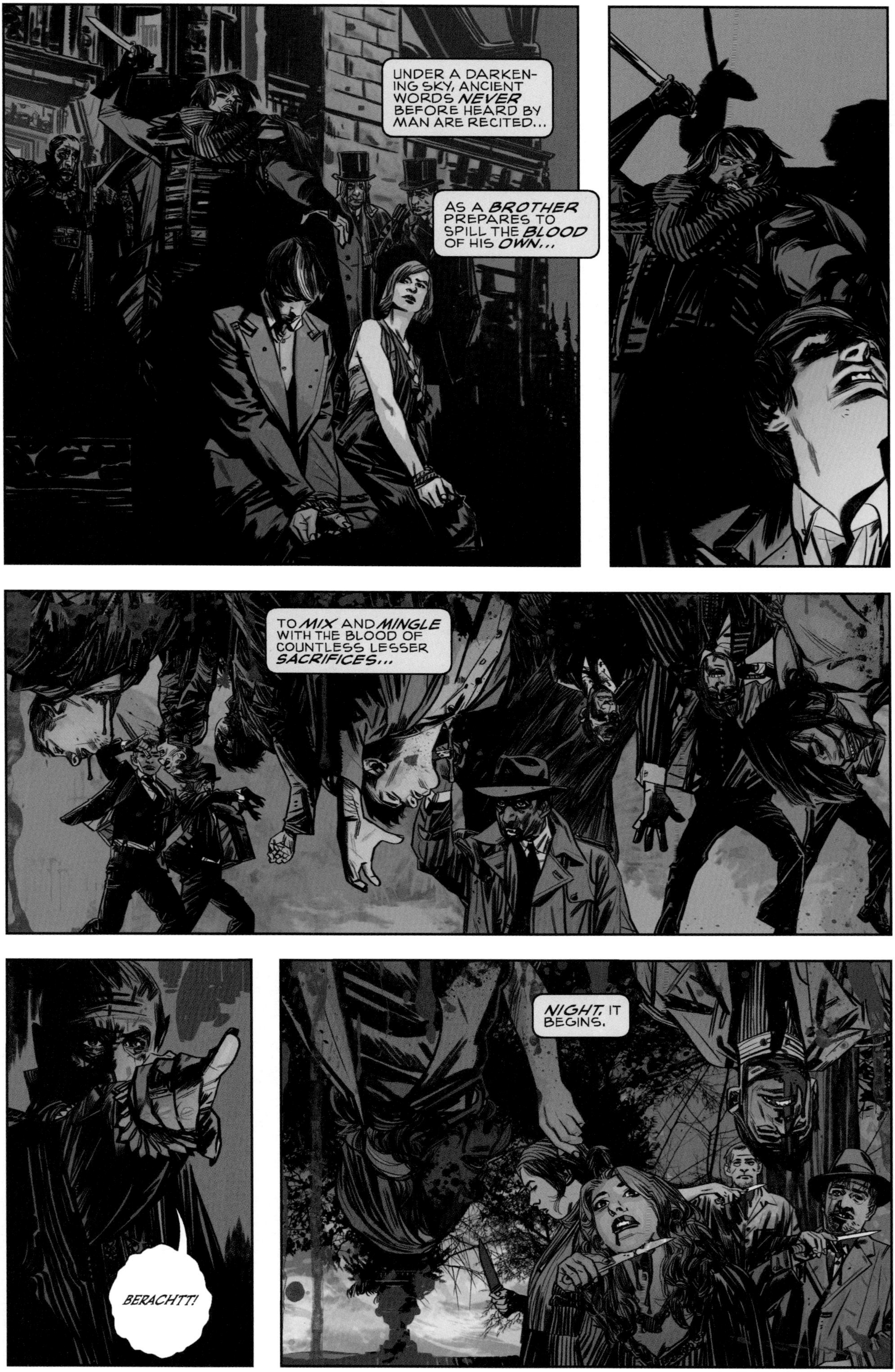
UNDER A DARKENING SKY, ANCIENT WORDS NEVER BEFORE HEARD BY MAN ARE RECITED...
AS A BROTHER PREPARES TO SPILL THE BLOOD OF HIS OWN...
TO MIX AND MINGLE WITH THE BLOOD OF COUNTLESS LESSER SACRIFICES...
BERACHTT!
NIGHT, IT BEGINS.

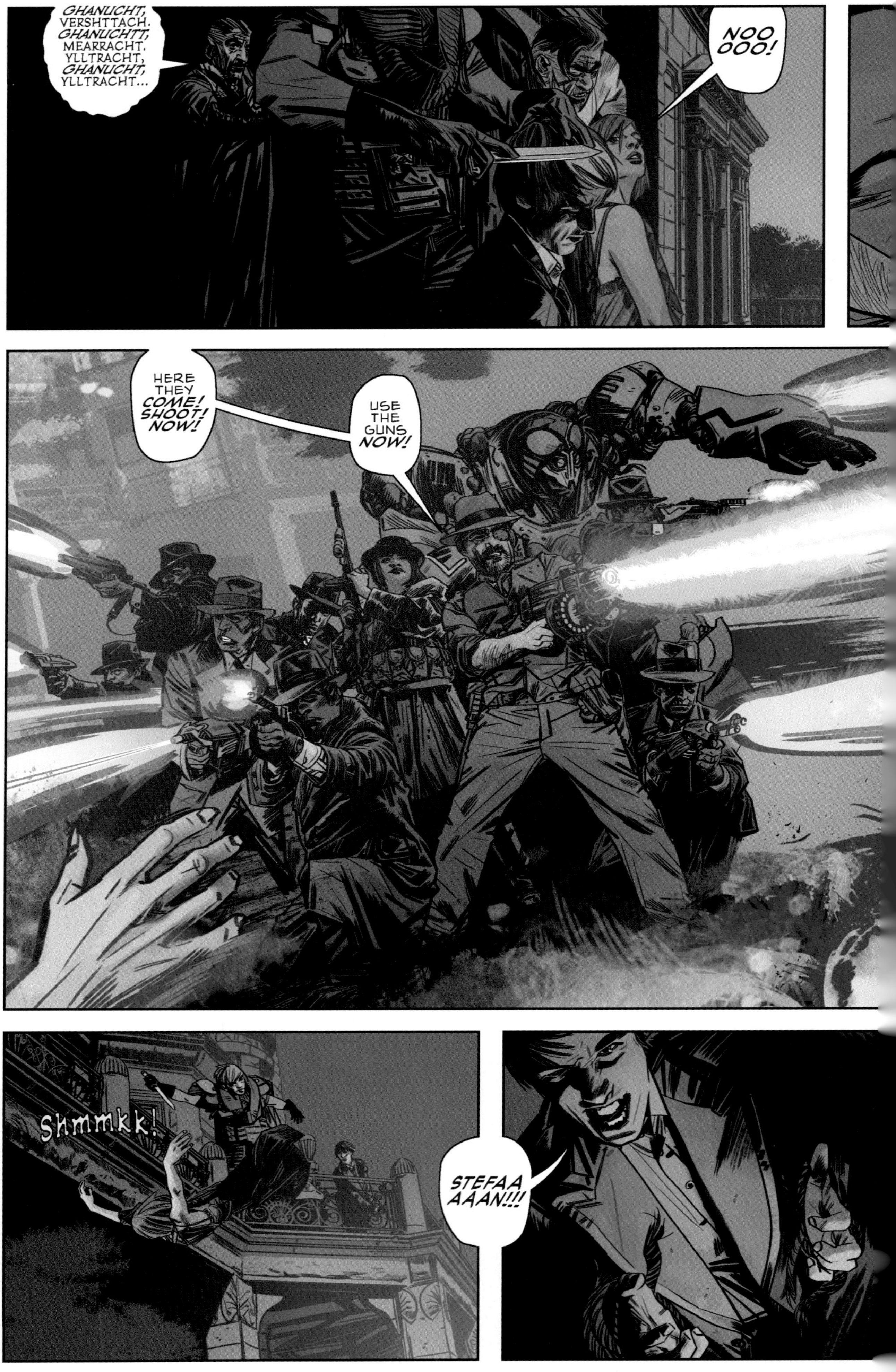
GHANUCHT, VERSHTTACH. GHANUCHTT, MEARRACHT. YLLTRACHT, GHANUCHT, YLLTRACHT...
NOO OOO!
HERE THEY COME! SHOOT! NOW!
USE THE GUNS NOW!
Shmmkk!
STEFAA AAAN!!!

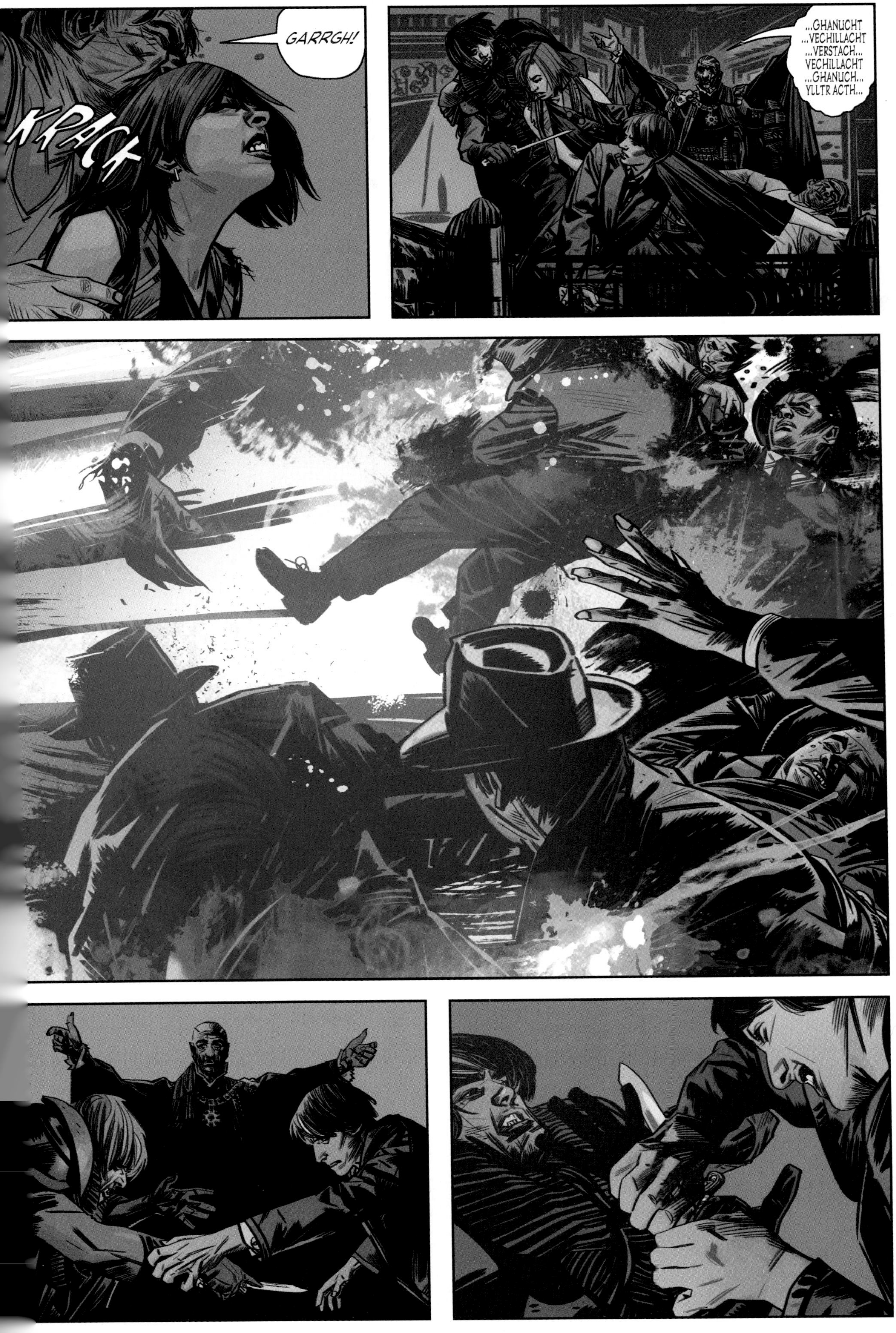
GARRGH!
KRACK
...GHANUCHT ...VECHILLACHT ...VERSTACH... VECHILLACHT ...GHANUCH... YLLTR ACTH...

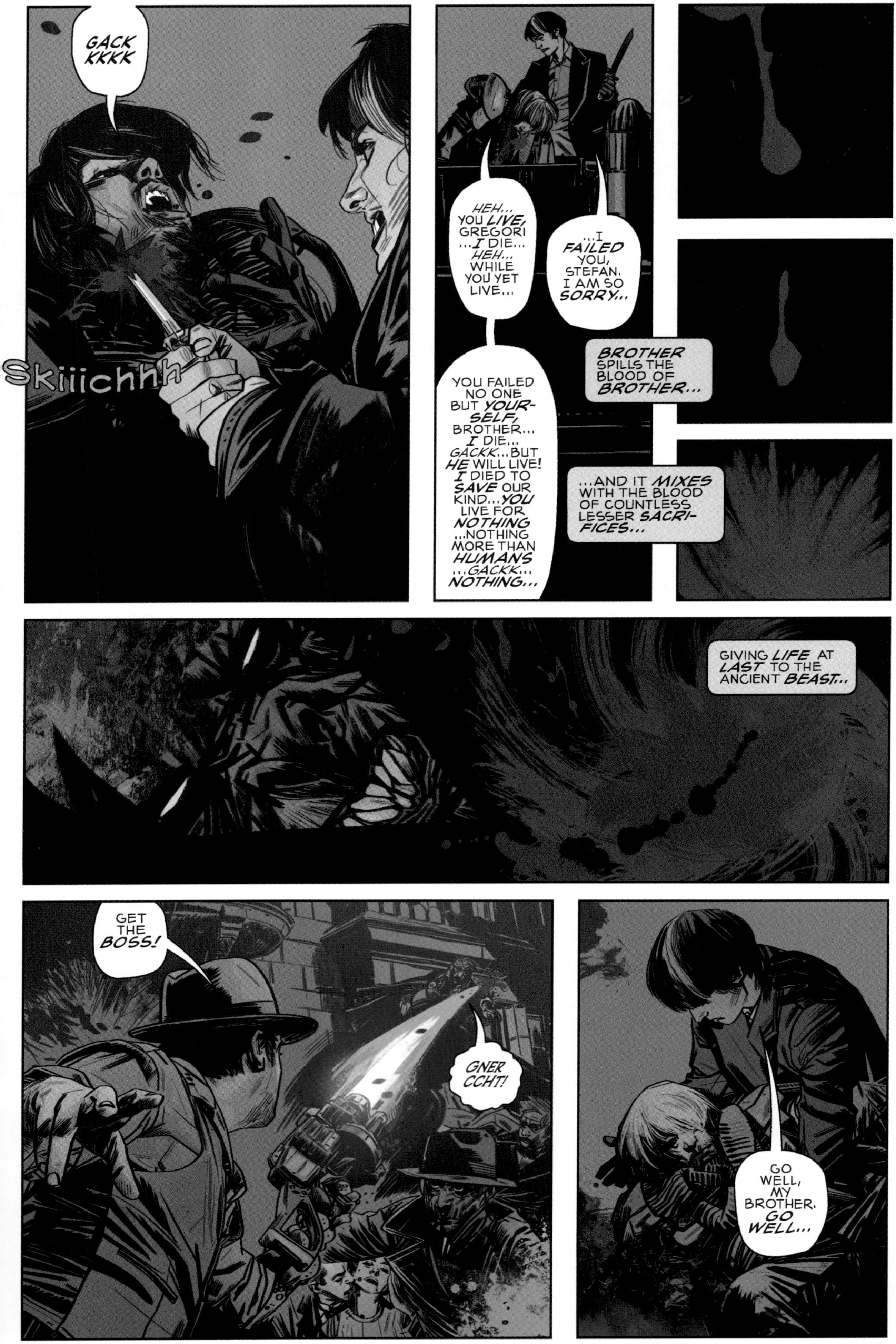
GACK KKKK
Skiiichhh
HEH... YOU LIVE, GREGORI ...I DIE... HEH... WHILE YOU YET LIVE...
...I FAILED YOU, STEFAN. I AM SO SORRY...
YOU FAILED NO ONE BUT YOURSELF, BROTHER... I DIE... GACKK...BUT HE WILL LIVE! I DIED TO SAVE OUR KIND...YOU LIVE FOR NOTHING ...NOTHING MORE THAN HUMANS ...GACKK... NOTHING...
BROTHER SPILLS THE BLOOD OF BROTHER...
...AND IT MIXES WITH THE BLOOD OF COUNTLESS LESSER SACRIFICES...
GIVING LIFE AT LAST TO THE ANCIENT BEAST...
GET THE BOSS!
GNER CCHT!
GO WELL, MY BROTHER. GO WELL...

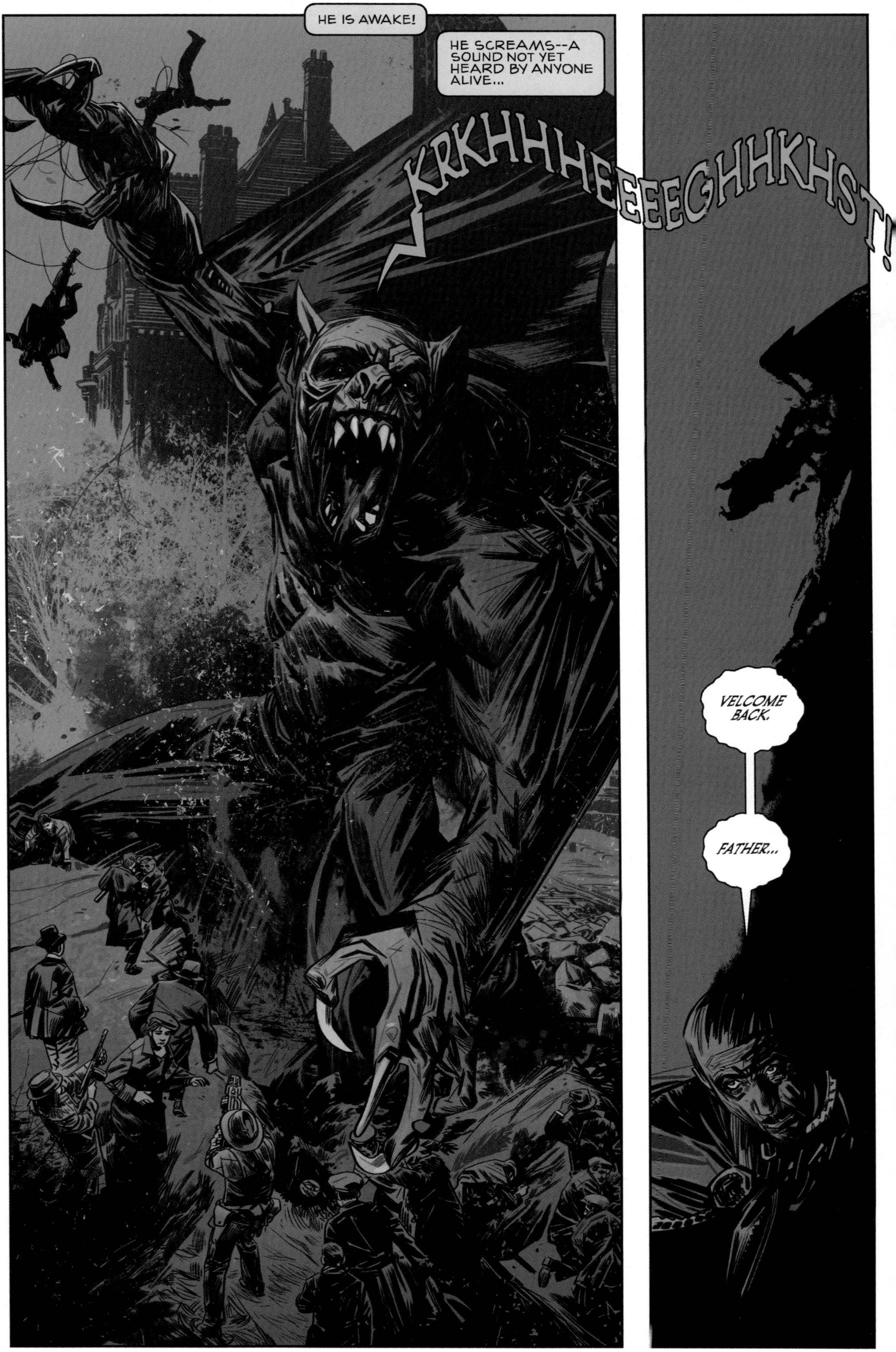
HE IS AWAKE!
HE SCREAMS--A SOUND NOT YET HEARD BY ANYONE ALIVE...
KRKHHHEEEEGHHKHST!
VELCOME BACK.
FATHER...

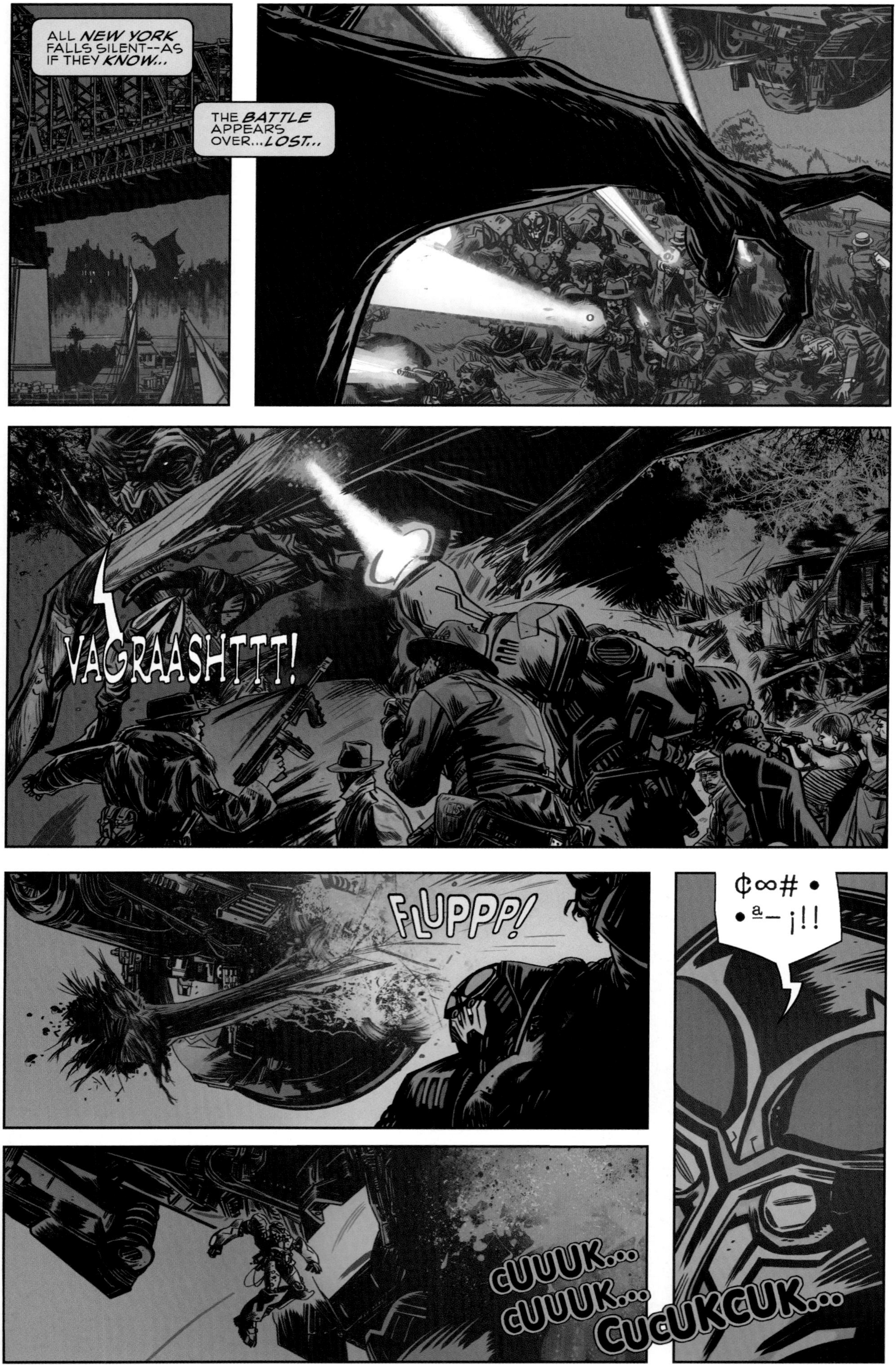
ALL *NEW YORK* FALLS SILENT--AS IF THEY *KNOW*...
THE *BATTLE* APPEARS OVER... *LOST*...
VAGRAASHTTT!
FLUPPP!
CUUUK... CUUUK... CUCUKCUK...

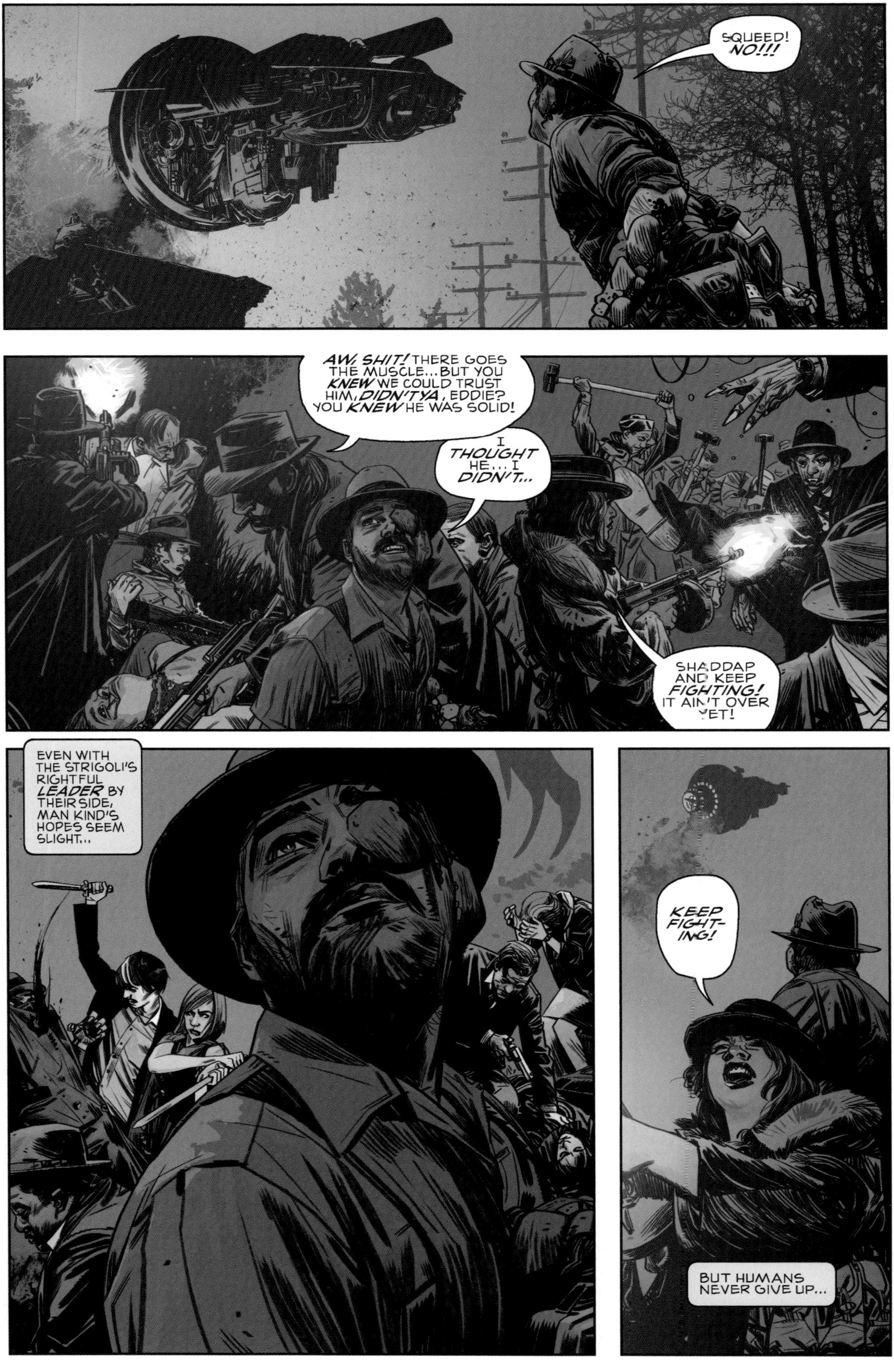
SQUEED! NO!!!
AW, SHIT! THERE GOES THE MUSCLE...BUT YOU KNEW WE COULD TRUST HIM, DIDN'TYA, EDDIE? YOU KNEW HE WAS SOLID!
I THOUGHT HE... I DIDN'T...
SHADDAP AND KEEP FIGHTING! IT AIN'T OVER YET!
EVEN WITH THE STRIGOLI'S RIGHTFUL LEADER BY THEIR SIDE, MAN KIND'S HOPES SEEM SLIGHT...
KEEP FIGHT-ING!
BUT HUMANS NEVER GIVE UP...

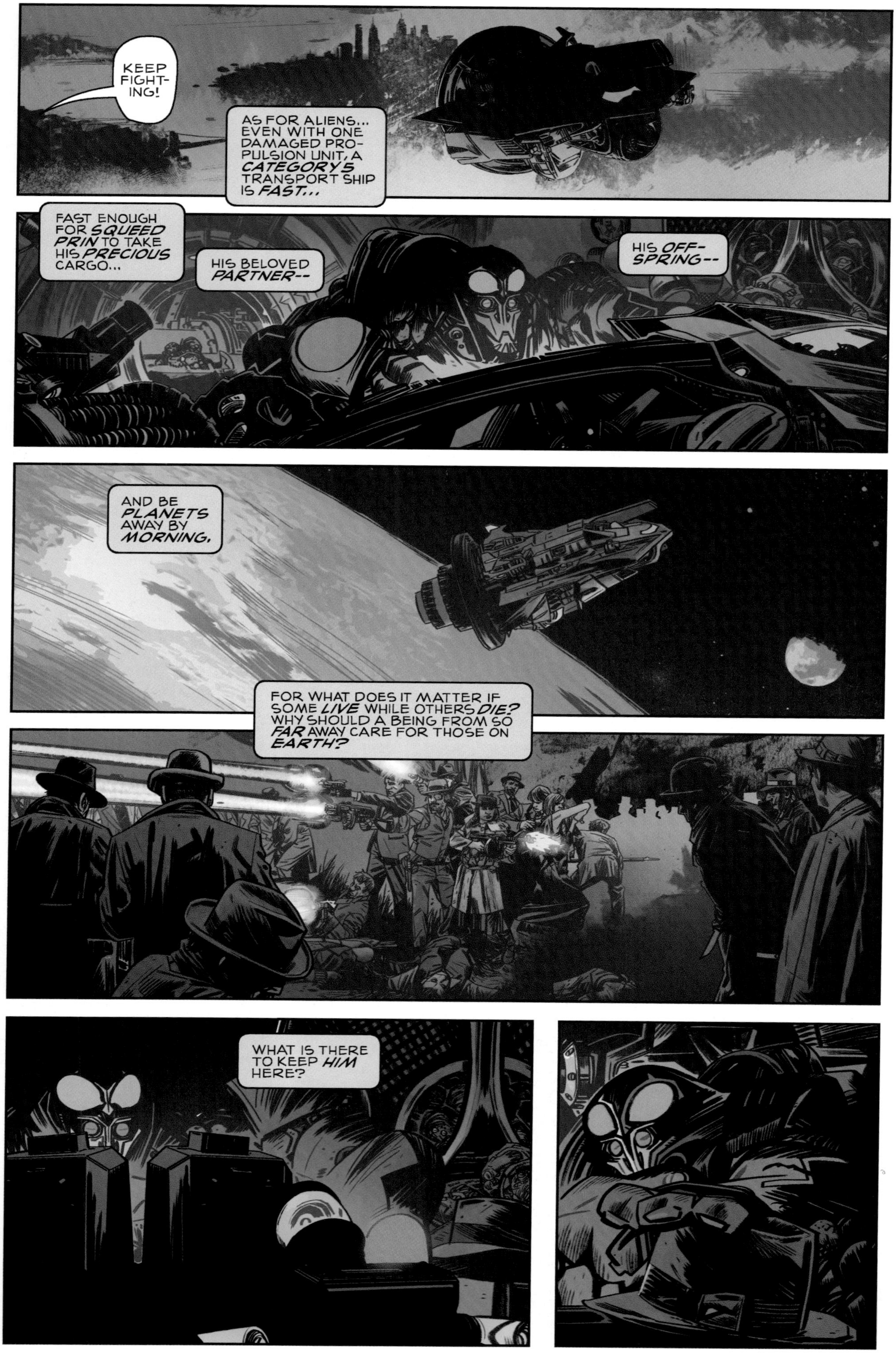
KEEP FIGHTING!
AS FOR ALIENS... EVEN WITH ONE DAMAGED PROPULSION UNIT, A *CATEGORY 5* TRANSPORT SHIP IS *FAST...*
FAST ENOUGH FOR *SQUEED PRIN* TO TAKE HIS *PRECIOUS* CARGO...
HIS BELOVED *PARTNER--*
HIS *OFF-SPRING--*
AND BE *PLANETS* AWAY BY *MORNING.*
FOR WHAT DOES IT MATTER IF SOME *LIVE* WHILE OTHERS *DIE?* WHY SHOULD A BEING FROM SO *FAR* AWAY CARE FOR THOSE ON *EARTH?*
WHAT IS THERE TO KEEP *HIM* HERE?

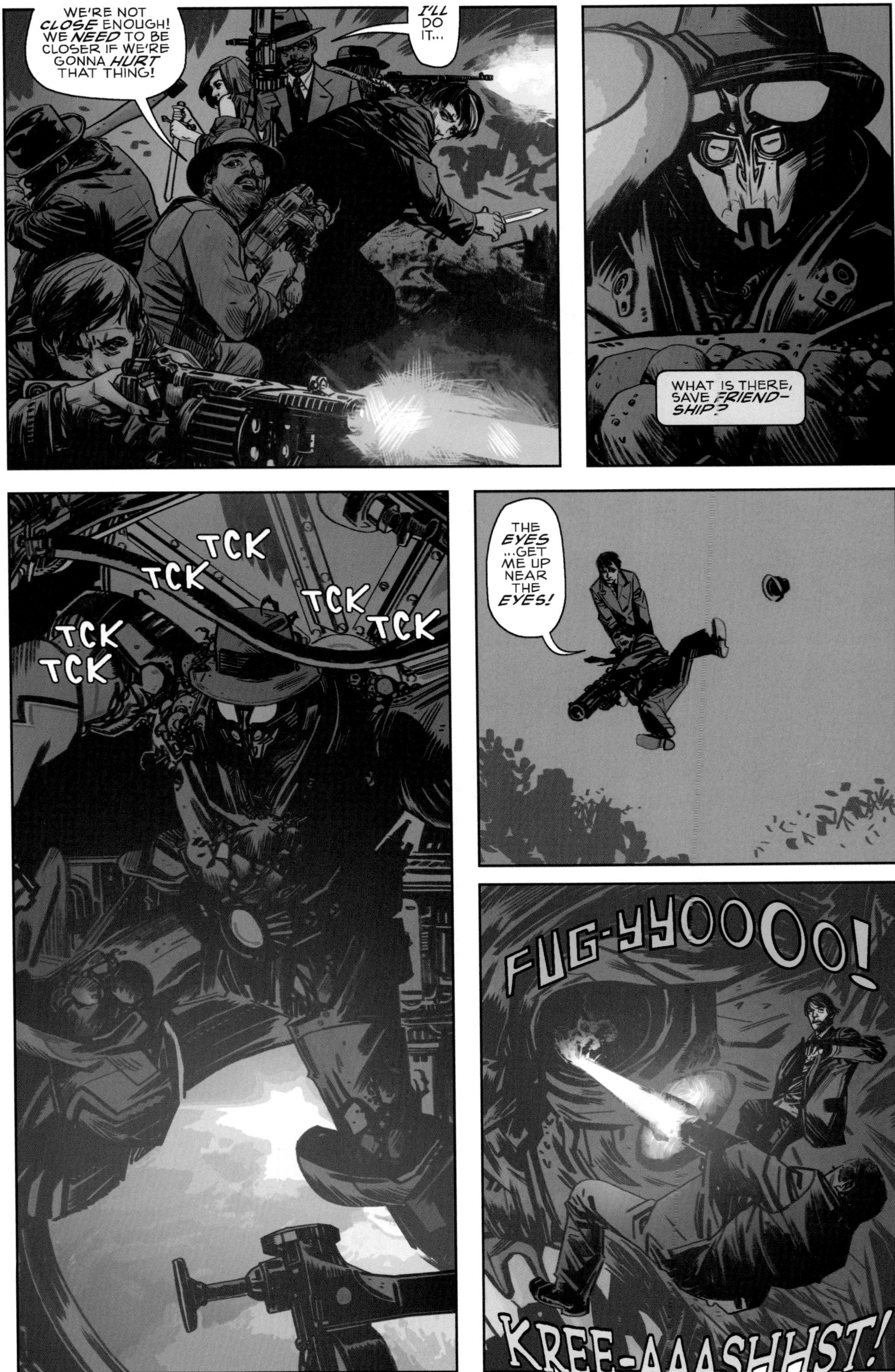

WE'RE NOT CLOSE ENOUGH! WE NEED TO BE CLOSER IF WE'RE GONNA HURT THAT THING!
I'LL DO IT...
WHAT IS THERE, SAVE FRIEND-SHIP?
TCK
TCK
TCK
TCK
TCK
TCK
THE EYES ...GET ME UP NEAR THE EYES!
FUG-YYOOOOO!
KREE-AAASHHST!

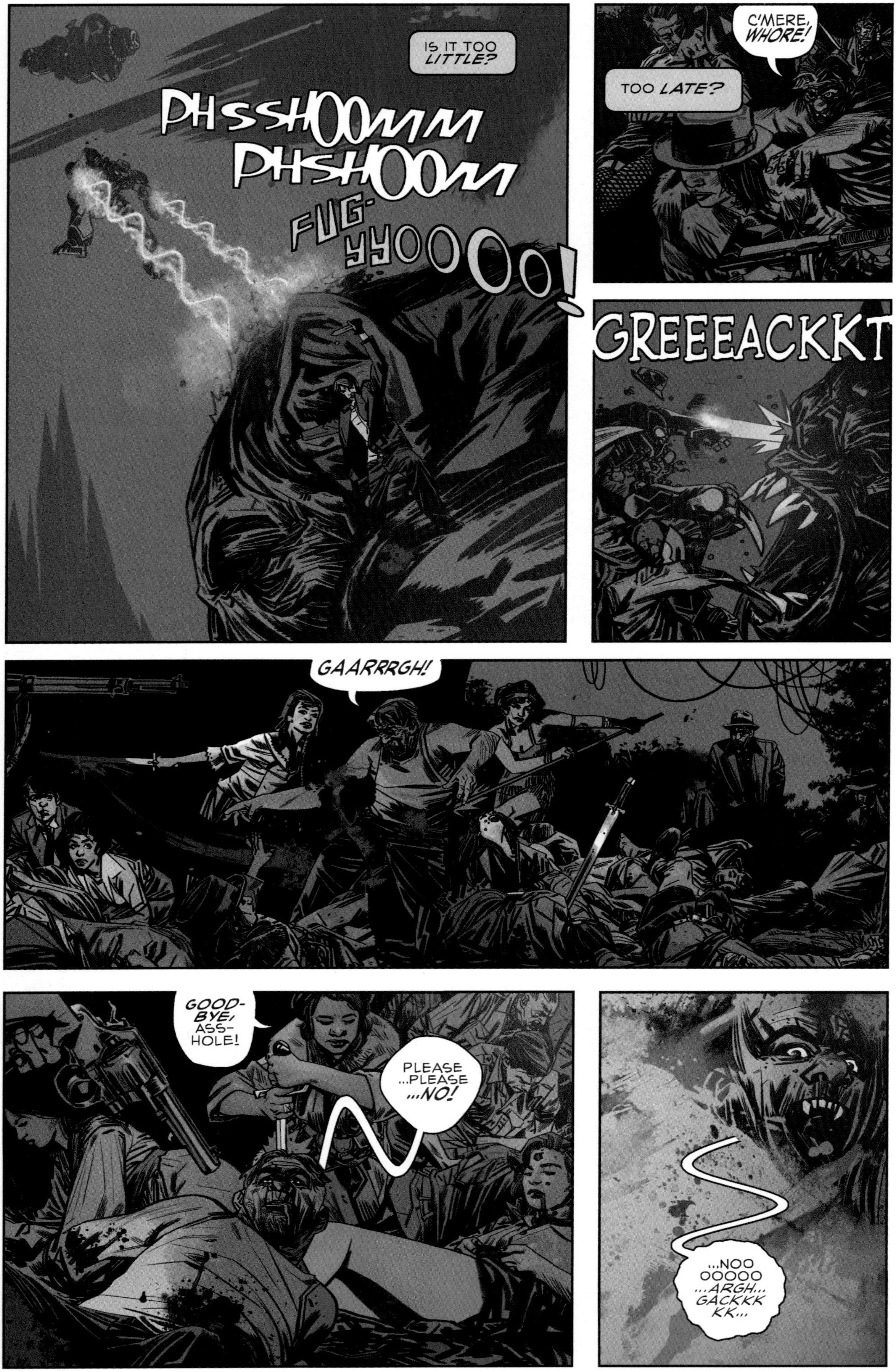
IS IT TOO LITTLE?
PHSSHOOMM
PHSHOOM
FUG-YYOOOOO!
C'MERE, WHORE!
TOO LATE?
GREEEACKKT
GAARRRGH!
GOOD-BYE, ASS-HOLE!
PLEASE ...PLEASE ...NO!
...NOO OOOOO ...ARGH... GACKKK KK...

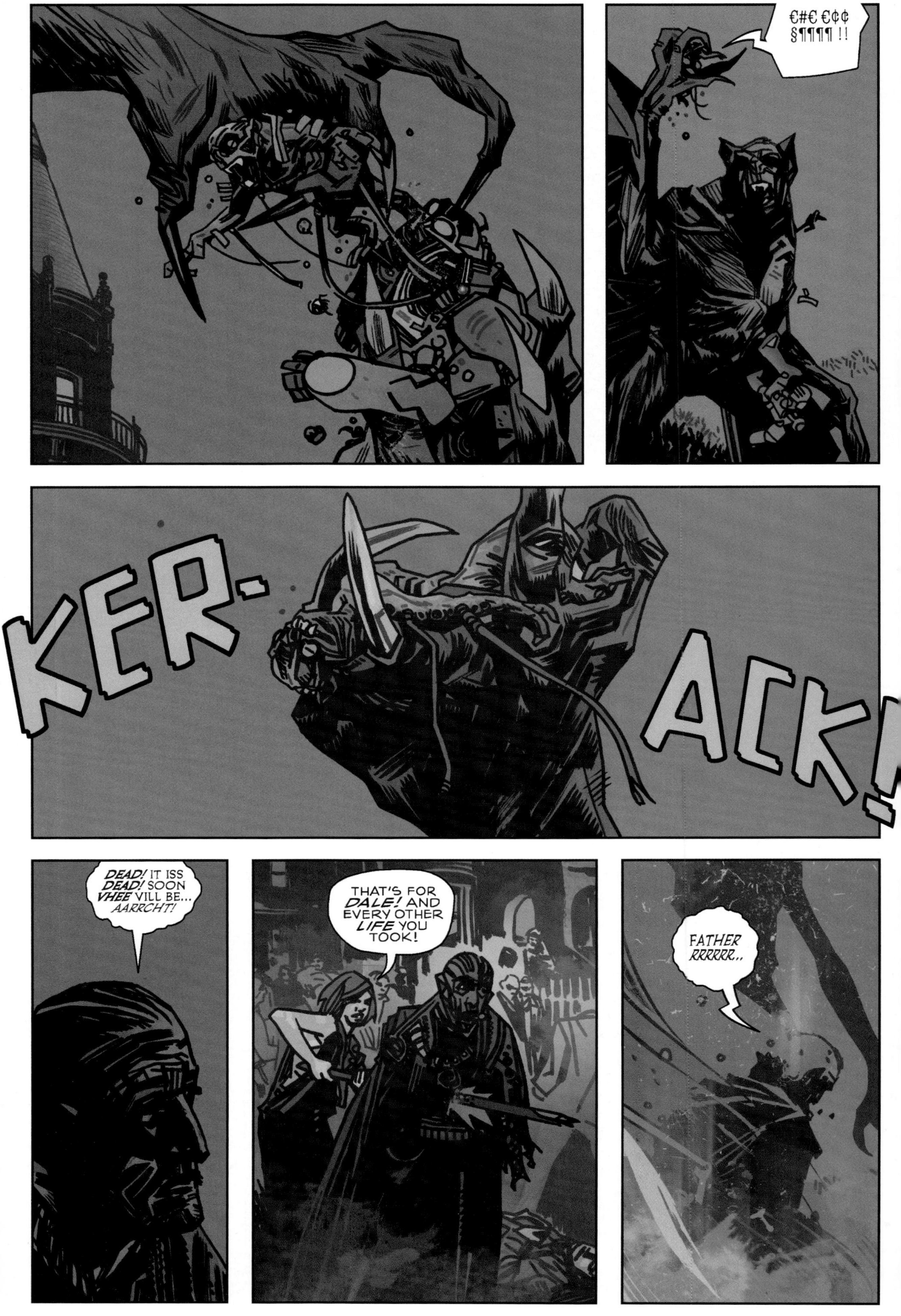
€#€ €¢¢ §¶¶¶¶ !!
KER-ACK!
DEAD! IT ISS DEAD! SOON VHEE VILL BE... AARRCHT!
THAT'S FOR DALE! AND EVERY OTHER LIFE YOU TOOK!
FATHER RRRRRR...

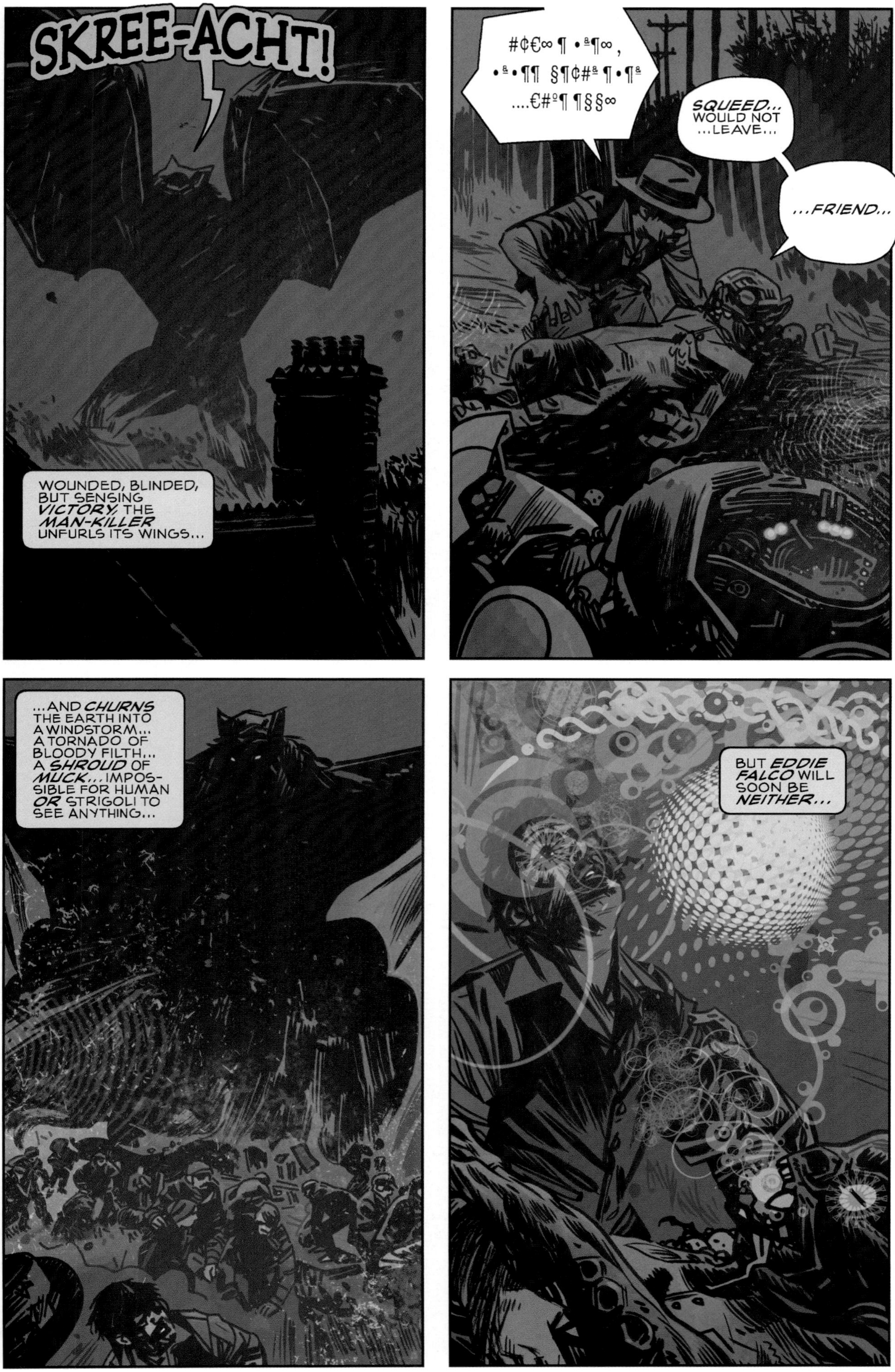
SKREE-ACHT!
WOUNDED, BLINDED, BUT SENSING *VICTORY,* THE *MAN-KILLER* UNFURLS ITS WINGS...
#¢€∞ ¶ •ª¶∞ , •ª•¶¶ §¶¢#ª ¶•¶ª ....€#º¶ ¶§§∞
SQUEED... WOULD NOT ...LEAVE...
...FRIEND...
...AND *CHURNS* THE EARTH INTO A WINDSTORM... A TORNADO OF BLOODY FILTH... A *SHROUD* OF *MUCK*... IMPOSSIBLE FOR HUMAN *OR* STRIGOLI TO SEE ANYTHING...
BUT *EDDIE FALCO* WILL SOON BE *NEITHER...*

TRAPPED IN THE *BLOOD-STORM*, THE HUMANS ARE *EASY* PREY FOR THE GIGANTIC *MAN KILLER...*

THE REMAINING STRIGOLI *FALL BACK* AS THEIR *NEW* LEADER—THE *FIRST* OF THEIR KIND—STRIKES *AGAIN* AND *AGAIN* AT ITS ENEMIES, FROM THE MURKY DEPTHS OF THE *MACABRE MAELSTROM...*

UNABLE TO *SEE*, UNABLE TO *BE SEEN...* BY ALL BUT *ONE...*

TCK

TCK

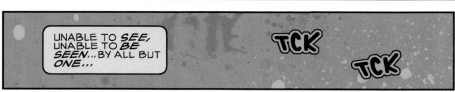

TCK TCK TCK TCK TCK TCK TCK TCK TCK TC

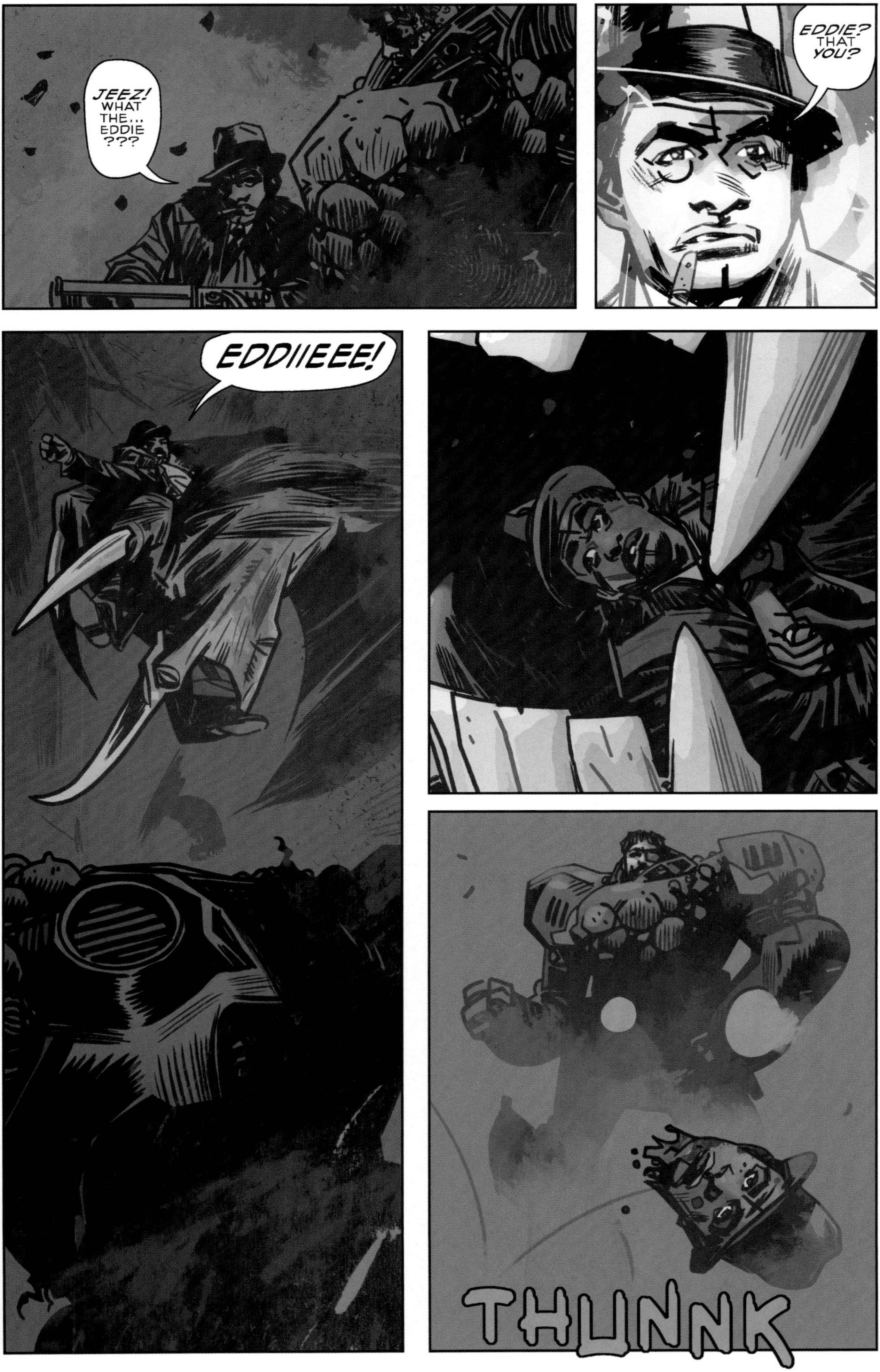
JEEZ! WHAT THE... EDDIE???
EDDIE? THAT YOU?
EDDIIEEE!
THUNNK

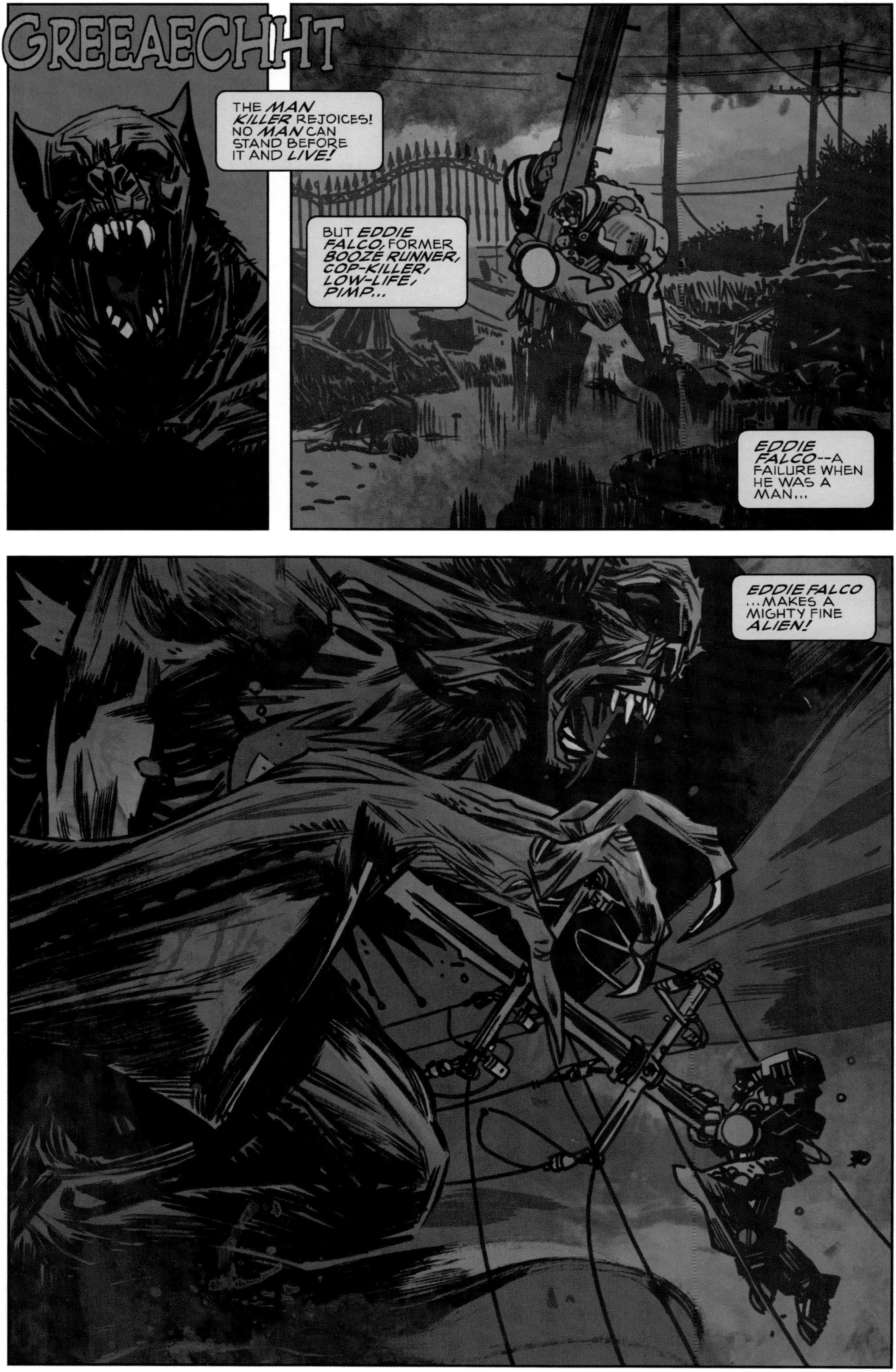
GREEAECHHT
THE MAN KILLER REJOICES! NO MAN CAN STAND BEFORE IT AND LIVE!
BUT EDDIE FALCO, FORMER BOOZE RUNNER, COP-KILLER, LOW-LIFE, PIMP...
EDDIE FALCO--A FAILURE WHEN HE WAS A MAN...
EDDIE FALCO ...MAKES A MIGHTY FINE ALIEN!

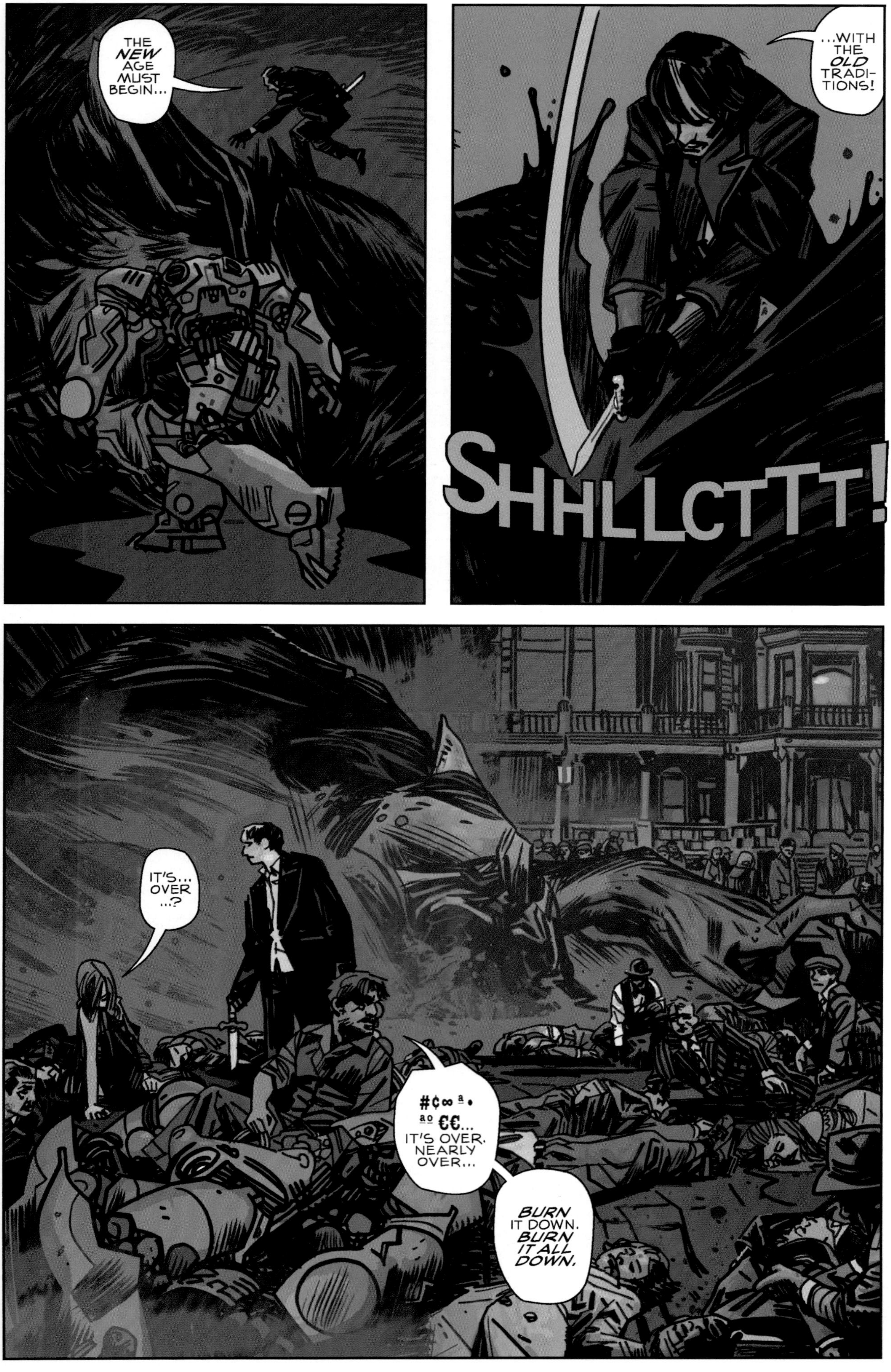
THE *NEW* AGE MUST BEGIN...
...WITH THE *OLD* TRADI-TIONS!
SHHLLCTTT!
IT'S... OVER ...?
#¢∞ª. ªº €€... IT'S OVER. NEARLY OVER...
BURN IT DOWN. *BURN IT ALL DOWN.*

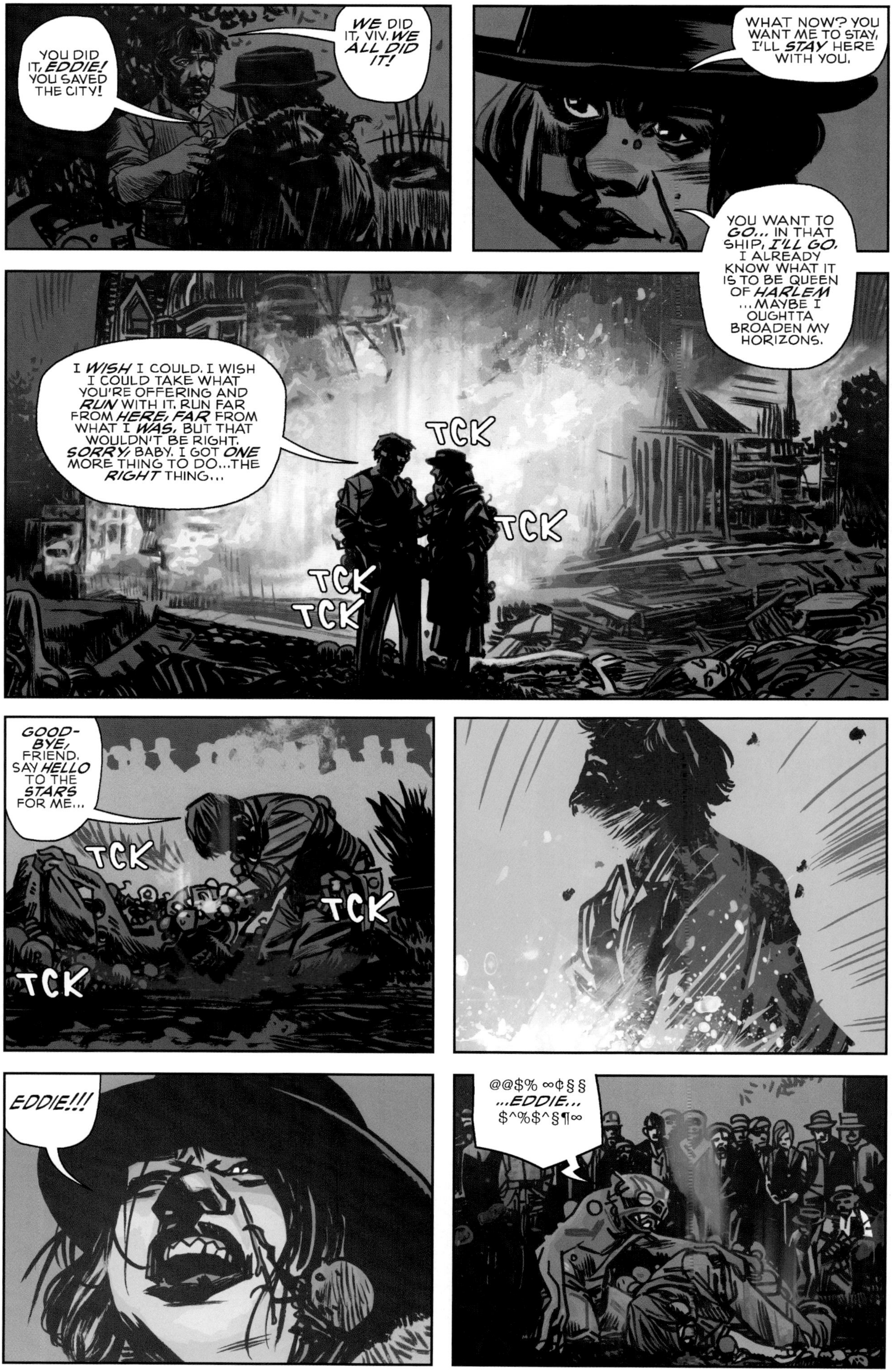
YOU DID IT, EDDIE! YOU SAVED THE CITY!
WE DID IT, VIV. WE ALL DID IT!
WHAT NOW? YOU WANT ME TO STAY, I'LL STAY HERE WITH YOU.
YOU WANT TO GO... IN THAT SHIP, I'LL GO. I ALREADY KNOW WHAT IT IS TO BE QUEEN OF HARLEM ...MAYBE I OUGHTTA BROADEN MY HORIZONS.
I WISH I COULD. I WISH I COULD TAKE WHAT YOU'RE OFFERING AND RUN WITH IT. RUN FAR FROM HERE, FAR FROM WHAT I WAS, BUT THAT WOULDN'T BE RIGHT. SORRY, BABY. I GOT ONE MORE THING TO DO...THE RIGHT THING...
TCK
TCK
TCK
TCK
GOOD-BYE, FRIEND. SAY HELLO TO THE STARS FOR ME...
TCK
TCK
TCK
EDDIE!!!
@@$% ∞¢§§ ...EDDIE... $^%$^§¶∞

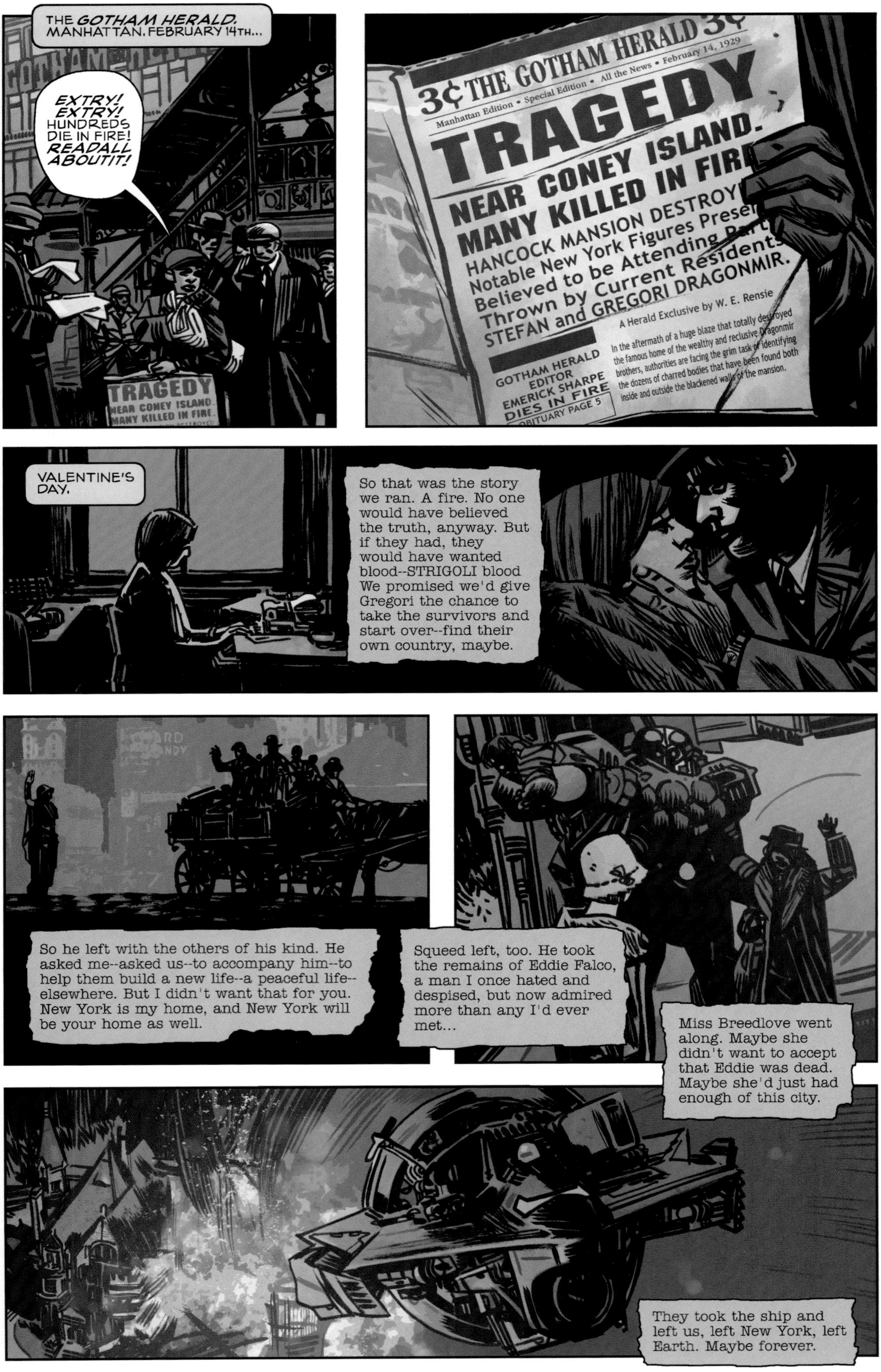
THE GOTHAM HERALD. MANHATTAN, FEBRUARY 14TH...
EXTRY! EXTRY! HUNDREDS DIE IN FIRE! READALL ABOUTIT!
TRAGEDY NEAR CONEY ISLAND. MANY KILLED IN FIRE.
3¢ THE GOTHAM HERALD 3¢
Manhattan Edition • Special Edition • All the News • February 14, 1929
TRAGEDY
NEAR CONEY ISLAND. MANY KILLED IN FIR
HANCOCK MANSION DESTROY
Notable New York Figures Prese
Believed to be Attending Part
Thrown by Current Residents
STEFAN and GREGORI DRAGONMIR.
A Herald Exclusive by W. E. Rensie
In the aftermath of a huge blaze that totally destroyed the famous home of the wealthy and reclusive Dragonmir brothers, authorities are facing the grim task of identifying the dozens of charred bodies that have been found both inside and outside the blackened walls of the mansion.
GOTHAM HERALD EDITOR EMERICK SHARPE DIES IN FIRE
OBITUARY PAGE 5
VALENTINE'S DAY.
So that was the story we ran. A fire. No one would have believed the truth, anyway. But if they had, they would have wanted blood--STRIGOLI blood We promised we'd give Gregori the chance to take the survivors and start over--find their own country, maybe.
So he left with the others of his kind. He asked me--asked us--to accompany him--to help them build a new life--a peaceful life--elsewhere. But I didn't want that for you. New York is my home, and New York will be your home as well.
Squeed left, too. He took the remains of Eddie Falco, a man I once hated and despised, but now admired more than any I'd ever met...
Miss Breedlove went along. Maybe she didn't want to accept that Eddie was dead. Maybe she'd just had enough of this city.
They took the ship and left us, left New York, left Earth. Maybe forever.

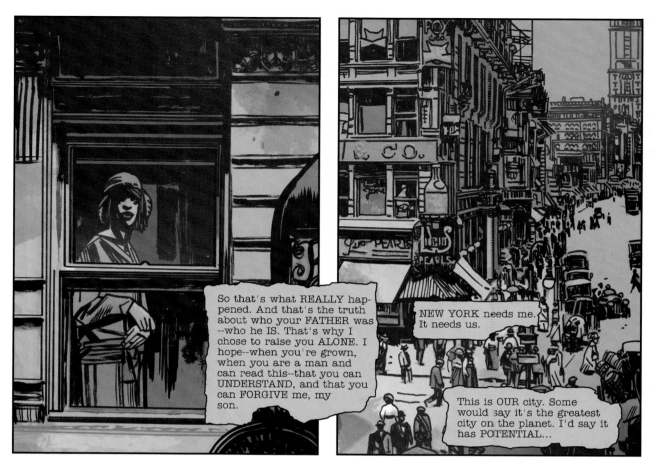

So that's what REALLY happened. And that's the truth about who your FATHER was --who he IS. That's why I chose to raise you ALONE. I hope--when you're grown, when you are a man and can read this--that you can UNDERSTAND, and that you can FORGIVE me, my son.

NEW YORK needs me. It needs us.

This is OUR city. Some would say it's the greatest city on the planet. I'd say it has POTENTIAL...

DONG... DONG... DONG...

PAPA LABRANCHE, WE ARE HERE, WE HAVE ARRIVED, PAPA, IT IS TIME.

C'EST BON! I WILL WAKE OUR ZOMBIES, ANY WHO STAND IN OUR WAY WILL BECOME A SLAVE, THIS CITY WILL SOON BE OURS, OURS AND OURS ALONE!

The END ?

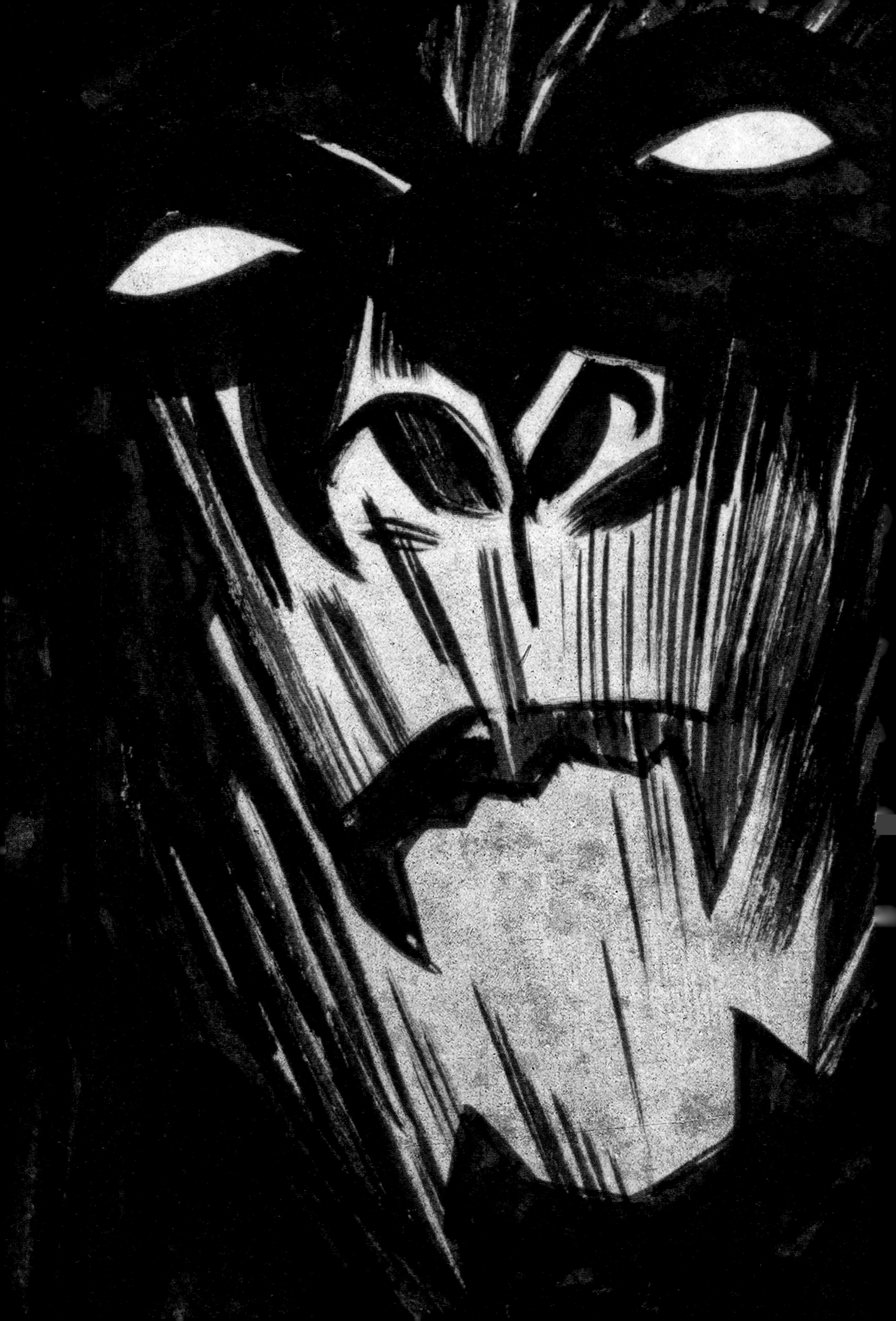

The
COVERS

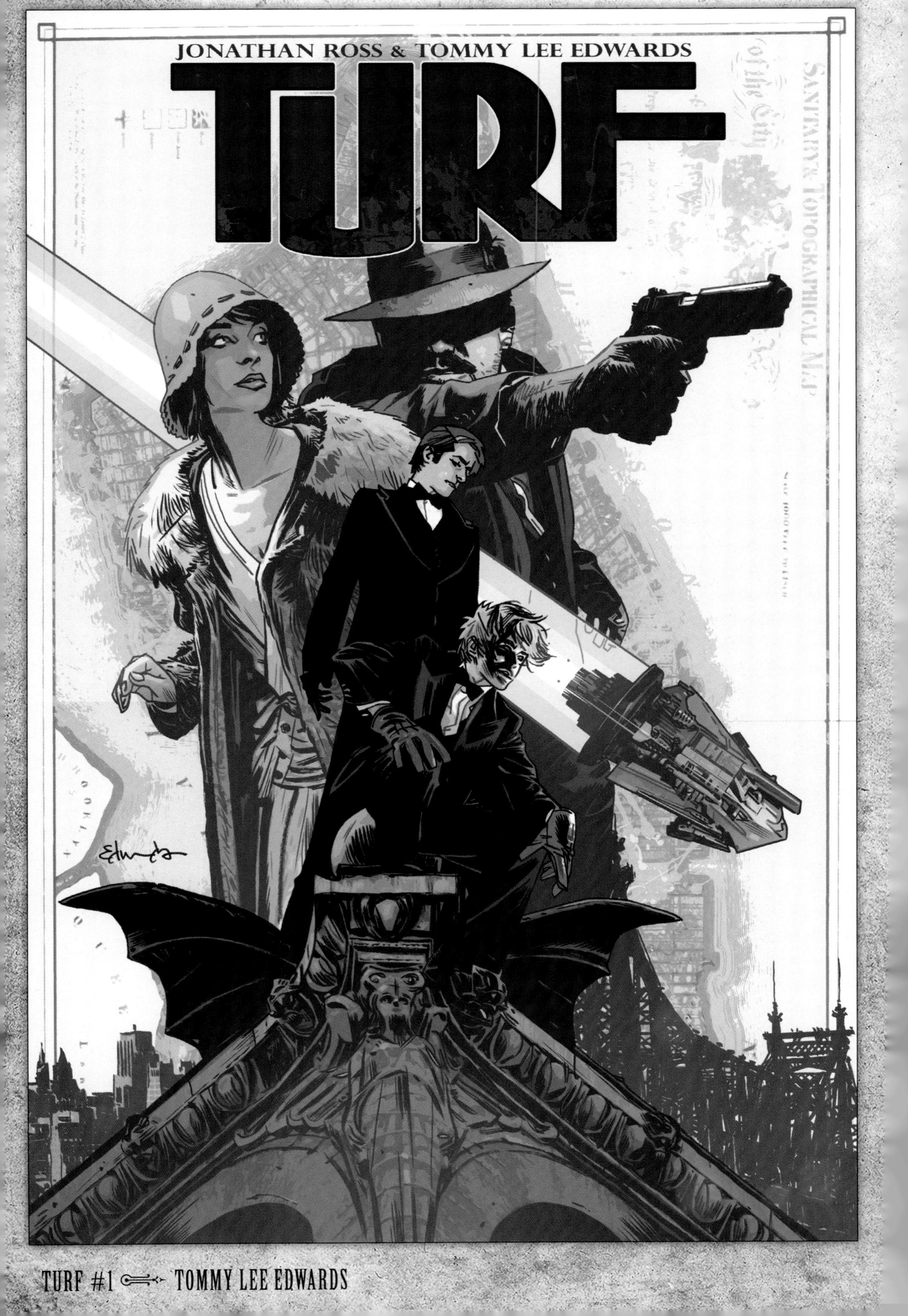
JONATHAN ROSS & TOMMY LEE EDWARDS
TURF
SANITARY & TOPOGRAPHICAL MAP
of the City

TURF #1 — TOMMY LEE EDWARDS

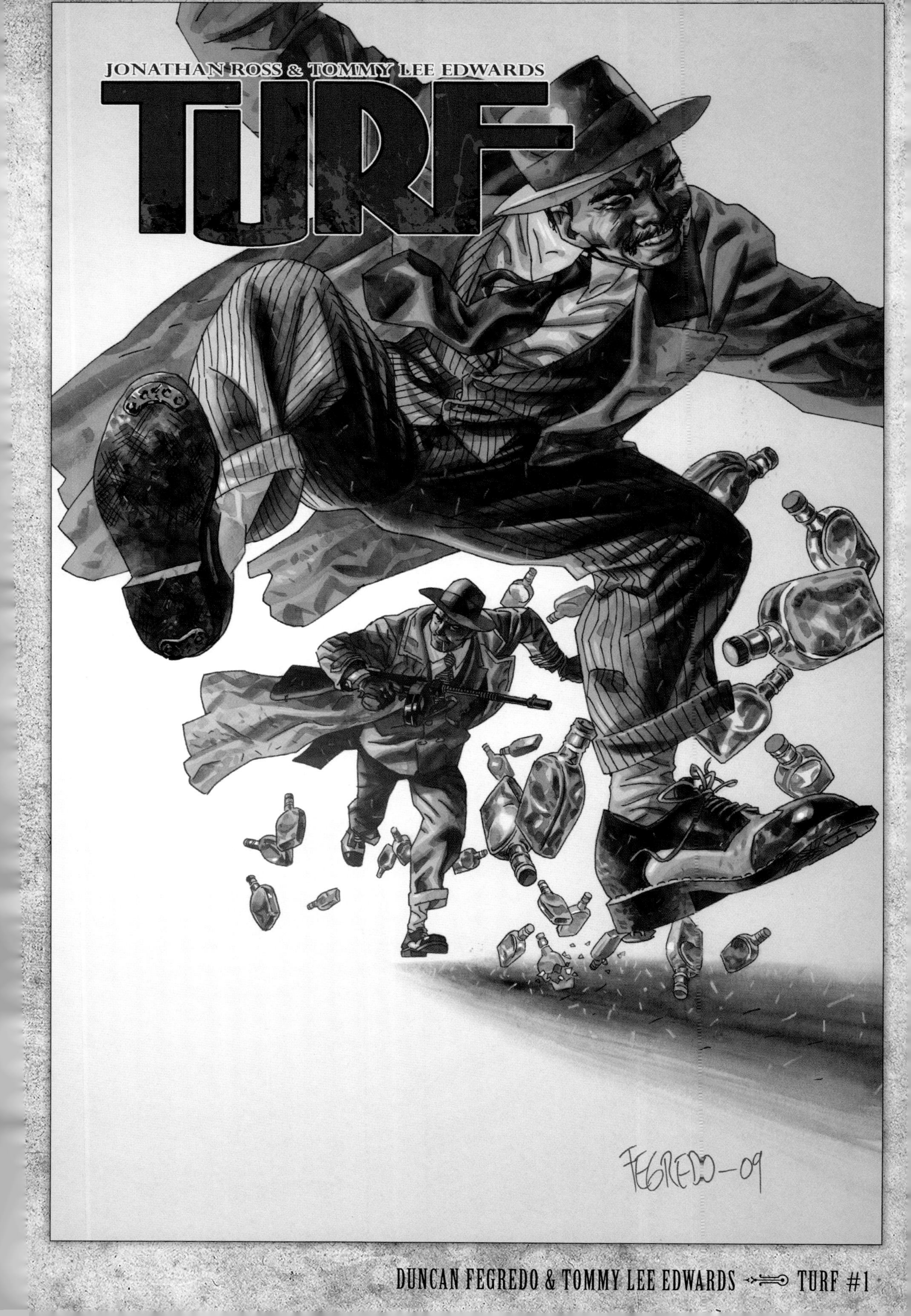
JONATHAN ROSS & TOMMY LEE EDWARDS
TURF
FEGREDO-09

DUNCAN FEGREDO & TOMMY LEE EDWARDS — TURF #1

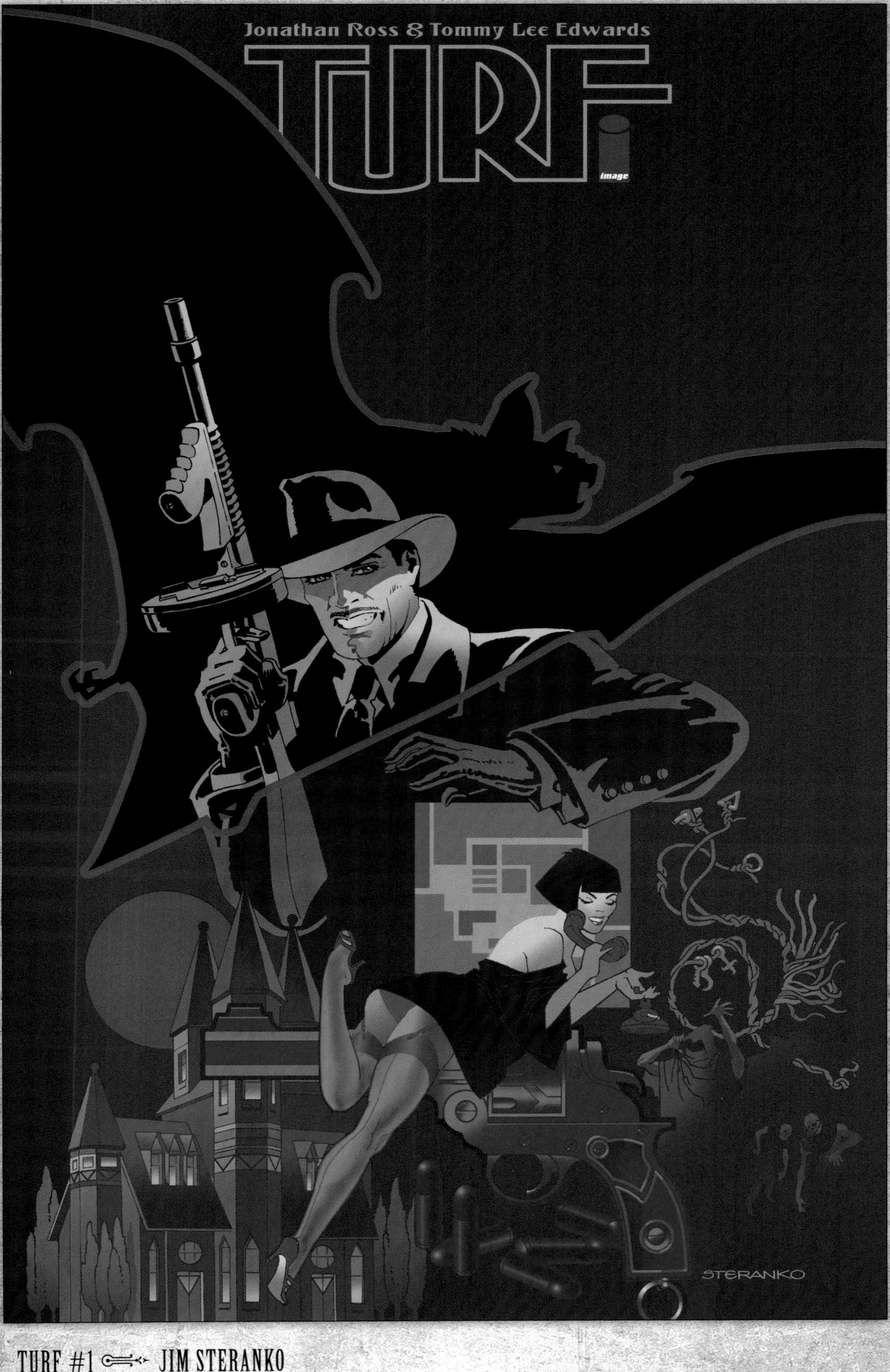

TURF #1 ⊶ JIM STERANKO

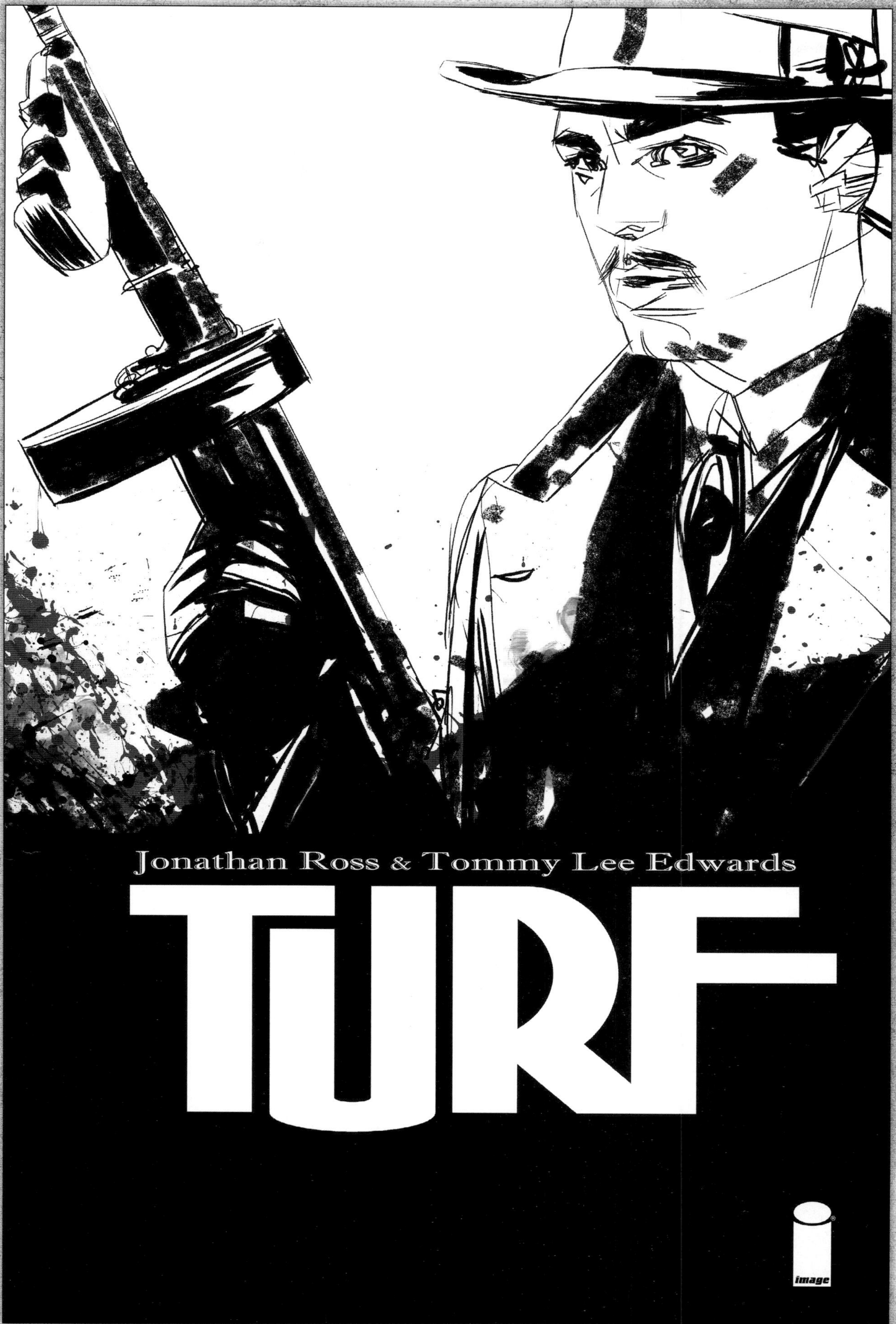
Jonathan Ross & Tommy Lee Edwards
TURF
image

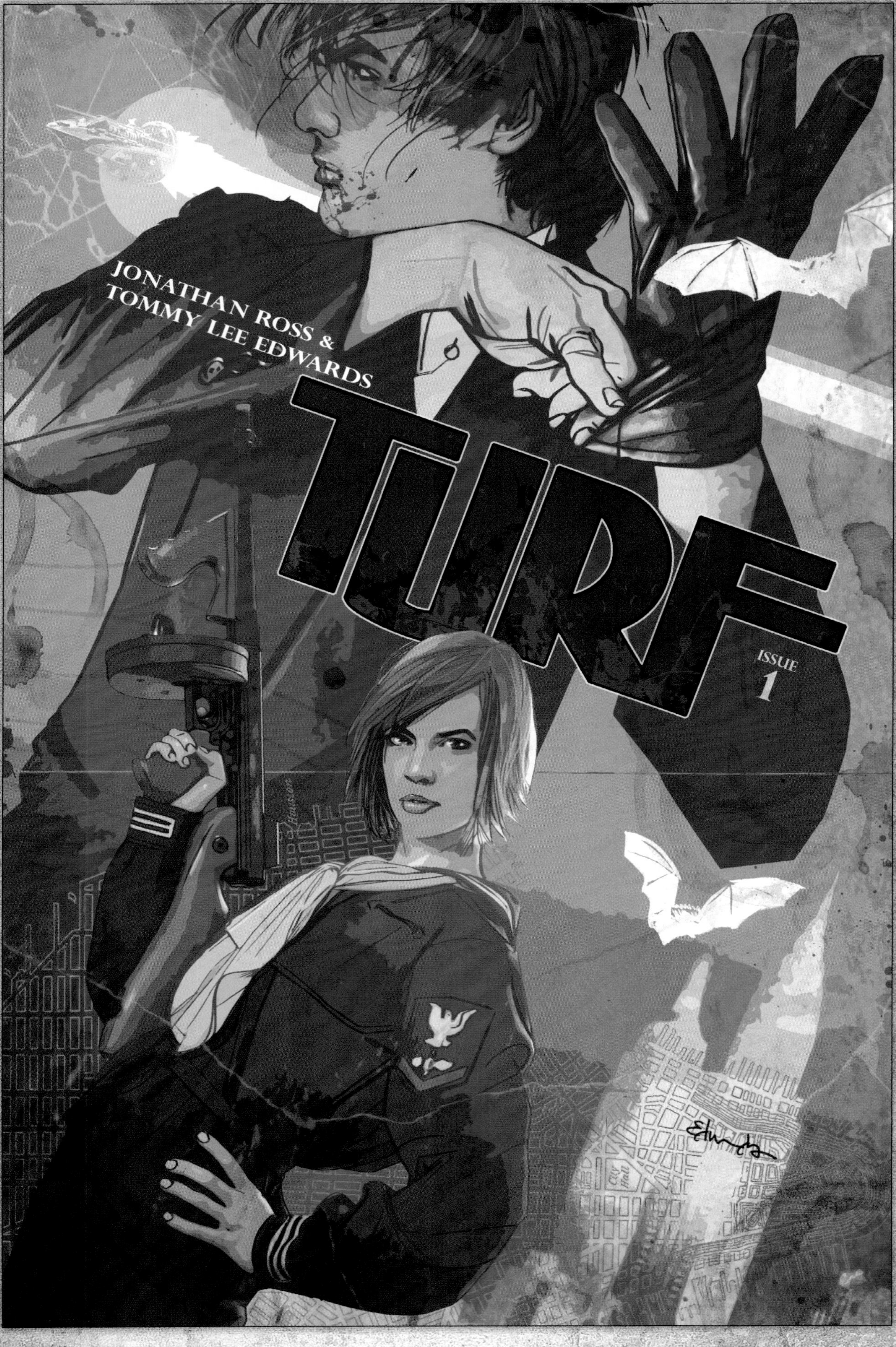
JONATHAN ROSS &
TOMMY LEE EDWARDS
TURF
ISSUE
1

TURF #2 ⊶ TOMMY LEE EDWARDS

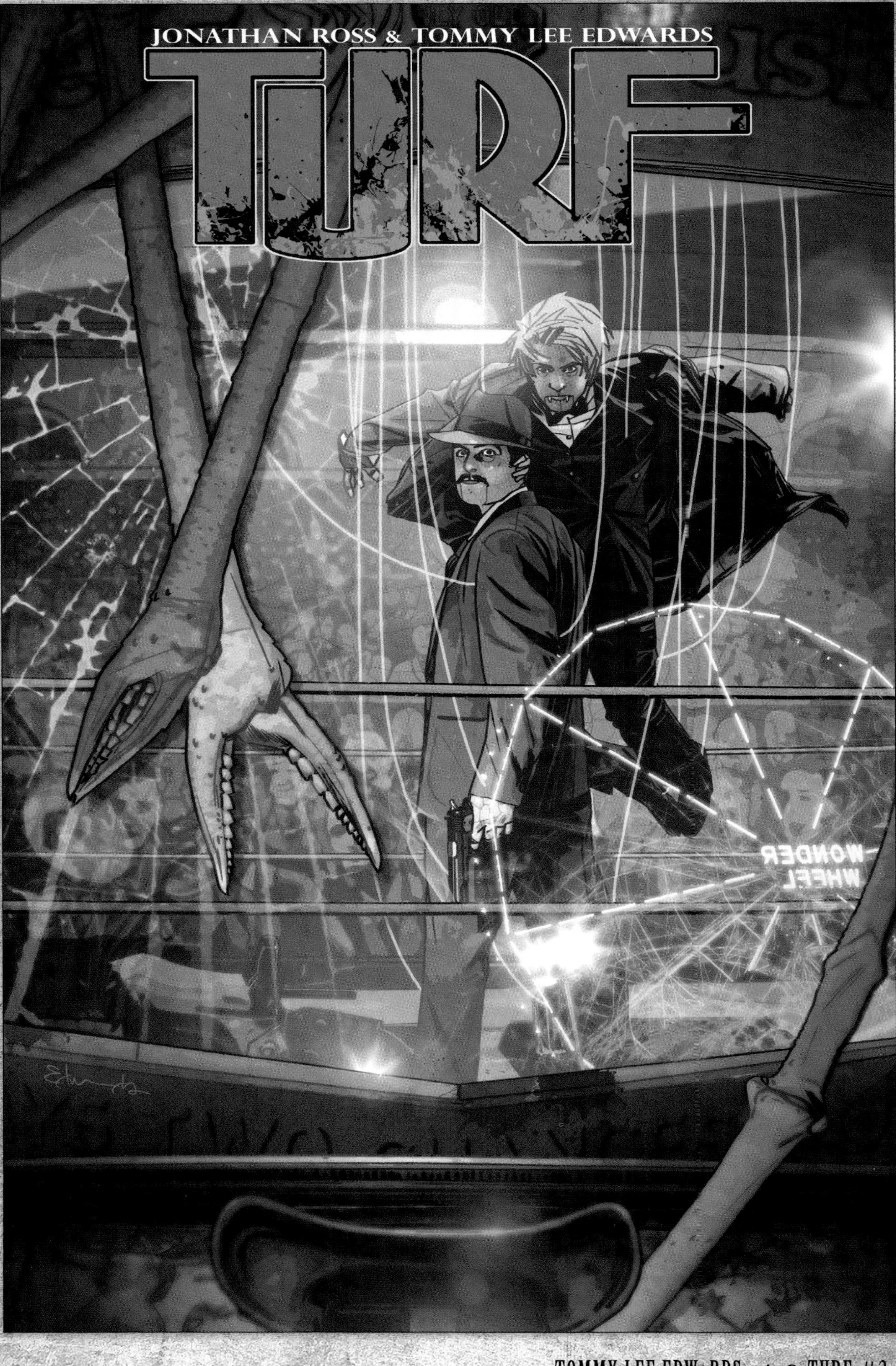
JONATHAN ROSS & TOMMY LEE EDWARDS
TURF
WONDER WHEEL

TOMMY LEE EDWARDS — TURF #2

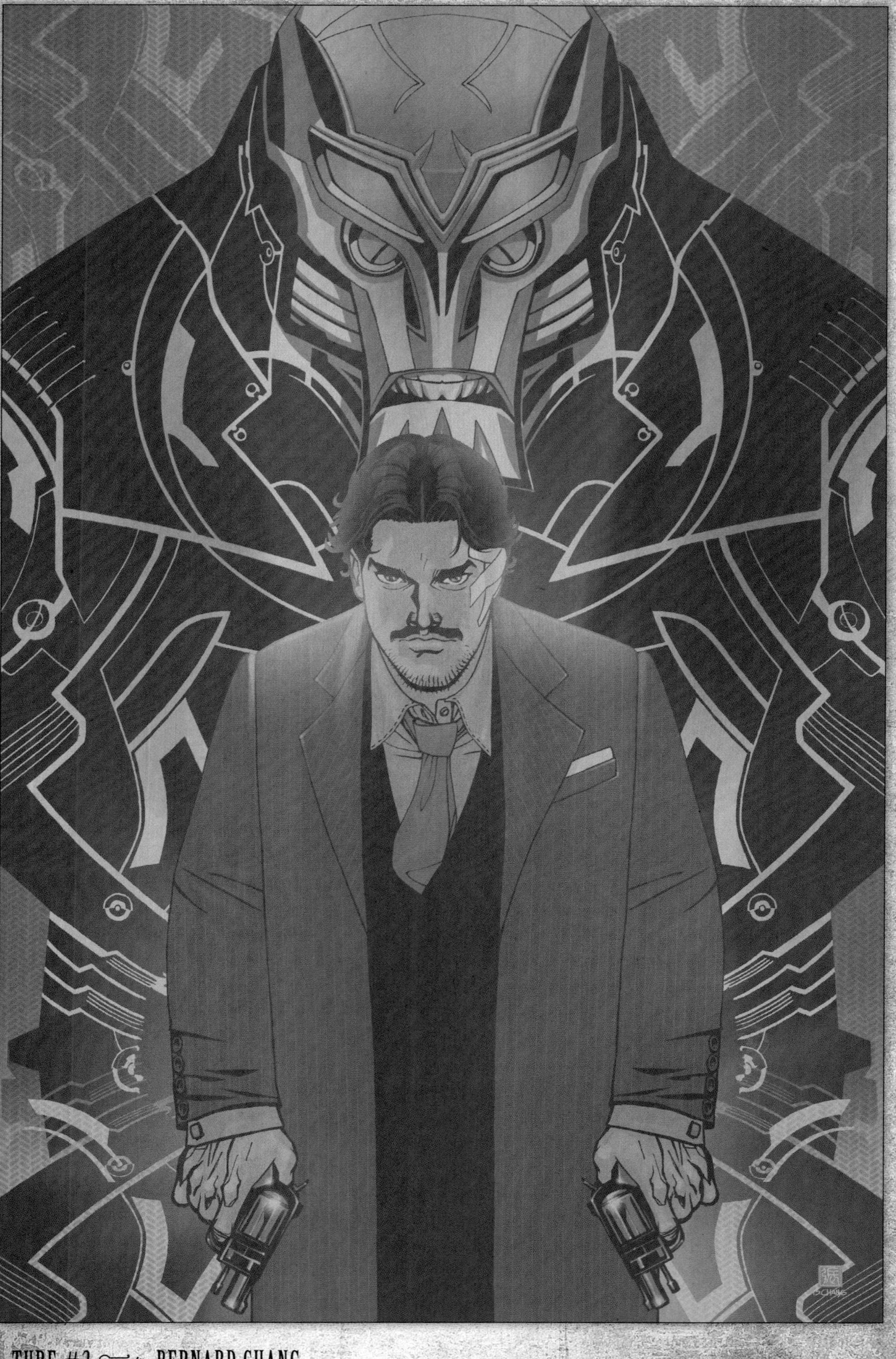

TURF #2 ⟜ BERNARD CHANG

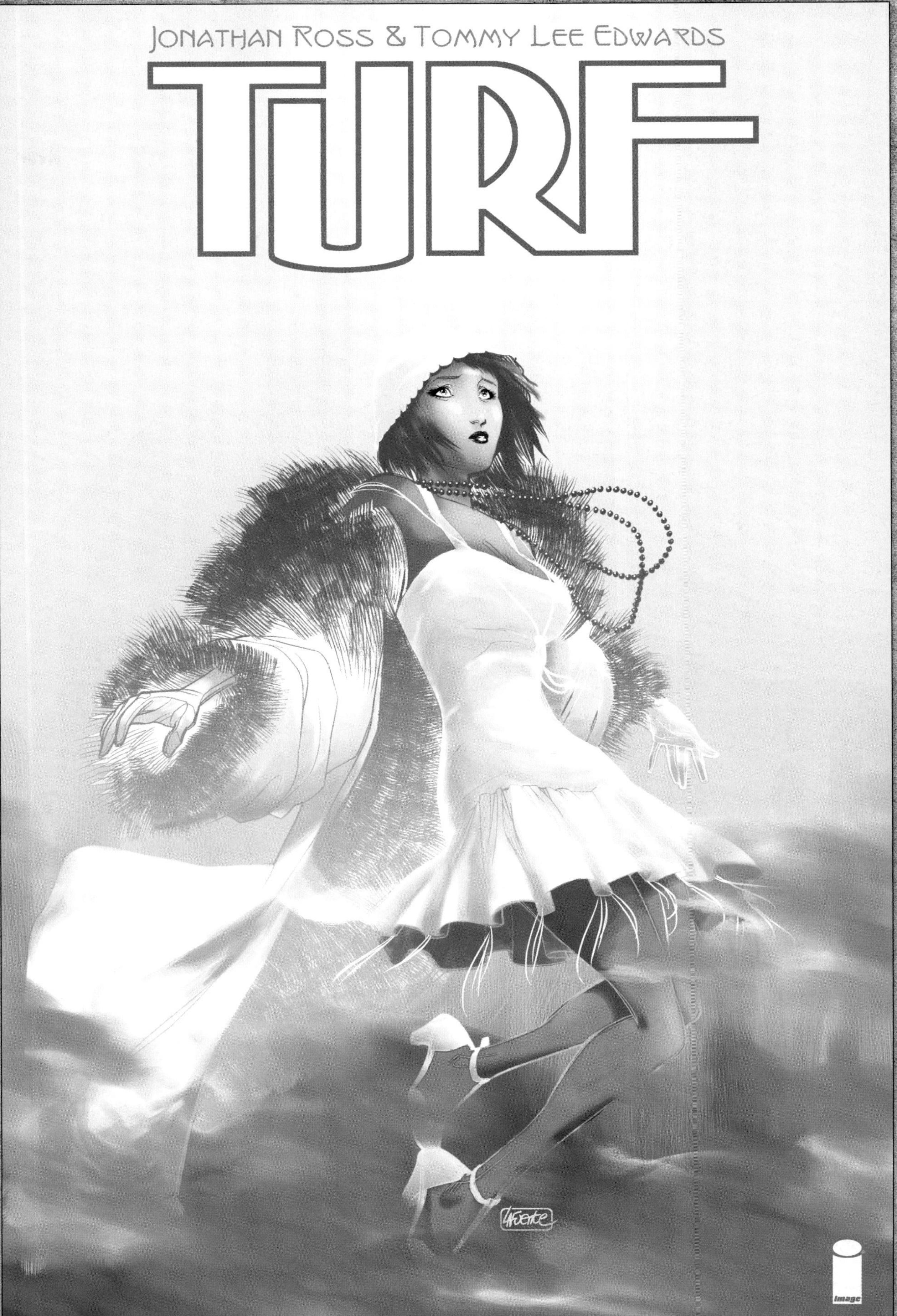
JONATHAN ROSS & TOMMY LEE EDWARDS
TURF

DAVID LAFUENTE — TURF #2

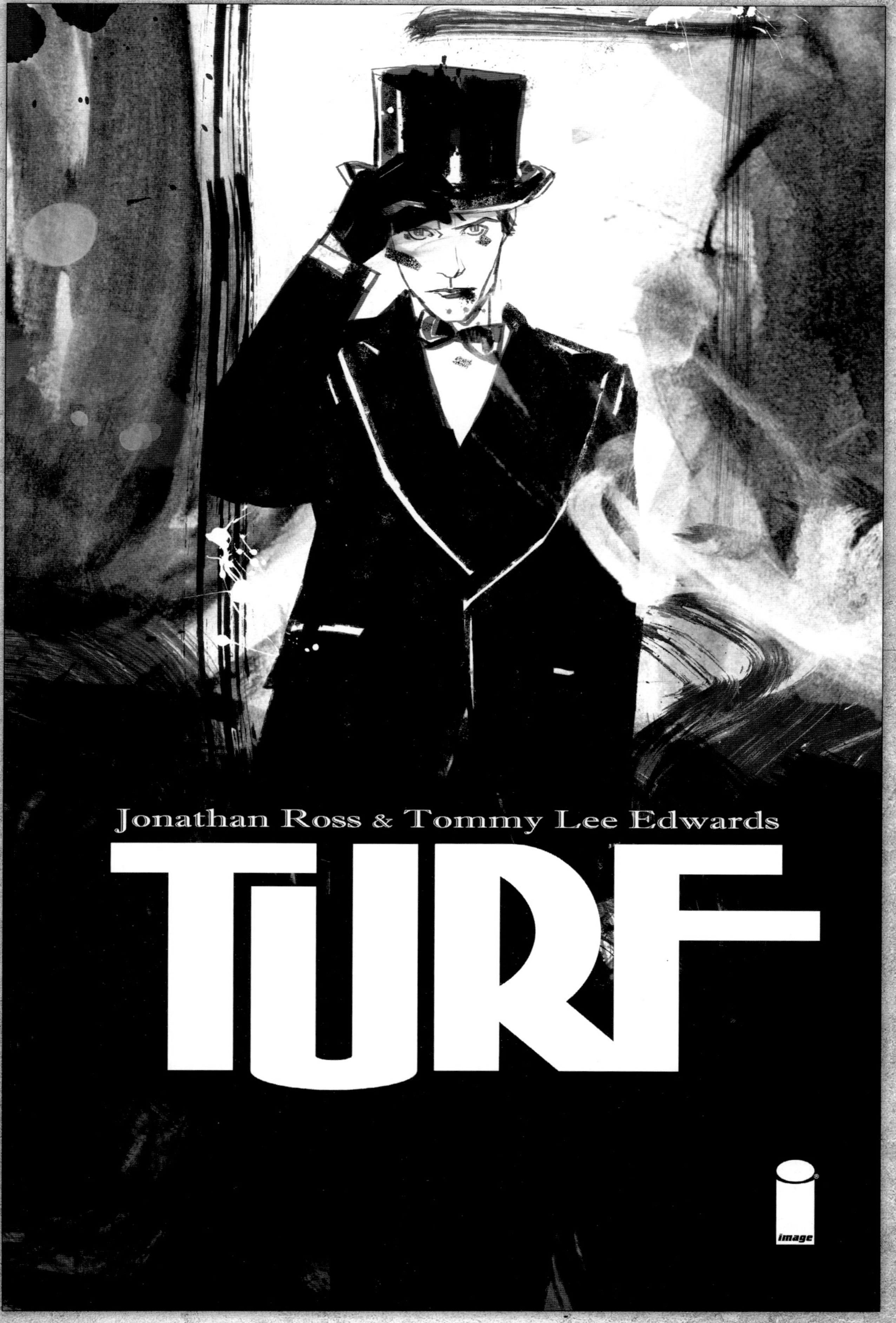
Jonathan Ross & Tommy Lee Edwards
TURF
image

TURF #2 ⟜ TOMMY LEE EDWARDS

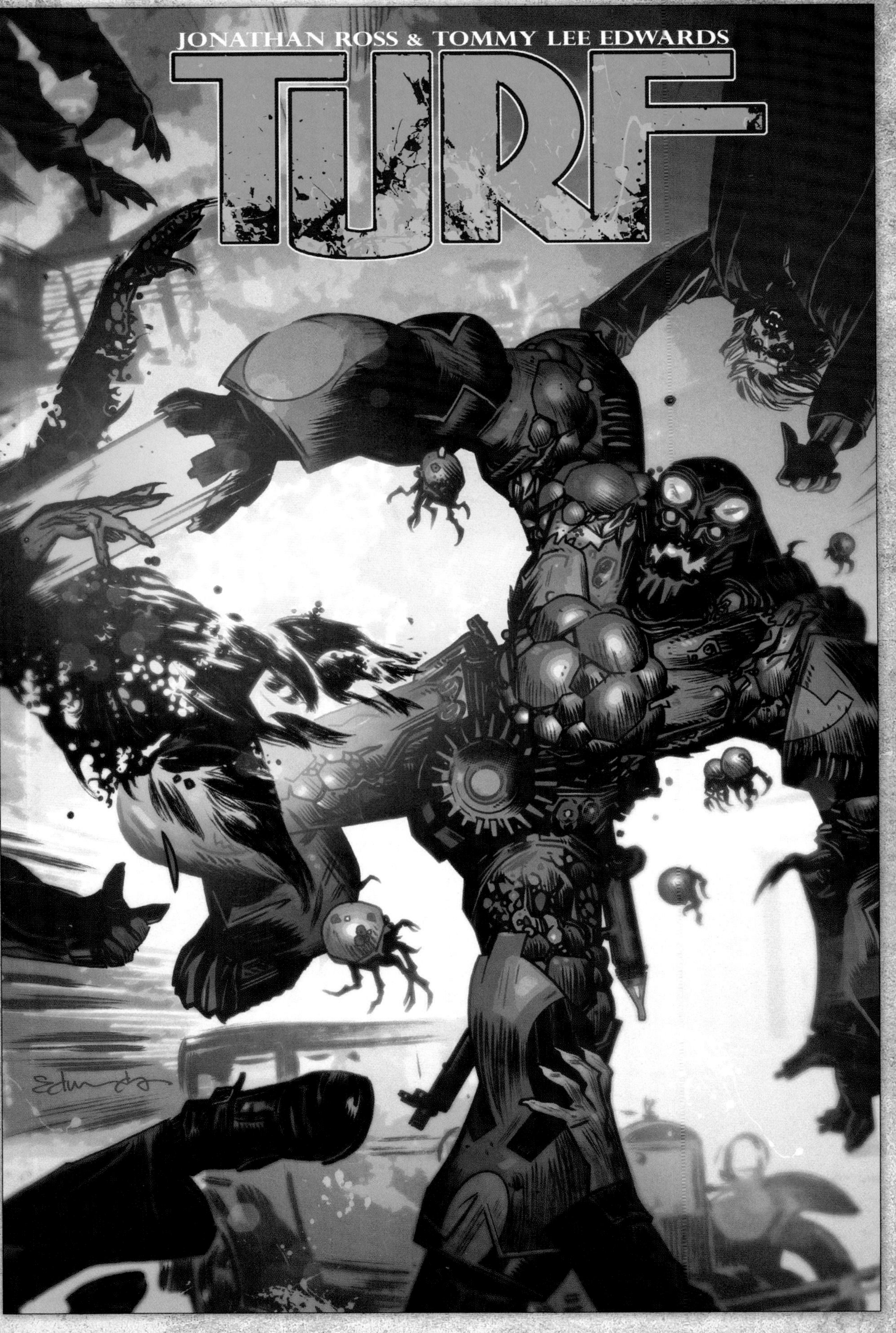
JONATHAN ROSS & TOMMY LEE EDWARDS
TURF

TOMMY LEE EDWARDS — TURF #3

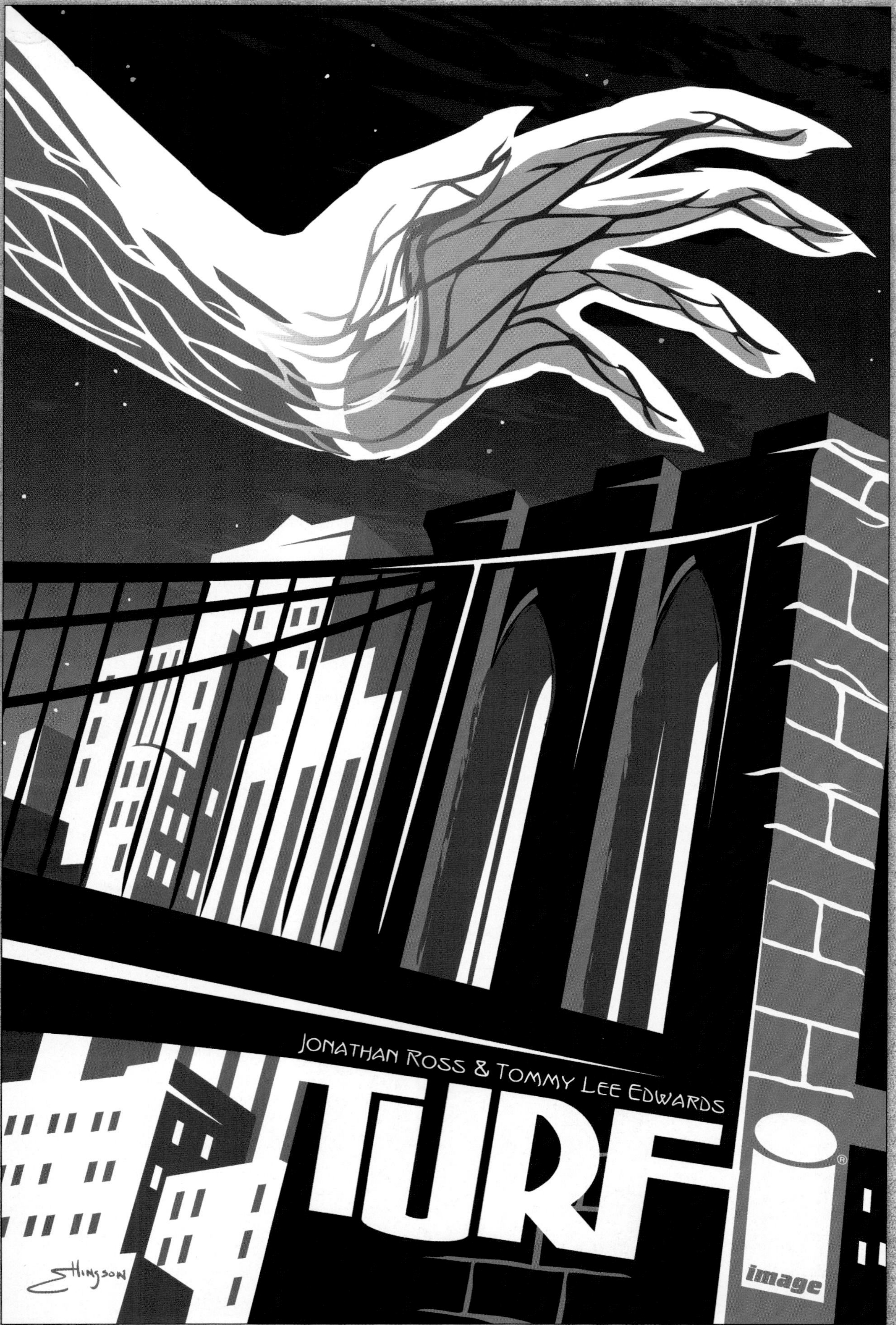
JONATHAN ROSS & TOMMY LEE EDWARDS
TURF
image
Ellingson

TURF #3 ⊶ JOSH ELLINGSON

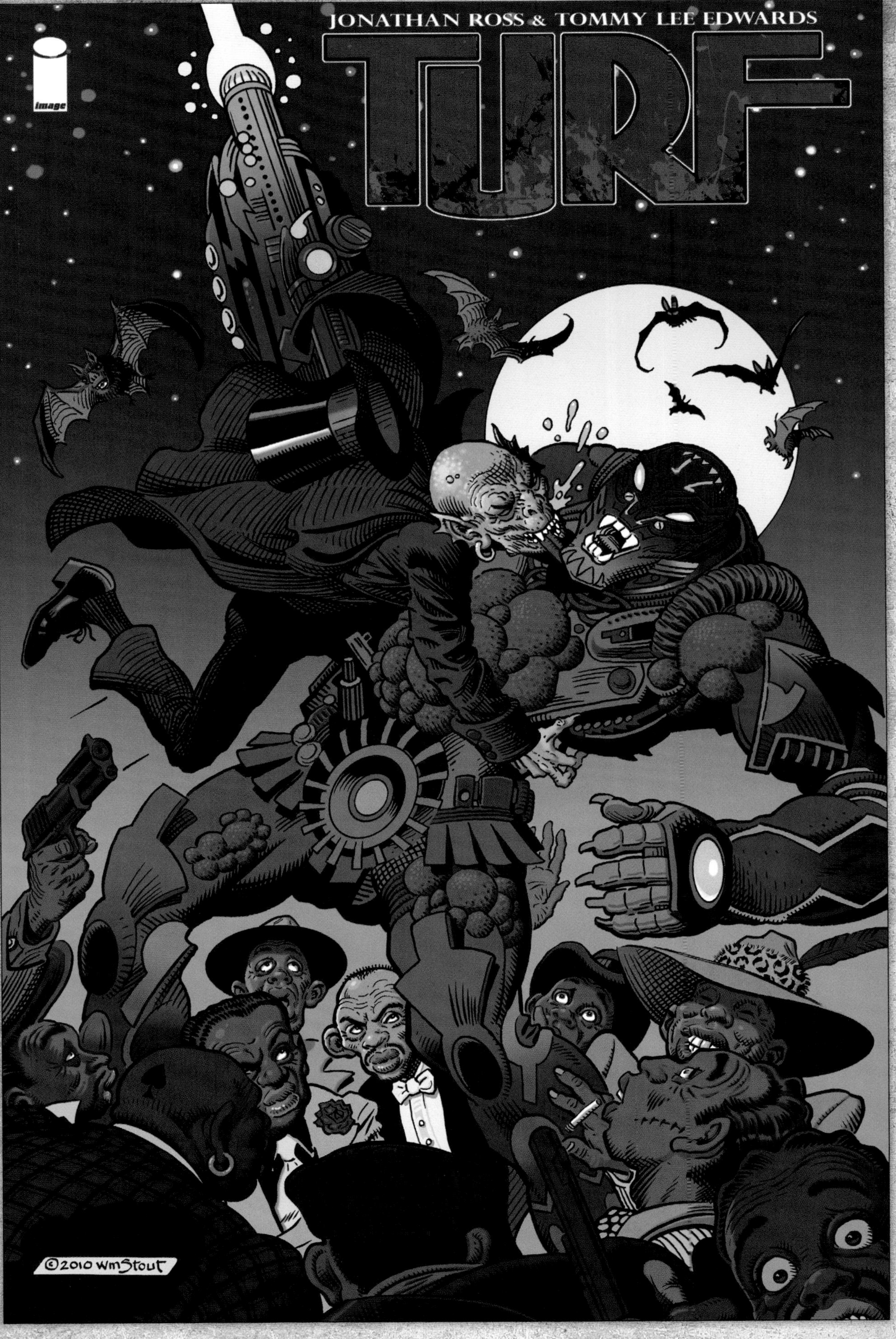
JONATHAN ROSS & TOMMY LEE EDWARDS
TURF
image
©2010 WmStout

WILLIAM STOUT — TURF #3

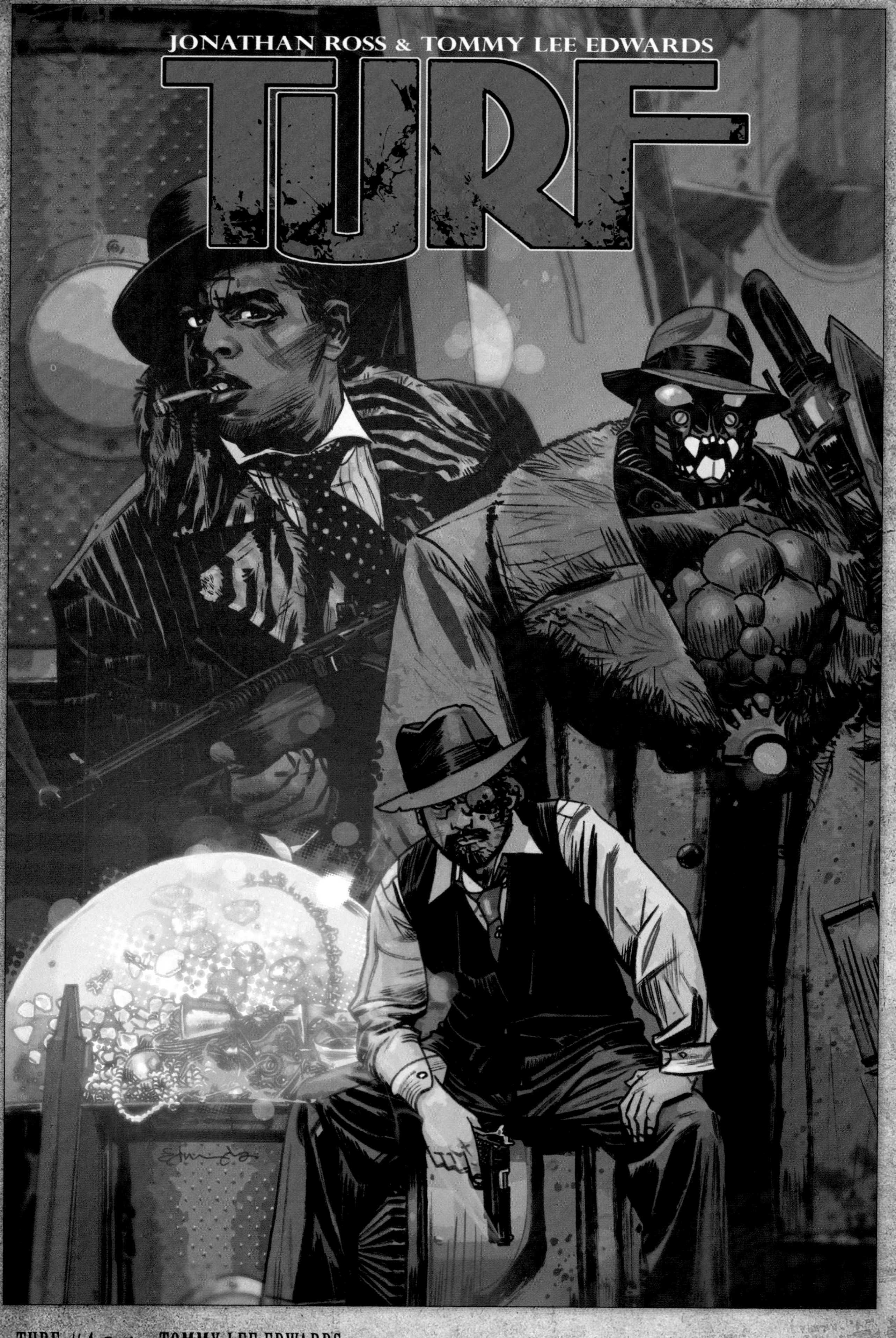
JONATHAN ROSS & TOMMY LEE EDWARDS
TURF

TURF #4 TOMMY LEE EDWARDS

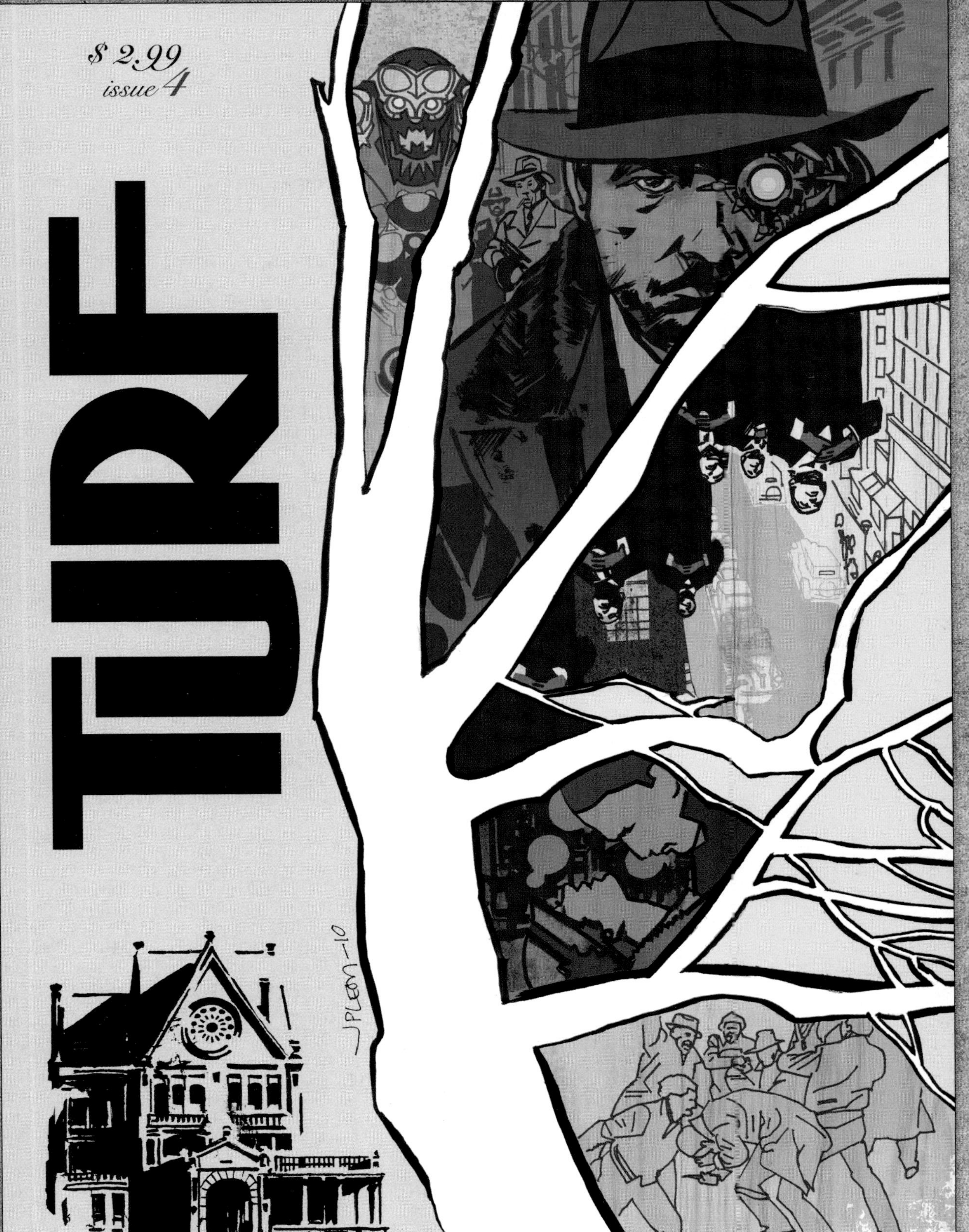
$ 2.99
issue 4
TURF
Jonathan Ross
& Tommy Lee Edwards

JOHN PAUL LEON ⟶ TURF #3

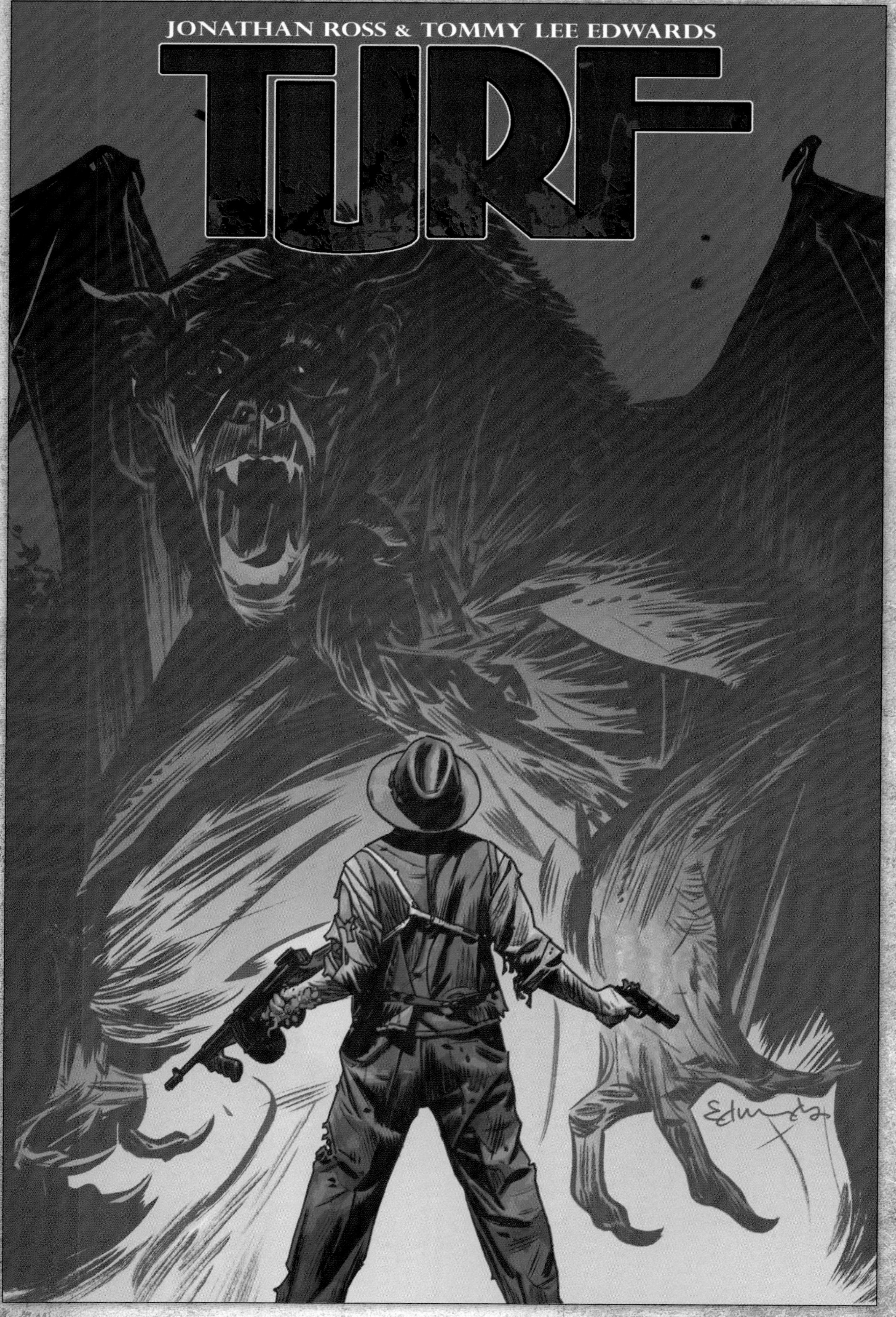
JONATHAN ROSS & TOMMY LEE EDWARDS
TURF
Edwards

TURF #5 — TOMMY LEE EDWARDS

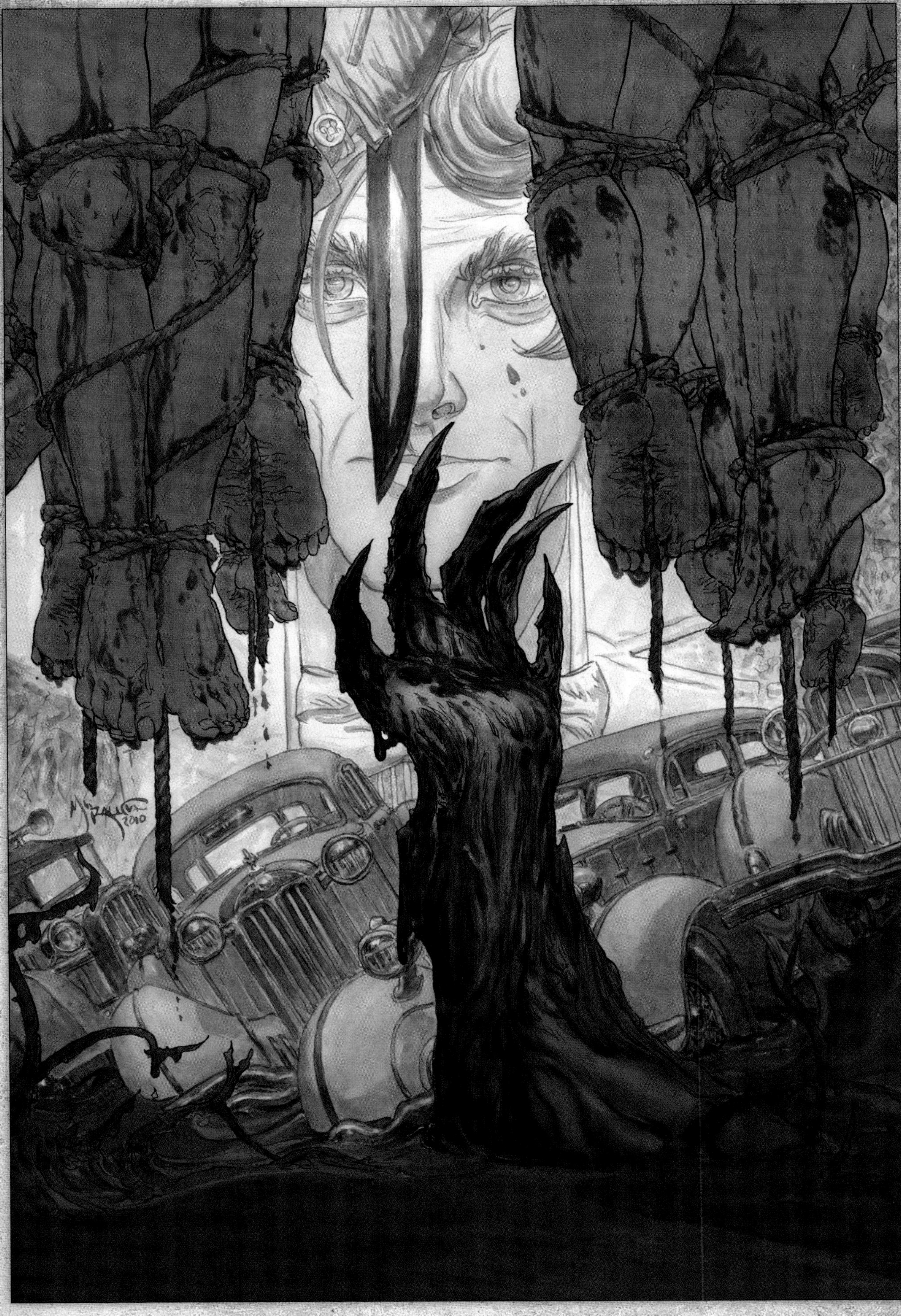

MICHAEL WILLIAM KALUTA ⟜ TURF #5

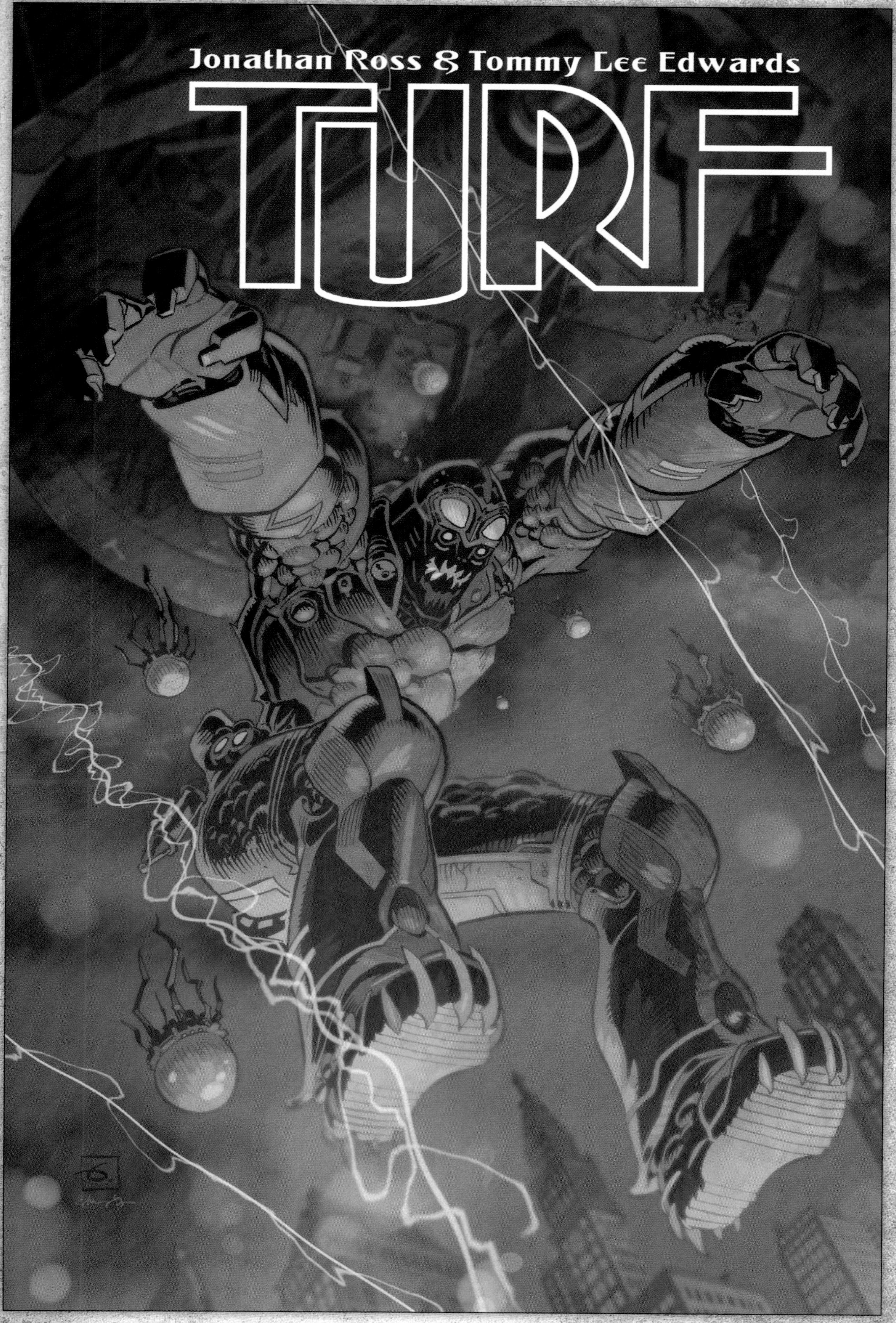
Jonathan Ross & Tommy Lee Edwards
TURF

TURF #5 ⊶ DAVE GIBBONS & TOMMY LEE EDWARDS

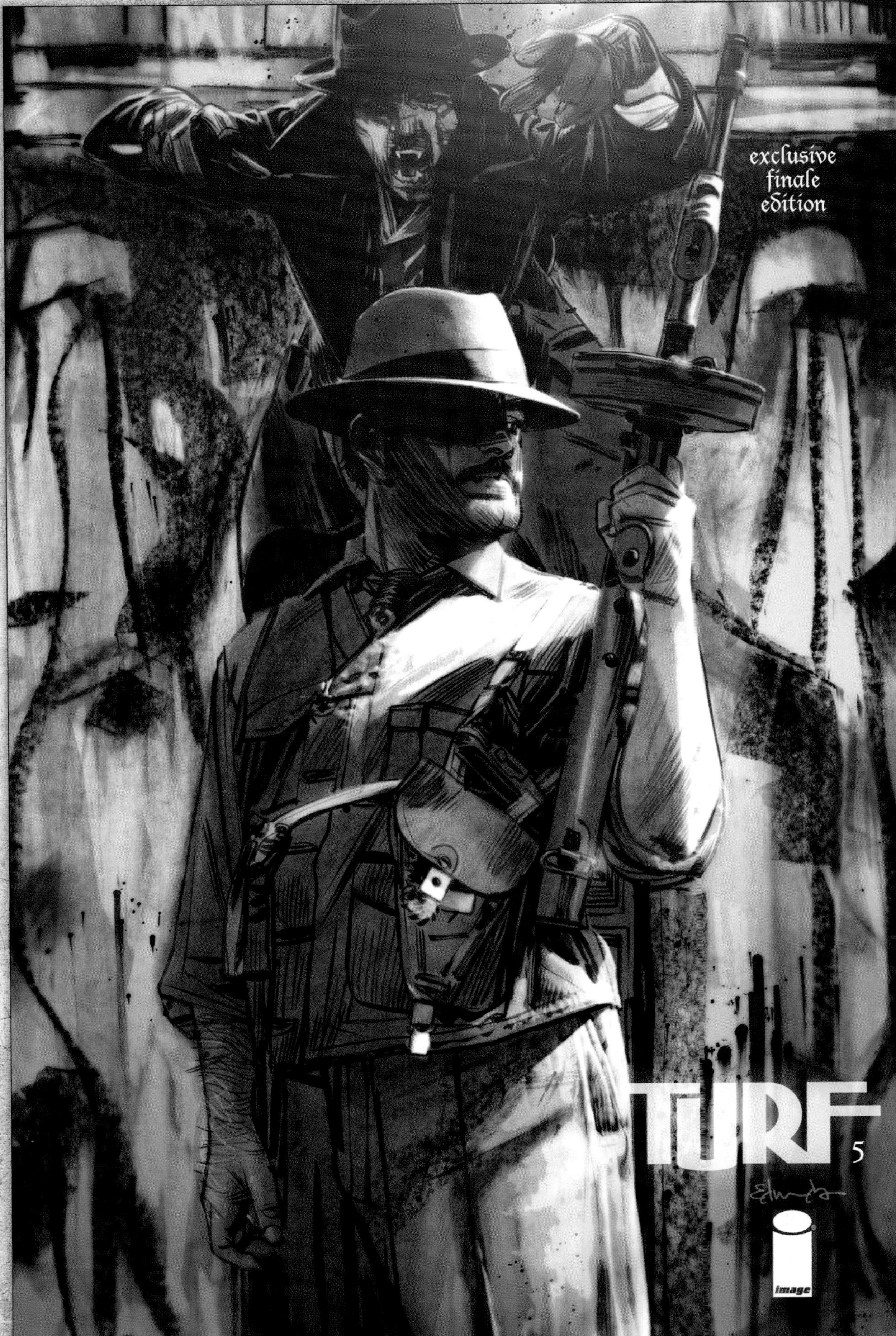
exclusive
finale
edition
TURF 5

TOMMY LEE EDWARDS — TURF #5

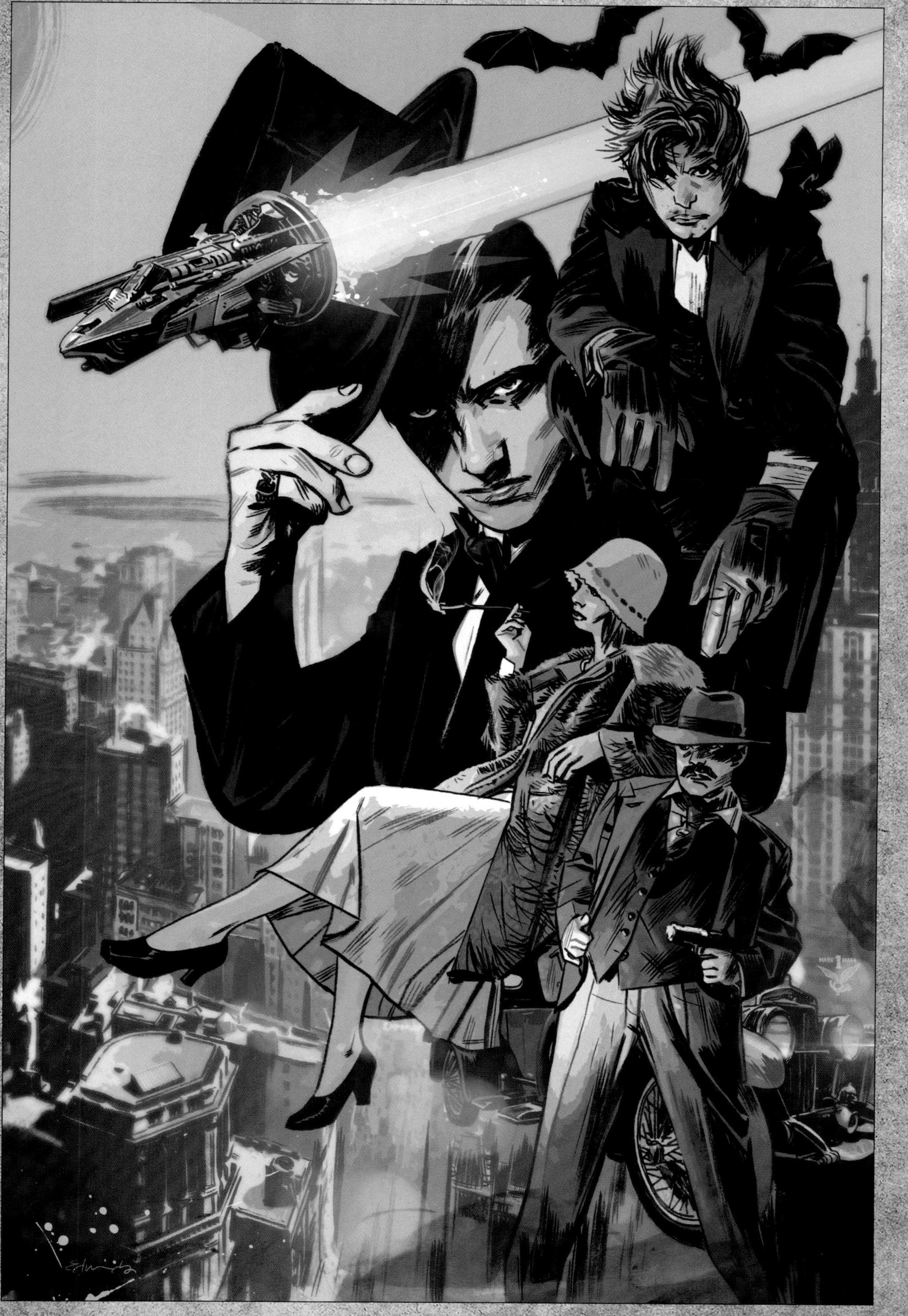

TURF POSTER ⊶ TOMMY LEE EDWARDS

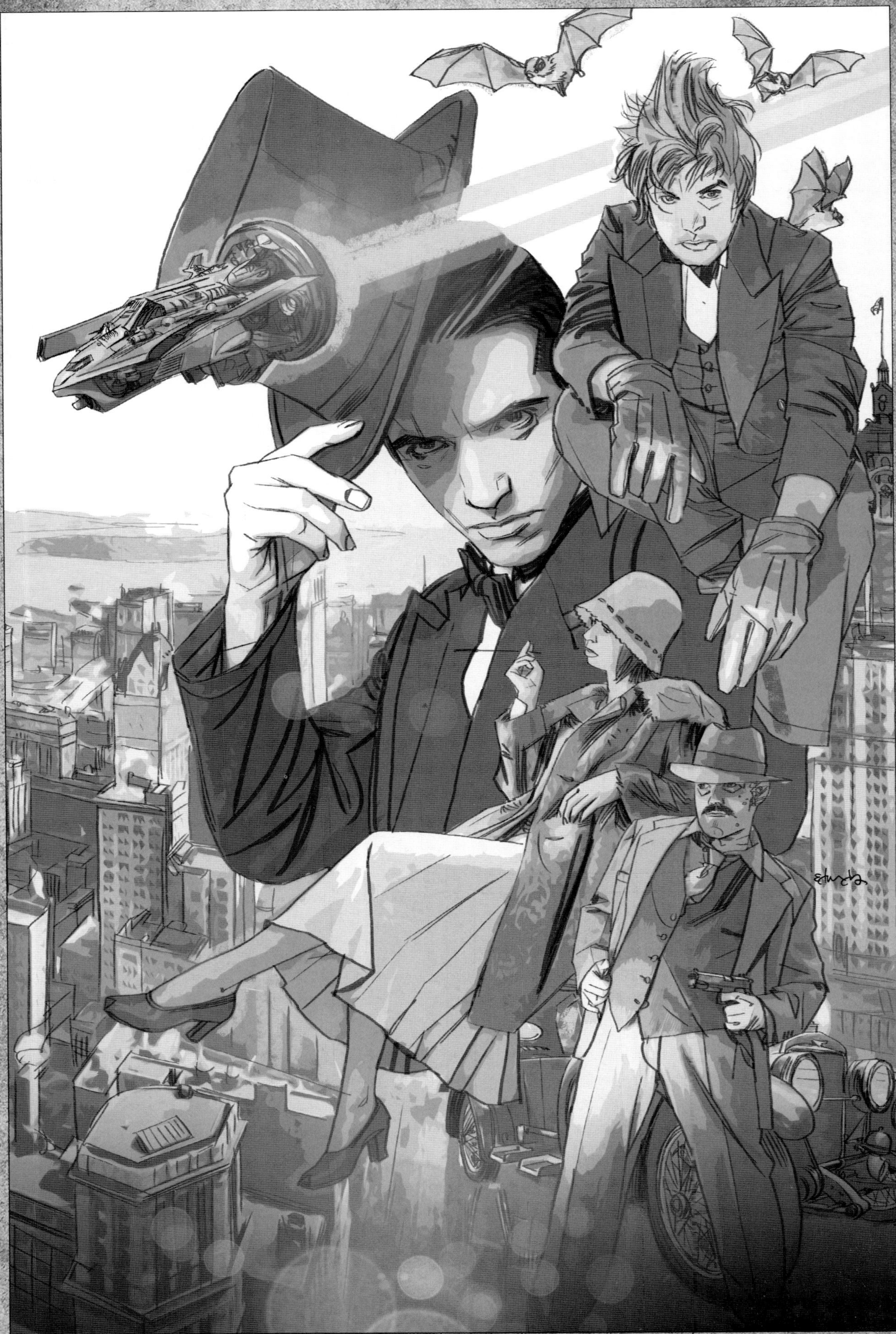

TOMMY LEE EDWARDS ⟶ TURF POSTER SKETCH

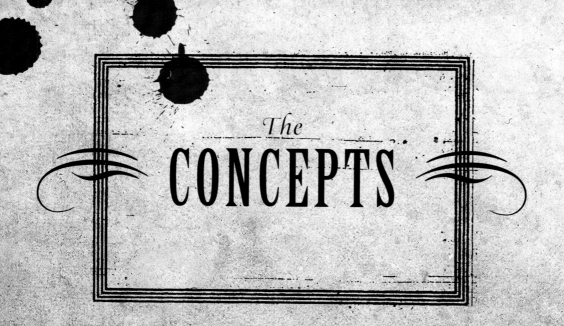

The
CONCEPTS

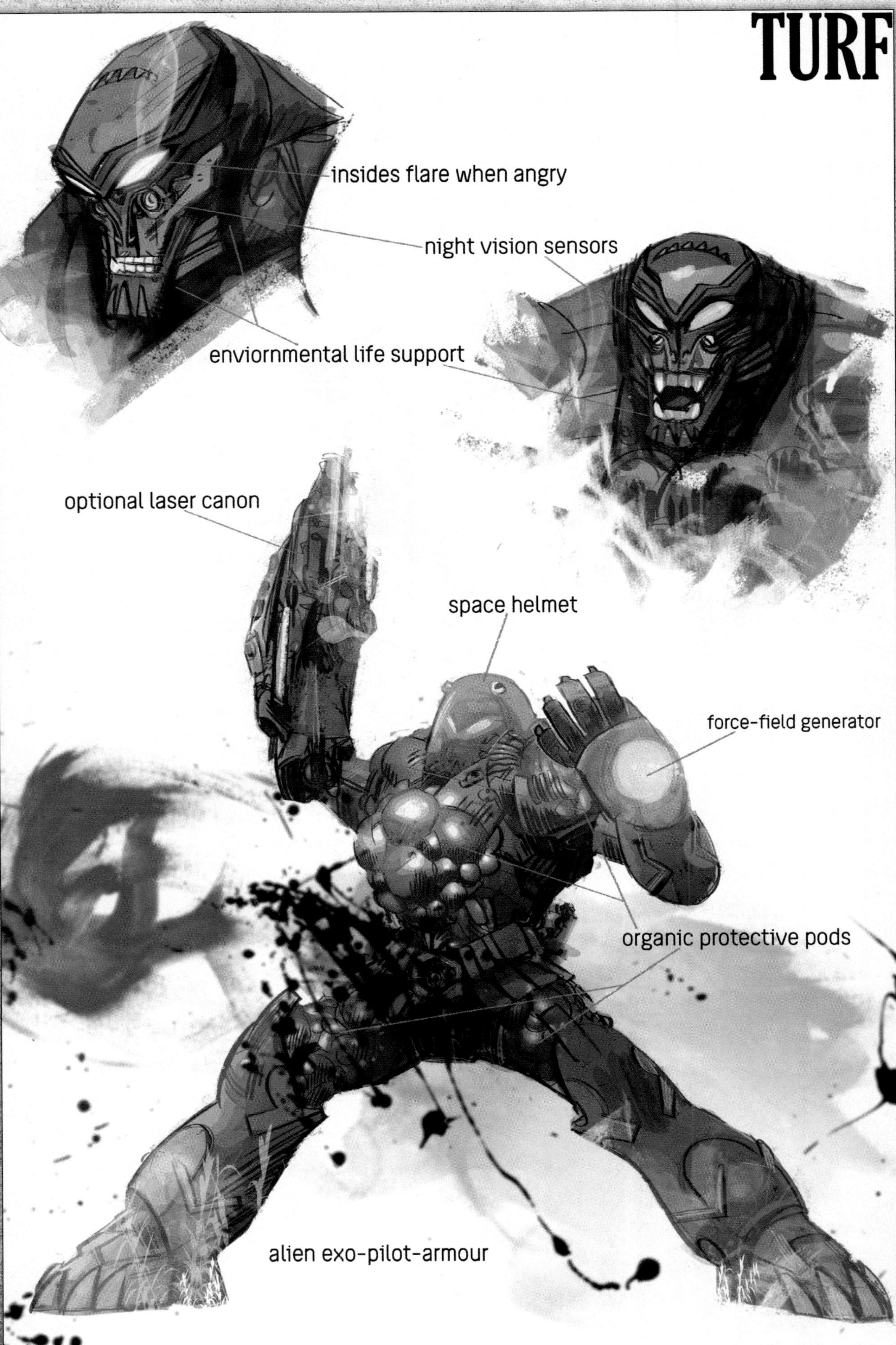
insides flare when angry
night vision sensors
enviornmental life support
optional laser canon
space helmet
force-field generator
organic protective pods
alien exo-pilot-armour

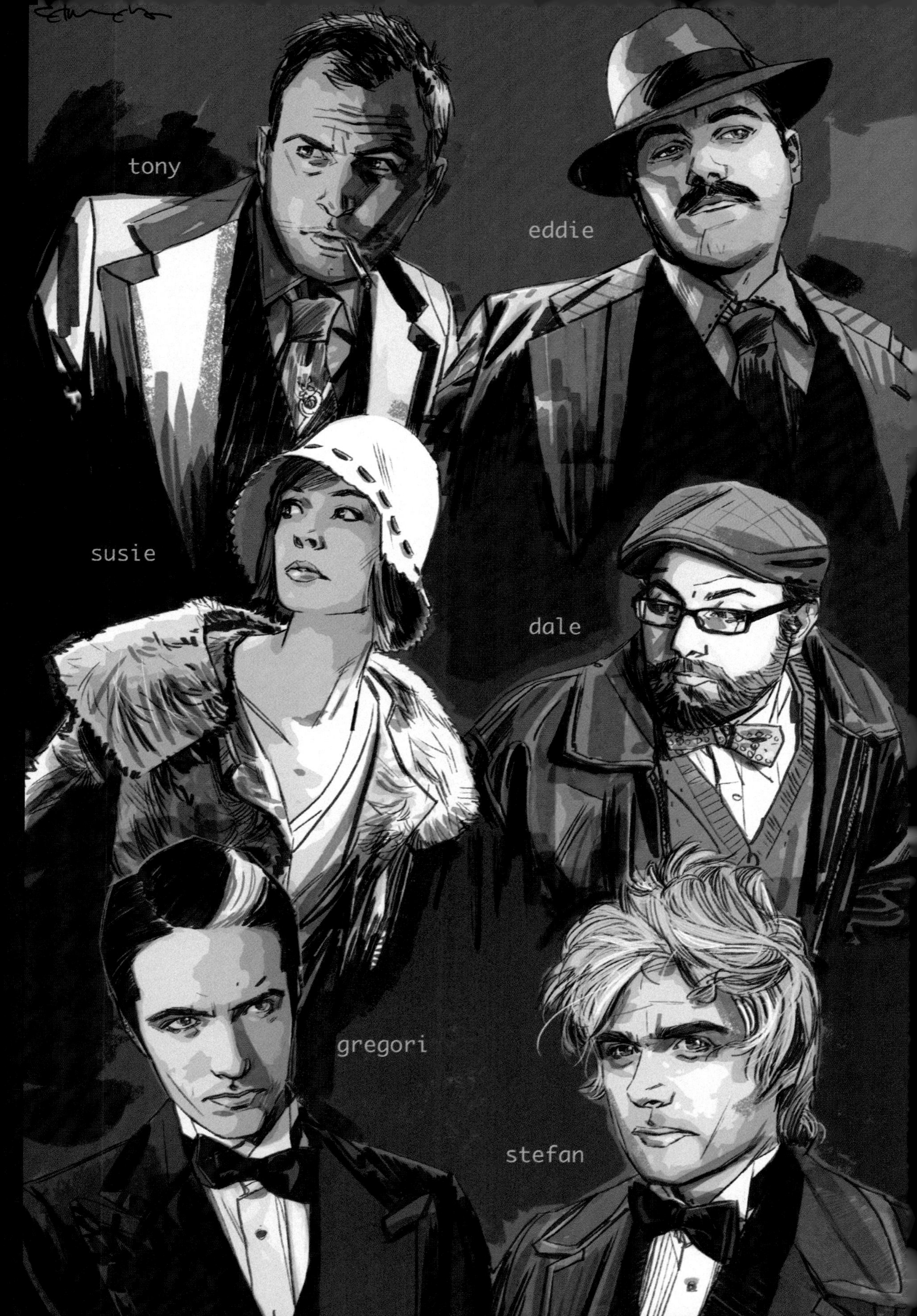

tony
eddie
susie
dale
gregori
stefan

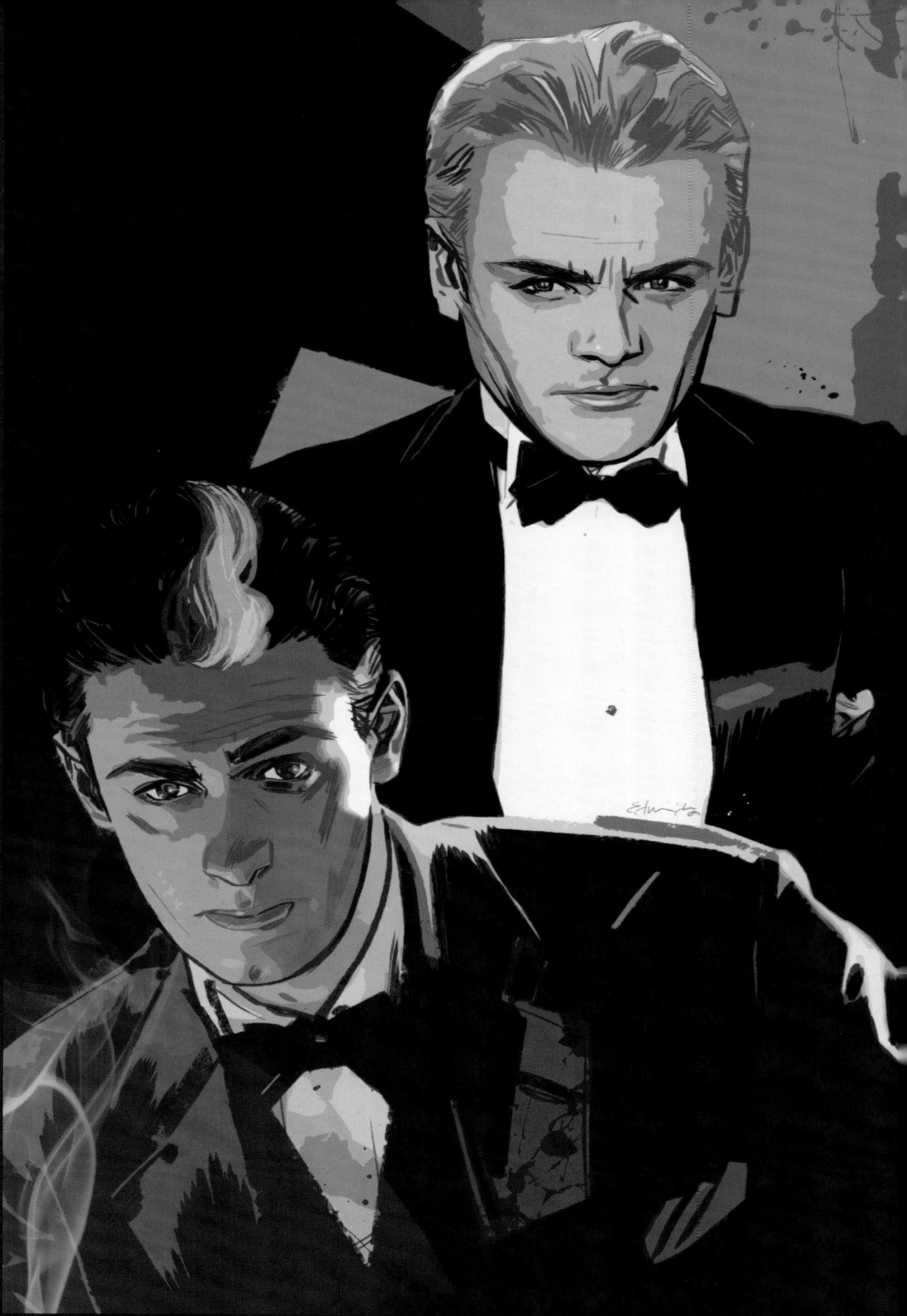

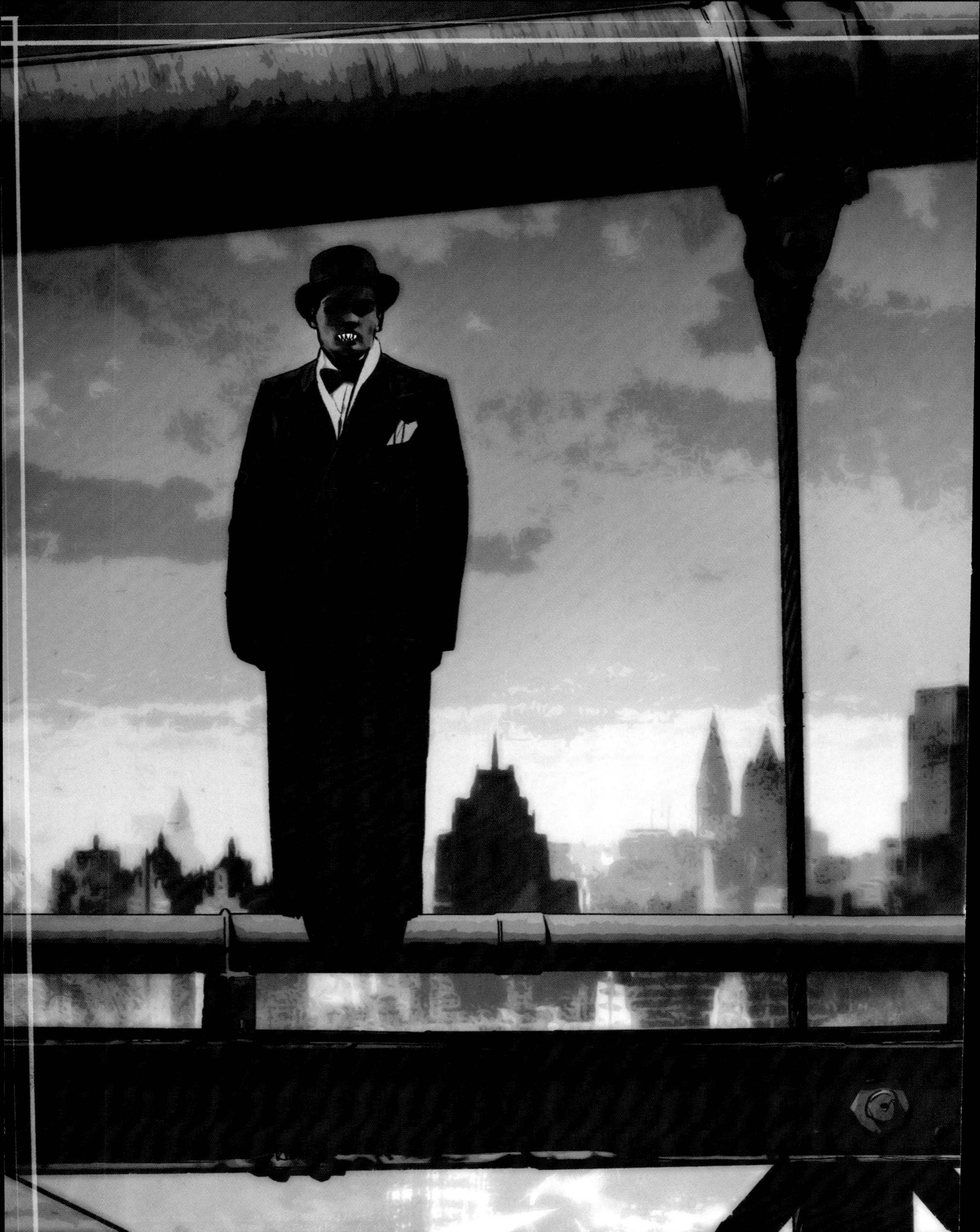

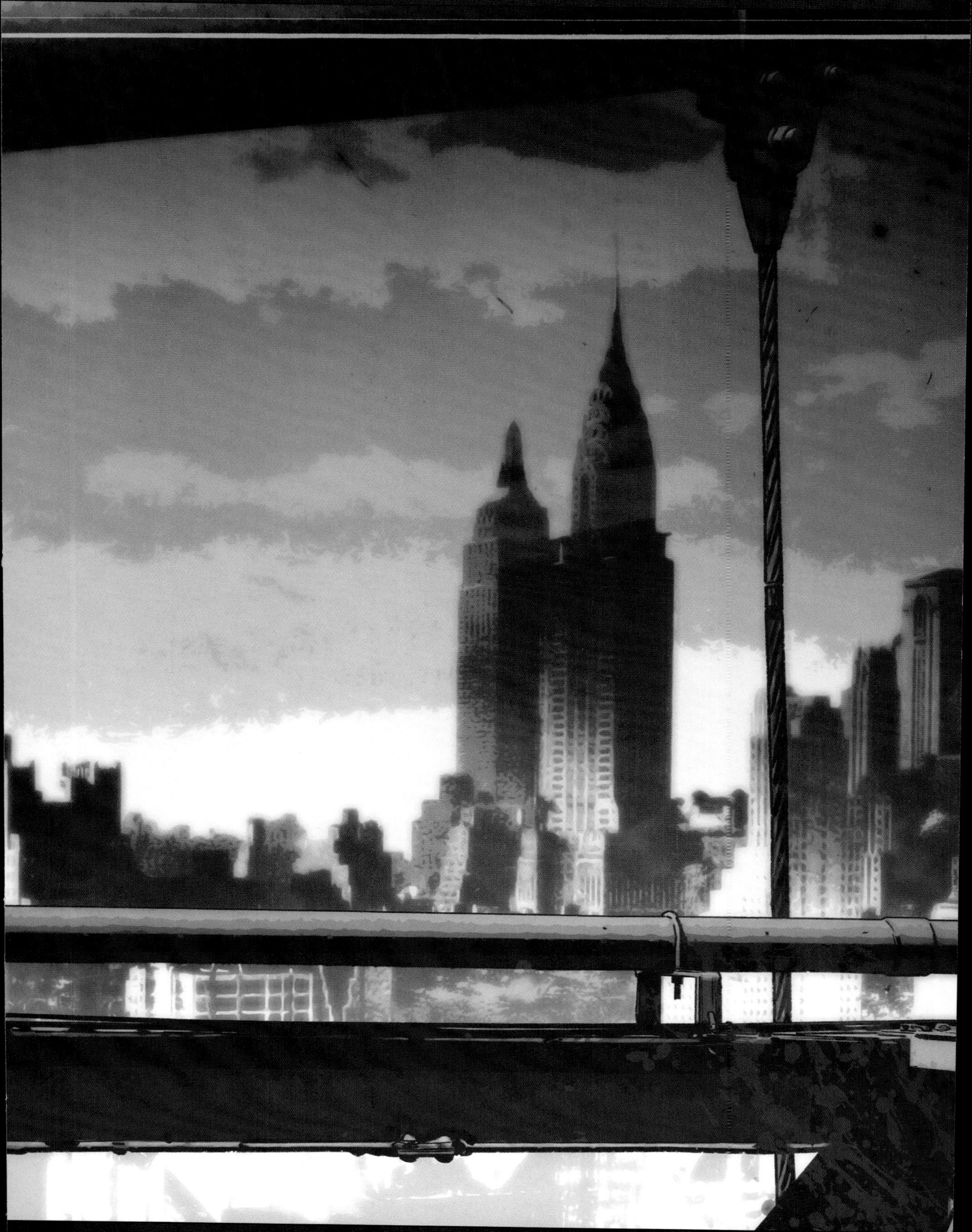

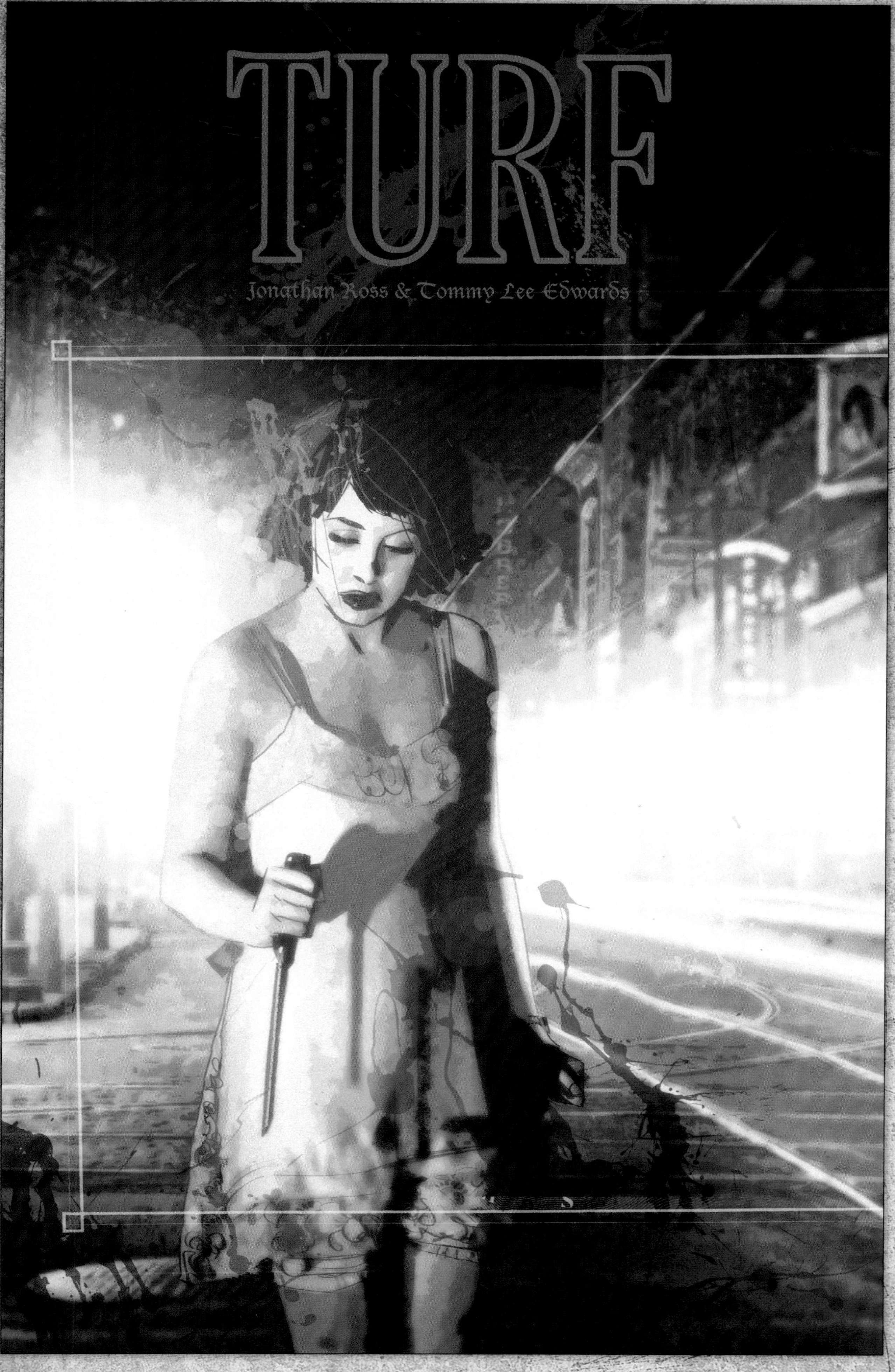
TURF
Jonathan Ross & Tommy Lee Edwards

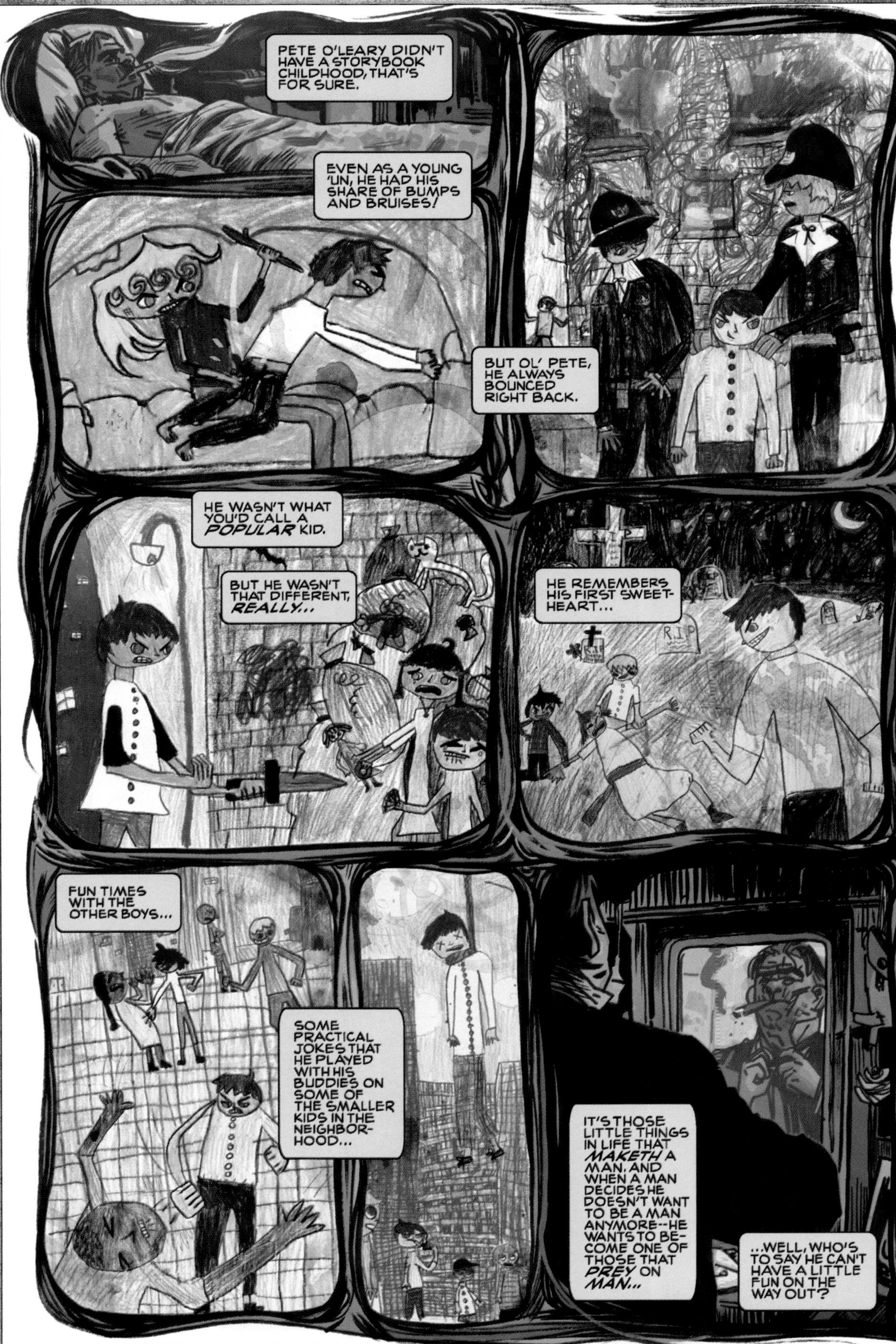
PETE O'LEARY DIDN'T HAVE A STORYBOOK CHILDHOOD, THAT'S FOR SURE.
EVEN AS A YOUNG 'UN, HE HAD HIS SHARE OF BUMPS AND BRUISES!
BUT OL' PETE, HE ALWAYS BOUNCED RIGHT BACK.
HE WASN'T WHAT YOU'D CALL A POPULAR KID.
BUT HE WASN'T THAT DIFFERENT, REALLY...
HE REMEMBERS HIS FIRST SWEET-HEART...
R.I.P
FUN TIMES WITH THE OTHER BOYS...
SOME PRACTICAL JOKES THAT HE PLAYED WITH HIS BUDDIES ON SOME OF THE SMALLER KIDS IN THE NEIGHBOR-HOOD...
IT'S THOSE LITTLE THINGS IN LIFE THAT MAKETH A MAN, AND WHEN A MAN DECIDES HE DOESN'T WANT TO BE A MAN ANYMORE--HE WANTS TO BE-COME ONE OF THOSE THAT PREY ON MAN...
...WELL, WHO'S TO SAY HE CAN'T HAVE A LITTLE FUN ON THE WAY OUT?

O'Leary's childhood was originally depicted by a nine-year-old, as seen through the eyes of Scarlett Edwards. The choice was ultimately made to have TLE emulate cartoons of O'Leary's youth for the final version.

The PROCESS

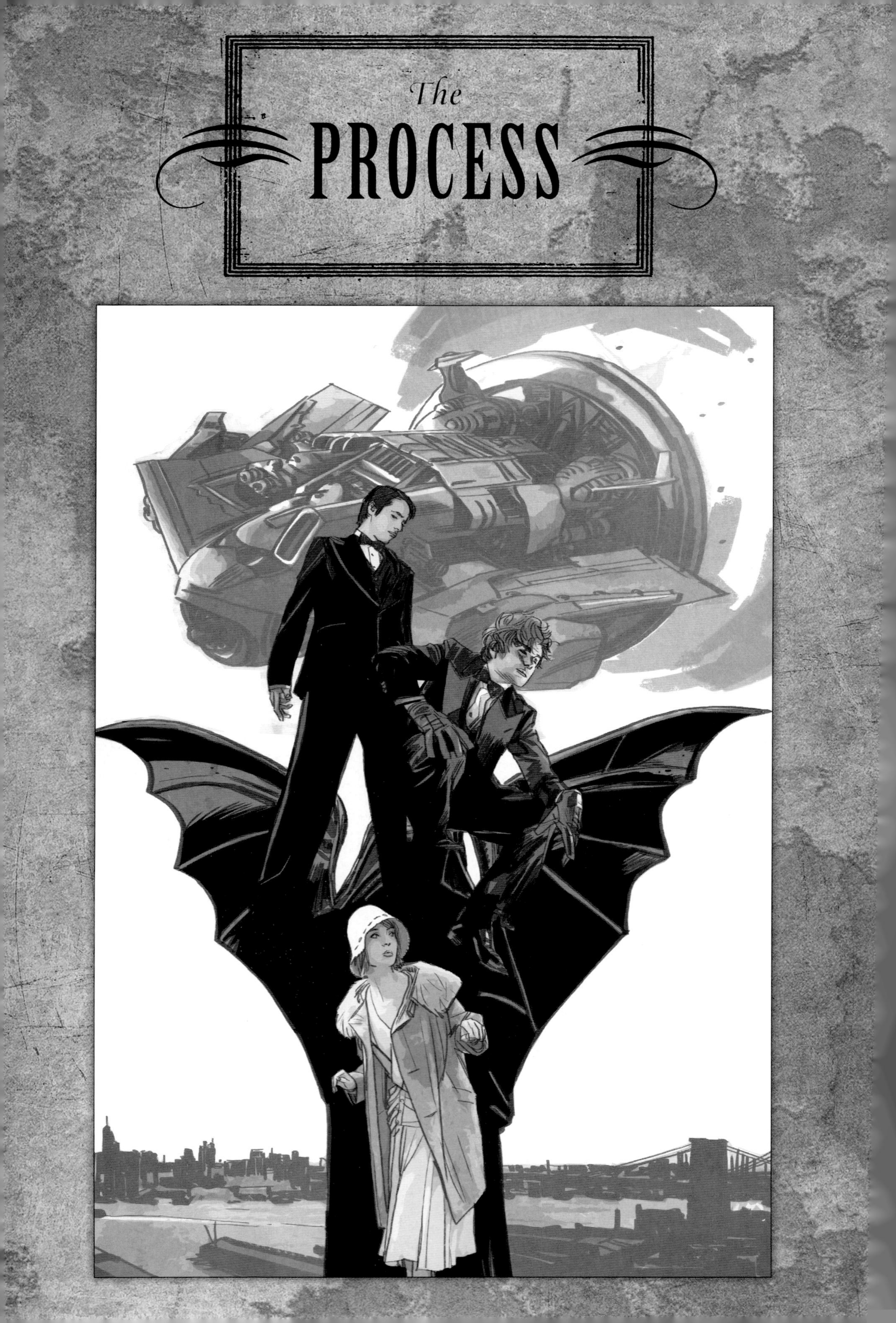

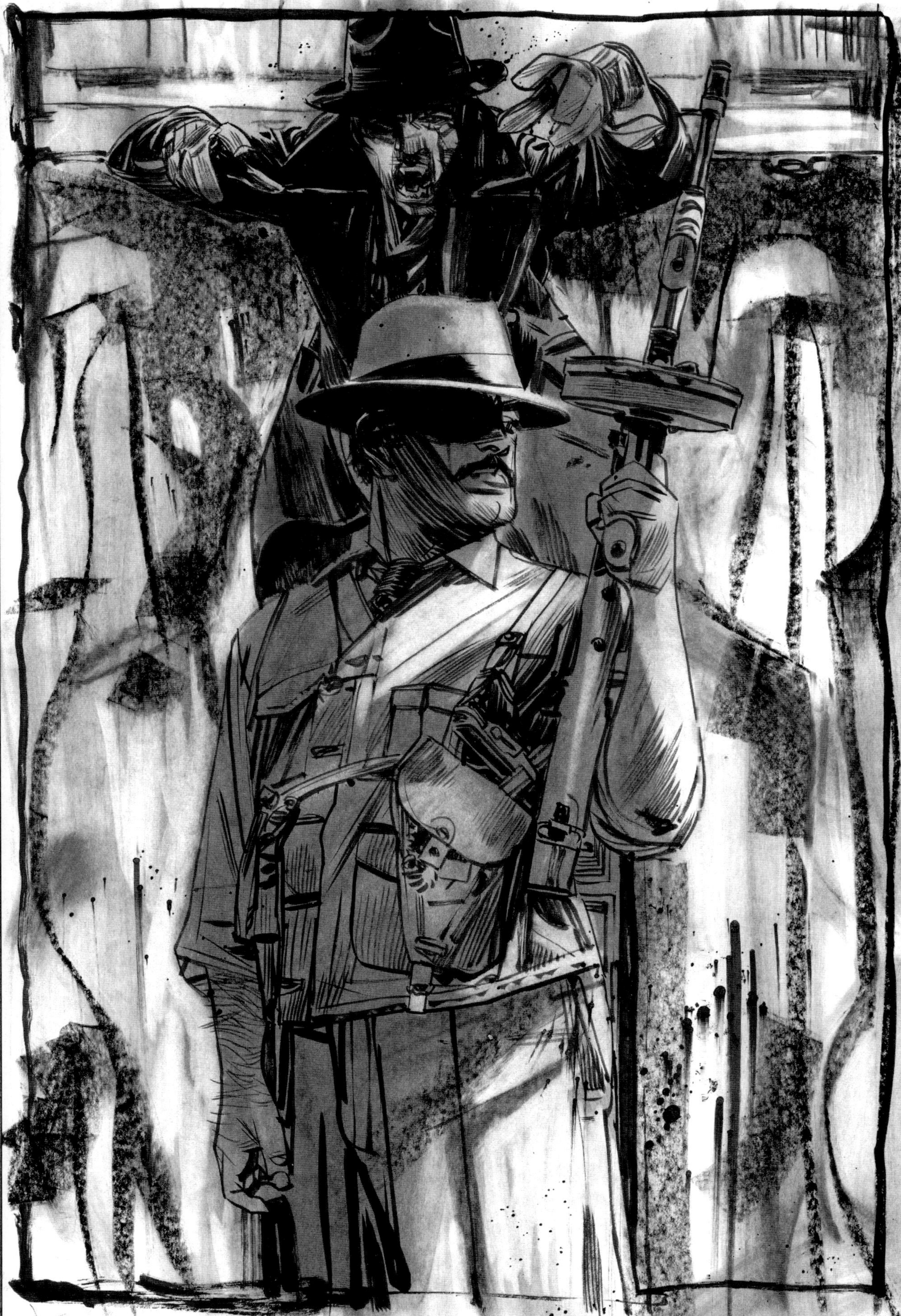

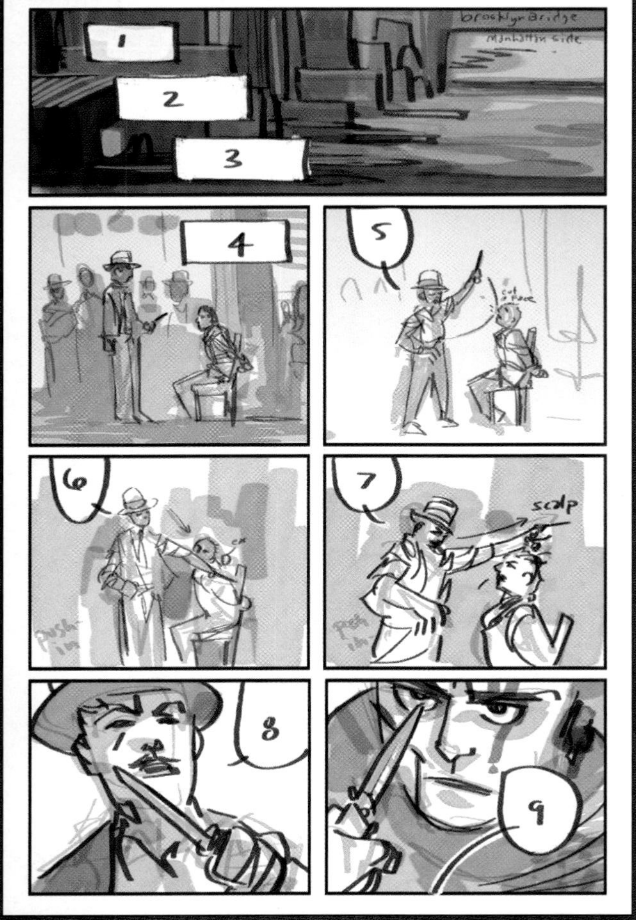
brooklyn bridge
scalp

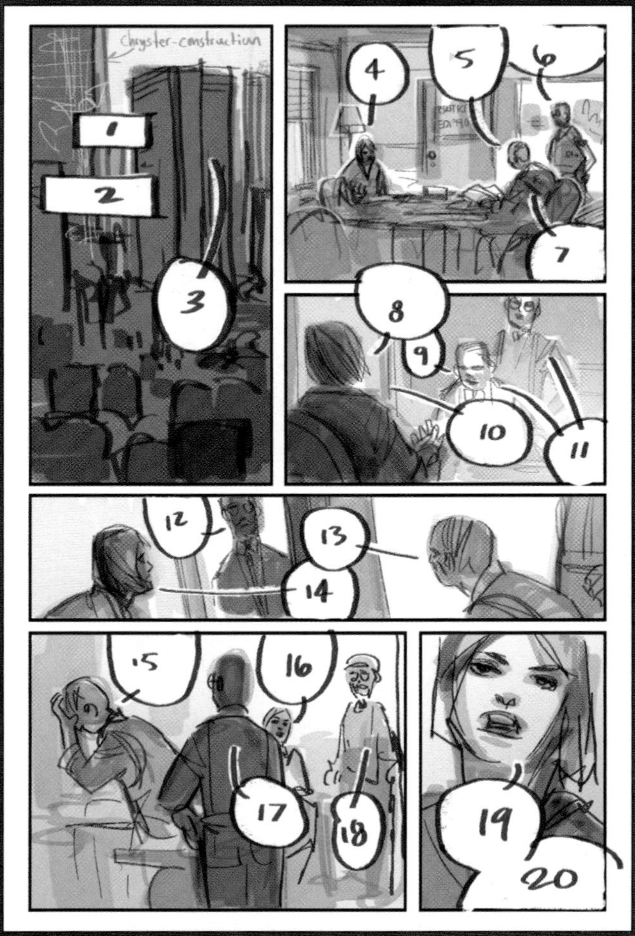

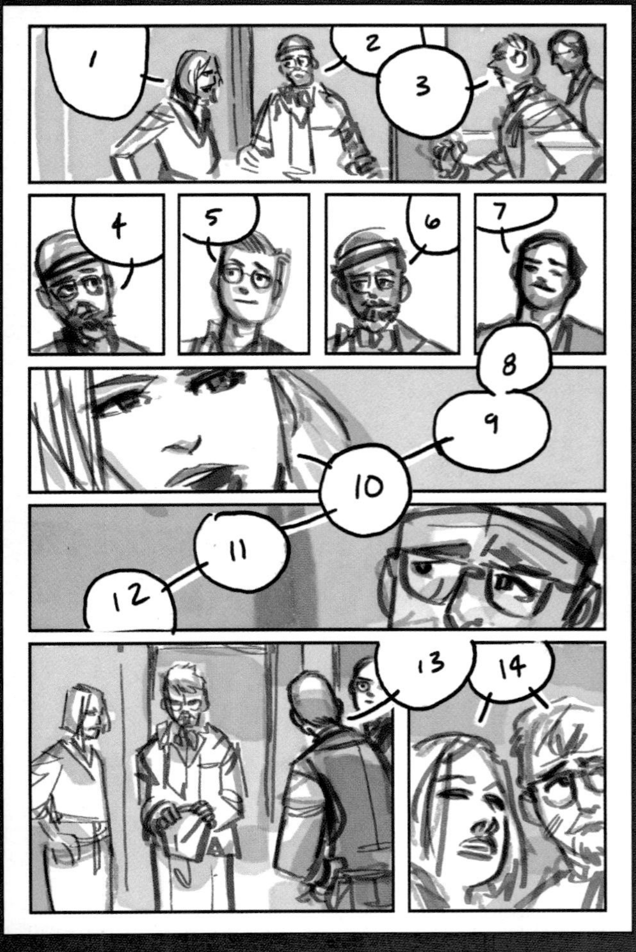

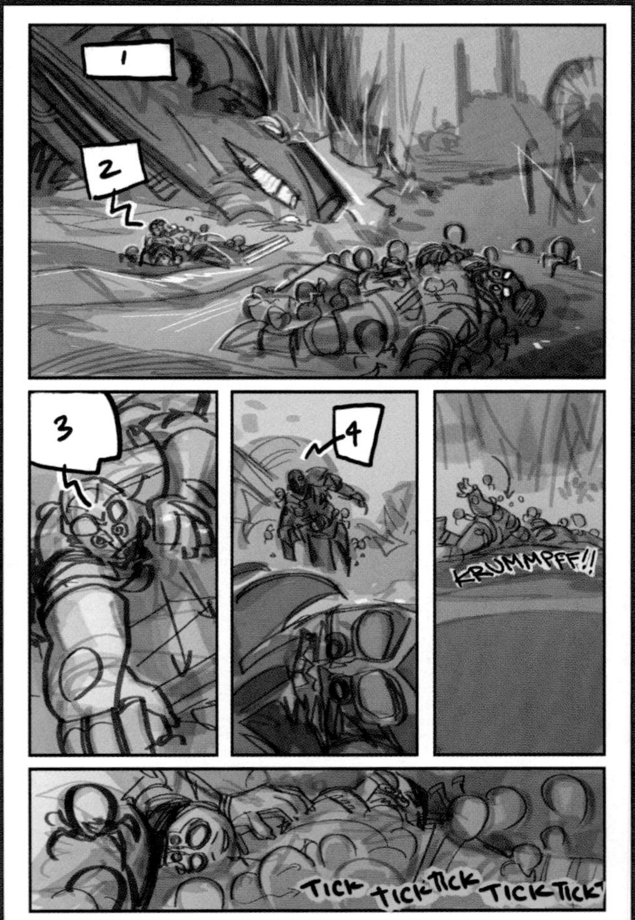
KRUMMPFF!!
TICK TICKTICK TICKTICK

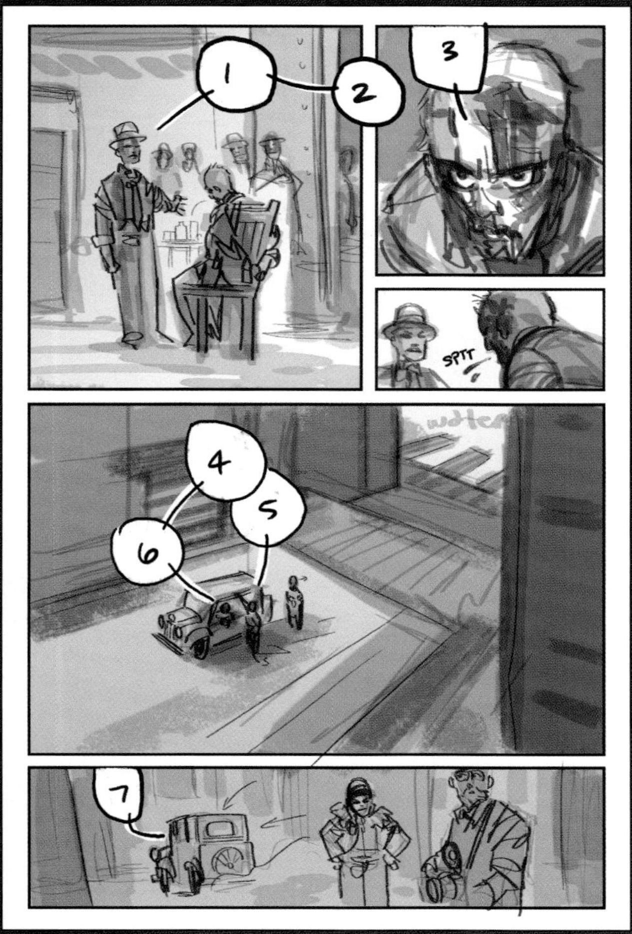
SPTT

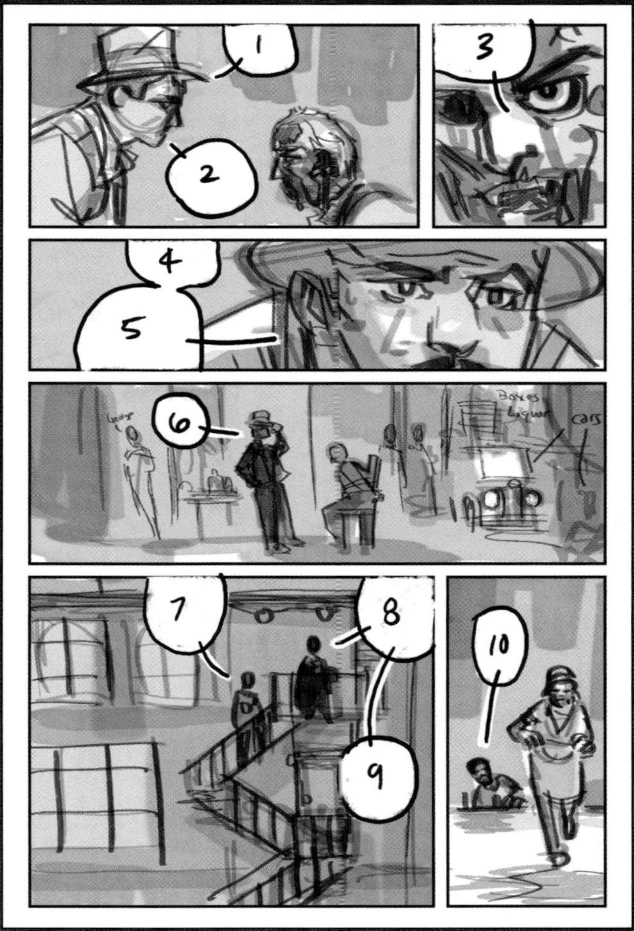
Boxes
Liquor
cars

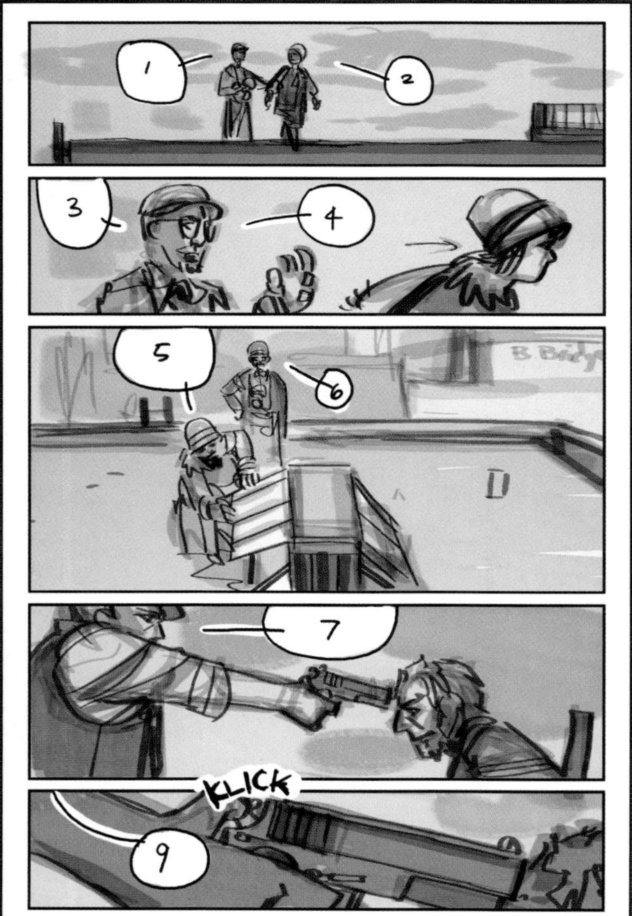
KLICK

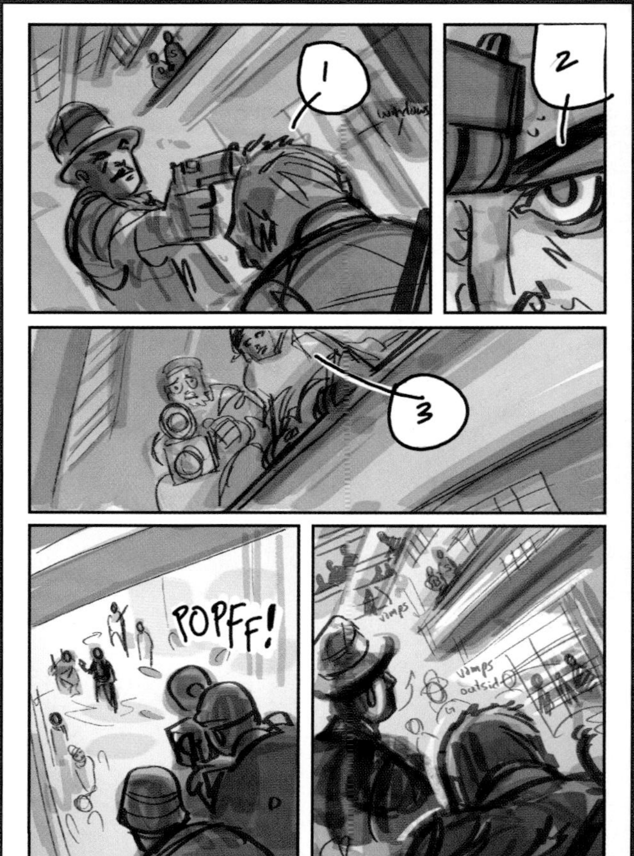
POPFF!

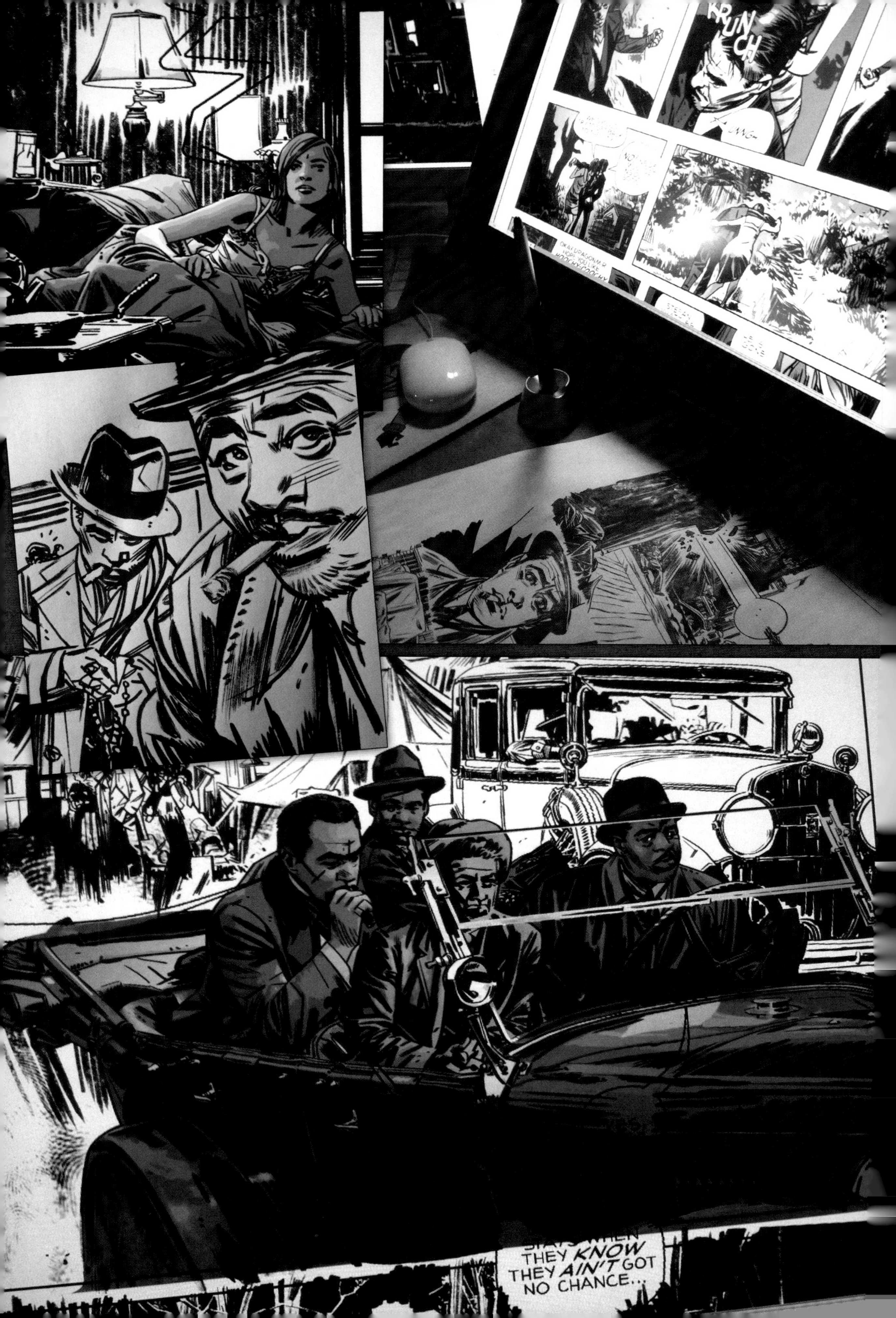
KRUNCH
THEY KNOW
THEY AIN'T GOT
NO CHANCE...

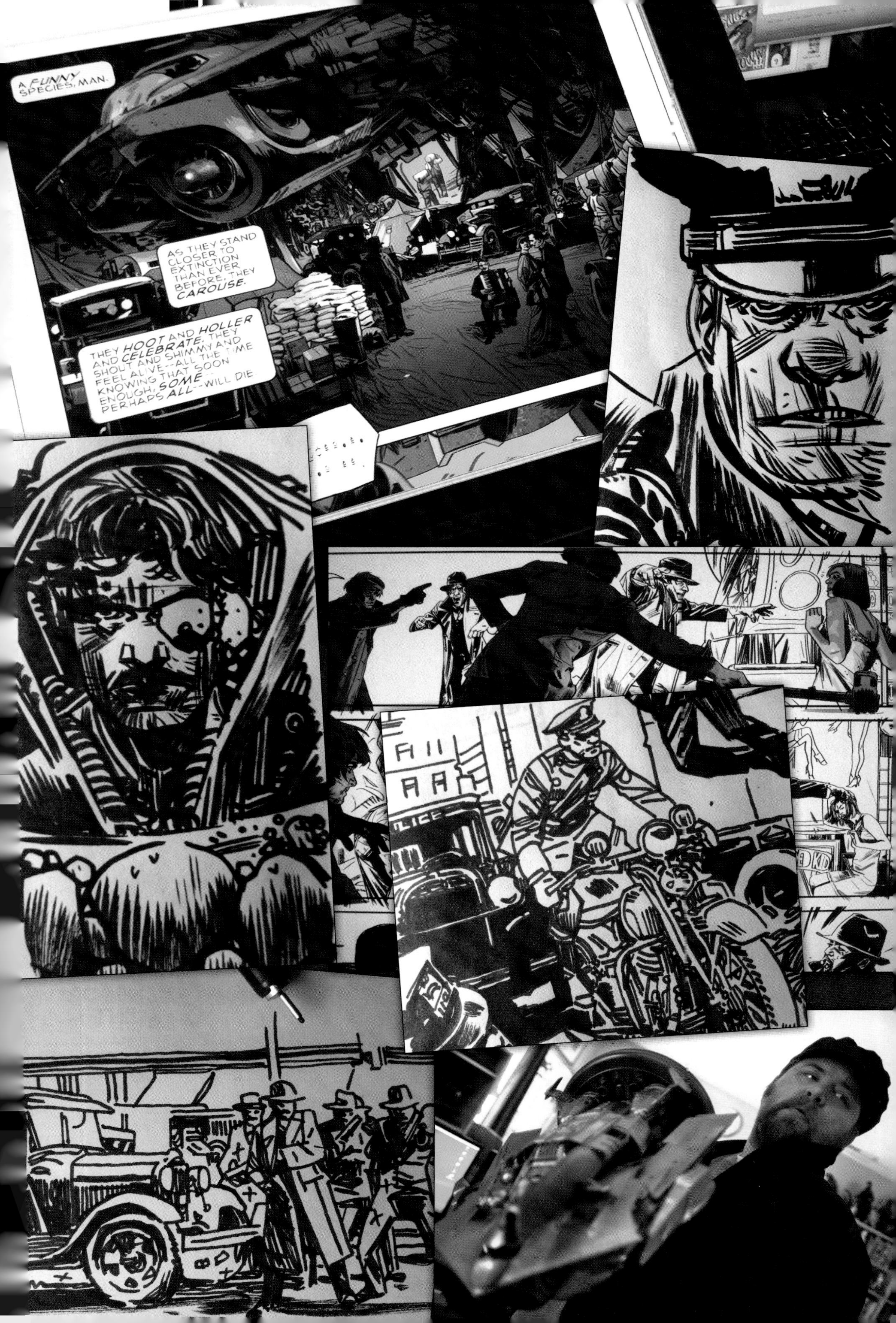
A FUNNY SPECIES, MAN.
AS THEY STAND CLOSER TO EXTINCTION THAN EVER BEFORE, THEY CAROUSE.
THEY HOOT AND HOLLER AND CELEBRATE. THEY SHOUT AND SHIMMY AND FEEL ALIVE--ALL THE TIME KNOWING THAT SOON ENOUGH, SOME-- PERHAPS ALL--WILL DIE.

The SPACESHIP

TLE and his two children turned Squeed's spaceship into a scratch-built family project.

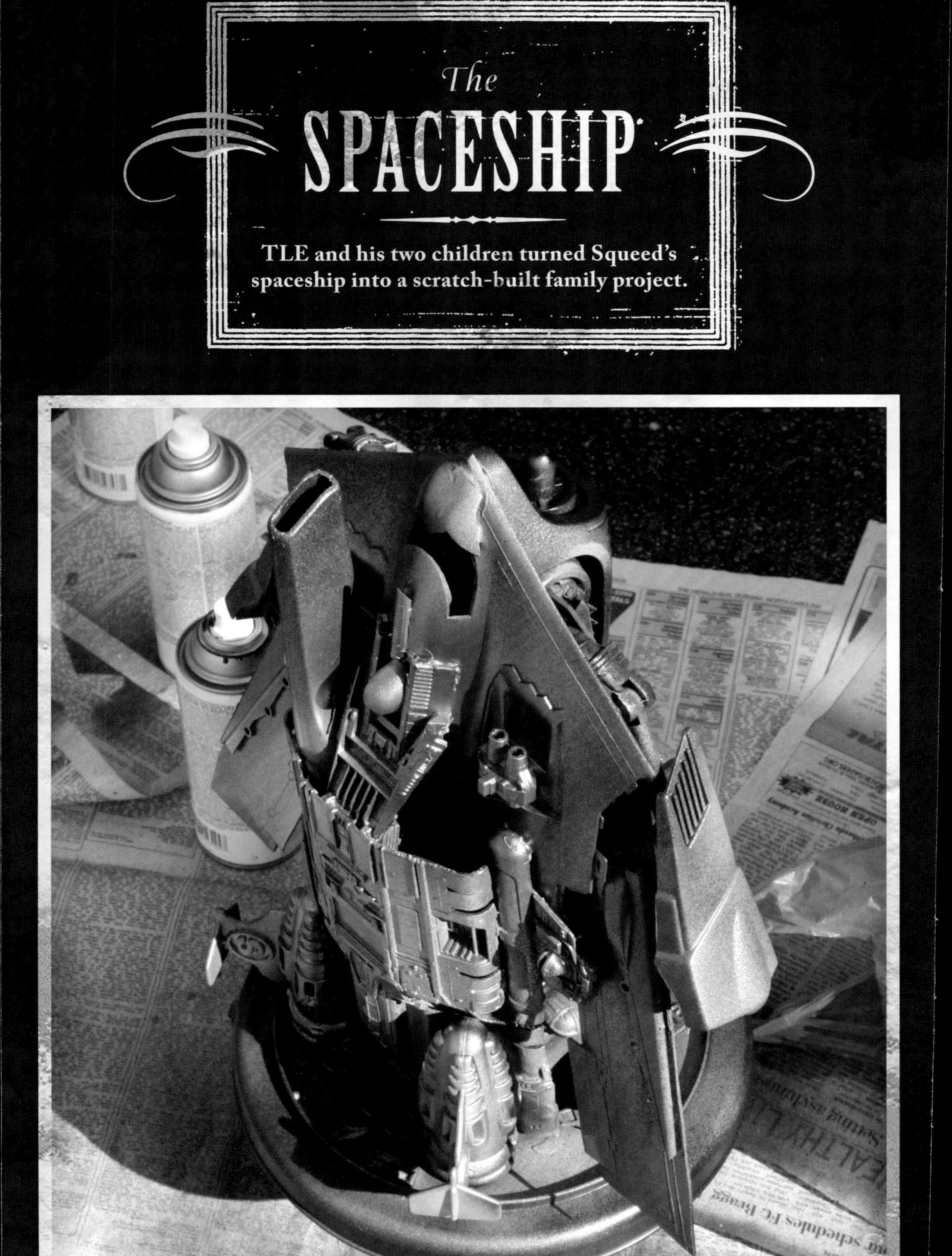

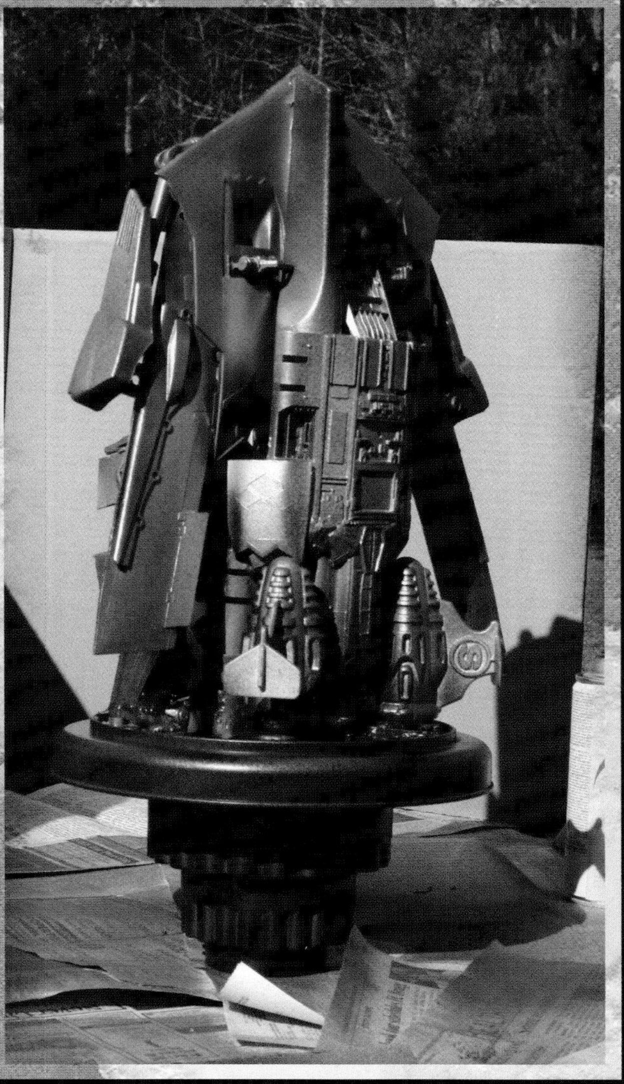

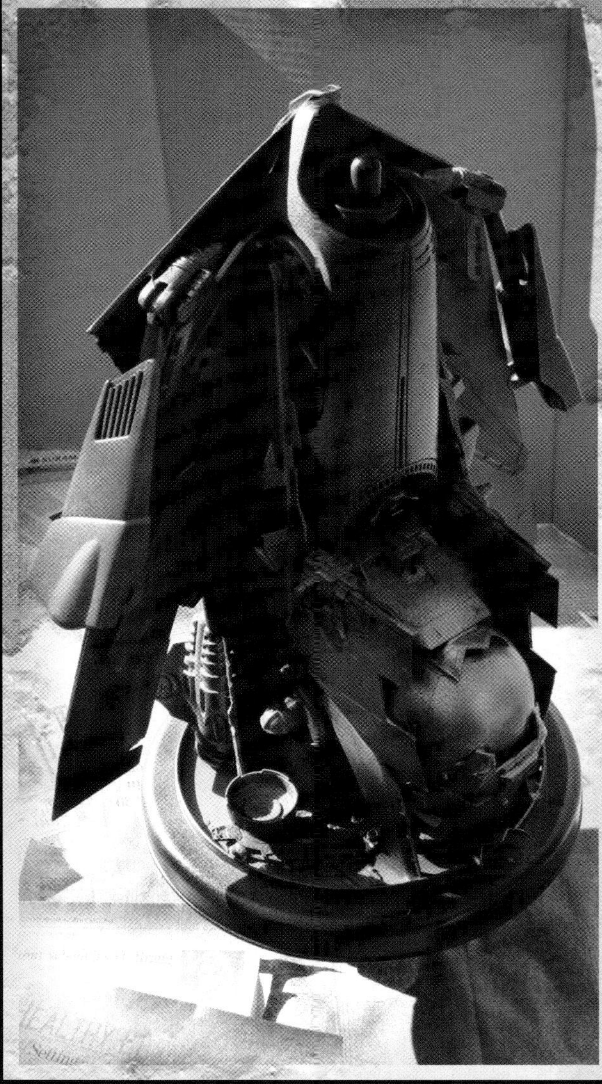

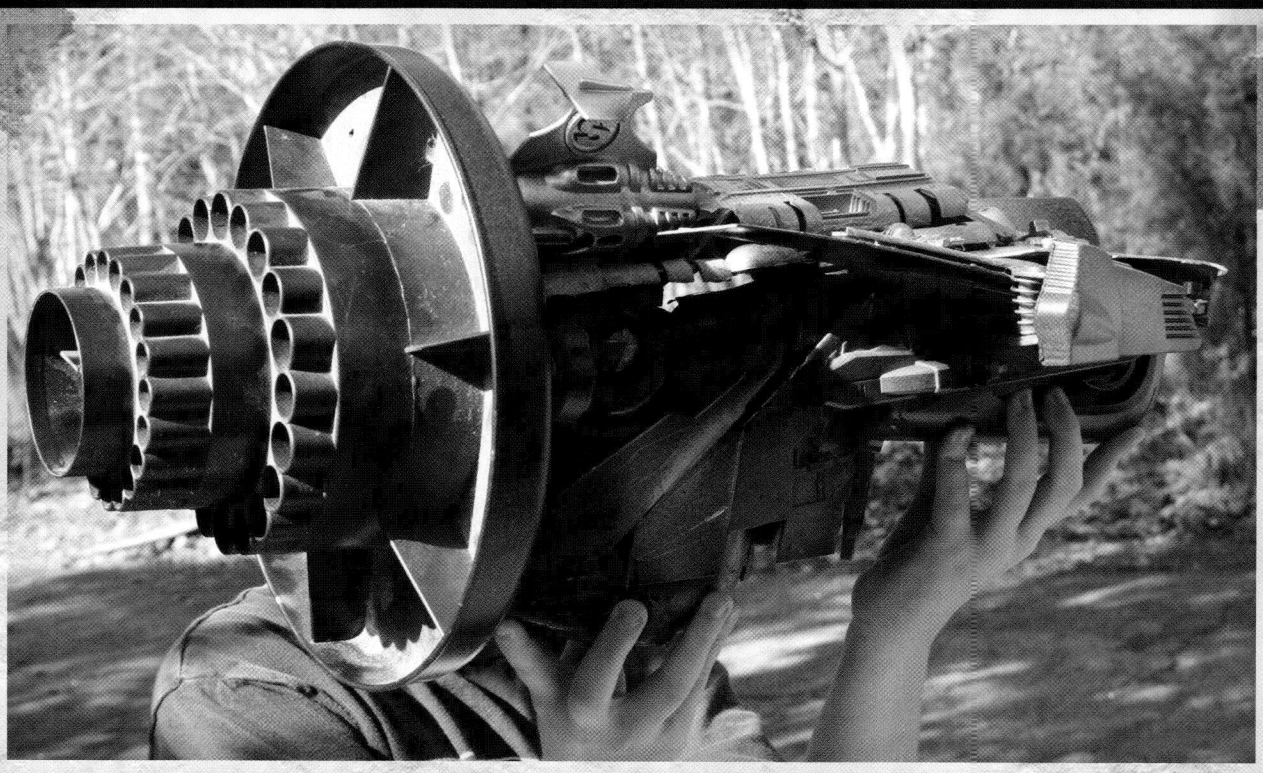

Photo by Sean LivingWater

Jonathan Ross

One of the highest profile broadcasters in the UK, he has hosted talk shows on all the major British Channels, and returns with *The Jonathan Ross Show* on prime time Saturday nights this fall. He has also worked in radio and has won lots and lots of pretty awards, none of which he knows quite where to put. He received the Stan Lee Best Newcomer Award for *Turf*. That made him very happy.

In a career that spans over twenty years Ross has often been associated with cult entertainment. His award-winning series *The Incredibly Strange Film Show* and it's sequel, *The Son of the Incredibly Strange Film Show* won a fan following that remembers them fondly to this day. He was responsible for the first western television interview with Jackie Chan, Tsui Hark and many other leading Hong Kong stars. He has authored programmes on subjects as diverse as Korean Cinema, Drive-Through Funeral parlours in Louisiana, and Steve Ditko. He has a collection of comics and original comic book art so large and valuable it frightens even him.

Tommy Lee Edwards

After studying film and illustration at the Art Center College of Design, Edwards took the comics industry by storm with his illustrations on such titles as *X-Men*, *Daredevil*, *Marvel 1985*, *Batman* and *The Question*. Proving to be one of the most respected and versatile artists working today, he has also designed video games like *Command and Conquer*, *James Bond*, and *Prey*. Edwards created the licensing style-guides for films such as *Harry Potter and the Sorcerer's Stone*, *Men in Black II*, *Superman Returns*, *Star Wars*, *Indiana Jones*, and *Batman Begins*. For Lucasfilm, he's created countless pieces for books, merchandise, magazines, and posters.

Edwards perhaps feels most at home putting his imagination and storytelling flare to the test while working as a conceptual and storyboard artist for film. He's collaborated with the Hughes Brothers on their Denzel Washington epic *The Book of Eli*, and has also contributed to the design of upcoming live action productions of *Akira* and *Masters of the Universe*. Currently Edwards is hard at work on *Golden Age*, his next creator-owned comic with Jonathan Ross.

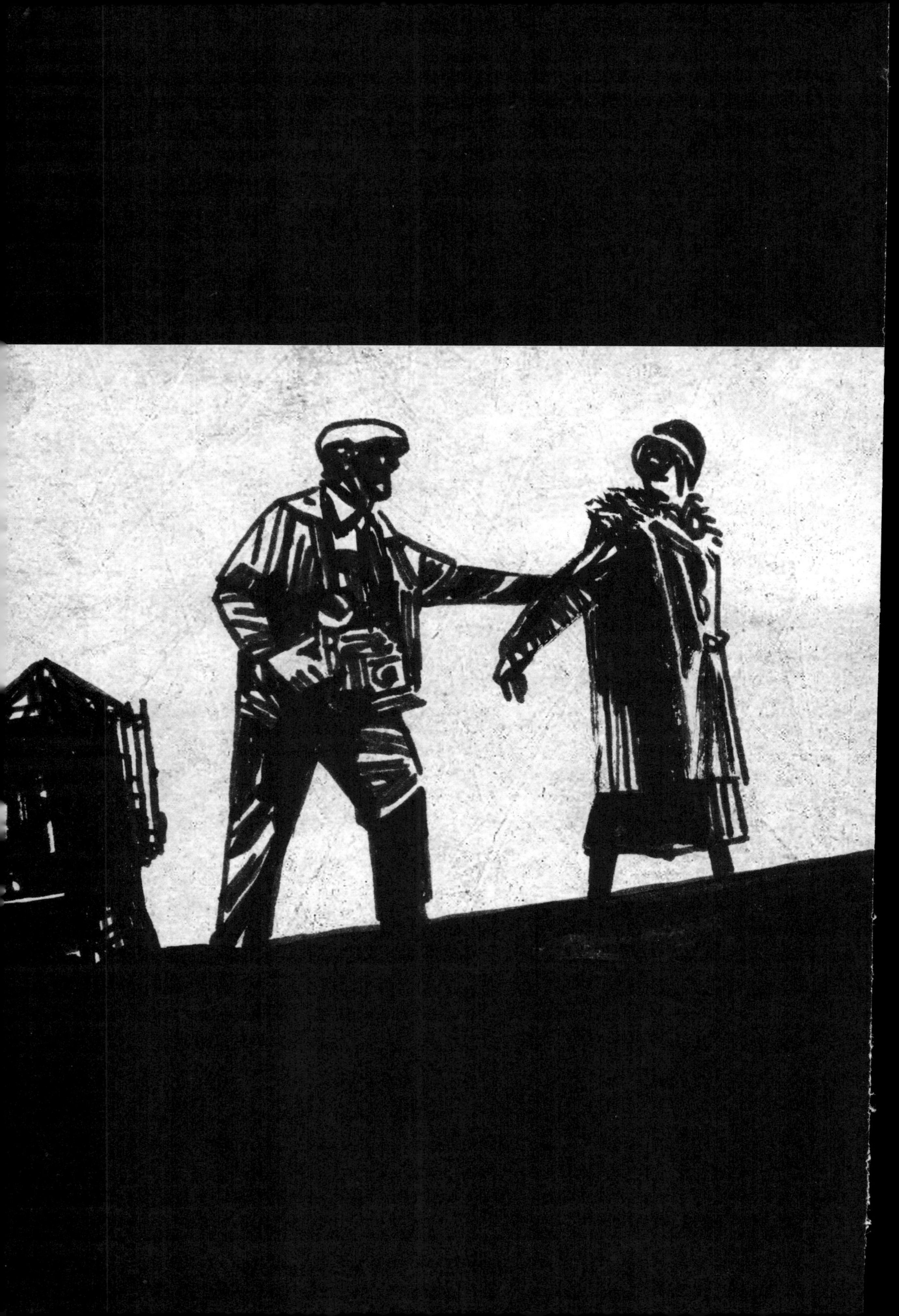